Whispered Consolations

Law, Meaning, and Violence

The scope of Law, Meaning, and Violence is defined by the wide-ranging scholarly debates signaled by each of the words in the title. Those debates have taken place among and between lawyers, anthropologists, political theorists, sociologists, and historians, as well as literary and cultural critics. This series is intended to recognize the importance of such ongoing conversations about law, meaning, and violence as well as to encourage and further them.

Series Editors:

Martha Minow, Harvard Law School
Elaine Scarry, Harvard University
Austin Sarat, Amherst College

Narrative, Violence, and the Law: The Essays of Robert Cover,
    edited by Martha Minow, Michael Ryan, and Austin Sarat

Narrative, Authority, and Law, by Robin West

The Possibility of Popular Justice: A Case Study of Community Mediation in the United States, edited by Sally Engle Merry and Neal Milner

Legal Modernism, by David Luban

Surveillance, Privacy, and the Law: Employee Drug Testing and the Politics of Social Control, by John Gilliom

Lives of Lawyers: Journeys in the Organizations of Practice, by Michael J. Kelly

Unleashing Rights: Law, Meaning, and the Animal Rights Movement, by Helena Silverstein

Law Stories, edited by Gary Bellow and Martha Minow

The Powers That Punish: Prison and Politics in the Era of the "Big House," 1920–1955, by Charles Bright

Law and the Postmodern Mind: Essays on Psychoanalysis and Jurisprudence, edited by Peter Goodrich and David Gray Carlson

Russia's Legal Fictions, by Harriet Murav

Strangers to the Law: Gay People on Trial, by Lisa Keen and Suzanne B. Goldberg

Butterfly, the Bride: Essays on Law, Narrative, and the Family, by Carol Weisbrod

The Politics of Community Policing: Rearranging the Power to Punish, by William Lyons

Laws of the Postcolonial, edited by Eve Darian-Smith and Peter Fitzpatrick

Whispered Consolations: Law and Narrative in African American Life, by Jon-Christian Suggs

Bad Boys: Public Schools in the Making of Black Masculinity, by Ann Arnett Ferguson

Whispered Consolations

Law and Narrative in African American Life

Jon-Christian Suggs

Ann Arbor

THE UNIVERSITY OF MICHIGAN PRESS

Copyright © by the University of Michigan 2000
All rights reserved
Published in the United States of America by
The University of Michigan Press
Manufactured in the United States of America
⊗ Printed on acid-free paper

2003   2002   2001   2000   4   3   2   1

A CIP catalog record for this book is available from the British Library.

Library of Congress Cataloging-in-Publication Data

Suggs, Jon Christian, 1940–
    Whispered consolations : law and narrative in African American
life / Jon-Christian Suggs.
        p.   cm. — (Law, meaning, and violence)
    Includes bibliographical references and index.
    ISBN 0-472-10651-1 (cloth : acid-free paper)
    1. Afro-Americans—Legal status, laws, etc.   2. Race
discrimination—Law and legislation—United States.   3. Justice.
I. Title.   II. Series.
    KF4757   .S84   1999
    346.7301'3—dc21   99-006889

For Seana, Heather, Joshua, and Quin

As a rule, a race writes its history in its laws and in
its records. Not so the Afro-American: he could make
no law; deprived of the opportunity to write, he could leave
no written word; he could only protest against the injustice
of his oppressors in his heart, in his song, and in his
whispered consolations to the suffering and dying.

Mrs. N. F. Mossell,
The Work of the Afro-American Woman, 1894

Contents

Preface

This book is interpretive and draws on law, history, and literature. Its intent is to describe something of the status and substance of African American life in the nineteenth and twentieth centuries by looking at texts by African American writers not usually discussed in conjunction with one another and at the legal and historical contexts in which they were produced. What follows is an introductory sketch of the relationships between American law and African American narrative, and between those two text-making enterprises and ideas about romanticism, identity, citizenship, and desire.

It is difficult to read the newspapers or the history books of this country without developing the sense that the primary relationship of African Americans to the rest of America is through the law. Property, crime, and the Constitution have dominated public discussion of African American life for the past two hundred years. This study of one aspect of that discussion, the textual relationships between American law and African American narratives, is derived from my teaching and my research. In the quarter-century I have worked at John Jay College of Criminal Justice in the City University of New York, I have been allowed and encouraged to teach and think across disciplinary lines, both in the Department of English and in the Interdepartment of Thematic Studies. That kind of intellectual space invites speculation, and I began this study by wondering how two narrative systems that privilege different proofs, or seem to do so, represent the common material of African American life. The interrelationships between these systems became my subject and my question, to which I wanted to suggest answers. In the following chapters I tease out what one is reading when one reads American law through African American narrative, and vice versa.

In my attempts my colleagues have been sources of information, methodologies, and inspiration on many fronts. It has been my good fortune over the last few years to have been in contact with people whose ideas have stimulated me. In no particular order I want to thank

Richard Weisberg, David Papke, Carla Kaplan, Judy Scales-Trent, Patricia J. Williams, Richard Yarborough, Brook Thomas, Paul Finkelman, Susan Sage Heinzleman, Aviam Soifer, Ariela Gross, Paul Lauter, William Wiethoff, Laura Hapke, Marc Bousquet, Gwen Matthewson, Robert Leitz, Joseph McElrath, Michelle Wallace, Reynolds J. Scott-Childress, Austin Sarat, and Martha Minow. John Paul Ryan gave me an opportunity to share an early version of this research at a conference sponsored by the American Bar Association. I particularly thank Michele Berger for her early interest in this project, her encouragement, and her intellectual comradeship.

A major portion of the research for this study was undertaken in 1994–95 while I was a scholar-in-residence at the Schomburg Center for Research in Black Culture. The residency was administered by the Center and underwritten by the National Endowment for the Humanities. For administrative and spiritual support during that year I must thank Howard Dodson, the chief of the Schomburg Center, and Diana Lachatanere, Curator of Rare Books and Manuscripts there and director of the Scholars' Program.

My colleagues at the Schomburg were invaluable to the growth of my understanding of African American history. Many heartfelt thanks go to Robert Hayden, Randolph Stakeman, Henry John Drewal, and Ula Taylor. The staff at the Schomburg are exemplary as professionals and I am indebted to them for a year and more of intellectual support. Peter Hobbs was my research assistant while I was at the Schomburg, and he was priceless. Kim Miller at the National Museum of African Art in Washington, D.C., did me a big favor, long distance.

Basil Wilson, the Provost of my college, who is a friend and colleague, has supported my research and my teaching by his example and a research grant. The Professional Staff Congress, our union, also provided financial support through its contractually defined research grant program. Ruth Misheloff is to be thanked for several kindnesses and encouragements.

It is impossible to even attempt a work like this without the help of librarians and archivists across the country. I would have even now only an idea with no material to support it were it not for the staff at the Schomburg Center, the librarians, colleagues all, at the Lloyd Sealy Library at John Jay College, library staffs at the Beineke Library at Yale University, the Harry T. Ransom Humanities Center in Austin, Texas, the Enoch Pratt Free Library of Baltimore, the City University of New York Law School Library, the Columbia Law Library, the Amistad Center at Tulane University, and Kate Anderson, research librarian at Memorial Library, the University of Wisconsin, Madison.

I have been helped immeasurably by being able to listen in on conversations on H-AMSTDY, H-LAW, SLAVERY, T-AMLIT, and AMLIT lists. The level of intellectual exchange through these lists was consistently high, providing me with bibliographic references and models of discourse otherwise unavailable to me.

Editors notwithstanding, I would not have been able to write this book without the active intellectual and emotional support of my wife and dear colleague, Nan Bauer-Maglin. She alone suspects what this study means to me.

This book began with the interest of Malcolm Litchfield when he was at the University of Michigan Press. I am grateful for his efforts on its behalf. When Malcolm left, Chuck Myers was as supportive and patient as one could want. Thanks to his management this book sees the light of day.

Signifying, Epistemology, and Ontology in Law and African American Narrative; or, A House of Laws on Fire

> "Guilty, or not guilty?" demanded the judge.
> "Not guilty," replied John. "I've owned that wagon ever since it was a wheelbarrow."
>
> Traditional—Texas

Innocence and irony fall under the law like feather and shot. In the everyday world one plummets, the other wafts. In the laboratory of the law each falls with equal weight, its measure taken. In the study of law and fiction in African American life, I have found myself tracking innocence and irony. Both are romantic. The American nineteenth century, romantic at its core, both insisted on and rejected the essential innocence of African Americans while ignoring the irony implicit in their position and central to their identities. The American twentieth century, no less romantic although at times less visibly so, dropped the insistence of innocence in African American life and gradually embraced its irony. These stances, or rather the records of them, are found in the annals of American law and in the texts of African American narratives. It is the job of this book to try to interleave narrative and annal.

When I first encountered Ralph Ellison's 1976 essay, "Perspective of Literature," written for a volume on American law, I was both interested and apprehensive. Interested because I was trying to find a place to start my inquiry into the relationships between American law and African American literature, apprehensive because I might find that Ellison had already said what needed to be said. I had not found any substantive discussion of the relationships anywhere else, and for all I knew it was because the word was out to everyone but me that Ellison had already been there, done that. To my surprise and, I must admit, relief, I discovered that if Ellison was to be my gauge, then African American literature's ongoing critique of American law was not only an untold story, it had been largely invisible to even the most implicated observers.

Ellison writes, as he opens his discussion:

> Recently a television dramatization of the *Scottsboro* case presented one of the judges that sat on the case as its hero. I was made aware of the snarl of personal and public motives, political and private interests, which had become the focus of the case. I was aware of the many factors locked in contention in the name of the purity of white womanhood, and as a writer I came to ask myself just why it was that American fiction had given so little attention to the law. ("Perspective" 325)

We now know that American fiction has indeed addressed "the law" in considerable detail. Even Ellison goes on in the essay to discuss such texts as "Benito Cereno," *Adventures of Huckleberry Finn, Pudd'nhead Wilson, Bartleby the Scrivener, Moby-Dick,* the novels of Henry James, and the Constitution, which he characterizes, quoting Paul A. Freund's words, as "a work of art in its capacity to respond through interpretation to changing needs, concerns and aspirations" (330).

But Ellison fails to mention even one work by an African American writer in his survey of the common ground of American fiction and American law. His discussion takes place as if no black American had ever written, even as he notes the ironic twists of law and culture that could make a lynching Scottsboro judge a hero. How could this have been so in 1976? And on what premises did he decide to reprint, unrevised, such a survey a decade later? Might Ellison argue that black Americans are untouched by the law and so are outside the purview of his exercise? That seems not to be his point, since fully half of his essay is devoted to showing how "race" emerged as a motif in American life from the arguments of the Declaration of Independence and the Constitution. He even notes that the multiple variations of such a motif do not necessarily translate into citizenship under the law: "Afro-Americans were strictly limited in their freedom to participate in the process of government. We could obey or break laws, but not make or interpret them. . . . Nor was it possible for me to ignore the obvious fact that race was a source of that rot [in the law], and that even within the mystery of the legal process, the law was colored and rigged against my people" ("Perspective" 321–22).[1]

Ellison argues that law and fiction are alike in that each consists of symbolic acts and each has some connection to defining social order. "Perhaps law and literature operate or cooperate," he writes, "if the term is suitable for an interaction that is far less than implicit; in their respective ways these two systems . . . work in the interests of social order. The one for stability—that is, the law is the law—the other striving to socialize those emotions and interests held in check by manners, conventions, and again, by law" ("Perspective" 329).[2]

Yet then to exclude from discussion any examples of literature written by black Americans seems peculiar. It is as if the transgressive characteristics of African American fiction are too strong to be contained comfortably within a symbolic system conceived of as "striving to socialize" disruptive emotions and interests. Ellison reaches for some accommodation of that transgressive power in quoting another passage from Freund:

> Does not law, like art, seek change within the framework of continuity, to bring heresy and heritage into fruitful tension? They are not dissimilar, and in their resolution, the resolution of passion and pattern, of frenzy and form, of contention and revolt, of order and spontaneity lies the clue to the creativity that will endure. ("Perspective" 329)

Although he says he cannot completely embrace Freund's position, Ellison wants to retain for the literary artist the right to "yell 'Fire' in crowded theaters" (330). That being the case, must we conclude that Ellison believed no African American writer ever warned the nation that its house of laws was on fire? Even if he looked no farther than his own lifetime, might he not have named Langston Hughes, Zora Hurston, Richard Wright, William Attaway, Willard Motley, Ann Petry, Chester Himes? Himself? Is Ellison innocent of the implications of his omission? Or is this just another irony of African American life under the law?

The purpose of this book is to consider how law and narrative, primarily fiction, combine in African American life. A few years ago, in pursuit of material for a course in law and literature, I was brought up short by the absence of any critical attention in print to this question. As a consequence I wrote an exploratory piece on law and epistemology in some African American fiction (Suggs, "Epistemology"). Because I wanted to discuss the work of novelists and of legal scholars whose use of literary devices to explore questions of legal history and theory I found suggestive, I used a very broad definition of fiction in that preliminary essay. That expansion led me part of the way into the investigation that became this thematically oriented, but historically situated, study. In it I have generally replaced "fiction" with "narrative" to encompass the discursive practices I have found most provocative.

Not all of the theoretical questions that inform this study are explicit in its realization. I will only mention briefly those which most centrally affect the story of an African American critique of American law. Central to all of them is the very basis of law in narrativity, the condition that the relationships under consideration in any construct of the law are accessible only as story, as a story told by someone to someone, and this is as true for legislation as for litigation.

The compounding problems of authority over and ownership of the text are also crucial; when proslavery whites, ante- and postbellum, wrote of the lives of those they had enslaved, who owned the story? For that matter, when abolitionists wrote or edited fugitive slave narratives as fact or fiction, who owned the story? Harriet Stowe or Uncle Tom? Harriet Jacob or Lydia Child? In the law, the question is similar. When there can be no black voice in the court and no black hand drafts the legislation, who owns the legal narrative of slavery? Of Jim Crow? The legally enforced illiteracy of enslaved blacks in America further compromised the question of the ownership of the narrative of slavery.

Who and what authorizes ownership of the narrative? At what point do you lose control of your own story? In a peculiar case of double indemnity, or serial appropriation, William Styron was pilloried by Jews who complained that he had violated the exceptionality of the Holocaust with the Catholicism of his protagonist in *Sophie's Choice* and by African Americans outraged over his portryal of the protagonist in *The Confessions of Nat Turner*.When Jeffrey Masson sued Janet Malcolm over her representation of him in a 1983 *New Yorker* profile, the case hinged on the extent to which her appropriation of his "voice" violated his ownership of his right to tell his own version of the story. Both Sherley Anne Williams and Toni Morrison have raised the question of the ownership of the text in contemporary accounts of North American slavery by calling their readers' attention to the role of white male amanuenses inscribing the lives of enslaved women of color in the antebellum South.

In a 1990 *PMLA* article, William L. Andrews noted that one task facing black writers of antebellum life was the creation of an authorized, authentic narrative ("Novelization" 23). One of the arguments of this book is concerned specifically with the complexity of that task in that the position of enslaved Africans in North America was socially and culturally inscribed in part by the denial to them of the capacity for "authenticity" by white romantic notions of identity. The formal denial of any self-authorized legal narrative to enslaved people and the severe circumscription of the legal statuses of free people of color are well known. Thus the establishment of an authorized African American narrative of any sort was problematic.

However "authorized" we might find any narrative, some poststructural readers might discover that under scrutiny *all* texts break down into incoherence and we might be better off prizing them for the risks they take or the panache with which they deconstruct themselves rather than for their authenticity or fidelity to reality or the integrity of their representations. Even if we don't completely accept the deconstructive moment as the end of all texts, we do have to look for a moment at one poststructural assumption: that language refers to itself and its system more than it refers to any "reality" outside the language system itself. That is, language isn't about things; it's about other words. Let's look at Ellison, above, as he quotes Freund on the Constitution: "a work of art in its capacity to respond through interpretation to changing needs, concerns and aspirations" ("Perspective" 330).

Are Freund and Ellison suggesting that the words of the Constitution are malleable in their meanings? Freund seems to suggest that he believes works of art mean different things at different times or under different kinds of scrutiny. He doesn't say what kinds of scrutiny but they seem to be those that emerge from needs, concerns, and aspirations that were not those of the artist. He is willing to grant the Constitution the status of art because it, too, offers up different meanings to different scrutinies. Poststructuralists, however, would say that *all* narrative, not just "art," has this characteristic and that Freund's belief in the exceptionality of art based on its ability to fix or release itself in relationship to meaning is mistaken. The error notwithstanding, the status of foundationalist texts in African American readings, particularly in the nineteenth century, is grounded specifically in this problem of how the Constitution and the Declaration of Independence threaten to offer up different meanings to different scrutinies.

Epistemologically, we are on shaky grounds if we want to know the truth at the end of a legal "event," whether trial or text. Think for a moment of the Simi Valley, California, trial of the officers who arrested Rodney King. Advocates for King were sure they knew what happened. Wasn't there a video of the whole arrest? After the defense got through with that tape, King was lucky not to have been charged with felonious assault as well as resisting arrest. The outcome of any case is what the grammar of the law will allow to be said about the conflict in question.[3] The court's desire, its charge, is to eliminate as much discrepancy between what actually happened and what can be said about what happened from the closure of the text of the case.

In African American narratives responding to the law's grammar, many voices choose to remain silent; others deliberately choose proofs, a grammar, and a vocabulary oppositional to the demands made by the court; others hypostatize the court's own language and elaborate its grammar. This production of a counterpositioned narrative to the law's story reveals the historical experience of blacks in America, that since the pursuit of judgment does not require that the entire story be told, law's closure is illusory. Just as the law as narrative often privileges the right of one or more of its narrators to withhold parts of the "whole" story, such as a defendant's prior criminal record, the historical legal narrative of African American life, from the slave coffle to the Supreme Court, is to a large part constructed on omission, on the ability of white legislators, lawyers, judges, policemen, and property owners to prevent the emergence of any narrative of African American life other than that which they authorize and narrate.

Finally, it is a truism in literary studies generally that narrative is also driven by character. In most realistic narrative, in which plausibility reigns, we readers must be able to imagine that the character of the protagonist produces the action that is powering the plot at the moment. But character/action relationships in fictions are reciprocal, and therefore our usual expectation for realistic fiction, and for the novel in particular, is that we see some evidence that action through the plot produces some perceptible change over time in the character under scrutiny. But character in the law functions more like setting than like character in the realistic novel. (Unless one were a deeply romantic novelist determined to present nature in harmony with your protagonist's emotions, so that it rains at funerals and coveys of quail take wing at every orgasm, giving setting the [e]motive force of character would be a serious burden to place on narrative.) The case in court, however, is driven by the act, not by character. You may not be convicted, in any formal sense, because of who you are. Character is established through testimony and is fixed in the legal narrative in the same way a grove of trees or a sandpit is fixed in a realistic novel. It is the context in which the act is presented, not the motive force behind the act.[4]

Thus the character of Larry Flynt, for example, is irrelevant to his standing before the court and under the First Amendment to the Constitution. So it is not necessary or useful to show if or how his character changes, in the pursuit of judgment in the suit brought against him by television evangelist Jerry Falwell. But in the film made about him, *The People vs. Larry Flynt*, which culminates on one level with that case, our moviegoers' judgment of him is based on what we understand of his character as its formation was represented to us in the course of the film. We find for him on the basis of our affection for his character as revealed to us.[5]

These questions about individual character and the differential privileging of the role of character in specific judgments are not the same as those about racially stereotyped ascriptions of character to classes of defendants, plaintiffs, or victims. If no one expects to see a change in character during the course of a trial-as-narrative, that is not the same as assuming that the racial chracteristics that the defendant exhibits at trial are immutable and causal; rather they need to be understood as the products of history, training, an ironic vision of life.

Charles W. Chesnutt contemplates the issue with no little irony in his 1899 short story, "The Web of Circumstance." In the scene in which Ben Davis is sentenced to five years in prison for larceny just after a white man has drawn only one year for manslaughter, Chesnutt observes:

> Human character is a compound of tendencies inherited and habits acquired. In the anxiety, the fear of disgrace, spoke the nineteenth-century civilization with which Ben Davis had been more or less closely in touch during twenty years of slavery and fifteen years of freedom. In the stolidity with which he received this sen-

tence for a crime which he had not committed, spoke who knows what trait of inherited savagery? For stoicism is a savage virtue. (260)

We will see that the presence of such attitudes toward African Americans in the courts, based on assumptions about African American character, affect African American narrative's critique of the law in somewhat predictable ways but in some surprising ways as well. As black writers in the nineteenth and twentieth centuries struggle against the romantic assumptions about African Americans held by most whites through the attempt to create "authentic" characters in authentic narratives, we will see them struggling also with the competing view of African Americans seen by whites through the lens of the law. Given the complexity of the issues I have just raised, it is impossible in this study to undertake a comprehensive account of the relationships among African Americans, their narrative practices, and the law under which they have labored. The story of "the law" in, and in relationship to, black popular culture alone would require multiple volumes. Beyond that, however, lies a more basic problem. As we recover the texts of a repressed literary past, the attempt at definition emerges as Sisyphean. It is a fool's errand to attempt to bring back any determined, essentialist text of African American life. My research uncovered novels and stories, cases and treatises that have yet to be discussed in any venue, not even this book. These versions of the life of the Race will, I am sure, eventually shape and give texture to some canon, literary or legal. In the meantime, I can only suggest, with attention to some thematic concerns in literary narrative, some questions about how it is that law and narrative interact to make meaning among the diverse positions of African American subjectivity.

While white American literature reserves a genre category or two for stories grounded in law—and ghettoizes those stories in separate review columns and bookstore and library sections—"classical" African American literature is universally grounded in law; in fact, all African American fiction carries the question of the legal status of blacks as its subtext. Whether one begins with slave narratives or intersects the historical line at the onset of the Black Aesthetic in the 1970s, the conflict between the substance of African American life and the status of that life under the law is the heart of the narrative challenge. Even when a Walter Mosley or Chester Himes writes a genre novel, say a detective story, the issues are identical to those at the center of the novels of Chesnutt, Delany, Harper, McKay, Hurston, Bambara, and Morrison.

How radically this situation differs from that of white American fiction cannot be overstated. The law's ability to shape—its historical force as the sole yet ever elusive determinant of African American social identity—presets the narrative base for all African American fiction. It might not be too much to say that much of what any of us, black or white, might understand by the term *Black Americans,* insofar as that status reflects a condition of citizenship, is not only socially constructed in a culture that masks its class determinants under mythic narratives of romance and individualism, but is determined and redetermined by the law. Consequently, there may not be a single novel in classical African American literature that does not contain a significant treatment of the question of the legal status of African Americans or have as its assumed and even unspoken ground the struggle over that status.

William L. Andrews separates the narrative voice of fiction from those of slave narrative and black autobiography. Because one argument of this study is that the center of all African American classical narrative is the question of legal status as a real and as a fictive condition, I will resist that set of discriminations. Andrews helpfully points out in the same article, however, a definition of *fictive,* borrowed from Barbara Herrnstein Smith (23), that sends me back to the earlier discussion of basic relationships between literature and law in this introduction:

> The marginal world of the earliest black American novels may be usefully termed a fictive world [as Smith] applies "fictive" to the subjects and objects of representation in various "mimetic art-forms" like poetry, the novel, or the drama. What is re-presented in these types of literary discourse are not "existing objects or events" but "fictive member[s] of an identifiable class of natural ('real') objects or events." (Andrews, "Novelization" 26)

But at the center of African American fictive narrative, as at the center of law's fictive nature, is not just the inscription of imagined representatives of an identifiable class of *objects and events* but of an identifiable class of *relationships.* I hesitate to attach Smith's qualifiers "natural ('real')" to the word *relationships* here because of the very relativity of relationships and the subjectivity of every description of them. That is, in the simplest relational structures the dyadic positioning of the participants invites conflicting analyses. For everyone on top, there is a someone on the bottom to whom the relationship feels quite different, although every bit as real and perhaps even natural. And it is this representation of relationships that is the structural core of the narratives we are going to try to examine. That difference of experience with the relational is what law and fiction negotiate; African American narrative fiction in particular negotiates that experience and at the same time interrogates law's negotiation of it.

To a considerable extent, in fact, one obvious interaction between the various texts of the law on one side and the various narrative categories of African American life is the interrogative effect of each narrational "event" on the other, an intertextual function. When one is read through the lens of the other, a third text emerges, as through a dialectical interrogation between oppositions. I would, however, modify the intellectually bureaucratic and linear tone that "intertextuality" imposes on what is actually a complex weave of interactions with the word *signifying*. My reasons for doing so are set out in Henry Louis Gates Jr.'s *Signifying Monkey*. Gates points out that the objects of his attention are African "metaphysical systems of order" in general and the act of signifying in particular. Signification, as Gates derives the meaning from experience and theory, means to comment on and through another discourse with your own more empowered one. He notes the stories of the mediator figure Esu and suggests that as the tales encode myths of man's relations to gods and humanity's place in the cosmic order, they at the same time embody and utilize language *above* ordinary language (4–6).

I am going to write as though what Gates says is true of the relationship between law and African American literature in the following ways. First, both law and literature "encode man's [sic] relation" to his gods, including those secular forces he obeys, and place him in the order of the cosmos of meaning as he sees it. Second, both law and literature operate at the level of meaning-about-meaning, meta-ontology, that captures what Gates describes as having been embodied in the Esu tales. Finally, when one is used as the device through which the other is read, the device signifies "on" the object text, speaking/reading through it and creating a third text that is a text of the experience of that particular reading. So American law and its history, in their particulars as well as in the shape of their combined presence in the national experience, take on new identities, hold new meanings, when the experience of the African American "nation" as embodied in its narrative fiction is used as the device through which case and statute are read. Even more dramatically, African American literature exhibits new concerns, other complexities, makes unheard statements in response to the interrogative signifying of the law.

So, to some extent, this work is a preliminary study of signifying on the law and of law as signifying discourse. It is also a theoretical and historical study of the relationships between two social texts, and it proceeds from the premise that both law and literature are mutually and inextricably responsible for writing the larger texts of social reality that define a period or region in American life. One attempts to understand how the dynamics of production of these two social texts define a historical or cultural moment by reading the interrogations of each by the other, watching the signifying make the real.

One consequence of reading such interrogations is to shift our gaze from the privileged inscriptions of social reality that are the products of the lives of white writers of legal and fictive discourses to the writing of African American experience, where lives, practices, and literatures are, even at this late date, still less familiar. This is particularly true with relationship to the lives of black Americans under the law. African Americans writing in the law and about the law offer an interrogative text that constitutes a parallel narrative often quite at odds with the canonical narrative of white American life. A study of that parallel narrative suggests, for example, how African American life is written and understood as an "amendment" to a privileged white status. We might also see how the law occupies a different site in African American life and specifically in African American narratives than it does in the life and literatures of white Americans.

Yet another metaphor for the relationship between American law and African American narrative is that of the palimpsest, in which one text is written over another. In this case I am interested to see how African American narratives overinscribe legal texts of the same issues, place, figures, events. I would even suggest that it is appropriate to see African American narrative overinscriptions as ironic, for signifying is an ironic act. In any case, I want to ask questions about some of the sources of the ontology of African American experience by looking at the meaning-making/text-making enterprise shared, however unequally at any given moment, by black and white Americans: participation, however dissimilar in action and effect, in the culture's dominant narrative modes, literature and law. The intertextualities, the palimpsests, the "signifying" considered here might be considered

epistemological moments that could lead us to understand the ontology. By "epistemological" I mean to suggest the problematic of both
law and literature as ways of knowing or certifying what is. More
specifically, I mean to consider how African American narratives, primarily fiction, signify on American law and allow us to judge it as a
way of knowing about African American life. At the same time, however, I mean to consider how American law operates to inject both epistemologies and ontologies into African American literature and life.

How the law and fiction, among other forms of narrative, functioned as epistemologies of desire, for example, is a complex story. It
begins and ends with the impact of romanticism.[6] By "romantic" in this
case I refer to typologies of self, imagination, community, property, privacy, individualism, authenticity, innocence, and irony that emerge in
American consciousness after Independence and that become the
unspoken premises from which white Americans in general reasoned
toward their understanding of the social body of the United States
throughout the nineteenth century.[7] This understanding excluded
African Americans from citizenship in the imagined national community and acted to suppress the expression of African American desire.[8]

In the America of which I am writing, matters of law are tied not
only to race but to property, as race in America itself is always already
a narrative of property. I would venture that romanticism served in the
emerging texts of our legal and cultural history to define self and property such that the fundamental assumptions upon which certain constitutional protections are based preemptorily excluded African Americans from any enjoyment of those protections that were not first
carefully and exhaustively argued. Because I find it highly unlikely that
the law, as one of the two primary texts of American life in the nineteenth century (literature being the other), would fail to exhibit characteristics of romanticism, the primary cultural paradigm in American
life in the nineteenth century, I think that an examination of the notions
of privacy, liberty, and the freedom to associate will show them to be
inscriptions of the romantic hero and that the obverse of each of these
will be seen to be inscriptions of the role of the "other" against whom
or which the hero struggles in the quest for autonomous identity, a role
reserved almost exclusively to the African.[9] I also want to note here that
the ongoing task of scholarship is not only recovering paradigms but
particularities, including the hidden records of gendered and sexual
"others." Much the same vocabulary that one uses to explore the condition of blacks under the law in nineteenth-century America can be

and is used in such work. Consider, for example, that Baldwin's themes achieve "an explicit exploration of the homosexual as the Other, to be granted or perpetually refused the golden promise of America's democratic dreams" (Porter 153). I note here that one of the limitations of this study is that it does not attempt anything like a comprehensive study of the relationships among designated "Others" and the conventions of their creation in American discourse of polity. As Bernard Bailyn notes, America as a wilderness was "a place where the ordinary restraints of civility could be abandoned in pell-mell exploitation, a remote place where recognized enemies and pariahs of society—heretics, criminals, paupers—could safely be deposited . . . and where putatively inferior specimens of humanity, blacks and Indians, could be reduced to subhuman statuses" (113). If the Mansfield decision in *Sommersett's Case* (1772) made any Negro free the moment his foot touched England, then the obverse of necessity was also true, that on the romantic western periphery of European consciousness, "restraint on brutal exploitation" should not hamper relationships between the colonial master and his property (114).[10]

Michael O'Brien argues that the new America became a romantic culture much sooner and with more alacrity than either France or Britain "because romanticism had special appeal for those who felt themselves on the periphery" (50). As a provincial culture in the throes of self-creation, the United States was receptive to romanticism as "the doctrine of the outsider" seeking to turn the isolation of the "parvenus, the migrant, the odd" into "a proclamation of self-worth" (51).

What, then, has been seen as an "Enlightenment" principle of rights for two hundred years might better be seen as a codification of desire, the romantic pursuit of autonomous identity, able of necessity, in the last instant, to stand apart from and to withstand community while longing for it nonetheless—more to my point, to withstand community's jurisdiction over private property.[11] It is in this way that romanticism in America is more clearly understood: as a colonial ideology. The combination of property relations as systematized violence and the "bizarre distentions" (Bailyn 114) of European culture that flourished in isolation at its far western reaches along with those relations produced in America the fullest realization of romanticism's colonialist impulses. Consequently, autonomous identity underwrites citizenship in America's romantic postrevolutionary republic and at the same time validates (even demands) its seemingly paradoxical postrevolutionary, internalized colonialism, slavery. And it is this same romantic autonomous identity that continued to underwrite citizenship in America's romantic republic and that was systematically denied to African Americans throughout the nineteenth century. While the legal history of this denial is, as Paul Finkelman notes, written in the "statutes, court decisions, and quasi-legal mechanisms for race control" that supported slavery ("Exploring" 90), the postwar rationales that undergirded the reapplication of slave codes as a "law of separations," first as "Black Codes" and then "Jim Crow," are grounded elsewhere. The relationships between this "law of separations," before and after Emancipation, and African American narrative are the objects of this inquiry.[12]

While epistemology, as a philosophical category, might turn out to be too restrictive for this discussion, it does provide a preliminary place to stand when one attempts to examine the tension in these texts between the reality of life for black Americans and the ability of the law to describe that reality. It also seems to be the case that these African American writers want to privilege the discussion of that tension through the use of specific literary forms, textual conventions through which they can approach the contradiction, perhaps the central contradiction, of their lives as lived. As a people who find themselves in this land, they find they are "of" this land only as they are defined through a system of laws designed and enacted in the first instance to incorporate their enslavement and only subsequently altered to admit their citizenship. The conflict resides in the fact that their enslavement was situated in the recognition of the "natural" right to property that was to be protected for all citizens while their citizenship is situated in a category of "status" that will always be textualized as an "amendment" to the "natural" rights that were to be embedded in the Constitution. And so black Americans will see themselves as strangers among strangers; always the objects being named, never the naming subjects. The law, one text of this disjuncture, can only amend and erase, but never capture, the life of the race. If it is, as Patricia Williams has argued, one task of lawyers to "un[do] institutional descriptions of what is 'obvious and what is not'" ("Spirit" 131), then the law as a narrative of omission and marginality cannot be let alone, centered among the social texts of American life, and one clear task of African American fiction is to undertake the decentering challenge of interrogating it.

One task of this book is to try to make that decentering visible. One way to do that will be to try to show not only how African American narrative signifies on "the obvious," but to try to reveal what is not obvious, in the "law" and in the narrative. Just for a moment, for example, we can divide the two centuries of black experience with the law at 1896, with *Plessy v. Ferguson*. We can argue that *Plessy* looks back to an Edenic text of American life but sets the type for a narrative of bondage and fallen grace. "Separate but equal" is an Edenic formulation; it limns an America as God might have made her, at the eve of that day when Adam and God had separated out all the beings of the world and given them names so that each would not be the other, just as God had separated day from night and land from sea, and then woman from man. Eden was that great good place where the evidence of an evenhanded Creation stood in its several separate and equal parts. So, said the Court, stood America on the brink of a new century. These are romantic images of a national past, an imagined identity with Creation, a privileging vision of the innocent genesis of property and race.

In 1954, another Court was drawn to the text of American origins and found another narrative. That Court read a tale of ironic bondage, made so by the illusion of equality. America, it read, had privileged separation at the expense of equality, maintaining at its heart contradictory and self-canceling texts, wounding itself through deception and forfeiting innocence. Double-tongued, like a serpent, America inhabited not Eden, but the prison-house of lies, holding half its people in bondage while proclaiming them free, holding that bound half responsible for the failure to produce the consequences of liberty while locking away the instruments of freedom when they entered the room.

Some understanding of how African Americans read and wrote America's genesis story is what we are after. How much romance, how much innocence, how much irony went into the composition of those narratives. Of course, innocence and irony are only parts of the story of law and fiction in African American life, but because of their ties to romanticism in American experience, they run throughout the narrative as, I have suggested, feather and shot, recurring entries in the logbook of the American experiment. One way to study the story of law and fiction in African American life is to treat it as a real text and to try to understand as much of the history of the production of that text as possible. I assume that the text is indeterminate or at least unfinished and has been worked on by several hands, encoding many voices. Along the way I want to note how these hands/voices have recorded their experimental observations of innocence and irony, and to consider alongside those matters others that will emerge, such as memory, property, privacy, and desire.

The epigraph to this book from Mrs. N. F. Mossell is relevant here. Although her limited knowledge of the published immediate past causes her to misstate the limits of black literacy in the nineteenth century, her primary observation is true enough: literate or not, African Americans were not admitted to the table where the composition of the text of American life was going forward. And illiterate in such large numbers, excluded in her time from representation by voice or hand in the accounts of their own lives, black Americans could only "whisper consolations" to their torn and dying selves. This study is an attempt to read even those texts of the law and fiction that have emerged in the light of her observation, to see how both law and fiction have operated as whispered consolations to a people and to uncover the narrative offered therein. To do that, I have assumed that there is a classical African American narrative whose chronological boundaries are roughly 1820 to 1954, and it is this narrative to which I will turn my attention, though in an epilogue I will suggest what happens to the classical narrative and what we might say about what succeeded it. The discussion of the classical narrative is undertaken in two parts, which I have arranged in eight subsequent chapters.

In the first four chapters I look at antebellum and postbellum matters and bring the account down to the first decade of the twentieth century. At the center of these chapters is the influence of elements of romanticism on the laws that circumscribed black American life and in the narrative responses to that circumscription. Strategic to that inquiry are matters of property, privacy, innocence, irony, authenticity, and personhood. I have tried to examine these matters as I read cases from colonial, antebellum, Reconstruction, and post-Reconstruction America, legislation from the same periods, narratives of fugitive slaves, debates, editorials, essays, stories, novels, and autobiographies. And I have tried to track one common effect of both slavery and post-Emancipation law, the suppression of African American desire.

The subsequent four chapters are less specifically keyed to legislation and litigation than to the shifting legal focus in African American narrative itself. The urbanization and consequential criminalization of everyday African American life under Jim Crow allowed black writers to finally shrug off the last of the affect of innocence and seek a realistic approach to the depiction of black life under American law. As African Americans moved into a "postproperty" world, they found it more than a little uncertain. No longer property de jure, they were often property de facto, and certainly they were nowhere near being "propertied." The irony of this life was explicit and unavoidable, and the nineteenth-century questions of personhood, citizenship, and authenticity had to be replaced with existential problems of "post-authentic" life—passing, purpose, and free will. Where once Innocence made you unfit for the franchise, now it meant not having to say you were guilty, if you could prove it.

And it was here that the "classical" African American interrogation of the law came to a close, with the inescapability of irony. The law, at first glance, ultimately abhors irony. The law appears to be a uniquely "innocent" institution in that it admits no middle ground. Even to be "guilty" is to be innocent—of ambiguity. That is why legal fictions abound in the law, to obviate irony. And African American narrative met the law on those grounds. But when modernism came to the African American novel, late as it did come, with Ellison's *Invisible Man*, the tone of the signifying changed. And the life of the Race under the law changed as well. As Derrick Bell, Patricia Williams, Ishmael Reed, Toni Morrison, James Alan McPherson, and a host of men and women novelists, story writers, essayists, memoirists, and legal scholars have testified since *Brown v. Board of Education*, the ironic power of the law still permeates African American life. In a final, epilogical chapter, then, I consider some aspects of a postclassical narrative and its relationship with American law since the advent of the modern civil-rights movement.

In general, one-half the book is the story of "romanticism, property, and the suppression of African-American desire." It emerges from and contradicts *Plessy*'s "Edenic America" and stretches its story from the first voice, that of America as "declared," to the birth of what Randolph Bourne called "trans-national America" at the brink of the First World War. It establishes the lines of innocence and irony across which black Americans and the law of the romantic republic that enslaved and then suppressed them spoke their pieces. It involves us with matters of identity, property, personhood, and citizenship. Ultimately it is a struggle over the right to desire.

The second half is the story of "law and the closing of the classical African-American narrative" and is about the consequences of the struggle over desire, the impact of the urbanization of African American life, and "postproperty" identity. In this part some African American desire becomes posited as criminal when not suppressed and becomes the hidden causative factor in the ironic racialization of urban pathology through the first half of the twentieth century. But a part of the story is of the emergence of the empowered ironic narrative that closes out the classical era of African American narrative despite the imputations of pathology. The period ends, as Ellison might appreciate, with his novel and the notice to Americans that, indeed, their house of laws is on fire.

CHAPTER 1

In Search of Justice and Jurisprudence

> It appears to your addressers that civil-rights doctrines are still in an imperfect, unsettled, mischievous state, and that the decisions of the courts are involved in an intricate tangle of verbal mysticism, the unravelling of which puts to confusion the legal acumen of even the most learned and skilful expositors of jurisprudence.
>
> Brotherhood of Liberty, *Justice and Jurisprudence*, 1889

Albany, a Negro belonging to Mrs. Carpenter, was burned to death June 12, 1741. Captain Marshall's Ben followed on the sixteenth. Cuffee, once owned by Squire Philipse, and Quack, who belonged to John Roosevelt—not John Walters's Quack—had been the first to die at the stake on May 30, but Caesar and Prince had been hanged on May 11, the very first to die. Accused of a conspiracy to fire and loot New York City, thirty-one free and enslaved Negroes were burned or hanged on orders of Judge Daniel Horsmanden's court (Horsmanden).[1] In 1755 in Massachusetts, a slave, Mark, convicted of aiding Phillis, was hanged and gibbeted; Phillis was burned at the stake for having poisoned their master, Captain John Codman. Described by Abner Cheney Goodell Jr., who discovered the transcripts of the trial in 1883, as the "only known instance of the infliction of the commonlaw penalty for petit treason, in New England," the sentence as carried out resulted in Mark's body hanging in chains from a scaffold at the corner of a public square in Charlestown, where Paul Revere reported seeing it some twenty years later, on the occasion of his famous ride (Goodell 3, 30).[2]

In the first of these accounts, Horsmanden, a New York landowner and later Tory sympathizer, compiled the notes, including his own, of the investigation and trial at which he had served as a judge. The rendering of the testimonies of the black defendants is his. No other records seem to have survived, and Horsmanden's account, fiction or fact, seeks to justify the course taken by the court, including the burning, hanging, and transportation of the various defendants. Horsmanden raises the specter of mass Negro riot and destruction to justify the excesses of his court. The Mark and Phillis case, conversely, reminds us that the effects of resistance to, and under, the laws of slavery were more often felt by the individual and within the household than by the system of slavery itself.[3]

While Horsmanden's trial account renders all discourse through the filter of a reportorial and perhaps self-serving white consciousness. In the preface to his account of the trial, Horsmanden argues that "negroes" in ordinary cases rarely give the same testimony twice.

> The trouble of examining criminals in general, may be easily guessed at; but the fatigue in that of negroes, is not to be conceived, but by those that have undergone the drudgery. The difficulty of bringing and holding them to the truth, if by chance it starts through them, is not to be surmounted, but by the closest attention; many of them have a great deal of craft; their unintelligible jargon stands them in great stead, to conceal their meaning; so that an examiner must expect to encounter with much perplexity, grope through a maze of obscurity, be obliged to lay hold of broken hints, lay them carefully together, and thoroughly weigh and compare them with each other before he can be able to see the light, or fix those creatures to any certain determinate meaning. (7–8)

While the Horsmanden record redacts the language of the defendants into a white colonial English, the transcript of the 1755 case of Phillis and Mark allows us to hear the voice of the enslaved/indicted directly. Even there, however, defendant and prosecutor sound exactly alike. The languages of suppression and resistance are modulated into a single toneless narrative, empty of any emotion. In Phillis's and Mark's testimonies as recorded, the nearest thing to a motive the reader will uncover is a general dislike of slavery and a desire for a better master (9). Phillis, who had been owned by Codman since she was a small child, testified that Mark, who had been bought by Codman as an adult, "told Phoebe and I that he had read the Bible through and it was no Sin to kill him if they did not lay violent Hands on him So as to shed Blood, by sticking or stabbing or cutting his Throat" (12). Mark was clearly dissatisfied with his lot and even convinced Phillis, or so she claimed, to set fire to Codman's buildings. Mark had worked for Codman in Boston, but Codman had brought him back to Charlestown. Phillis testified that "Mark first proposed it, to Phoebe and I; and the reason he gave us was that he wanted to get to Boston, and if all was burnt down, he did not know what Master could do without selling us" (13).

Beyond the matters of the crime, however, Phillis's testimony sketches the outlines of a life in colonial slavery, one in which children are bought and sold, limits are placed on public gatherings of non-whites, servants are known by the possessive forms of their owners' names, and conversations among slaves are carried on in a local code based on years of experience in the same community. Even small lessons of household management can be extracted from the record, as Phillis and Mark describe the routines against which their resistance was formed. We even begin to sense how the community of the enslaved circulated its own news, its own common understanding of the world, when we learn that one assumption of the plotters was that "Mr. Salmon's Negros poisn'd him, and were never found out, but had got good masters, & so might we" (9). But such documents are rare.[4] Goodell cites other cases the outcomes of which are reported but from which the voices are absent. Here, too, the events are matters of arson, poisons, and the resentment of the enslaved.

The many and the few. In any number, Africans and their descendants in America have been defined and circumscribed, segregated and trivialized by the laws of the land since their arrival here in the seventeenth century. As part of that record, for example—between Horsmanden's account of a colonial revolt that may never have existed and the post-Reconstruction fantasy of black nationalism, *Imperium in Imperio,* Sutton E. Griggs's 1899 novel of a plan to seize Louisiana and Texas for the black race—lie some 160 years of American law and African American narrative.[5] For the first half of that considerable stretch both the law and the literature, as prose genres that have narrative at their center, belonged primarily to whites. The text of that dominance was broken only occasionally by the eloquent but sporadic and ineffectual petitions for freedom from anonymous Africans enslaved in northern states[6] or the novelty of a tale of Christian conversion and escape from slavery, usually published in England.[7]

But with the appearance, in the 1820s, of domestically published slave narratives and autobiographies, black writers began to engage both literature and the law, usually by representing the latter through the former. There were black voices in the texts of the law, earlier, but these were subalternate voices, voices mediated through the representations of their masters, in the cases of enslaved people, and through the writs of their lawyers if they were free persons of color.[8] Even more often we find the causes, but not the voices, of antebellum African America in the records of appellate court decisions at state levels throughout the Old South.[9]

While there were cases of national interest involving Africans in America prior to the Civil War,[10] the great body of narrative dealing with African American life before the middle of the nineteenth century is contained in more ordinary case records and in the published accounts of black life in and out of slavery written or authorized by those who lived the lives. As historians have begun to recover the stories of enslaved blacks and free people of color in the courts, the legal outlines of those lives, and some of the specific content, become visible. Melton A. McLaurin's recovery of the story of Celia, who murdered her owner in rural Missouri, is an example of the kind of scholarship that pays its respects to the impact of narrative on the record of the past. Another is Victoria E. Bynum's study of black and white women in antebellum North Carolina.[11] Bynum reveals that while enslaved people, and especially women, had little access to the law as plaintiffs, the records of local courts contain narratives of crime, violence, domestic "frisson," and social unrest enough to fill several novels.

> In March 1836, for example, the superior court of Granville County charged Hannah, the slave of Col. John G. Hart, with murdering her son Solomon by slashing his throat with a knife she had obtained the night before from the plantation dairy. She also slit her own throat in an unsuccessful attempt to kill herself. As she lay bleeding, she called out to a black man passing by to "come there and put her away." Hannah survived to face trial and conviction on murder charges (40 n. 17).

> In 1843, William Russell of Granville County accused his slave Dilcy of trying to poison his entire family, but the court found no evidence on which to indict her. Candis, an Orange County slave, languished in jail for more than two months in 1853 before being found innocent of charges that she had set fire to the home and barn of Aaron Jones Jr., a white man (40 n. 18).

> In Orange County, Silvia Chavis, a free black mother, became so outraged by a slave's attempt to entice her teenage daughter into prostitution that she successfully sued the slave and his master in the county court (80 n. 84).

Work by legal and cultural historians indicate that African American access to the courts before and after the Civil War varied from jurisdiction to jurisdiction. In fact, the range of cases in which blacks, whether free or enslaved, figure in the antebellum South alone goes beyond the predictable category of petitions for freedom. No one can even estimate the number of cases in which Africans in America appear as plaintiffs, victims, or defendants, or in which their interests are represented by second parties, during this period (Catterall; Fede; Finkelman, *Slavery and the Law*; Morris; Schafer; Stroud; Tushnet, *American Law*).

In 1837, George Parnham, a Virginia slaveholder, wrote to a local magistrate complaining of the treatment of Juba, one of his elderly slaves, at the hands of patrollers. Juba was wakened in the middle of the night and dragged into the yard to receive three hundred lashes for an unspecified offense. Only the intervention of the slaveholder's sister prevented the attack from being carried out:

> Mr. Wm. B. Stone, July 25th 1837, Sir—On Tuesday night the 18th of July Ins't between 10 & 11 o'clock Mrs. Goodwin being with me, & both of us having gone to bed, Mrs. Goodwin was roused by a rap at the window, when a servant told her that the patrol were killing Juba (my negro (Man) and requested her to go to the quarter.

When the beating began, Mrs. Goodwin threw herself between the patrollers and Juba:

> Ten blows were deliberately lain on (as Mrs. Goodwin counted, sitting in the door. There was a pause. Mrs. Goodwin thinks she then heared my voice raised in remonstrance. The blows then commenced again in rapid succession. Six were struck, as Mrs. Goodwin says, when she rose from her seat determined to rush between the man & the blows, & receive, in her own person, the blows which remained to be inflicted.

The old man Juba, an epileptic who was obviously in the care of his owner, was seriously injured, and a doctor was sent for. Parnham decided to take legal action:

> These three men professed to be on a patrol. I wish to commence a civil suit against the three. I suppose it is to be a case for a Jury, &

that therefore the County Court is the proper tribunal at which to bring the suit. So, please to issue a writ against them I suppose that it would be proper to say that these men came forcibly upon my premeses [sic] and injured my negro, by means of which I lost his services for a period of time. The facts of the case are that I am not only losing his services at this time, but am employing a physician for him.

You will probly [sic] be able from the statement of facts which this communication contains to make out the declaration & prepare the matter in all aspects [as] it should be prepared. I supposed [sic] it will be necessary to have Mrs. Goodwin summoned to appear as a witness. Dr. C. Lancaster is the physician who attends Juba. If you deem it necessary, have Dr. L. summoned.

> Yours respectfully
> Geo. D Parnham

Just as Parnham's letter suggests the quasi-legal field of contestation onto which enslaved people could be thrown by their mere presence in a household, even a "caring" one as Parnham's seemed to be, it also suggests how hard it would be to overestimate the number and the impact of local and state statutes accumulating "on the books" in the slaveholding states, and beyond, prior to 1865, concerned solely or in the main with the presence of enslaved and free blacks in this country (Finkelman, *Statutes on Slavery* and *Slavery in the Courtroom*; Morris). What needs also to be remarked is how absent from any of these texts is the direct voice of African American experience. The story of Juba above literally cries out for the old man's voice. How did he feel, awakened in the night to be dragged and beaten? Was he befuddled, angry, frightened, resigned? Did he know the cause of any of it? What would his lawsuit have claimed? Parnham's claims loss of service.

How different Parnham's account of the beating is, sympathetic though he might be to Juba's plight, from these accounts of violence against slaves from black authors of autobiography and novel. First, Frederick Douglass:

> Before he commenced whipping Aunt Hester, he took her into the kitchen, and stripped her from neck to waist, leaving her neck, shoulders, and back, entirely naked. He then told her to cross her hands, calling her at the same time a d——d b——h. After crossing her hands, he tied them with a strong rope, and led her to a stool

under a large hook in the joist, put in for the purpose. He made her get up on the stool and tied her hands to the hook. She now stood fair for his infernal purpose. Her arms were stretched up at their full length, so that she stood upon the ends of her toes. He then said to her, "Now, you d——d b——h, I'll learn you how to disobey my orders.!" and after rolling up his sleeves, he commenced to lay on the heavy cowskin, and soon the warm, red blood (amid heart-rending shrieks from her, and horrid oaths from him) came dripping to the floor). (*Narrative* 26)

And from another recounting, a half-century later, by African American novelist Pauline Hopkins:

With all his mighty strength he brought the lash down on the frail and shrinking form. O God! was there none to rescue her?

The air whistled as the snaky leather thong curled and writhed in its rapid, vengeful descent. A shriek from the victim—a spurt of blood that spattered the torturer—a long, raw gash across a tender, white back. Hank gazed at the cut with critical satisfaction, as he compared its depth with the skin and blood that encased the long and tapering lash. It was now Bill's turn.

"I'll go you one better," he said, as he sighted the distance and exact place to make his mark with mathematical precision, at the same time shifting his tobacco from the right to the left cheek. Again the rawhide whistled through the air, falling across the other cut squarely in the center. Another shriek, a stifled sob, a long-drawn quivering sigh—then the deep stillness of unconsciousness. Again and again was the outrage repeated. Fainting fit followed fainting fit. The blood stood in a pool about her feet. (*Contending* 68–69)

Parnham's interests (and those of the owners of the enslaved bodies described by Douglass and Hopkins in their later narratives) are addressed quite clearly in this 1748 Virginia statute which limits responsibility for the death of a slave: "An accidental homicide during correction of a slave does not make one liable for prosecution or punishment, unless the slave is killed wilfully; on a manslaughter verdict, there is no forfeiture or punishment" (Guild 156). By 1792, however, while there was no help for the slave, the owner had gained the right to recompense: "The owner is not barred of his remedy when his slave is

killed by another person . . . or other person undertaking the dismemberment in case of a slave so punished by court order. . . . The value of
a slave [who dies by or at law] shall be paid by the public to the owner"
(Guild 160).

Eventually, the "object voice" silenced in these texts emerges as the
"subject voice" in the sixty-five slave narratives published prior to the
Civil War and persists, in a variant tone, in another fifty or so published
between the end of that war and the 1930s (Andrews, "Representation"
63). The very premise of the escaped slave's tale is that she or he has
broken the law. In many cases, the law broken is not only one or many
of those local ordinances that support the practice of slavery in any
jurisdiction, but in cases of active resistance to return, the violation is of
a federal statute, either of the two Fugitive Slave Acts passed prior to
the outbreak of hostilities between the North and the South. James L.
Smith, who had escaped to freedom in 1838, was haunted by the power
of the law more than a decade later. He wrote in his account of his life,

> After the Fugitive Slave Law was passed, terror struck the hearts of
> those who had escaped to the free States, as no earthly power
> could prevent them from being returned to their masters. Very
> many were taken back. For my part, I was very much frightened,
> and was continually haunted by dreams which were so vivid as to
> appear really true. One night I dreamt my master had come for me,
> and, as he proved property, I was delivered up to him by the
> United States Marshal. In the morning I told the dream to my wife.
> She said she "believed it would come true," and was very much
> worried. (203)

As novelist and autobiographer William Wells Brown would comment
in his own story, even removal to England failed to erase the fear that
one's master might appear, writ in hand, to take you back. Because the
Fugitive Slave Act applied in practice to every person of African
descent in the United States, its impact on African American narrative
cannot be ignored (G. E. Walker 19).[12]

Out of these contexts, African American attitudes toward the law
emerge as a complex welter of hope, cynicism, trust, and clear-eyed,
even ironic, understanding. Smith, for example, writing at the end of
the century about events having taken place decades before, extols the
promises of the law implicit in the Civil Rights Acts of 1866 and in the
Fifteenth Amendment to the Constitution but reminds his readers on

several occasions that slaveholders and slave catchers operated under the aegis of the law as well. The Reverend G. W. Offley, in his own narrative, argues to his fellow men and women of color that the law is arbitrary and a man-made instrument that they should ignore when determining their own worth in the world, quoting St. Paul to the effect that "where there is no law there is no transgression. Then the moral guilt rests on the oppressor and not on the oppressed" (136).

Offley's narrative, one of the shortest published, is informative about the legal complexity of a slave's life. Each of the complexities revealed in this personal narrative has a parallel in case law in virtually every slaveholding state. As he tells it, his mother was born a slave, married, and had three children. She was freed at the death of her master by his will, and her children were to be free at the age of twenty-five, except that the youngest child was named in a second will that was destroyed by the master's wife, and he was held as bound for life. Offley's father, a free man of color, bought that son and a sister and freed both of them, the boy at sixteen and the girl at twenty-five. Offley himself was held to work with his father until he was twenty-one. In a scene that reflects the desperation of the slave Hannah cited above and anticipates the case of Margaret Garner of Kentucky, whose actions formed the core around which African American author and Nobel Prize winner Toni Morrison built her 1987 novel, *Beloved*, Offley's mother confronted her dead master's family over their original refusal to allow the father to purchase his own children's freedom. Told that the master's family would buy the children themselves and shoot her husband dead on the auction ground if he tried to stop them, she replied, "[B]uy them and welcome, but you had better throw your money in the fire, for if you buy one of my children I will cut all three of their throats while they are asleep, and your money will do you no good" (131).[13]

But these are extraordinary moments, or so they seem to most readers, recorded instances of extreme conflict. The place of law in African American life and narrative is much more ordinary and yet so totalizing. The evidence of case law, legislation, and antebellum slave narrative gives compelling weight to an argument that black Americans, enslaved and free, have lived under the law at a level of imbrication unknown to any other citizen or even any alien visitor or resident. Occasionally, as in the instances of Mormons in Missouri and Illinois in the 1830s, or of foreign nationals or American residents of foreign "extraction" in time of war, acts are passed to limit the presence or activities of one group of people. Those moments pass, and the great majority of Americans never experience them. But black Americans under the law in the nineteenth century seem never to escape it.

To read, for example, "Linda Brent"'s *Incidents in the Life of a Slave Girl* is to read a template for the centrality of law in the slave narrative. Her narrative opens with a statement of legal status, "I was born a slave," and the opening paragraph is a catalog of legal issues: the terms under which her father hired out his work; the denial of his request to purchase his own children; her description of herself as "merchandise" redeemable on demand; manumission laws and the right of resale; inheritance law and the lack of legal protection of children by their enslaved parents. The paragraph ends with this bitterly ironic comment on the denial of the right to make binding contracts: "The reader probably knows that no promise or writing given to a slave is legally binding; for, according to Southern laws, a slave, *being* property, can *hold* no property. When my grandmother lent her hard earnings to her mistress, she trusted solely to her honor. The honor of a slaveholder to a slave!" (Jacobs 4).[14]

It is informative, even if you might think it superficial, to read through slave narratives and note the numbers of times "the law" is mentioned directly and then to add to those instances the references to property and to justice. What would strike you rather soon, I think, is how unlike anything in white literature is this obsession with the law and with legal status. In literature written by white Americans the closest parallel I can imagine is with the fascination psychotherapy and various forms of self-realization holds in much of twentieth-century fiction.

In "Brent"'s account, for example, her status as property is the center of her identity on almost every page, and the legal context of that "property-ness" is reiterated again and again:

> But I was her slave, and I suppose she did not recognize me as her neighbor. . . . I try to think with less bitterness of this act of injustice. . . . These God-breathing machines are no more, in the sight of their masters, than the cotton they plant, or the horses they tend. (Jacob 6)

> I spent the day gathering flowers and weaving them into festoons, while the dead body of my father was lying within a mile of

me. What cared my owners for that? he was merely a piece of property. (8)

And her children were property as well:

> She had forgotten it was a crime for a slave to tell who was the father of her child. (12)

> His threat [to sell her child] lacerated my heart. I knew the law gave him the power to fulfil it; for slaveholders have been cunning enough to enact that "the child shall follow the condition of the *mother*," not of the *father*; thus taking care that licentiousness shall not interfere with avarice. (78)

Finally, the law denied her the right to the disposal of her own body and emotions:

> For my master, whose restless, craving, vicious nature rove about day and night, seeking whom to devour, had just left me, with stinging, scorching words; words that scathed ear and brain like fire. . . . When he told me that I was made for his use, made to obey his command in *every* thing; that I was nothing but a slave, whose will must and should surrender to his, never before had my puny arm felt half so strong. (16)

> Pity me, and pardon me, O virtuous reader! You never knew what it is to be a slave; to be entirely unprotected by law or custom; to have the laws reduce you to the condition of a chattel, entirely subject to the will of another. (56)[15]

"Brent" continues chapter after chapter with discussions of the Fugitive Slave Law, with accounts of local slave law in action, with discussions of the true nature of justice and of the illegality of her master's actions against her. Even at the end of her troubles she is unable to avoid the condition of property and the laws that bind her to it. Her friend Mrs. Bruce buys "Brent"'s freedom, and she responds:

> "The bill of sale!" Those words struck me like a blow. So I was *sold* at last! A human being *sold* in the free city of New York! The bill of

sale is on record, and future generations will learn from it that
women were articles of traffic in New York, late in the nineteenth
century of the Christian religion. It may hereafter prove a useful
document to antiquaries, who are seeking to measure the progress
of civilization in the United States. I well know the value of that bit
of paper; but much as I love freedom, I do not like to look upon it.
I am deeply grateful to the generous friend who procured it, but I
despise the miscreant who demanded payment for what never
rightfully belonged to him or his. (206)

Black essayists, memoirists, autobiographers, novelists of the century
were all responding to the single most salient fact of their lives as
Americans, enslaved or free: that they were creatures of the law and
their stories were stories of the law. William Wells Brown's 1853 novel,
Clotel, or The President's Daughter, opens with a discussion of slave law
and maintains a running discourse on life under the law for 190 pages:

In all the slave states, the law says:—"Slaves shall be deemed, sold,
taken, reputed, and adjudged in law to be chattels personal in the
hands of their owners and possessors, and their executors, admin-
istrators and assigns, to all intents, constructions, and purposes
whatsoever." A slave is one who is in the power of a master to
whom he belongs. The master may sell him, dispose of his person,
his industry, and his labour. He can do nothing, possess nothing,
nor acquire anything, but what must belong to his master. The
slave is entirely subject to the will of his master, who may correct
and chastise him, though not with unusual rigor, or so as to maim
and mutilate him, or expose him to the danger of loss of life, or to
cause his death. The slave, to remain a slave, must be sensible that
there is no appeal from his master." [*sic*] Where the slave is placed
by law entirely under the control of the man who claims him, body
and soul, as property, what else could be expected than the most
depraved social condition? (55–56)[16]

Brown's novel, in various editions and revisions, inscribes and
reinscribes the conflict between the ironic self-knowledge of his characters and the dehumanizing texts of American slave law.[17]

To begin to explicate how deeply enmeshed in the law are both African
American life and the fictions that represent it, it will be necessary to

give up any idea of simply moving chronologically through American legal history or providing some simple accounting of "instances" of the law in African American fiction. A good place to start a more complex reading of the "intertext" of law and African American fiction in the nineteenth century is with an account of life under the law late in the century, written by black hands, that is as polemical, as creative, and as idiosyncratic a mixture of the conventions of law and narrative as the century will produce.

In 1889, in Philadelphia, *Justice and Jurisprudence: An Inquiry Concerning the Constitutional Limitations of the Thirteenth, Fourteenth, and Fifteenth Amendments* was published. The 578-page text bore no author's name; it was identified only as having been commissioned by "The Brotherhood of Liberty." We now know that this was the Mutual United Brotherhood of Liberty, an organization of Baltimore ministers, lawyers, and laypeople, all African Americans, dedicated to the "advancement of the African race in America" (Brotherhood of Liberty, i) through the full application of the law to Negro life. Aside from a few names and cases in which they were involved, we know little more.[18] Nevertheless, it is clear that this volume represents the core of their concern about national citizenship, its benefits to the African American community, and the threats to it from an activist court seeking to obscure, elide, and eliminate the protections of the Fourteenth Amendment (ii). As such, it adds to our understanding of the centrality of the question of life under the law in the minds of the African American middle class through the period that pioneer black sociologist Rayford Logan so aptly christened "The Nadir." That this work builds its arguments through the deployment of an array of literary and rhetorical devices previously unseen in any legal texts of the period adds to its significance. For it is the response of African Americans to the law through narrative, as though the law was a narrative form as amenable to manipulation as the novel or the short story, that attracts us.

The only sustained argument against the abrogation of the legal protection of citizenship produced to that time by any African American or group of African Americans, *Justice and Jurisprudence* presents evidence of the existence of a deep-seated commitment to an American identity on the part of a determined, even militant, African American bourgeoisie.

The arguments in *Justice and Jurisprudence* and the language and compositional style in which they are couched indicate that the Brotherhood of Liberty believed in the commitment to rationality of its white audience. The author(s) of the preface assumed that

> if the complex constitutional questions and the perplexing social problems involved in the much mooted race-question could be examined and their deep, broad, ethical and political significance demonstrated by an interesting discussion, free as possible from dry abstraction, sectionalism, and partisanship, public opinion might become disentangled from the many knotty disputes by which it is now obscured, chiefly through the chicanery of a narrow system of vicious politics. (i)

The execution of the text, and its scope, are scarcely hinted at by the formalistic language of the preface. The argument and the appendix, identifying every case and every piece of legislation bearing on the rights of African people in the United States since 1862, range across labor relations, religion, moral and legal philosophy, political science and political economy, ancient and modern history (including legal history), and even the emerging field of anthropology. All of these are framed in the literary device of the dialogue, employing a dream sequence, and each episode is introduced by copious citations from classical and modern literature and philosophy, as an anonymous chief justice of our Supreme Court is visited by a student/lawyer from another culture and is asked to clarify some rather peculiar observations the traveler has recorded. The visitor is also allowed to have a conversation with a journalist about the same matters.

Here is what the writers of the preface have to say about this narrative strategy:

> *Justice and Jurisprudence* opens with a colloquy of absorbing interest between the Chief Justice of the Supreme Court and a foreign jurist "void of the intellectual and social bias generated by slavery." The character of the foreign student's subsequent interview with an eminent representative of the American press is an original conceit, executed with consummate skill, and the striking narrative which ensues is constructed with no *apparent* labor or art: it is interwoven with law and history—with philosophy and politics. There are no digressions, unnecessary descriptions, or long speeches; grace, incisive wit, sometimes bitter but never malignant sarcasm, distinguish the fanciful allegories of the journalist, as well as the

more sober reflections of the Chief Justice. . . . There is a marvelous picturing power displayed in the imagery of the student's dream, a noble extravagance in the sudden conjuring up and representation of the spirits of Fame, Ambition, and Destiny, so weird and yet so majestic do they appear as they approach Mr. Blaine[19] with thoughts intent upon his doom. The augury of his future, by the ministers of the fates, is a masterpiece.

The authors of the preface go on for two-thirds of a page more about the role of headnotes and epigraphs and close that segment thus:

The satiric reprehension, the tart irony of some of these selections may appear too bold and uncharitable, and others may exhibit human infirmities in a somewhat humourous light, but these weapons have been used only on the side of truth. The husband-man has scattered broadcast these seeds of knowledge, and it is humbly hoped that they may effectually contribute to the improvement of the rising generation, by affording the opportunity of becoming familiar with the axioms and sentiments of renowned Christians, patriots, statesmen, philosophers, historians, and poets. (ii–iii)

The vagaries of literariness notwithstanding, a desire to hold fast to citizenship and to "moot" the race question through a meeting of black and white minds was not peculiar to black Baltimoreans. T. McCants Stewart, a black lawyer also writing in 1889, but from New York, reminded his race that reason was on their side. After all, he noted, speaking of white working men, "If we have been slaves, they have been slaves; if we have been beaten and oppressed, they have been beaten and oppressed; if we have at times been cruelly murdered, without judge or jury, they were once like as we were once. They have risen; we are rising" (31). Stewart's implied identification with white workers by virtue of a shared experience was not, however, particularly reciprocated.[20]

In most communities, the white working man, taken en masse, was a monopolistic threat to black labor. In Baltimore in the 1880s, competition for jobs between black and white working men was a source of civic tension; black canmakers, brickmakers, longshoremen, blacksmiths, carpenters, painters, ship caulkers, and grain haulers vied for the same work. *Justice and Jurisprudence* charged the "lords of labor" and "labor monopolies" with excluding black workers from a fair share of the labor market, referring for the most part, it seems, to the trades guilds. One of the goals of the Brotherhood of Liberty was an integrated trades union system in Baltimore. Beginning in 1882, the Knights of Labor had begun recruiting Negro workers in Baltimore. Espousing labor solidarity regardless of color, the Knights promoted the organization of the skilled and unskilled in Baltimore into local assemblies— some of which were integrated. In 1884 Maryland exempted labor unions from the state's conspiracy statutes, and subsequently black workers, eager to demonstrate their solidarity, as Stewart's analysis suggested, joined the Knights. In 1886, a year when, nationwide, some sixty thousand members of the Colored Farmer's Alliance were members of the Knights of Labor, twenty-five thousand workers in Baltimore marched in an integrated Labor Day parade (Brotherhood of Liberty, chap. 3; Callcott 47; Meier 46; Paul 352–53). Nevertheless, the general decline in the fortunes of the Knights of Labor affected its Baltimore alliances as well, and by 1889 the author(s) of *Justice and Jurisprudence* would argue that not even the Fourteenth Amendment could protect the black laborer from "the merciless clutches of the monopolistic labor class, which has condemned him to the unremunerative pursuits of caterer, cook, coachman, porter, drayman, scrubber, carpet-beater, hod-carrier, stevedore, or bootblack" (Brotherhood of Liberty 14).

A similar situation existed a decade later in Wilmington, North Carolina. There, in one of the last of the integrated cities of the Reconstruction South, both public and private sectors of the economy saw free black participation. African Americans owned ten of eleven restaurants, twenty of twenty-two barber shops, were bootmakers, were 25 percent of the fish dealers, one-third of the meat wholesalers, one-half the tailors. Blacks were lawyers, mechanics, furniture makers, jewelers, painter-plasterers, plumbers, locksmiths, stonemasons, brickmasons, and wheelwrights. One consequence of this prosperity for blacks was a high unemployment rate for whites, resulting in an embedded resentment among working-class whites that was exploitable by Democratic Party insurgents, who fomented a riot and seized the city government from its black and white Republican officeholders (Prather 1–49). As we will see later, the events that exploded in Wilmington in 1898 became the bases for two quite dissimilar African American novels. Similar economic issues propelled events in Philadelphia in the 1830s and 1840s and are reflected in Frank J. Webb's 1857 novel, *The Garies and Their Friends*, discussed in chapter 2.

Still, T. McCants Stewart's sentiments about a tide of black fortune were shared by much of the black middle class of his day. They are echoed, for example, in Mrs. N. F. Mossell's poem, "Tell the North that We are Rising," published the same year as Stewart's article. In invoking the sentiment of ascension with the trope "we are rising," both Mossell and Stewart were referring to an almost folkloric episode that had occurred at a Sunday School service at the Storrs School, a forerunner of Atlanta University, in 1868, apotheosized in John Greenleaf Whittier's poem, "Howard at Atlanta."[21] At the close of his remarks to the children of the school and their families, General Oliver Otis Howard, the commissioner of the Freedmen's Bureau, had asked his audience, in Whittier's version, "What shall I tell the children / Up North about you?" A boy stood from the seats and answered, "General, / tell 'em we're rising."[22] The boy's phrase swept black America as an anthem.

A decade later, Mrs. Mossell closed her poetic commentary on the event with these verses, an unequivocal claim to a place in American life for her people:

> But we still would send the message
> To our friends where'er they roam,
> We are rising, yea, have risen:
> Future blessings yet will come.
>
> Noble son of noble mother,
> When our hearts would shrink and falter,
> We yet treasure up your message
> Laying it on Freedom's altar.
>
> We will [sic] courage strive to conquer,
> Till as England's Hebrews stand
> We are neither slaves nor tyrants,
> But are freemen on free land.

(65)

If it was not clear enough that some segments of the black bourgeoisie saw their race's future in the paradigm of American citizenship guaranteed by law and that "rising" meant progress within a shared American nationalism, Alexander Clark's 1886 analysis of the revolutionary movement in Europe and America left no doubt where he, an "Africo-American" lawyer, stood:

That we may not be confounded and misled by the ambiguity of terms and possibly become involved in the plots of anarchists and other evil designing men, is it not well that, as Africo-Americans, we remain standing face to face, and in faith with Providence who is the great counsel and help of nations as well as individuals, and continue our trust in that genius of American liberty, which struck the shackles from four millions of our people and lifted legislation to the summit of Sumner's magna charta of our Civil Rights? We want nothing of socialism or the commune, the strike or the boycott, the mob or the riot. For us be it sufficient that we emulate the spirit and faith of Lincoln, Grant, Sumner and their noble compeers, men devoted to liberty and justice, but equally the friends and champions of law and order as the benign agencies of man's highest good. Let us be beguiled into following no flag of murky hues, or strange device, but stand, unbound by any complications, with free consciences, in the simple dignity and loyalty of American citizens, and giving our heart's whole allegiance to God and country. (54)

Clark's belief in the efficacy of the law of Lincoln, Sumner, and Grant as a source of order and justice was typical of his class position and his concomitant American Protestantism. As we will see in a subsequent discussion of the characteristics of the peculiar American romanticism that affected both black and white Americans around matters of race, its central tenets were both "localist" and rural, and a tension between the communalism of romantic ideology and the individualism of romantic "psychology" was constantly being negotiated. Barry Alan Shain has argued that the local, communal, and rural aspects of this tension are specifically Protestant in origin.[23] Despite some common origins with white middle-class ideology of the period, however, black bourgeois attitudes toward white stewardship of the law exhibited more than a little ambivalence. In Mrs. F. E. W. Harper's eponymous novel, *Iola Leroy* (1892), Iola Leroy's friends are not revolutionaries; they are black intellectuals and Christians.[24] Nevertheless, while they hope for a Christian grace to grip their white antagonists, they do not expect it. Rather, their talk constantly returns to self-help and growth and the promise of a world of their own under law.

Dr. Gresham, Iola's white suitor, is allowed to speak what many in the book feel: "The great distinction between savagery and civilization is the creation and maintenance of law. A people [and here he means white America] cannot habitually trample on law and justice without retrograding toward barbarism" (218). Later, Dr. Latimer, the mulatto hero who wins Iola's hand, addresses his friends on the same subject: "Law is the pivot on which the whole universe turns; and obedience to law is the gauge by which a nation's strength or weakness is tried. We have had two evils by which our obedience to law has been tested—slavery and the liquor traffic" (249–50).[25] Iola's family and circle of intellectual friends create their specific identities through a resistance to attacks on their sense of selves as citizens by serving their people, turning from the white world to the community of race, and through faith in law. This "turning from" does not, in the case of the romantically noble characters of Harper's genteel world, imply a separate nationalism based on racial affinity, however. Rather, Iola Leroy and her circle seem intent on creating a more American America than whites can envision. The "we" in Dr. Latimer's peroration of the evils of slavery and alcohol seems to be both the race and the nation, with the race enduring far more beneath the lash of both evils than the nation, but with the nation just as sorely tested as to its essential worthiness. The nation under white stewardship barely retained its soul, and certainly, the novel implies, African Americans could guide an America more true to the ideals of the Republic than whites were able to sustain at the end of the century.[26] The novels of Harper and her contemporaries at the end of the century are congruent in their despair over the ways of white people. Each expresses clearly that somehow the great promise of America has been aborted by these whites who have corrupted the law, that great civilizing force, into a tool of oppression.[27]

In fact, to understand black bourgeois attitudes toward citizenship at the end of the nineteenth century, it is necessary to recognize that a shift in reference had taken place in the African American community during Reconstruction. Prior to Emancipation, the essential civil document to which all questions of rights were referred by blacks was the Declaration of Independence. More so than the Constitution and its preamble, the Declaration of Independence stood as the text of equality in American consciousness, as blacks in America read that consciousness.[28] Even prior to the framing of that document black voices in the colonies had spoken for its principles. In the anonymous petitions for freedom presented to the Massachusetts authorities in 1773 and 1774, Africans held against their will argued that

> your Petitioners apprehind we have in common with all other men
> a naturel right to our freedoms without Being depriv'd of them by
> our fellow men as we are a freeborn pepel and have never forfeited
> this Blessing by aney compact or agreement whatever. . . . Nither
> can we reap an equal benefit from the laws of the Land which doth
> not justifi but condemns Slavery or if there had bin aney Law to
> hold us in Bondege we are Humbley of the Opinion that never was
> aney to inslave our children for life when Born in a free Countrey.
> ("Slaves Petition" 30)[29]

To the new nation's enslaved people of African descent, the Constitution's failure to address such petitions and end slavery underscored, rather than provided relief for, their condition of servitude. As a symbolic comment on that reality, white abolitionist William Lloyd Garrison burned a copy of the Constitution at an antislavery rally in Framingham, Massachusetts, on July 4, 1854, to the cheers of thousands of supporters. Garrison's *Liberator* carried on its masthead the motto "No Union with Slaveholders; The US Constitution is a Covenant with Hell and an Agreement with Death" since the 1840s.[30] Garrison's antagonism to the Constitution drew the condemnation of many other white abolitionists but may have actually only reflected the grave misgivings of blacks in the movement. In 1851, for example, debate at the State Convention of the Colored Citizens of Ohio had centered on a proposition that it was impossible for a "colored man" to "consistently vote under the United States Constitution." H. Ford Douglass, arguing for the resolution, condemned the Constitution and its offspring, the Fugitive Slave Act:

> I hold, sir, that the Constitution of the United States is pro-slavery,
> considered so by those who framed it, and construed to that end
> ever since its adoption. . . . You might search the pages of history in
> vain, to find a more striking exemplification of the compound of all
> villainies! It shrouds our country in blackness; every green spot in
> nature, is blighted and blasted by that withering Upas. (*Minutes*
> 316–17)

Douglass was followed by William Howard Day, who rose to speak for the Constitution by arguing that *the* Constitution was not its construction or how it might be construed in its particulars. Rather, he insisted, its essence resided in its intent, or rather the purpose of the framers toward certain eternal values. "I consider the Constitution the foundation of American liberties, and wrapping myself in the flag of the nation, I would plant myself upon that Constitution, and using the weapons they have given me, I would appeal to the American people for the rights guaranteed" (318). Although Day's position carried the vote, the response of C. H. Langston came closest to the emerging consensus on the Constitution as the day-to-day violence of slavery increased in the South:

> I perfectly agree with the gentleman from Cuyahoga (Mr. Douglass) . . . that the United States Constitution is pro-slavery. It was made to foster and uphold that abominable, vampirish and bloody system of American slavery. . . . But whether the Constitution is pro-slavery, and whether colored men "can consistently vote under that Constitution," are two very distinct questions; and while I would answer the former in the affirmative, I would not, like the gentleman from Cuyahoga, answer the latter in the negative. I would vote under the United States Constitution on the same principle, (circumstances being favorable) that I would call on every slave, from Maryland to Texas, to arise and assert their *liberties*, and cut their masters' throats if they attempt again to reduce them to slavery. Whether or not this principle is correct, an impartial posterity and the Judge of the Universe shall decide. (319)[31]

As late as 1853 William Wells Brown, in the preface to the first edition of *Clotel*, would write,

> In fifteen of the thirtyone states, Slavery is made lawful by the Constitution, which binds the several States into one confederacy. . . . The entire white population of the United States, North and South, are bound by their oath to the constitution, and their adhesion to the Fugitive Slave Law, to hunt down the runaway slave and return him to his claimant, and to suppress any effort that may be made by the slaves to gain their freedom by physical force. (xvii–xviii)

He notes further, in the memoir with which he introduces the novel, that in his own experience, the Constitution was the document he most feared. "By the constitution of the United States he was every

moment liable to be arrested, and returned to the slavery from which
he had fled. His only protection from such a fate was the anomaly of the
ascendancy of the public opinion over the law of the country" (38).
Only by fleeing to England did he feel liberated from the tyranny of the
text. "My old master may make his appearance here, with the constitution of the United States in his pocket, the fugitive slave law in one
hand and the chains in the other, and claim me as his property; but all
will avail him nothing" (41).[32]

But the three civil rights amendments and the enabling legislation
that followed the Civil War changed the reputation of the Constitution,
and of "the law" in general among black Americans, such that it
replaced the Declaration of Independence as the governing document
of black claims to citizenship.[33] Natural rights, after all, were not secur-
able in nature but had to be secured by government for the people.
Thus one role of the United States Supreme Court after *Marbury* was to
guard against incursions upon natural rights of citizens inscribed in the
Constitution.[34] When black Americans turn to the Constitution, postbellum, they also turn to the Supreme Court, for protection of those natural rights alluded to in the Declaration and written into the Constitution, particularly the access to the natural rights of the first ten
amendments that was secured in the postwar amendments. The Declaration had stated the universal principles, based on natural law, that
should embrace all humanity. But American positivistic law, under the
Constitution's umbrella, enforced not universals but specific identity
through the evolution of case law in which status defined standing. The
importance of the postwar amendments to black Americans in general
was that they established the viability of rights defined by standing
rather than by specific litigation, rights accruing to one as a member of
a group with standing before the law.

That is not to say that there were still no reservations on the part of
some Negro commentators as to the ability of the Constitution to match
the rhetorical promise of the Declaration of Independence. In *Imperium
in Imperio* (1899), Sutton Griggs gives the following speech to his protagonist, black lawyer Belton Piedmont:

> [Y]ou know that there is one serious flaw in the Constitution of the
> United States, which has already caused a world of trouble, and
> there is evidently a great deal more to come. You know that a
> ship's boilers, engines, rigging, and so forth may be in perfect con-
> dition, but a serious leak in her bottom will sink the proudest ves-

sel afloat. The flaw or defect in the Constitution of the United States is the relation of the General Government to the individual state. The vague, unsettled state of the relationship furnished the pretext for the Civil War. The General Government says to the citizen: "I am your sovereign. You are my citizen and not the citizen of only one state. If I call on you to defend my sovereignty, you must do so even if you have to fight against your own state. But while I am your supreme earthly sovereign I am powerless to protect you against crimes, injustices, outrages against you. Your state may disfranchise you with or without law, may mob you; but my hands are so tied that I can't help you at all, although I shall force you to defend my sovereignty with your lives. If you are beset by Ku Klux, White Cappers, Bulldozers, Lynchers, do not turn your dying eyes on me for I am unable to help you." Such is what the Federal Government has to say to the Negro. (181–82)[35]

Griggs's characters so mistrust the Supreme Court that whenever a case involving African Americans or their interests comes before it, the Imperium itself considers the case in parallel deliberations (G. E. Walker 29).

It would not be until *Brown v. Board of Education* (1954) that the Declaration of Independence would, in effect, be written back into a reading of the Constitution. Between 1883 and 1954, courts generally upheld a localized, antifederal reading of the purposes of the basic document and its amendments. The author(s) of *Justice and Jurisprudence* challenged the right of an activist court to so undermine the grand sweep of the postwar amendments, but they did not recognize as clearly that the threats of exclusion from the national discourse of citizenship came from sectionalism, partisanship, and narrow politics and not simply from a misapprehension by whites of the Constitution as amended. Awash as even they were in the ethoi of their time, black activists as militant as the membership of the Brotherhood of Liberty could not appreciate how the cultural assumptions of the century's long march away from the Enlightenment had created a matrix of premises that supported Negro enslavement and after Emancipation excluded blacks from any real role as citizens. What they did recognize, however, was that the Court of the 1880s was the enemy of the natural rights of blacks as American citizens.

The body of law that eventually spelled out the citizenship of African Americans was contained in constitutional amendments, federal and state legislation, and litigation after 1865 and was, the Brotherhood felt, under sustained assault by 1889. The organization had been struggling, with some success, on the local front in Baltimore but believed that some national effort was necessary if a disaster for the race was to be averted. Rev. Harvey Johnson, the principal organizer of the Brotherhood, had been in contact with T. Thomas Fortune, but differences in focus prevented the Brotherhood and Fortune's Afro-American League from allying in any formal manner.[36] As the Brotherhood saw things, cases such as *Hall v. DeCuir, Miles v. Railroad Company*, and the Civil Rights Cases of 1883 set the stage for local and state imposition of abridgments to the national citizenship rights and privileges of black Americans. However wide-ranging in the African American community the discussion of a separatist black nationalism was at the moment, such abridgments of an American citizenship were not acceptable to the activist bourgeoisie of Baltimore.[37]

These critiques, from Wells, Griggs, and Harper among the novelists, from the state and national conventions of black men, from lawyers, ministers, and fugitive slaves centered on the proposition that there was a documentable commitment on the part of the nation to the legal status of citizenship for African Americans and that that commitment was based in both natural and positive law. It seemed also clear to these commentators that white Americans could not be trusted as the stewards of either the commitment or the documents that backed the commitment.

As for the Brotherhood of Liberty, their search for justice for black Americans and a jurisprudence on which it could be based was also predicated on the determination that theirs was an American identity and an American future:

> [I]n this age neither social abhorrence of the colored population, nor unintelligent, retrogressive, pro-slavery heresies, obsolete views of a day that is dead, nor myopic, pride-begotten prejudices, can be substituted for the widening character and the growing force of American thought, the sublime mission of which is to restore peace and order to human hearts and human society, by the establishment of the fundamental principle of the civic equality of all American citizens; that in the Atlantic States south of the thirty-sixth parallel of latitude, the relations of the races are interdependent; that eight millions of Afro-Americans can neither be annihilated nor transported. (Brotherhood of Liberty v)

CHAPTER 2

Romance and Resistance

"I thank God, then there is still some hope! My lot is cast
with that of my race, whether for weal or for woe. . . ."
"Woe be unto those devils of whites, I say!"

Martin R. Delany, *Blake, or The Huts of America*

While "the law" was only one text of African American experience, and
although it was true that throughout the nineteenth century blacks
were creating other narratives about their sojourn through slavery to a
freedom that promised but did not easily yield citizenship, the "raw
material" of these narratives was identical to that of the law. It would
seem useful, then, to describe some of the interaction between literature
as a text of identity and desire for African Americans and the law as the
text against which African Americans and their self-texts had to react
yet within which they also had to reside.

The concentration of the effect of law on desire exposes in the relationships between black life and American law what Armstrong and
Tennenhouse argue is a common but obscured nexus of power and
identity, the ideological function of desire:

> And is it not this very knowledge of ourselves as the subjects and
> objects of desire that we have been taught to discover in literature?
>   . . . such expressions of desire in fact constitute ideology in its
> most basic and powerful form, namely, one that culture designates
> as nature itself. . . . Because redefinitions of desire often revise the
> basis of political power, or human nature itself, one might say that
> changes in the understanding of desire, the practice of courtship,
> and the organization of the family are culturally antecedent to
> changes in the official institutions of state. . . . [W]here this rela-
> tionship between personal and public experience can be shown to
> hold true, we must set representations of desire, neither as reflec-
> tions nor as consequences of political power, but as a form of polit-
> ical power in their [sic] own right. ("Literature" 2)

In the first instant, therefore, the ground of all conscious activity in the African American texts I will mention here is the law. It would be hard to overstate how fundamentally law permeates both fiction and "nonfiction" texts, although this importance is not immediately apparent. The grounding presence of the law escapes notice in the fictions primarily because it *is* so fundamental, because all these fictions promote, argue, defend, lament, put case for, and premise every action on the question of the legal status of African Americans. Further, it is upon this constantly contested status that all substantial African American life is based. So even when a novel is not, for a moment, contemplating the law, it is waiting for the next legal moment. Seen another way, the law in African American novels of the nineteenth century is similar to the overwhelming snowlike presence of whiteness that settles on and around Bigger Thomas's life throughout Richard Wright's 1940 novel, *Native Son;* it is the condition on which action is predicated and to which reaction is inevitable.

Consequently, all resistance in these texts is resistance to the law and/or to the constraints of legal status. It is the law that sets blacks apart from whites; we see this in the massive legal history of African Americans, from the first seventeenth-century civil codes defining the terms of service of returned runaways (whites would serve out their terms; Africans were assumed to serve for life) through the framing of the Constitution, *Scott v. Sandford,* the Black Codes, Reconstruction, Jim Crow, *Plessy, Brown v. Board of Education,* the Civil Rights Acts of the 1960s to 1990s. We can see this in African American fiction as well. Therefore it is essential that we realize that just as this history is a powerful counternarrative to the legal history of whites, novels of African American life create a narrative alongside the privileged inscriptions of their white counterparts (Barrett; Castronovo; Ernest; V. Smith; Stepto). The functional effect of this narrative is to challenge the historically obvious discourse on citizenship on the basis that the relationship of African Americans to American law is substantially different from that within which white (males) have operated.

The fundamental difference is that which is established because the Constitution assumes the rights of white males to hold citizenship and to exercise its prerogatives, and assumes the referentiality of common law to be always and naturally to white males. The assumptions privilege white males in the text of American positive law as natural beings and so gives them status as situated in a condition extant prior

to the law itself. African Americans, on the other hand, are amendments to the natural narrative of American legal and social reality, and
their individual and collective existences must always be argued rather
than assumed.[1]

A less obvious difference, one embedded in the matrices of influence of romanticism on American culture and law, is a product of the
cultural reinforcement of the legal textualization/marginalization of
African American life through the romantic notion of "the other." The
socioeconomic position of the African American in the nineteenth century during slavery is easily understood through this particular lens.
What needs to be understood as well, however, is the impact of "other-
ness" as a romantic notion after Emancipation operating to keep
African Americans at the margins of American community. Just as the
"natural" position of white males as antecedent to the law privileges
them in the Constitution and other political texts as a consequence of
eighteenth-century rationalism in the ideological service of status made
up of race, gender, and class,[2] so the centering of the white male in
romantic cultural narratives of emotional, social, and economic self-
realization writes the lives of African Americans "under erasure." As
legally construed, this centering can be said to assume and expect a
property interest in whiteness that reproduces black subordination
(C. I. Harris 1731). The "saving remnant" of white Americans notwithstanding, we seek some reading of American law and African American literature that sheds light on the amazing recuperative power of
white (male) hegemony.

The literary evidence, and the consequences, of this centering in
antebellum America are apparent inasmuch as

> what seemed to be on the "mind" of the literature of the United
> States was the self conscious but highly problematic construction
> of the American as a new white man. Emerson's call for that new
> man in "The American Scholar" indicates the deliberateness of the
> construction, the conscious necessity for establishing difference.
> (Morrison, *Playing* 39; see Hardack for a parallel position)

But Emerson, however good he is on the care and feeding of the subject,
sees little of the intersubjective. So little, in fact, that he can scarcely
assess the social effects of oppression.[3] So the figure of the enslaved
person of color is appropriated to the agenda of white identity. As

Judge Beverly Tucker of Virginia put it in 1838, "It is certainly well cal-
culated to inspire the humblest white man with a high sense of his own
comparative dignity and importance, to see a whole class below him in
the scale of society" (Owens 18). The antebellum romantic assumption
that the same natural laws of innate divinity would be accessible to the
merchant and to the frontiersman, farmer and judge, was clearly limited in its applicability to white males. As David R. Roediger has noted,
"[T]hat blacks were largely noncitizens will surprise few, but it is
important to emphasize the extent to which they were seen as *anti-
citizens,* as 'enemies rather than as the members of the social compact'"
(57). Even after Emancipation, the literary function of the slave as a sign
of alterity remained unchanged. In the works of post-Reconstruction
nostalgists of slavery Thomas Nelson Page, Frances Hopkinson Smith,
Harry Stillwell Edwards, and James Lane Allen, "only those aspects of
the slave's life and thought that delineate the nature of the white man
and his institutions" were allowed to represent anything fundamental
in slave character (Andrews, *Literary* 49).

This episode in cultural construction had originally taken place in
the context of confrontation with a physical and social reality that epit-
omized romantic sensibility. North America was the physical site, and
colonial and postcolonial America was the sociological site whereon
the problematics of a nonhierarchical freedom could be worked out by
Euro-Americans, the paradigms of the virtues of newness written and
refined, and the primacy of the private over the public postulated as
liberty.[4] I would argue that it is on that notion of the private that a conscious difference was constructed and that the black American was the
necessary "other" against which both privacy and difference were
posited, first as the *property* "other" that one had the liberty to own and
secondly as the *social* "other" against whom one could assert the right
not to associate, a sort of "negative capability," to borrow a term from
nineteenth-century romantic poetics, inherent in the First Amendment.

Looking ahead to *Plessy v. Ferguson* (1896) from this kind of discussion, for example, allows us to realize that case as a textualization of
the desire to regain paradise. As I suggested in the introduction to this
study, "separate but equal" is an Edenic formulation; it promises an
America as the Judeo-Christian God of white people might have made
her, that great good place where the evidence of an evenhanded Creation stood in its several separate and equal parts, the site of "Adamic
multigeneity," to use a phrase popular in eugenics theory of the late
nineteenth century.[5] White Americans had gone out of Eden, so to

speak, during Reconstruction, but a revitalized spirit of racial exclusion
was abroad in the land, and Eden could be regained.

From the vantage point of this discussion we can also understand
the retrogressive power of Christian conversion of slaves. Baptism casts
them into "innocence"—the Garden state prior to knowledge, absent
any sense of distinct self (i.e., not separated from God/master in Christian terms) or of irony—because the Garden is a romantic, not an ironic
place. Thus enslaved heathens made into Christians are "innocent" and
unironic—childlike in their faith and without passion, hence without
authenticity, all characteristics, as we shall see, of romantic identity as
humans. Without those qualities, for all their innocence, they remain
property.

The antebellum novel that best captures the poignancy of life within
this tautology is Frank J. Webb's *The Garies and Their Friends* (1857). The
preface to the novel, provided by Harriet Beecher Stowe, assures the
reader that the author is a "coloured young man, born and reared in the
city of Philadelphia" (v). The story that Webb tells, of black and interracial life in Georgia and Philadelphia, turns on property and law, on
ownership and identity, on innocence and forbearance, the heroic black
entrepreneur balanced by the villainous white lawyer using the law of
contracts/property to make an (extra)legal fortune from black misfor-
tune and the biracial family caught in the snares of the law.

The novel opens in the 1830s, and most of its action occurs in that
decade. The story should be read against the historical record of Nat
Turner's rebellion and the consequent increase in harsh treatment of
slaves throughout the South, although almost no events crucial to the
plot take place in the slaveholding states. The historical placement of
the action, however, defines one of the key elements of the plot, the
legal problem of manumission.

In his youth, Clarence Garie bought and fell in love with Emily, a
mulatto. Forbidden by the laws of his state to marry her, he nevertheless lived with her as her husband, and they had two children. Garie
inherited wealth and more slaves and lived content with himself until
one day his "wife" asked to speak to him about the future of their children:

> I know you do not treat me or them as though we were slaves. But
> I cannot help feeling that we are such—and it makes me very sad
> and unhappy sometimes. If anything should happen that you

should be taken away suddenly, think what would be our fate. Heirs would spring up from somewhere, and we might be sold and separated for ever. (53–54)

"Mrs." Garie goes on to recount the story of Celeste, a mulatto woman in the same position. The father of Celeste's children was killed on a business trip and it was discovered that all his property was heavily mortgaged "to old MacTurk, the worst man in the whole of Savannah" (54). Celeste and the children were remanded to the slave-pen to be sold.

Identifying with Celeste and pregnant with her third child, "Mrs." Garie fears that the times are closing in on her family:

"And I have such a yearning that it should be born a free child. I do want that the first air it breathes should be that of freedom. It will kill me to have another child born here! its infant smiles would only be a reproach to me. Oh," continued she, in a tone of deep feeling, "it is a fearful thing to give birth to an inheritor of chains"; and she shuddered as she laid her head on her husband's bosom. (55)

Mr. Garie had never had a scruple regarding the ownership of slaves, but when he considers his "wife's" concerns, he realizes that although he is the father as well as the master of his children, it is out of his power to manumit them.[6] He plans to take them all to Philadelphia, where a community of free blacks to whom "Mrs." Garie has ties will welcome them. The Ellises, at the center of that community, anticipate their arrival by buying and furnishing, as their agents, a house from Walters, a black investor.

All of these characters will, in the course of the novel, confront the contradictions of race and citizenship in the free North. But for the moment, the Garies see only the possibilities of personal liberty. As Mr. Ellis tells his wife, "I rather imagine he purposes emancipating his children. He cannot do it legally in Georgia; and you know, by bringing them here, and letting them remain six months, they are free—so says the law of some of the Southern states, and I think of Georgia" (65).[7]

The fortunes of the Garies and their friends run hot and cold in Philadelphia, basically at the hands of the evil Stevens, a "Philadelphia" lawyer (315) and a pettifogging attorney, who derived a tolerable income from a rather disreputable legal practice picked up among the courts that held their sessions in the various halls of the State-house. He was known in the profession as Slippery George, from the easy manner in which he glided out of scrapes that would have been fatal to the reputation of any other lawyer. Did a man break into a house, and escape without being actually caught on the spot with the goods in his possession, Stevens was always able to prove an *alibi* by a long array of witnesses. In fact he was considered by the swell gentry of the city as their especial friend and protector, and by the members of the bar generally as anything but an ornament to the profession. (125)

Stevens arranges for the murder of Garie and causes the death of Mrs. Garie, by then legally married, and her unborn child. Stevens then inherits Garie's fortune as a collateral heir and is kept from selling Garie's children, as in the tale of Celeste, only by the law that Ellis had noted earlier. Years later, when the children have become adults, the murder is uncovered (a corrupt coroner had ruled the deaths of Mr. and Mrs. Garie accidental), and all property is restored, all possible parties are married, and the elderly preside over almost Pickwickian domesticities.

What marks this novel is the very desire for domesticity it champions. In every episode the center is the attempt by one person of color or another to establish or maintain a legal household. And in every illustration of the desire for domesticity is the countervailing legal or extralegal impediment. Garie and "Mrs" Garie are not married, and his uncle suggests: "As long as you live here in Georgia you can sustain your present connection with impunity, and if you should ever want to break it off, you could do so by sending her and the children away; it would be no more than other man have done, and are doing every day" (100). Clarence Garie replies: "I feel that Emily is as much my wife in the eyes of God, as if a thousand clergymen had united us. It is not my fault that we are not legally married; it is the fault of the laws" (100–101). We are told,

Prior to their emigration from Georgia, Mr. Garie had, on one or two occasions, attempted, but without success, to make her legally his wife. He ascertained that, even if he could have found a clergyman willing to expose himself to persecution by marrying them, the ceremony itself would have no legal weight, as a marriage between a white and a mulatto was not recognized as valid by the laws of the state. (133)

In fact, while the novel portrays interracial alliances as tragic in their consequences because of both law and custom, the lovers themselves are not portrayed as essentially flawed, as is suggested in Martin Delany's *Blake* two years later or in Sutton Griggs's *Imperium in Imperio*, forty years later. Webb's criticism of miscegenation takes two forms. One, the issue of its legality or illegality as an impediment to true love has been mentioned. The second is more complex because it exposes the ambiguous impact of notions of romantic love.

In the novel, Garies's son, Clary, grows to manhood passing for white in a northern boarding school. His excessively romantic love for a white woman blinds him to the legal and customary restraints of his condition and to the chances for happiness and love that await him in the black community. Clary's fate is to sicken and die for love once his "secret" has been revealed to Birdie, his beloved. Only at his death are they reconciled as she rejects the racism of her family. Even so, she arrives at his bedside too late to have even a word with him.

Clary is contrasted not only with his sister, who marries within the race, joining fates with charismatic Charlie Ellis, but with George Winston, a figure introduced and removed early in the book but whose example looms over Clary's choices and creates part of the historical frame for the novel. Winston's story also reveals another complex issue for the novel, the ambivalence of the text toward the South as a context for self-realization in issues of race.

George Winston was freed by Mr. Moyese, his New Orleans master, as a reward for the good work he did. By contrasting George's freedom in Louisiana with the implacable enslavement of "Mrs." Garie and her children, the novel calls attention to the truly "local" and customary quality of slave law. Even given the "charity" of Louisiana manumission law, however, we are reminded that freedom, once given, is not always freedom retained. Moyese's lawyer, Ketchum, draws up the papers for George and then returns to the case he is handling for another client: "The note [had] found Mr. Ketchum deep in a disputed will case, upon the decision of which depended the freedom of some half-dozen slaves, who had been emancipated by the will of their late master; by which means of posthumous benevolences his heirs had been greatly irritated, and were in consequence endeavouring to prove him insane" (10–11).[8]

Winston travels through the North and finds that while he can pass for white and does so on one occasion, the practice is distasteful to him, and he chooses to live as a person of color. Clary's weak romanticism contrasts with Winston's heroic embrace of race over illusion. Webb makes the contrast clear by having Winston besieged by young white women of society, all of whom he rejects. Clary has obviously been ruined by his environment, in this case the New England boarding school in which he was surrounded by white classmates who thought him white as well. His sister, as light as he, stays home and in the loving care of the black community finds happiness and domesticity.

Life in the North for black people, even when surrounded by the community, is nevertheless circumscribed by legal and quasi-legal boundaries. Mr. Ellis tells Winston of an episode involving his friend Walters, the wealthy black Philadelphia entrepreneur whose financial support is essential to the Ellises and later to the Garie children:

> I met him the other day in a towering rage: it appears that he owns ten thousand dollars worth of stock, in a railroad extending from this to a neighbouring city. Having occasion to travel in it for some little distance, he got into the first-class cars; the conductor, seeing him there, ordered him out—he refused to go, and stated that he was a shareholder. The conductor replied, that he did not care how much stock he owned, he was a nigger, and that no nigger should ride in those cars; so he called help, and after a great deal of trouble they succeeded in ejecting him. (50)

Winston asks if there was any chance of redress.

> No, none, practically. He would have been obliged to institute a suit against the company; and, as public opinion now is, it would be impossible for him to obtain a verdict in his favor. (51)

Later in the novel, Mrs. Bird, a kindly white woman, is taking Charlie Ellis to the country and encounters Jim Crow on the railroad when the conductor rouses sleeping Charlie and tries to force him to leave the car. Mrs. Bird indignantly shows their tickets and tells the conductor, truthfully, that the boy is sick:

> "I don't care whether he is sick or well—he can't ride in here. We don't allow niggers to ride in this car, no how you can fix it—so come, youngster," said he, gruffly, to the now aroused boy, "you must travel out of this."
>
> "He shall do no such thing," replied Mrs. Bird, in a decided tone; "I've paid full price for his ticket, and he shall ride here; you have no legal right to eject him."
>
> "I've got no time to jaw about rights, legal or illegal—all I care to know is, that I've got my orders not to let niggers ride in these cars, and I expect to obey, so you see there is no use to make any fuss about it." . . .
>
> "You had better let the boy go into the negro car, madam," said one of the gentlemen, respectfully; "it is perfectly useless to contend with these ruffians. I saw a coloured man ejected from here last week, and severely injured; and in the present state of public feeling, if nothing happened to you or the child, you would be entirely without redress. The directors of this railroad control the State; and there is no such thing as justice to be obtained in any of the State courts in a matter in which they are concerned." (110–11)

It is a characteristic of this novel, as it would be of its successors as novels of black domestic life forty years later, that characters speak directly to the point about the impact of law on personal life:

> "It is a dreadful long walk," replied Mrs. Ellis. "How provoking it is to think, that because persons are coloured they are not permitted to ride in the omnibuses or other public conveyances! I do hope I shall live to see the time when we shall be treated as civilized creatures should be."
>
> "I suppose we shall be so treated when the Millennium comes," rejoined Walters, "not before, I'm afraid; and as we have no reason to anticipate that it will arrive before tomorrow, we shall have to walk to Winter Street, or take a private conveyance." (64)

Much later, under attack by Irish criminals hired by Stevens and his associates who seek to drive blacks out of a choice real estate section, Walters and the Ellises barricade themselves in Walters's house and gather weapons:

> "I wish we were well out of this: it's terrible to be driven to these extremities—but we are not the aggressors, thank God! and the results, be they what they may, are not of our seeking. I have a right to defend my own: I have asked protection of the law, and it is too weak, or too indifferent, to give it; so I have no alternative but to protect myself." (208)

These speeches have the appearance of set pieces, and they should be understood as part of the didactic machinery of the text. That they occur with such straightforwardness and frequency signifies how central to the conscious narrative of black life the law remained. Webb even adds a footnote in the midst of the fiction to clarify a point about the law he does not want his readers to miss, explaining why Garie is surprised at seeing Negro children with schoolbooks in Philadelphia: "It is a penal offense in Georgia to teach coloured children to read" (120).

The novel taken as a whole argues clearly that the law is no refuge for free persons of color if they are without the necessary financial power to make it speak for them. Money, it seems, is necessary to offset the advantage skin color allots to whites. This is quite clear in the representation of George Stevens's ability to use the law to protect the Irish ruffians he hires to burn out the Negro community and kill Garie, to steal the inheritance of the Garie children, and to cover his tracks for twenty years. Only the wealth of Walters sustains the Garies and their friends over those twenty years until circumstance and time catch up with Stevens. Inasmuch as Walters's wealth is based in real estate and equities, the centrality of private property as a bulwark against the law is interesting because it is unique in African American narrative of the nineteenth century.

Because Webb's portrayal of the fortunes of the Garies in the North can be contextualized to a particular time and place, Philadelphia between 1830 and 1855, it is possible to look at matters of race, class, property, and legality with some specificity. For instance, the black population into which the Garies moved sometime in the 1830s was young: 50 percent of black Philadelphians were under age twenty-four; it was female: 58 percent were women; it was of considerable size:

twenty thousand; residence was not rigidly segregated: blacks lived in all twenty-four of the city's wards by 1860, although the "community" did tend to concentrate in the city's four central wards, which held about 64 percent of the black population.

As for fidelity to the reality of class and property, it appears that Mr. Walton would seem to be something of a fiction to be sure, a black millionaire in a city in which the total amount of property owned or mortgaged by African Americans in 1847 was only five hundred thousand dollars, and that amount divided among 315 families. The 1850 census shows that only 4 percent of all blacks held property in Philadelphia, and the mean value of that property was $103. Webb's re-creation of race relations, however, coincides with Philadelphia's history. The Anglo upper classes used Irish economic and racial insecurities to keep black Philadelphians in line. Blacks and Irish competed for the same jobs and occupied the same rung of poverty. Sixty percent of black Philadelphians possessed real or personal property of only sixty dollars in the 1830s and 1840s, and some 80 percent of black Philadelphians were unskilled laborers; 16 percent were skilled workers who also competed with recent white immigrants for work; 4 percent were professionals and businessmen.

The record notes four instances of major racial violence in the decade in which the crucial events of the novel occur and to which Webb was probably alluding. In 1831 whites attacked and beat blacks at a Fourth of July celebration; in 1834 whites led a three-day riot in which black churches, associations, and residences were attacked and burned and during which black refugees fled to the countryside (whites identified themselves to the mob by placing lighted candles in their parlor windows); in 1838 a mob of three thousand whites burned a black meeting hall, a black orphanage, and attacked blacks on the street; and in 1842 a parade of black temperance and antislavery marchers celebrating the anniversary of the abolition of slavery in the British West Indies was attacked by whites led by a local Irish mob. The whites, several thousand in number, overwhelmed the twelve hundred black marchers and chased them through the city, beating individuals and breaking into black homes, destroying property and beating the inhabitants, finally burning meeting halls and a church in the black community. This and the 1834 riot seem the events most like that in which Mr. and Mrs. Garie are killed.

In court, blacks in Philadelphia were on no safer ground than they were in the streets. An 1837 suit brought by whites had resulted in a decision that disenfranchised blacks, and the next year the Pennsylvania constitutional convention voted to make the disenfranchisement statutory, a move that was ratified in a statewide referendum in October 1838. After the 1842 riot, the grand jury blamed the black temperance marchers and refused to indict any whites. The effect on the black community was palpable. Black leaders began to despair of finding acceptance by white Philadelphians, and gradually the black population of the city dwindled in proportion to that of whites. Whereas the black population had grown from two thousand to twenty thousand between 1790 and 1840, the free black population decreased between 1840 and 1850. Philadelphia's black population dropped from 7.4 percent of the total for the city in 1840 to under 4 percent in 1860.[9]

The issue of privacy, exemplified in *The Garies* by Stevens's anger at having the Garies as his neighbor and the attempts by Stevens and other whites to manipulate the real estate market by driving blacks into ghettoes through arson and violence as well as by the potential power of private property, is placed in contradistinction to that of community in the novel. This contradistinction reflects a tension at large in the nation throughout the century. The ideological bases of that tension lie in the apparent assumption that privacy must be premised on a "monadic" personality that can stand outside of community, since privacy demands a setting aside of the commune in an abrogation of the many's rights, consequent to privileging the rights of the one; the very notion of such a personality is a romantic conception. Further, the emergence of ideas of personal liberty seems the product of romantic sensibility insofar as it [the emergence of the idea] is predicated on recognizing some potentiality *inherent* in privacy, since liberty is, for the Framers first and foremost the agency through which we are to exercise our "right" to own and dispose of productive *private* property, that is, property held apart from the community. This property, of course, included slaves.

The notion of property, or of "proving property" in others, as in proving one's property interests in another being, was fluid in antebellum America as it pertained to black people. The wall between person and slave, between free man or woman and enslaved man or woman, was far too permeable to offer any protection to the unenslaved. In *State v. Harden* (So. Car. 1832), Judge John B. O'Neall had found that

> Free negroes belong to a degraded caste of society; they are in no respect on an equality with a white man. According to their condi-

tion they ought by law to be compelled to demean themselves as inferiors, from whom submission and respect to the whites, in all their intercourse in society, is demanded; I have always thought and while on the circuit ruled that words of impertinence and inso-lence addressed by a free negro to a white man, would justify an assault and battery. (Wilson 27 n. 25)

In states throughout the slaveholding South from 1832 to the eve of the Civil War, local courts and state appeals courts found there to be no reason to see the free black person as anything other than a legal fiction, and not a particularly well-wrought one at that. In Tennessee Judge Nathan Green ruled,

Free negroes have always been a degraded race in the United States . . . with whom public opinion has never permitted the white population to associate on terms of equality and in relation to whom, the laws have never allowed . . . the immunities of the free white citizens. (1839 *State v. Claiborne*, qtd. in Wilson 36 n. 53)

But it was the Georgia Civil Code of 1861 that best expressed the conditions under which free blacks lived:

The free person of color is entitled to no right of citizenship except as such are specially given by law. His status differs from that of the slave in this: No master having dominion over him he is enti-tled to the free use of his liberty, labor and property, except so far as he is restrained by law.

All laws enacted in reference to slaves, and in their nature applicable to free persons of color, shall be construed to include them, unless specifically excepted. (Ga. Civil Code 1861 pars. 1612–13, qtd. in Wilson 35 n. 50)

I would summarize the implications of these arguments about privacy and property for the legal status of African Americans as follows.

Privileging the individual right to privacy with its extracommuni-tarian implications constructs a rationale for the status of slaves as being "those entities not entitled to liberty because as property they are unable to stand alone, outside community, by choice or will." That is, they are unable to exhibit the characteristics of a romantic personal-ity. A corollary to this rationale, and one equally damning to the enslaved person, is the conclusion that because of all that has gone before (status as property, inability to stand alone outside the community of slaves), the slave has no *need* for privacy, and it may be withheld from him or her. This point is interesting because it allows us to argue that if one is not allowed to choose privacy, then one is not allowed to choose company or community; that is, there is no choice. And the opposite would hold as well; to be able to choose one is to be able to choose the other. Thus it would appear that the freedom to associate depends from a notion of privacy, and the First Amendment becomes, in such a reading, a romantic text of the right to choose not to have community as much as it is of the right to have whatever community one chooses. In any case, none of these romantic "rights" are available to the slave, and only occasionally are they available to a free person of color. It follows then, that as whites under law could not see the antebellum free person of color as a citizen of the romantic republic, they would be unable to see that status applicable to or assigned to the postbellum freedman.[10]

I find this line of argument compelling because I understand the basis of the traditional *non*economic argument for white resistance to association with people of color to be set in the right of citizens to choose with whom they are to associate. In extreme cases, whites argued that "they" (meaning African Americans) want to live with "their own kind." I say *extreme* cases because the essential quality in the argument for whites is "choice," based on a notion of "privacy as agency" that is itself rooted in the romantic ideal of the singular personality developing through a context of will over circumstance. Whites were generally loathe to extend that choice to blacks. I have used the past tense here, but I believe that one explanation for some contemporary white attitudes toward African Americans is that the heritage of slavery and post-Reconstruction Jim Crow life contains the deeply held belief that black people are not entitled to the choices emanating from privacy because they historically occupied a status, by custom and law, by definition and statute, alien to the paradigm of individuation in which the romantic life of the citizenry was grounded.

I would also argue that the inability of nineteenth-century white Americans to imagine the African American at the center of narratives of romantic development, because of his/her predetermined role as the "other" against which the self-realization of the romantic hero must work, parallels and reinforces the unwillingness of white Americans to

accept the African American at the center of legal, political, and economic texts, that is, citizenship. If the African American could never be
situated as the self-realizing subject, how could he or she ever truly be
"American"?[11] That was the terrible implication of the Fugitive Slave
Act of 1850, that there were no rights that could not be denied, even to
a man or woman exhibiting the same desire for freedom that legend has
ascribed to the revolutionary colonists. It is the power of that threat,
added to the near-total control slavery claimed over the lives of
enslaved blacks and free persons of color as well, that is at the center of
the struggles of Martin Delany's hero, Henry Blake, in his antebellum
novel *Blake, or The Huts of America.*[12]

The great advantage Henry Blake has throughout the novel is the
inability of whites to recognize his capacity for self-directed action.
Blake is an American romantic hero in the Cooper mold. He appears in
this novel fully formed and never undergoes change because he is
Delany's vision of pure black humanity with every human capacity
raised to heroic levels. Henry Blake is pure of heart as well as pure
racially; he is courageous, multilingual, handsome, and intelligent. As
Blake plans his nationwide slave rebellion, travels to every slaveholding state to establish revolutionary cells at every major plantation, frees
his closest friends and leads them to Canada, tracks his enslaved wife
to her new master in Cuba and installs himself at the head of an indigenous liberation movement there, he never falters and never fails to
exhibit the characteristics of a fully "enfranchised" American hero,
despite the fact that he is a fugitive.

Houston A. Baker's observation about the relationship between
legality and narration has relevance to Delany's depiction of his hero:

> In the black narrative, the judgment rendered by the white world
> manifests itself in a pattern of extralegality. Moving from an ini-
> tially limited position, the black protagonist often finds himself out-
> side the dictates of a society that attempts to confine him, and his
> expanding consciousness leads to the realization that it is not
> humanism or moral righteousness that brings about the adverse
> rulings of the white world, but a quest for personal power and a
> desire for psychological stability purchased at the price of a dis-
> torted image of the black American. Once the protagonist has
> moved beyond the limits of his society, however, he is not assured
> freedom. According to the standards of the world he has rejected,

he is a criminal. The shades of the prison house are likely to close at any moment, and a renewed captivity is always imminent. (*Singers* 16)[13]

Delany's unique vision was of how it was possible and necessary to appropriate the role of the always-incarcerated and reject it. Henry Blake as laborer/slave/revolutionary was like no other figure in African American fiction to that day. One can read virtually any other black text of the period and recognize both the evidence and the ability of white desire to reincarcerate the African American, to write him, as Toni Morrison says in *Playing in the Dark,* as both the "not-free" and the "not-me" (38). Only in *Blake* is that white imperative not matched by the ability to realize it.

Delany is able to visualize such agency for his hero because he presents slavery as an economic system rather than a system of racial oppression. In the slavery Delany describes, all the players seek negotiable and negotiating space. Blake himself is seen constantly renegotiating his relationship to the means of production as he trades on his formal status as a free man, on his literacy, his guile, and his romantically conceived qualities of moral and physical superiority. Thus Blake sells and buys himself in and out of various degrees of bondedness as he plans his rebellion and seeks his wife. Similarly, his picaresque journey through the slaveholding South, to Cuba, and to Africa surveys the range of economic relationships within the rubric of slavery as it was practiced at midcentury.

As an economic text, Delany's version of slavery contradicts many black narratives of the antebellum period but corresponds with the development of relations between black Americans and white America in the postwar period and beyond. For if the central issue of African American narrative prior to 1865 was slavery as a personal experience that stood for but scarcely explained the complexities of a national system of economic privilege, after Emancipation the issue was citizenship and it had been clear since the founding of the republic that citizenship was an economic issue. The true roots of that issue, however, lie in the implications for ideas of property and citizenship in a slaveholding nation posed by some aspects of "romantic" thought. Although the terminus of a more traditionally understood American romanticism is usually posited in the 1850s, the attitudes it produced had effects that were felt through the entire century.

As an exercise in speculation on the extent of the influence of romantic attitudes throughout the century on matters of both race and citizenship, I would suggest the peculiar juxtaposition of Mary Shelley's *Frankenstein* to, among others, the problem of slave literacy and the development of the notion of "personhood" under the Fourteenth Amendment.

In 1818 Mary Shelley published *Frankenstein, or The Modern Prometheus* with this epigraph from book 10 of *Paradise Lost:*

> Did I request thee, Maker, from my clay
> To mould Me man? Did I solicit thee
> From Darkness to promote me?–

The novel turned on the desire of man to breathe life into dead or non-human form, to make out of the inhuman, the almost-human. Shelley's book was almost the last of the gothic romances to find a wide audience, but it defined for Eurocentric culture perhaps once and for all how the dream of mastery over the principle of life itself was situated at the heart of all desire for autonomous power. In an ironic way, the premise of the novel, entangled as it is with both the Enlightenment and with romanticism, glosses an important part of the relationship between African American life and the law. And the nexus of relationships that bind African Americans and American law is tangled also with attitudes and assumptions of both the Enlightenment and romanticism.

There are two analogies to be drawn between Mary Shelley's book and life as it was lived by African people, enslaved or free, in America. In one we are made aware once again of the centrality of language in romantic notions of self-creation. Shelley's monster's story is like nothing so much as a slave narrative, an account of finding oneself in bondage and liberating oneself from it through language and action.[14] It is tempting to read Shelley's entire romance as though it were about slavery, but it will be enough now to point out that the monster's narrative describes the hard-won acquisition of first a representative and then a symbolizing performative language that both sets him free of a too-literal world and provides him with the capacities to exhibit both imagination and irony. Even so, the narrative is about the failure of language to save him. Whoever he has become, he never overcomes the physical differences between himself and his creator, nor can he even share that hated difference with another, since the doctor who made him refuses to make another with whom he might find companionship; he is denied even the "whispered consolations" of the community of sufferers. Ultimately, action alone can serve him, and he both pursues and flees his master, vanishing into the whiteness of the far north.

It is not necessary to claim any influence of one text on the other to find suggestive the parallels between the monster's narrative and the "type" of the antebellum slave narrative. In the "Romantic agon, the life-and-death contest of the spirit of revision against all that represses it," as William Andrews describes the slave experience that is depicted at the heart of the slave narrative before the war, literacy is

> the ultimate form of power . . . for at least two reasons. First, language is assumed to signify the subject and hence to ratify the slave's humanity as well as his authority. Second, white bigotry and fear presumably cannot withstand the onslaught of the truth feelingly represented in the simple personal history of a former slave. ("Representation" 64, 65–66)

But as in Shelley's romance, the romance of the slave narrative represents the failure of the word as well, as when Frederick Douglass finds that it is not his ability to read but his will to fight with the white slave-breaker Covey that liberates his manhood. To violate the laws against slave literacy is a protoemancipatory act, it seems, but however free the mind, the body remains trapped in a difference that is untouched by the ability to read or write about it. The "liberating subjectivity" of literacy (Andrews 65) did not extend to the body of the slave. To fight leads ultimately to flight, to the north where there are other laws and where language can become a part of the reconfiguration of self. Just as it is the monster's narrative told in the north, not his creator's, that makes him come alive for us, so the telling of one's story itself becomes a liberating subjectivity in the life of the escaped slave, so much so that many, Andrews would claim, "treat their arrival on the abolitionist lecture platform or their acceptance of the anti-slavery pen as the fulfillment of their destiny" (65).

While one might say that the slaves lived lives that represented a striking *inversion* of the Frankenstein premise (that is, that which was *human,* the African, was made *inhuman,* property), after the Civil War, the Fourteenth Amendment was added to the Constitution to rectify that gothic irony and affirm African American humanity. This was to be done by drawing that population into the community of citizenship through an assignment of status under the law. In point of historical fact, however, African Americans have had to argue the applicability of that amendment time and again as citizenship slips in and out of their grasp. And if the legal status of enslaved people had been an inverted shadow of Mary Shelley's gothic dream, the Fourteenth Amendment failed to right it, at least in the nineteenth century.

Nevertheless, in this second analogy, the Fourteenth Amendment *did* alter American history in a way no one anticipated, finally fulfilling the promise of Mary Shelley's book by realizing the dream of the creation of life from inert matter and doing so ultimately at an ironic cost that did not go unremarked by African Americans. In 1886, *Santa Clara County v. Southern Pacific R.R.* was decided, a case that provides a kind of relief against which the status of the African American in the nineteenth century should be read. Seventy years after Mary Shelley had begun her romance, *Santa Clara County* wrought a truly Frankensteinian miracle. With a stroke of the pen, American corporations, creatures of foolscap and ink, were declared persons under the law and entitled to the protection of the Fourteenth Amendment just like any (other) flesh and blood citizen.[15] The struggle over "corporate personification" had begun with the Dartmouth College decision of 1819,[16] just a year after the publication of Shelley's romance, and the long-ensuing debate over corporate identity and property rights emerged as one of the most puzzling to legal theorists of the nineteenth century. *Dartmouth* held that "a corporation was an artificial person that owed its existence more to government than to its corporators and, as a creature of positive law, had only the rights and privileges that obtained from the government's grant."[17] This holding should be seen as an inversion of the position of enslaved people at the same time, and the discussions that followed it parallel the arguments over the "person-ness" of Africans in America, enslaved or free.

As mirrored inversions of corporations now seen as legal persons, slaves were not *legal* persons, but were *moral* entities; while corporations as artificial persons had only a contractual identity, slaves as moral beings only had no contractual existence. As one court put it:

> It is clear that slaves have no legal capacity to assent to any contract. With the consent of their masters they may marry, and their moral power to agree to such a contract or connection as that of marriage, cannot be doubted; but, whilst in a state of slavery, it

cannot produce any civil effect, because slaves are deprived of all civil rights.[18]

However, this court believed that the limitation on the contracting "self" was an imposed condition and could, in law, be alleviated. "Emancipation," the court went on to note, "gives to the slave his civil rights, and a contract of marriage, legal and . . . valid by the consent of the master and moral assent of the slave, from the moment of freedom, although dormant during the slavery, produces all the effects which result from such contract among free persons" (293).

Not that the issue was so easily resolved everywhere. In North Carolina in 1853, Polly Delaney, a slave, was married to a free black man. When he died, she was not allowed to inherit his farm and material holdings because she was a slave. Because the condition of children followed that of their mother, the children of the marriage were also slaves and could not inherit the property. But the courts did make her and her children work off her dead husband's debt. "Polly's legal treatment confirms the contention of Orange County former slave Thomas Hall that 'getting married an' having a family was a joke in the days of slavery, as the main thing in allowing any form of matrimony among the slaves was to raise more slaves'" (Bynum 63).

Nor was the issue of marriage as contract necessarily clearer for free blacks, particularly for women. The "contractual" status of women in "free" marriages was not necessarily an unmixed advance from enslavement in the first half of the nineteenth century. Thus, while the right to marry as a contractual right was significant to men who had escaped, as we can see in the life of Frederick Douglass, it was less so for women. Linda Brent's anger at having her freedom bought seems to extend to her attitude toward marriage by the end of her narrative.[19] The transfer of one's sense of property in oneself to yet a third party after enslavement is no emancipation. That Brent closes her account with the declaration, "Reader, my story ends with freedom; not in the usual way, with marriage" (Jacobs 207), signals the unresolved conflict between women's experience and the rhetoric of liberation.[20]

Not all courts held the same assumptions about "selfhood" and enslavement. The problem lies, usually, in the court's language; the idea of the slave as a "moral" being remains singularly undefined. In many jurisdictions, local attitudes toward slaves and slavery influenced the choice of language in such decisions. One school of legal history, the "personalist" approach, suggests that the life experiences of justices, including the moral ecology of their childhood, education, and adult practices have much to do with their decisions in cases dealing with slaves and slavery.[21] How "local" jurisdictions experienced slavery should be expected to vary greatly, from the harsh legal climates of Georgia and Florida to the less malignant courts of Louisiana and North Carolina. Thus, what was meant by *moral*, as in *moral being*, must be grounded in the local experience of master-slave relationships. As one South Carolina judge put it to the jury in an 1872 case, "Slavery owed its origin to force; to the dominion of the strong over the weak; to the rule of power without regard to right. . . . Wherever it has existed as an institution it reposed solely upon the local law, with that and by that it rose or fell" ("Slave Contracts" 309).

If then the slave was not a "legal" person but a "moral" entity and the very ideations of "legal" and "moral" under slavery were the products of local experience and local values, such a set of expectations about identity suggests we consider the importance of the romantic concept of "belonging" to the idea of "the local" in the traditional defense of slavery as a municipal, that is, local, institution, and not a federal one.[22] If we as "readers" of the text of these localized relationships assume that the white, male land- and slaveholding citizens of the United States were exposed to and drew on the same ideas and assumptions we identify now as elements of "romanticism," we ought to expect that these influences would also participate in shaping attitudes toward such relationships as community, place, belonging, and the other terms associated with the problems of self, legal and moral identity, and citizenship posited earlier.[23]

Entry to a discussion of the role of "belonging" in the influence of romanticism on American attitudes toward citizenship and the idea of local autonomy begins with a fundamental premise about "imagination" in romanticism, that imagination is both *responsive* and *creative;* our sense of reality (our response to an external condition) is felt to be inseparable from our creative capacity/impulse. Consequently, imagination and reality do not *confront* one another but together *constitute* what we experience and how we do so. This simple dialectic relationship lies beneath at least some of the issues that follow.

We can locate the origins of "belonging" as a romantic notion in the thought of the eighteenth-century philosopher Johann Gottfried von Herder, who saw belonging as generated from our apprehension of some value or set of values—cultural values of the Good and the

Right—of which we are inclined to say, "To this we wish to belong—this is the way of life that is us." Such values are *not* the product of autonomous intellectual choice but arise from our awareness of the rootedness of our *local* experience.[24] This situating of value in the "local" also suggests that the idea of belonging to a site of value responds to an impulse toward moral certainty, as in a notion of the moral authority of the people of a place *because* of their experiential relationship of that place. Such moral certainty becomes a central element in the legal defense of slavery in the South and manifests itself later as the presumed authority for the "states' rights" movement in the South.[25] It is this effect of challenging the potential decentering and thereby destabilizing effect of the Enlightenment emphasis on the universality of human experience, particularly in the realm of morals or virtue, this reactionary aspect of romantic thought, on which I want to draw for some of the following discussion.

These local nexuses of value not only situate the moral subject in a specific place, but can support a commitment to some expression of romantic nationalism in which the individual feels one with the people of another or larger place, even an imaginary place.[26] At the same time, this sense of being "rooted in" constitutes a part of the romantic reaction to Enlightenment "reason" by providing the experiential base for moral life. That is, romantic community and Enlightenment rationality are incompatible because one cannot stand back from one's own context to analyze without losing all guidance. Reason is a tool for testing, not a source of belonging, and can give no base for moral conviction; only local experience with a world of moral choices configured as arrangements of value ascription can do that. That is, one might reason one's way to an acceptance of the notion of a universal human community but, from a romantic perspective, one could scarcely "belong" to it through the exercise of reason alone.

The play of imagination and reality, noted above, seems essential to "belonging" when one wants to move that concept from the experientially local to some larger "local" community of values, because the product of that play is implicit in the figuring forth of any assumed community of values to which one would belong. Benedict Anderson, for example, begins a deconstruction of the idea of the "nation" with a definition of it: "An imagined political community—and imagined as both inherently limited and sovereign" (6; Wald; Berlant; Gleason). The community is imagined because no one member will know all the members—so each must imagine his or her relationship to another member, to the "nation," and to the characteristics of membership (6). This is less so in the context of the "local" community. There, what is imagined is the identity of purpose, as though not only one's country-men but all their intentions could be known to you. It seems reasonable to see such imagined knowledge as the base from which one feels authorized to write law.

If you cannot, or will not, imagine any or all of these relationships and characteristics of a person, he cannot be a part of your imagined political community—as blacks have not been imagined by whites in America from the seventeenth through the twentieth centuries.[27] It is obvious, I think, that one characteristic of any member of that commu-nity, from the perspective of any other member, would be that he or she would be capable of participating in the creation of community through imagined congress with everyone else on all levels. As Peter Goodrich has said, "the establishment of an identity, the constitution of a community and the capture of subjectivity are first a matter of estab-lishing a collective or national identity whose virtue will be matched only by the evil of those who do not belong to it." (n.p.)

Consequently, if some persons, black Americans, are denied par-ticipation in the public imaginative acts of a community, the reading and writing of its texts of record, its literature, history, or laws, then they can never be *of* that nation, being unable to imagine it or to partic-ipate in the constant imagining of it. The debates in the early nineteenth century over the very possibility of an American literature, after all, were crucial to the public sense of the nation. This was so because "America" as a community distinct from its European cousins could come fully into existence only through the romantic relationship between imagination and citizenship. Therefore, to legislate black illit-eracy under local laws of slavery was to legislate black exclusion from the nation, from the imagined community, by preventing the not-imag-ined (by whites) black American from imagining him/herself in or of the nation, from imagining the nation at all.[28] And by being held illiter-ate, one is excluded from the acting civic/cultural community (unable to read law, write history, keep accounts, etc.) as well as from the imag-ining one. Thus, we err to see laws against literacy for slaves as *only* economically instrumental by design, or even *only* to prevent blacks from having ideas of freedom; rather they functioned to prevent blacks, free and enslaved, from imagining an America with themselves in it as imagining subjects, rather than as imagined property objects.[29] That such an effect was ultimately not successful is a matter of record and is the point of this book. But the struggle to overcome the effects of these romantic impediments has been long and hard. Even a century after Emancipation, African American lawyer and Pulitzer Prize winner James Alan McPherson would declare that a "mind needs media to reinforce a sense of self. There are no imaginations pure enough to be self-sustaining" ("Elbow Room" 227).

Just how important could writing and reading be? Writing as a reproduction of self, of one's body and one's sensibilities, can have an effect on one's readers. Not only might the literate slave be able to imagine him- or herself a part of the national design, but the text of that imagined identity could convince a readership of the validity of the identity. Armstrong and Tennenhouse argue in connection with Samuel Richardson's 1740 protonovel *Pamela*, for example, that the ability of the eponymous heroine to write was somehow causal in arousing the interest and affection of English readers (*Imaginary* 200). It was, they suggest, the task of the novel to overcome class biases on the part of Richardson's readers against the general unworthiness of the life of the English serving girl. Because she was seen primarily as a drudge by her mistress and as a target for sexual exploitation by every male member of the household, her sensibilities were both invisible and unimaginable by Richardson's public. But by reproducing such a life through letters, in the imagined voice of such a young girl, Richardson succeeds in making his readers care about the fate of the physical body of the girl, as the embodiment of the voice they come to know:

> During the course of the novel . . . the repeated assaults upon Pamela's chastity cause her body to disappear along with her status as servant. She stops working and does nothing but write personal letters. As she does so, she ceases to exist as a sexually desirable woman and becomes a unique source of written speech. The transformation proves curiously self-empowering. (199)

Some such effect was the purpose of all antebellum narratives made by Africans in America: slave and ex-slave narratives, novels, and testimony. The fundamental power of such narrativity is underscored in studies by H. Bruce Franklin, as well as by Armstrong and Tennenhouse (*Imaginary*), who seek to identify themes of American captivity in discussions of the early novel. Franklin includes the slave narrative in his study of American prison literature, and Armstrong and Tennenhouse argue that the American captivity narratives of the seventeenth and early eighteenth centuries are the sources of women's narrative voices for the early English novel. Both genres were widely read, and each changed the way the reader considered his or her understanding of the national design (G. Smith). For each subject in these narratives spoke to his or her situation as a citizen held in captivity, absent from the protections and expectations of a citizen's lot. The reader who responded sympathetically to the English woman held captive by savages in a strange yet English place, and the reader who responded sympathetically to the African American held captive by a barbaric institution in a familiar land, each had to emerge from the experience with a new notion of national identity. Just as Pamela's plight alerted the English readership of the mid–eighteenth century to a new design of English nationhood, one in which "the future of the ruling class—their suitability for rule—would continue to hinge on their adherence to courtship procedures that demonstrated extraordinary concern for the feelings of otherwise quite ordinary women" (Armstrong and Tennenhouse 201), so slave literacy, especially slave narrativity, functioned to create a text of concern for the plight of otherwise untextualized and hence unimagined citizens, Africans.

If, then, writing creates identity, in the case of the development of the novel it is the role of the woman to create for herself an identity based on her ability to tell her story, and the same is true for the slave narrative. This suggests that one function of narrative, and perhaps the key to its appeal, is to give voice to the marginalized object, transforming it into the voiced subject. If this is the case, then we can argue that narrative fiction parallels law because the Anglo-American system of closure through confrontation eliminates the category of object and situates all parties as subjects *when they testify*. It is true that there is a subject position under the law that is infinitely better to occupy than the object position, but the whole struggle of the law is to seize the text of the case through the combined narratives of parties, witnesses, evidence, and the law itself. In the process of testifying, each party acts in the subject position. African American literacy in the nineteenth century, then, would be hardly imaginable to whites who could find no subject position in the law for slaves or free persons of color.

Similarly, eighteenth-century reading practices in the law and in literature reflect the power of literacy to create the acting subject. Susan Sage Heinzleman has pointed out that both the emerging novel form and English common law in the eighteenth century required a disciplined reader—the common law because it was not a self-sufficient text, and the novel, I would add, because as an emerging rather than established set of conventions of representation it lacked a full context. In both cases, Heinzleman argues, any epistemological advantage to having encountered the text had to depend heavily on the experience and "discipline" of the reader. In effect, the reader acting on the text was responsible for creating some sort of ontological order. Again extrapolating to the conditions faced by enslaved people in North America, I would argue that the very discipline of reading implied a status of subjectivity that was disallowed by every other law governing slavery, even if a law forbidding reading had not existed. Enslaved people were held in an epistemological bondage that forbade them to either read themselves into the law or write themselves into it. Or into history. Or into literature. Part of the material text of American life, slaves were to be no part of any text other than an inventory, if the system that slavery had become were to work.

Similarly, restrictions on literacy limit the ability of the individual to own her own text or, and perhaps even more importantly in some situations, to enhance the text of oneself-as-property through more complex relationships with other texts.[30] As the situated "other" in texts of white supremacy, she cannot own her own story. Just as the enslaved person is prevented from occupying the subject position in the law, she cannot occupy the subject position in a "literary" text of her life until she has the ability and right to write it. So narratives are immediately recognizable as private property in this romantic sense, but property productive of a public effect, quite as private productive property produces effects in a capitalist society as it is put to work.[31]

Even this last idea, private productive property, is itself an imagined thing; that is, no such thing exists in nature. Rather, it is the creation of the application of human imagination to the notion of identity (the property of a thing) in things. Prior to the early modern period, "property" as we understand the term did not appear in English common law. Over time, the law came to "imagine" that one can have stewardship of the property of things (Seipp). By the dawn of the period we are considering, human imagination applied to property—which was no longer a characteristic of the thing but had become the thing itself—was believed to create new value, new reality; property became real in a new way by being owned. That is, it cannot be owned by another or others without becoming something newly else, something rooted not in community or belonging, but in individuality, in this case the individuality of ownership by this person and not by that person. This is evident in the tradition of designating slaves by the possessive forms of their owners' names, as in "Smith's Cuffee" instead of Cuffee or even Cuffee Smith.

It should be clear that this is a difficult construct to overcome when a slaveholding culture ceases to be so. Could whites suddenly stop seeing blacks as property and recognize in them the "property" of being able to own property? This was of course complicated by the previous existence of laws forbidding the ownership of property by blacks. And this is one more of the imaginative acts purposefully denied to the enslaved black object, the right and therefore the opportunity to imagine himself as other than property, to imagine the life of property not as bondage but as capital. The shadow of that inhibition still obscures African American participation in American life (P. J. Williams, *Alchemy*; Staves; Radin; C. I. Harris).

The antebellum black novelist who saw this problem with the greatest clarity was Martin R. Delany. Unlike his contemporary Frank J. Webb, Delany saw no benefit accruing to his characters from property, since they were the property objects themselves. Delany's approach in *Blake* was to posit the problem of slavery as one of labor oppression, with race as the class designator. Delany was clearly a "race" man in its most pristine sense; his novel demonstrates his preference for the "pure" African over the mulatto character. Nevertheless, he understood slavery as an economic system based on racial controls, not as mere expression of white racism. As a consequence, there is little in Delany's novel that speaks to or for the citizenship or the "Americanness" of enslaved negroes. In fact, the strong emphasis on the "international" character of slavery established by the amount of space given in the novel to Cuban affairs and to Blake's sojourn in Cuba, including his Cuban origins, contradicts the "local" quality of the practice of slavery. The slavery that appears in *Blake* is an international system of oppression-through-property supported by national policies implemented locally. As such, it demands a response that matches it in sophistication. Blake's plan for rebellion was to be such a response.[32]

The legal center of the novel is the issue of American citizenship, nevertheless. It is from the impossibility, as Delany sees the future in the 1850s, of any truly participatory citizenship for African Americans that the need for revolution springs. In chapter 15, within polemical discussions of the Dred Scott case and the Missouri Compromise, the Fugitive Slave Laws, and the "rights" of free Negroes, Delany engages the distinction between "suffrage" and "franchisement." The passage, a conversation among two southern slaveholders and a northern judge who owns slaves in Cuba, bears reproducing in part here.

"How about the Compromise measures, Judge? Stand up to the thing all through, and no flinching."

"My opinion, sir, is a matter of record, being the first judge before whom a case was tested, which resulted in favor of the South. And I go further than this; I hold as a just construction of the law, that not only has the slaveholder a right to reclaim his slave when and wherever found, but by its provision every free black in the country, North and South, are [sic] liable to enslavement by any white person.[33] They are freemen by sufferance or slaves-at-large, whom any white person may claim at discretion. It was a just decision of the Supreme Court—though I was in advance of it by action—that persons of African descent have no rights that white men are bound to respect!"

"Judge Ballard, with this explanation, I am satisfied; indeed as a Southern man I would say, that you've conceded all that I could ask, and more than we expected. But this is a legal disquisition; what is your private opinion respecting the justice of the measures?"

"I think them right, sir, according to our system of government."

"But how will you get away from your representative system, Judge? In this your blacks are either voters, or reckoned among the inhabitants."

"Very well, sir, they stand in the same relationship as your Negroes. In some of the states they are permitted to vote, but can't be voted for, and this leaves them without any political rights at all. Suffrage, sir, is one thing, franchisement another; the one a mere privilege—a thing permitted—the other a right inherent, that which is inviolable—cannot be interfered with." (60–62; Crane)

At this point in the discussion, the matter of Cuba is raised and the position of blacks in that Spanish colony compared to practices at home. Judge Ballard as a property owner in Cuba introduces the political issue on which the last half of the novel will turn:

"I don't like it at all, and never could be reconciled to the state of things there. I consider that colony as it now stands, a moral pestilence, a blighting curse, and it is useless to endeavor to disguise the fact; Cuba must cease to be a Spanish colony, and become American territory. Those mongrel Creoles are incapable of self-government and should be compelled to submit to the United States." (62)

In effect, the entire novel is a response to the legal and political issues set out in this chapter. While the immediate problem for any individual enslaved person was freedom, the two longer-range problems were the destruction of slavery as a system of property and the acquisition of the "franchise" by all emancipated people. Delany underpins the narrative with references to local and federal cases and legislation regarding each of these as well as Spanish colonial law and British Admiralty law. As Henry Blake travels through every slave-holding state, through the North, Canada, and Cuba, Delany's book reads more and more like a "legal" picaresque and less and less like the novel of domestic manners of his contemporary, Webb, or his successors at the end of the century, Hopkins, Harper, Dunbar, and Chesnutt.

By the 1880s, Delany was near the end of his life, and he had shifted his energies from internationalism and colonization to the struggle for enfranchisement. The aftermath of the Civil War had turned the issue of black economic exploitation into a matter of localized practices. In April 1882, a progenitor group to the Brotherhood of Liberty met at Baltimore's Ebeneezer A. M. E. Church to condemn "the Republicans for their silence on the bastardy law and the proscription against Negro lawyers, and for the party's failure to honor the Negro's need for employment opportunities through the [sic] patronage" (Paul 200). According to the *Baltimore Sun* reports of the meeting, Martin R. Delany addressed the gathering and urged them to organize independently of the Republicans and the Democrats and to protect their civil rights. Delany's antebellum separatist views had changed after the war and Emancipation, but he was not sanguine about any real power without a political base (Kahn). He advised them to neither "elbow the whites nor be elbowed by them" (Paul 200n. 49).[34]

The Brotherhood's energies eventually went into the effort to get black lawyers admitted to the Maryland bar and to ensure the ability of the black community to bring cases in civil court and to defend itself in criminal court and in every instance on appeal, even to the highest level, that "grave of liberty," the United States Supreme Court (Wakeman 26).[35] It was in the context of the risks to black citizenship, the "franchise" that had been granted by the Thirteenth, Fourteenth, and Fifteenth Amendments, that the Brotherhood of Liberty understood the challenges posed by the direction the courts had taken. They realized that their only protection against the implications of the past was in the vigorous insistence on present-day rights at every level and in every sphere, primarily through litigation and electoral politics.

It was in pursuit of this legal stratagem that the Brotherhood sought an analysis of the implications for the three postwar amendments of the Court's "activist" approach.[36] The result was the 578-page treatise on civil rights law through whose arguments the constitutional and social problems of the "much mooted race-question" might be ameliorated.[37]

The arguments posited in *Justice and Jurisprudence* are remarkable not only for their very existence but for what they reveal of the issues confronting the imagined community of which the Brotherhood sought to be representative, and for how they are presented to readers, primarily whites who made up the larger national community. The Brotherhood aspired to gain membership in this community for all people of color in the country:

> As a generalization, this work may be said to consist of two parts. The first concerns the Positive Law of the Fourteenth Amendment, by which the whole power of the American state is pledged to maintain the equality of civil rights of every American citizen by Due Process of Law. The second discloses the transparent veils of legal fiction under cover of which the civil rights of all races are slowly being undermined. It shows how judicial construction has so impaired the *lex scripta* that, although the letter may remain, yet the heart has been eaten out. (i)

The Brotherhood of Liberty placed its hope for the future of the race in the constitutional protections afforded them by law, but feared the "hypochondriac alarm and valetudinary longevity of race prejudice" they saw afflicting even the highest court (10). The methodological sin through which the 1883 Court erred, in the Brotherhood's analysis, was "juristic innovation," "judicial construction," and causing "an unconstitutional drift of the courts and public sentiment away from the

Fourteenth Amendment" (i, ii). The counter-Reconstruction Court of 1883 "made" law, as far as the Brotherhood could see, and that was clearly unconstitutional— the amendments were clear and binding and unabridgeable except by the duly constituted process of repeal. Nevertheless, the Brotherhood sensed that white American tolerance for a restrictive reading of the conditions under which citizenship might be practiced by black Americans was growing and that the ideological barriers to full citizenship that had been present since the founding were being erected once again at every intersection of black and white life.

Nowhere are those barriers more evident than in the question of racial identity itself as property. At the end of the century white novelist and lawyer Albion Tourgee constructed an argument for his client in *Plessy v. Ferguson* based on the essentialist argument that racial identity is property.[38] In Tourgee's argument, the privileges of association guaranteed by the Constitution were distributed racially by the offending Louisiana statute such that Plessy, a man seven-eighths white and one-eighth black, lost the properties guaranteed by the national document to his majority "part," the whiteness of him that held, as property, the right to sit in a specified car. This was to be understood by the Court as a violation of due process (Olsen, *Thin*; Bell, "Xerxes"; C. I. Harris).[39] That the Court rejected the argument despite its record of support for property rights suggests the validity of the assumption stated above, that white Americans could not, after Emancipation, easily make the transition from the legal *or* psychic ownership of blacks to any recognition of blacks as propertied subjects. To the 1896 Court, blacks were beings apart from whites and shared no intrinsic characteristics with them. Equality was an "extrinsic" assignment that could be relegated to secondary importance when the law was assumed to address fundamental human qualities such as racial identity and could be circumscribed when the issue at hand turned, as the Court reasoned it did, on matters of intrinsic difference rather than extrinsic identity.

These distinctions without differences on which whites traded after 1883 become the fundamental subject matter of African American fiction for the next twenty years. The causal argument is almost syllogistic; it is premised on the centrality of property in romantic and capitalist thought and develops through the construction of a legal base to support the exercise of that centrality. When African Americans achieved nominal subject status under the law and in the culture, the narratives they produced, both legal and fictive, addressed the concept of property. As a mirror of white legal and fictive narrative, which had imagined a world in which whites owned the relations of production and held black people as part of that property, black legal and fictive narratives imagined a world in which African Americans were no longer owned but were instead actively propertied beings, owning not only real property but legal standing.

CHAPTER 3

The Romance of Desire and Identity

> In giving this little romance expression in print, I am not actuated by a desire for notoriety or for profit, but to do all that I can in an humble way to raise the stigma of degradation from my race. . . . The colored race has historians, lecturers, ministers, poets, judges and lawyers,—men of brilliant intellects who have arrested the favorable attention of this busy energetic nation. But, after all, it is the simple, homely tale, unassumingly told, which cements the bond of brotherhood among all classes and all complexions.
>
> Pauline M. Hopkins, *Contending Forces*

Desire: Citizenship and Sexuality

The voice of Pauline Hopkins in the preface to her novel *Contending Forces* is painfully restrained. What is the "stigma of degradation" she wants to erase with her "simple, homely tale" introduced in such a ladylike manner? It is the reputation of the Negro woman, and through it, that of the race itself. By 1900 black women carry the weight of more than two centuries of white male rapaciousness on their backs, and the advent of Jim Crow has brought with it the public humiliation of black character.[1]

By the late nineteenth century, not just Hopkins but all African American novelists were struggling to find some common ground between desire, as an element of human personality, and the legal circumscription of African American life by white racism. Constrained by the conventions of melodrama and the novel of manners, their fictions reflect the struggle in the living world between African American desire (and participation in the romantic impulse still present in American culture) and Jim Crow legislation designed to control, limit, and even eliminate the expression of that desire in American life. For most whites, blacks were recognized only as beings without agency and without desire—only appetite (Somerville 140).[2] In African American novels of the nineteenth century, however, heroes of the race are without appetite, but filled with desire. The desire is for honor, home, and freedom. And in a nation in which the demonic racism of whites seemed intent on overpowering the good that is possible in all humans, it was civil solace to which blacks in literature turned, and the text they read for an understanding of how one ought to be in America was the law. The bulk of the talk and the action in these books is directed at the legal structure that surrounds the characters and of which they are so aware.

Just as property-ness as a legal status was a condition of antebellum life for blacks in America, so property as a legal concept also influenced the context into which African Americans emerged out of the strictures of slavery. This is particularly true for the African American family, the foundation on which black life is represented in nineteenth-century African American fiction. The centrality of marriage in African American novels of the late nineteenth century reflects its importance as a marker of citizenship, as a legal institution in which blacks were finally allowed to participate (Grossberg 129–36). The skein of social relationships between whites and blacks beginning in the antebellum period is tangled to say the least: free and not-free people on the same land, families and "not-families" begetting children, particularly as property became a part of the infrastructure of the "republican" family.

As the "economic moorings of the [postcolonial] household shifted from production toward consumption," the nature of the family as a unit within the citizenry began to change. The slaveholding family, while engaged in a family "business" of production, did less and less of the actual producing and in the larger holdings consumed rather more than it as a discrete unit produced. Production was the function of the slave as private productive property held by the family, the slaveholding variant of the "more clearly defined use of private property as the major source of domestic autonomy" (Grossberg 6) that was changing the economic base of the republican family in general. Slaveholders were, therefore, unable to accept the existence of slave marriages and families; for slaves to become consumers rather than producers would be antithetical to the very basis of slavery, production.

The compromise to the paradigmatic dissonance caused by the desire of enslaved people to enter into a social relation not conceptually admissible by their enslaver was the general practice, localized in its forms, of allowing "marriages" that carried no legal or contractual force or benefits. The ironic implication of this compromise is that it posits for enslaved people the purest motives for marriage. Unlike whites, black slaves could not marry for money or status, nor to ensure a family line, nor to join two dynasties, nor to ensure against incriminating testimony in court. All that would be left as reasons for marriage would be love, companionship, care, empathy. These reasons are the stuff of our romantic notions of the family.[3]

Another way of saying this is to say that slave marriage was denied as a way of denying family and family was to be denied because of the special role of the family in republican ideology: as the crucible in which the nation, like the moral and ethical character of its citizens, is formed. Since blacks were property—and if human at all, certainly not humans fit to be citizens—their having families was not just unnecessary but dangerous, since no one would want to allow the effects of family into the worldview of slaves. But it was some version of this republican family, amended first by romanticism and then by Victorian domestic gentility, that African Americans replicated after Emancipation and that African American novelists at the end of the century sought to re-create in their stories. In those texts, as in the lives they reflected, family had come to be the repository of a core of moral and civic values, "'the permanency of marriage, the sacredness of the home, and the dependence of civilized life upon the family. None of these ideas were new, but they did not become universally accepted until the Victorian era, when they quickly received such general support that men found it impossible to believe that customs had ever been otherwise'" (Grossberg 10; O'Neill 89).[4]

Marriage as a contracted relationship is at the heart of the nineteenth-century African American novel, even in those dealing with slavery. From *Our Nig* (1859) through *Contending Forces* (1900), black characters love, marry, raise children, suffer agonies of separation and powerlessness in the face of the violence of enslavement, resist enforced violations of their vows. In Delany's *Blake,* for example, it is the sale of his wife that sets Henry Blake on a course to alter history. To regain her he will plan a general uprising of slaves across the nation and even into Cuba. In every state Blake sets up cells of insurrection, each situated in the household of a married couple, counting on the stability and discipline of the relationship to hold the center of his revolution in place. In Frank J. Webb's *The Garies and Their Friends* (1857), domesticity as a function of family relationships is the desired condition for all of the African American characters, and the extended family of black men, women, and children in a free community cradles and nurtures generations of black fortune.

Through these families at the heart of any civilized life are imagined, at least in part, the "deep horizontal comradeship" and the web of relations it subsumes that characterize the experience of community, despite "the actual inequality and exploitation that may prevail" (B. Anderson 7). Yet inequality and exploitation, however invisible to the imagining white mind in search of community, were fashioned into badges and indices to mark the bearer as not of the community. So whites in the late nineteenth century could imagine a nation as a web of comradeship and equity and at the same time identify certain persons among them as not of that community, although the excluded had been among them for three hundred years.

The ironic counterevidence to white assumptions that blacks were not of, or capable of, such a community was always available to them, but probably never so straightforwardly as in the novels of black bourgeois life written in the last decade of the century. Frances E. W. Harper's *Iola Leroy* (1892) chronicles the life of a heroine of such purity of purpose that one worries she will refine herself out of the possibility of any human community, black or white. But at the last moment, she realizes she is in love with the man who loves her, and we are showed that her acceptance of him authenticates his fitness for life in the new world of black dignity and worth. As she contemplates her decision, she rejects her white suitor, Dr. Gresham:

> She had admired Dr. Gresham and, had there been no barrier in her way [his race], she might have learned to love him; but Dr. Latimer had grown irresistibly upon her heart. There were depths in her nature that Dr. Gresham had never fathomed; aspirations in her soul with which he had never mingled. But as the waves leap up to the strand, so her soul went out to Dr. Latimer. Between their lives were no impeding barriers, no inclination impelling one way and duty compelling another. Kindred hopes and tastes had knit their hearts; grand and noble purposes were lighting up their lives; and they esteemed it a blessed privilege to stand on the threshold of a new era and labor for those who had passed from the old oligarchy of slavery into the new commonwealth of freedom. (271)

It is in this mixing of the personal and the public telos that African American novels of the period, so many of them indebted to conventions found in "women's" novels of a previous generation, differ from those models. Instead of the interpretation of experience figured forth solely in modes of personal relationships, excluding class or caste, black novels generally showed events and their reconciliations as matters of race informed by the other conventions of the novel, for example, the transcendence of the physical world (experienced as the suppression of all physical desire) and the surrogation of physical pleasure into duty, discipline, self-control, and sacrifice, all moral and useful strategies for guiding one's community through an inhospitable world.

In order to understand the relationship between the domestic and the common weal as an element of African American narrative's critique of American law, the nation as both limited and sovereign (B. Anderson 7) remains to be considered. In such a finite entity, not "coterminous with mankind" (7), the citizen imagines a state of freedom, which if directly overseen by God, is at least directly so, and therefore the citizen/state exists in a special relationship with God, unmediated by hierarchy. Thus, the position of "citizen" assumes a sacralized quality.[5] "Negroes" as heathens, even those converted to Christianity, could never be imagined in this unmediated space by whites. It is interesting, for example, how the paternalism of southern slavery distinguished it so clearly from that of the northern states and from European serfdom. At its least inhumane, southern slavery saw Negroes as ignorant, permanent children between whom and the rest of all experience, including that of God, the slaveholder stood.

It is some combination of this unsacralized condition and the very unimaginability of the Negro as part of the belonged-to-community that lies at the root of the fear of miscegenation (or cohabitation or amalgamation), a relationship the laws of which have plagued both races for three hundred years.[6] In commenting on miscegenation in the imagined homogenous community, Anderson inadvertently points us to a peculiar contradistinction—how in some contexts the product of miscegenation is looked on as becoming like "us," and therefore acceptable, but later, or even simultaneously, is seen as being debased or even evil. He cites an early nineteenth-century Colombian liberal, Pedro Fermin de Vargas: "[I]t would be very desirable that the Indians be extinguished, by miscegenation with the whites, declaring them free of tribute and other charges, and giving them private property in land" (13–14; Lynch 260).

Anderson notes that the method of extinction is by impregnation with "white, 'civilized' semen" and the awarding of private property. This, Fermin believed, was the only way to "hispanicize" Indians and, as a consequence, expand the agricultural base of Colombia (13). Miscegenation as eradication was, in fact very much on the minds of the black middle class in the United States at the end of the nineteenth century. In 1885, the Reverend H. Edward Bryant, writing in the *A.M.E. Church Review*, pointed to the conflict between race and citizenship by warning against the appeal of "race mixing":

> [W]e have a large number of leading men who are ashamed of the word, Negro, and rise up in holy horror and righteous indignation when we are called Negroes. They reply: *"Look here, sir, I am an American and my race are Americans, not Negroes."* I readily admit we are Americans in nationality, but raceologically I am willing to be called a Negro, and I shall labor to make that word honorable. . . . Those little philosophers who are searching for some alchemy or panacea which will turn the Negro race white, I suppose are in favor of applying the only remedy yet discovered, ruinous as it is in the end, viz: miscegenation, amalgamation, and that shameful system of immorality which has prevailed so long in this country (in the past by compulsion,) and even now almost by compulsion, because of the circumstances of our people. (262–63)[7]

But a quarter of a century later, the following ironic perspective on the problem, informed by over two decades of experience with Jim Crow laws, is found in the black newspaper, the *Savannah Tribune:*

> There is much discussion going on in the white newspapers of this section over what seems to be a decrease in the percent of increase in the population of the negro race, comments the *Colored Alabamian* of Montgomery. We would respectfully call their attention to the fact that whatever increase is made in the negro population is perfectly "natural," for there is practically no immigration of blacks from other countries to the United States. On the other hand there are hundreds of thousands of whites who come to this country each year.
>
> We would also call the attention of the whites who seem to be a little happy over the situation to the fact that there are thousands of negroes going over to the white race each year. Many negroes move from one state to the other and send their children to white schools and join white churches. Conductors on street cars and trains can't tell negroes from whites sometimes. We have seen negroes with whom we are well acquainted pass for white right here in the city of Montgomery. When the census is being taken all

such negroes are counted in with white people and the totals are made up and published showing that the negro race is dying out, etc. If they will give us back our white negroes, we will make a better showing in 1920. There are laws against the intermarriage of whites and blacks; and other laws against whites and blacks sitting together on trains and in street cars, and a thousand other barriers, but this whitening process is still going on. ("Give Us Back Our White Negroes," June 15, 1912, n.p.)

Fear of miscegenation and the idea of the loss of self survived the era of slavery such that it not only, as we see above, proved a constant barrier to one form of "integration" of the society in the minds of both whites and black Americans, but also came to stand, as an issue, for the circumscription on African American life in general. The matter of human sexual desire between the races, particularly as felt by blacks for whites, came to be synecdochic for the general desire of black Americans to participate in the country's life at all, with at least one interesting consequence, the masking of African American "desire" in narrative.

A powerful example of the shaping effect of both law and customary belief about miscegenation on African American fiction during this period is seen in Sutton Griggs's *Imperium in Imperio* (1899). Into the argument for the political and physical separation of his race from white America that sits at the center of the novel Griggs inserts the dedicated "race woman"'s fear of miscegenation. Viola Martin is loved by Bernard Belgrave and loves him in return. He has asked her to marry him and leaves her door with every hope for their future. When he returns the next day, he finds she has killed herself. Here are excerpts from the letter she leaves, as Griggs has composed it to explicate the issue of miscegenation:

In 18—— just two years prior to my meeting you, a book entitled, "White Supremacy and Negro Subordination," by the merest accident came into my possession. That book made a revelation to me of a most startling nature.

While I lived I could not tell you what I am about to tell you. Death has brought me the privilege. That book proved to me that the intermingling of the races in sexual relationship was sapping the vitality of the Negro race and, in fact was slowly but surely exterminating the race. It demonstrated that the fourth generation

of the children born of intermarrying mulattoes were invariably
sterile or woefully lacking in vital force. It asserted that only in the
most rare instances were children born of this fourth generation
and in no case did such children reach maturity. . . . I looked out
upon our strong tender hearted manly race being swept from the
face of the earth by immorality, and the very marrow of my bones
seemed chilled at the thought thereof. I determined to spend my
life fighting the evil. My first step was to solemnly pledge God to
never marry a mulatto man. . . . When you came, I loved you. I
struggled hard against that love. God, alone, knows how I battled
against it. I prayed Him to take it from me as it was eating my heart
away. . . . But it was not to be. I had to choose between you and my
race. Your noble heart in its sober moments will sanction my
choice. I would not have died if I could have lived without proving
false to my race. Had I lived, my love and your agony, which I cannot bear, would have made me prove false to every vow. (173–75)

Viola asks Bernard, a lawyer and leader of his people, to continue
her work in dissuading the young from intermarriage and, should per-
suasion fail, to lead the race physically from "this accursed land" (175).
At the novel's climax, we find Bernard leading the Imperium as it plans
to seize Texas and create a black nation, fulfilling his duty to the
woman who had signed her suicide note as she could never have done
in life, "Your loving wife, Viola Belgrave."[8]

The representation of the African American woman as a heroine of
discipline and sacrifice was crucial to the agenda of the fiction-writing
black bourgeoisie of the Nadir. Calumnied in white folklore as a creature of sexual desire and gratification, the black woman was rewritten
in the novels of Frances E. W. Harper, Pauline Hopkins, Griggs, and
others as a bulwark of respectability and a center of family and race solidarity and stability. In Griggs's portrait, for the good of her race she
forgoes even a happy marriage and the fulfillment of her physical and
social desires by performing the ultimate expression of denial, the
removal of physical desire completely, by killing it and the organism,
her own body, that houses it. The consequence of that act is played out
in the novel as the renunciation of the desire for American citizenship,
renunciation of integration into the life of the American family, a symbolic killing of the desire to be embraced by the American body politic.

Unlike heroes of traditionally romantic American novels by white
authors, however, the men and women of these novels do not separate

themselves from all community in order to resist a heartless system. White romance heroes Natty Bumppo, Huck Finn, and Ishmael each seeks an understanding of natural, romantic law by moving to the margins of civil life and becoming fast friends with a person of color who teaches him how to read the text of the universe. The heroes of these African American novels, however, reverse this action, turn to community and family and seek no associations with whites, learning nothing of value from them about how to be in the world except what can be learned from the bitter experience of having survived the worst whites could do. In fact, in these novels the African American characters serve as moral exemplars for whites, a version of their role as guides to right living and survival in romantic novels written by whites.

Still, in their attempts to figure forth the solidarity required to save the race, these novels' depictions of the lives of black people *are* romanticized. Characters everywhere are paragons of authenticity. Here passions are not for sex or liquor or power. Everyone is committed to the uplift of the race.[9] The least educated are still wise and honorable, endearingly warm and funny; the most educated are gravely brave and dedicated to good works. In one scene in which too much dedication is argued, unsuccessfully, to be a bad thing, Iola Leroy is invited out to a *conversazione*. She had feared it was to a dance:

> "I am glad it is not to a hop or a german . . . but something for which I have been longing."
>
> "Why, Iola," asked Robert, "don't you believe in young people having a good time?"
>
> "Oh, yes," answered Iola, seriously, "I believe in young people having amusements and recreations; but the times are too serious for us to attempt to make our lives a long holiday." (243)

Like most American novels of the Victorian period, these by African Americans lack much of the ironic edge of the modern novel. But each does carry the ironic component of the reflexive, self-created character at the heart of romantic theories of the self. From Martin Delany's eponymous hero Blake through the black bourgeois citizenry of Charles W. Chesnutt's 1901 novel of the Wilmington, North Carolina, race riot, *The Marrow of Tradition,* black men and women fashion themselves out of resistance to a hostile, and to them often irrational, white world. The white "others" against whom they react are corruptions of human spirit and are the exact opposite of the helpful companions of color of white romance, of the Uncases, the Queequegs, the Jims, the Uncle Toms; they are rather more the equivalent of the demonized blacks of later white fiction of the post-Reconstruction period. Just as the romantic hero in white American novels acts out of some organic imperative, doing naturally what he must do, not what he is entitled to do, so, too, do the heroes in African American novels of the period. Such an imperative is fundamental to romanticism, in which the very laws of nature, for example, are set aside so that the romance hero can fulfill his desires. The language of romanticism is always the language of desire, of individual need written as categorical imperative. For this reason, romance and the imperative of heroic desire are often the masks for mythologies of "Destiny," "the Nation," or even "the Race."

How the issue of desire and renunciation was tied directly to the issue of black citizenship under law for the black bourgeoisie can be even more clearly seen in the positions spelled out by characters created by Pauline Hopkins in her 1900 novel, *Contending Forces* (Marcus). In a collection of set pieces framed by a meeting in Boston of the American Colored League, a fictional version of T. Thomas Fortune's Afro-American League, Hopkins's characters debate the best responses to the "race" issue at the end of the century, prompted by a recent lynching incident that has been represented in the press as a case of white revenge for miscegenation.

What might first strike a reader not familiar with the kinds of positions on miscegenation already discussed in this chapter is the unanticipated "admission" made by the single white speaker at the meeting, a Republican politician named Clapp, that one solution to the problem of the color line is miscegenation: "All history shows that two races, approaching in any degree equality in numbers, cannot live together unless intermarriage takes place or the one is dependent and in some sense subject to the other" (246). But Clapp goes on to argue that miscegenation by law would never occur in the United States, and so blacks must accept subordination to whites. Clapp's unique logic is further complicated when miscegenation as voluntary and consensual relations between the races is conflated with rape, and sexual subordination is conflated with racial subordination.

Clapp and his conservative black counterparts addressing the meeting condemn lynch law but qualify their condemnation by accepting the argument that the victims of lynch law are, in every case, rapists, perpetrators of forced miscegenation. The solutions they propose to the problem follow a line of conservative thought running from adherence to a "natural law" that demands quick retribution (while eschewing mob law, somehow), to gradual socialization of the most degraded of the race, to the "humanizing influence of the dollar" applied to vocational education, to looking to the federal government for legal protection from the overzealousness of white lynch mobs. Each of the conservative speakers, including a Booker T. Washington surrogate, a Dr. Arthur Lewis, condemns black political activism and blames the drive for political equality for blacks for the tension between the races.

A clue to Hopkins's position on these propositions is in her depiction of the audience's response to them:

> As [Clapp] finished and returned to his seat, a sigh like a broken moan seemed to come from the very heart of the multitude, but not a movement broke the stillness. . . . [Lewis] ceased speaking and sat down amid murmurs of applause, mingled with disapprobation. Some among the audience began to grow restless. Was this what they came to hear—an apology, almost a eulogy upon the course pursued by the South toward the Negro? . . . Scarcely had [Langley, a mulatto lawyer] taken his seat amid suppressed murmurs of discontent, when a tall, gaunt man of very black complexion arose in his seat among the delegates, and in a sonorous bass voice uttered the solemn protest of Patrick Henry, so famous in history: "Gentlemen may cry 'Peace! Peace!' but there is no peace!" (248, 251, 254)

Hopkins's voice in the argument is carried through two speakers at the meeting, Luke Sawyer, the tall, gaunt man above, and Will Smith, the closing speaker. Sawyer turns the coin on the previous speakers with a devastating tale of lynching for profit meant to drive blacks out of economic competition with whites and another of sexual brutality and degradation imposed by whites upon black women. Sawyer's view of the evening's arguments seems to represent Hopkins's view as the novel frames it:

> I want to tell the gentlemen who have spoken here tonight that conservatism, lack of brotherly affiliation, lack of energy for the right and the power of the almighty dollar which deadens men's hearts to the sufferings of their brothers, and makes them feel that if only *they* can rise to the top of the ladder may God help the hind-

most man, are the forces which are ruining the Negro in this country. It is killing him off by thousands, destroying his self-respect,
and degrading him to the level of the brute. *These are the contending
forces that are dooming this race to despair.* (256)

The audience is so moved as to be hushed while Sawyer poses his
response to the issues to the day: a call to arms. Sawyer compares the
conditions of blacks that day with those of the American colonists who
had taken up arms against "a tax too heavy placed on tea and things
like that." How would they have acted had they suffered as blacks did
at the close of the nineteenth century? Peace may be desirable, argues
Sawyer, but justice was undeniable. Peace may come only with the
grave (262). By associating Sawyer's cause with those of the Founders,
Hopkins reflected the deeply held belief of the black bourgeoisie that
they could and should claim the full heritage of American citizenship
through the equitable application of the law for which the Founders
had fought.[10]

As stirring as Sawyer's message is to the crowd, which breaks into
song when he finishes, it is Will Smith, the W. E. B. Du Bois avatar in
Contending Forces, who adumbrates Hopkins's final position on miscegenation, lynching, and citizenship.[11] The Negro, Smith maintains, not
interested in mixing the races, "dwells less on such a social cataclysm
than any other race among us." He rejects miscegenation, lawful or
unlawful (264). The real issue, he maintains, is how the Negro can live
as a citizen. To Smith's, and to Hopkins's, mind, the Negro must
embrace politics and pursue education rather than mere industrial
training. Emigration and other schemes of black nationalism must be
resisted, and the depiction of Negro men as rapists must be challenged
with the facts of white violations of Negro women and the economic
and political motives behind most lynchings.

"For the sake of argument," Hopkins has Smith say,

we will allow that in one case out of a hundred the Negro is guilty
of the crime with which he is charged; in the other ninetynine cases
the white man gratifies his lust, either of passion or vengeance. . . .
Lynching was instituted to crush the manhood of the enfranchised
black. Rape is the crime which appeals most strongly to the heart
of the home life. Merciful God! Irony of ironies! *The men who created
the mulatto race, who recruit its ranks year after year by the very means
which they invoke lynch law to suppress,* bewailing the sorrows of vio-

lated womanhood! . . . If the Negro votes, he is shot; if he marries a white woman, he is shot; if he accumulates property, he is shot or lynched—he is a pariah whom the National Government cannot defend. But if he defends himself and his home, then is heard the tread of marching feet as the Federal troops move southward to quell a "race riot." (270–71)

The answer to these depredations on the truth, Smith tells his audience, is simple: "We must *agitate!*" Rejecting brute force for a long-range effort to sway public opinion, Smith calls his people to preach as the abolitionists had done: "Appeal for the justice of our cause to every civilized nation under the heavens. Lift ourselves upward and forward in this great march of life until 'Ethiopia shall indeed stretch forth her hand, and princes shall come out of Egypt'" (272).

While the discussion of miscegenation embedded in this investigation of the romantic impulses behind white and black attitudes toward matters of family, law, and citizenship has taken us through a complex weave of attitudes toward desire as well, it is crucial to remember that while miscegenation as a matter of *policy* was not pursued in the United States, in practice, on a local, personal scale, a version of Fermin's argument for the homogenization of Colombia was carried out here. The consequence of miscegenation in the slaveholding South was the challenge to the racial basis of slavery as a system by the stream of cases involving petitions for emancipation on the basis of paternity. Most of these were settled by application of the English common-law rule that the condition of the child follows that of the mother. Still, skin color taken as evidence of white descent was often enough to allow local courts to entertain the argument that one or more of plaintiff's parents might have been free persons of color as a consequence of consanguineal promise.[12]

A good example of miscegenation's complexity can be seen when miscegenation and amalgamation are placed in the context of incest. In her study of the representation of miscegenation, Eva Saks quotes an antebellum Mississippi statesman: "The same law which forbids consanguineous amalgamation forbids ethnical amalgamation. Both are incestuous. Amalgamation is incest." What produces each of these crimes and links them, in the South of the nineteenth century, is the "invisible father," the aporia caused by the law's provision that condition follows the mother (53–54; Samuels). Hence no father exists for mulatto children—they are the children of nobody. Under such conditions the practical and, if you will, metaphysical potentiality of incest increases.

The implications for citizenship of the incest/miscegenation identification are considerable. In the first instance, such an identification forecloses the possibility that the children of miscegenation, lawful or unlawful, could aspire to full citizenship, since they seemed to be considered complicit in a felonious act rather than the products of it. The Mississippian who declared that "amalgamation is incest" clearly had as his purpose the exclusion of the children of such unions from white society. The assumption behind such a statement is that miscegenation is always the act of race mixing between white men and Negro women, since were it otherwise, and white women cohabited with Negro men, the children of such unions would be white by virtue of the previously noted rule that the condition of children always follows that of the mother.[13] By this point in the argument, however, any rational meaning that could be attached to the term *incest* has been lost.

The assumption is hidden, of course, because stated openly it would be challenged, but it is the hidden premise of white male aggression toward black men: fear of their sexuality. That fear, as Will Smith argued to his friends, also serves as a cloak for white economic aggression and aggrandizement. One of the more startling cases of the interweaving of sexual and racial politics at the end of the century turned exactly on such a challenge and had as its stakes the practice of Negro citizenship in a southern city. The city was Wilmington, North Carolina, and the event was the "riot" of 1898 in which armed white insurgents overthrew an elected, biracial city government and installed an all-white conservative one in its place (Prather).[14] The "riot"—in fact a coup d'etat—was engineered to put an end to one of the last Reconstruction-style city governments in the Old South and was premised on an insult to southern white womanhood published in a Wilmington black newspaper. That the "insult" had been published sometime earlier and that it was in fact not a gratuitous attack on white women but an editorial response to a public speech meant little to the whites who were looking for ways to disenfranchise blacks in the city.

The editorial that provided the excuse for armed insurrection was written by Alexander Manly and published in the *Wilmington Record* on August 18, 1898. Manly's editorial was part of his ongoing defense of black men from defamatory attacks in a white propaganda campaign during the off-election year of 1898, an important campaign in which Democrats, sensing the implications behind the recently decided *Plessy v. Ferguson,* and smarting under Republican dominance, hoped to win control of the North Carolina legislature. Part of the strategy was to raise the specter of black rapists violating white women. Maniy's editorial specifically was a response to the position of Rebecca Felton, wife of a former congressman. Mrs. Felton gave a speech in Tybee, Georgia, in August 1898, in which she proposed,

> When there is not enough religion in the pulpit to organize a crusade against sin, nor justice in the courthouse to promptly punish crime, . . . [and] if it needs lynching to protect woman's dearest possession from the ravening human beasts—then I say lynch, a thousand times a week if necessary. (Prather 71)[15]

Manly's response was, in effect, that if the laws were enforced evenly, protecting black women as well as white, blacks would support Felton's position. But they were not, and, Manly noted, any sexual or affectionate relationship between black men and white women was punished as rape, even when the attraction was mutual (Hodes). In fact, the crux of his defense of black men was the simple observation that in the New South, as in the Old, white women had and would continue to fall in love with black men and had and would act on that emotion.[16] To his mind, these relationships were what lynchings were designed to mask. The reverse was never the case, that is, when white men and black women had relationships. Manly warned whites that "you cry aloud for the virtue of your women while you seek to destroy the morality of ours. Don't ever think that your women will remain pure while you are debauching ours. You sow the seed—the harvest will come in due time."[17]

While there was some controversy in Wilmington when the editorial was published, none of it was extraordinary. Nevertheless, conservative Democrats in Wilmington who were seeking an issue with which to inflame the white working-class population against the city's integrated government and services realized that when other state and local political issues were in alignment, the editorial could be used to push the white populace into violent reaction against the black citizens of the town who were the primary supporters of the biracial administration. It is likely that behind the rebellion was the "legal" presence of blacks in Wilmington, that is, in positions of authority, criminal, civil, and regulatory, over whites. Some of white Wilmington disliked appearing before a Negro judge, being arrested by a Negro policeman or being handcuffed to a Negro, under the control of a Negro officer. Wilmington's four Negro lawyers got most of the business in criminal courts. White women complained of having their homes inspected by Negro sanitation officers, and white schools (the system was segregated) reportedly were inspected by Negro school commissioners (although it is unlikely that this happened since there were two separate school commissions). Negro overseers of the public roads controlled the work of white laborers (Prather 56–57; Clawson).

The Democrats filed the editorial away for a later day. When that day came, two months later, the editorial was dusted off and republished, this time in the white newspaper. In three days the coup was over and the white Democrats were in control of the city. Sixteen Negroes were dead, and more were run out of town. The black middle class in Wilmington was decimated, and black city employees and officials were removed from their jobs. There was no official inquiry into the events, nor did federal or state governments respond to requests for protection for black citizens after the violence had ended. Later that year the state legislature "ratified" the new city government.

It is important to note here that this violent disenfranchisement of Wilmington's black citizens could be predicated on the issue of rape and miscegenation because the black population of eastern North Carolina at the time was greater than the white population, and many Negro citizens lived middle-class lives in what was essentially a commercial and laboring urban center. These conditions made white fear of Negro domination even more intense than it ordinarily would have been in an area in which slaves had been held only by the largest landowners, as was the case in the upland Piedmont areas of the rest of the state.

Charles W. Chesnutt centers his fictional treatment of the coup on the issue of the color line for a Negro doctor and his light-skinned wife, half sister to one of the leading white women of the town.[18] Ironically, it is the doctor's civility in contrast to white manipulations of images of black rapacity, his civic quality in the face of the worst provocation, that marks the moral climax of the novel. Still unconsoled from the loss of his own child in the rioting, the doctor is asked to save the life of the son of his wife's half sister and antagonist.[19] That he does so may be read as a mark of the superheroic counterstereotyping African American novelists felt they had to employ to counteract white propaganda, but the doctor's ability to transcend his own grief ought more properly to be read as an example crafted by Chesnutt, to whites, of the true nature of civility and citizenship, one more argument from the black bourgeoisie that the lines of color that separated them from full citizenship under law, however those lines had been laid down, were totally arbitrary.

Chesnutt's focus on the doctor's civility is not the most striking aspect of the novel, however. Given the history of the actual events from which the story was fashioned, the absence of any real discussion of miscegenation as the catalyst in the political reaction of Wilmington's whites is remarkable. Chesnutt displaces the political volatility of the miscegenation/rape issue as it appeared in Wilmington's political stew to the realm of family tragedy, casting it in the conventional trope of the inherited consequences of slavery's generational sin.[20]

Thus, in the African American fiction of the last half of the nineteenth century, the civic consequences of miscegenation—the "color line" in law and property—occupy the center of the narrative. It is in this second half of the century that African American literature emerges as part of the national text, that part in which African Americans create the record of their imagined American-ness, or of their resistance to it. That identity is essentially that of the American citizen. As Dickson D. Bruce Jr. notes, "The genteel literature produced by post-Reconstructionist black writers was a measure of their optimism" that "[r]acial barriers were not . . . impregnable" (32), but we must not forget that the genteel suppression of human desire, however equally visited on black and white Victorian society and through which black authors sought to secure themselves and their black audiences to white Americans of similar Christian and bourgeois empathies, was only a part of the machinery of the suppression of that same romantic imperative that could still be felt in America. In the cases of black Americans, laws *mandating on pain of imprisonment* the exercise of restraint on their part provided for the levying of corporal and capital punishment on the part of the "authorities" if they failed to suppress their desire.

Identity: Self and Reality

The effort to deny citizenship in any active, meaningful sense to people of color by demanding through law the suppression of their civic and private desire was also the effort to deny the right to identity. In the terms of this analysis, romanticism's relationship to questions of the self and identity, personal and national, lies in part in the realization that romanticism is ultimately about self-creation—and the self's creation of reality by acting on the outside (of self) world through under-standing created by the understanding self. Underlying this statement of relationship between self and reality are two primary elements of romantic individualism: *authenticity*—the ability to act in one's own behalf sans hierarchy (and thus sovereign and thus sacralized); and *irony*—the reflexive capacity for unmediated knowledge of the self within the structure of the external (to the self) world. It is crucial to realize that it was *both* these components of romantic individualism that American society sought to deny African Americans in the nine-teenth century.[21]

Denial of the Authentic Romantic Self

The "authentic" romantic self is both spontaneous and responsive and, therefore, "natural," as opposed to wrought. In the truly romantic per-son/self, this natural authenticity finds its expression in passion, that is, emotion both spontaneous and responsive.[22] At the end of the period I am discussing, Henry James wrote,

> The romantic stands, on the other hand, for the things that, with all the facilities in the world, all the wealth and all the courage and all the wit and all the adventure, we never can directly know; the things that can reach us only through the beautiful circuit and sub-terfuge of our thought and desire. (xvi)

From antebellum America to this century, the denial of authentic-ity to blacks consisted of *(a)* attacks on the spontaneity and naturalness of the black "self" by trivializing and infantilizing it, by rendering it grotesque and devoid of meaning, incapable of "the beautiful circuit and subterfuge" of thought and desire; and *(b)* defining black passion as demonic, as unnatural, or as inhuman and limbic, as appetite only. Such reductionism relegated African Americans to the simple surface of the everyday, devoid of complexity, lacking any access to the beauti-ful or the sublime.[23]

The effect of this conscious reductionism in white portrayals of black "passion" and "naturalness" is the denial of these essential com-ponents of the romantic self to blacks. Put another way, a paradigm for self-construction whites claimed for themselves was excluded from the ideology used by whites to explain the presence of blacks in the world. That this was done through every medium of cultural construction, including law and literature, explains how fundamental the exclusion of blacks as authentic "selves" from the common consciousness of whites became.

The effect on African American fiction was specific: the denial of desire produced a hyperrationalized gentility of tone and spirit that was undercut by black writers' abilities to manage irony. That tone was cut as well by the influence of melodrama, a heightening of tensions through the employment of mutually exclusive moral positions signified by speech and action and suggesting "an underlying Manichaeism . . . putting us in touch with the conflict of good and evil played out under the surface of things" (Brooks, *Melodramatic* 4).[24] The conventions of melodrama not only contradict the tone of the African American novel of manners at the end of the century but force the reader's consciousness beneath the denial of desire suggested by their gentility, "into deeper sources of being" (4). Melodramatic convention in late-nineteenth-century African American fiction, constituting "a form that facilitates the 'circuit' of desire," allows its fabricator to seize access to "'the romantic' as the realm of knowledge reached through desire . . . permits its break through repression, brings its satisfaction to full expression" (154). This is perhaps how these fictions should be read, as narrative resistance to the "real-time" legal suppression of desire.

Susan Gillman argues correctly that we should understand these novels as examples of the appropriation of melodramatic form as "a narrative instrument for managing social tension and conflicts" (224).[25] In the preface to *Contending Forces*, Pauline Hopkins declares,

> Fiction is a great value to any people as a preserver of manners and customs—religious, political and social. It is a record of growth and development from generation to generation. *No one will do this for us; we must ourselves develop the men and women who will faithfully portray the inmost thoughts and feelings of the Negro with all the fire and romance which lie dormant in our history,* and, as yet, unrecognized by writers of the Anglo-Saxon race. (14–15)

Hopkins's story of families, history, miscegenation, and desire is melodramatic, but the reader's impulse to disregard the coincidences of plot and event not only misses the importance of the appropriative act but ignores a fact of nineteenth-century African American life: families sundered, identities blurred, racial lines were crossed, the "dead" returned. These were the conditions of history for enslaved people, particularly after Emancipation and the war. The "stuff" of white melodrama was the matter of living for black Americans. For example, the "motif" of the family reunited and the dead returned had its codification in laws and rules regulating marriage by former slaves in areas controlled by the Freedmen's Bureau (Edwards).

One Bureau document contained five sections governing eligibility to marry, who may permit marriage, who may "solemnize" marriages, first marriages and reunions, and rights of wives and children. After noting that previously unmarried people may marry, the document reads:

> —All married persons who shall furnish satisfactory evidence of either the marriage or divorce of all former companions, according to the usages of slavery, or of their decease, will be eligible to marry again.
> —All married persons, producing satisfactory evidence of having been separated from their companions by slavery for a period of three years, and that they have no evidence that they are alive; or, if alive, that they will ever, probably, be restored to them, may be allowed to marry again. ("General Orders," 1)

What constituted "satisfactory" evidence was not spelled out, and the qualifying passages citing "no evidence that they are alive" and "ever, probably, be restored" suggest how complex the task of regularizing relationships was. Persons already married were recognized. The rules, however, are predictably ambiguous. The marriages of "all parties living together as husband and wife at the time of obtaining their freedom, or solemnized since obtaining it" were recognized, but those "whose marriage was only a mutual agreement between themselves" had to get a certificate from some authorized venue. The same was true for those who claimed to be married but were separated by slavery and had no records (3).

The greater problem, however, was in those cases where everyone survived but had already made new alliances. A man living alone was required to "receive" a wife "restored" to him unless he could prove moral causes. The same was true of husbands restored to wives. If either refused to receive the other and no moral or legal grounds could be found, the bonds could be dissolved by a proper agency and provisions made for support of any children. If a man "find two wives restored to him by freedom, the one having children and the other not, he shall take the mother of his children as his lawful wife," except on moral grounds. The rules do not say what is to be done if both women have his children. The most ambiguous passage has to do with any case in which a man with a wife finds another restored to him. The rules say that if the resident wife has no children by him, he *may* take the first wife if she has children by him, if she have no other known living husband, and if "his present wife assent to such change of their marriage relations" (3).

It should be noted that the rules are remarkably evenhanded in their treatment of men and women. A woman could choose among two restored husbands, could reject any and all, would be provided for if set aside for reasons not moral or legal, and could insist on support by a former husband she rejected for moral causes. Men were required to support children of all marriages unless a former wife with children remarried. Men marrying women with children were required to support those children (3–4).

In general, the rules reflect the best of a bureaucratic attempt to deal with a problem none of its managers had ever seen. The document states the purpose of the rules:

> To correct as far as possible one of the most cruel wrongs inflicted by slavery, and also to aid the freedmen in properly appreciating and religiously observing the sacred obligations of the marriage state. . . . The sacred institution of Marriage lies at the very foundation of all civil society. It should be carefully guarded by all the agents of this Bureau. It is hoped these rules may do something to correct a monster evil which meets us at the very threshold of our work. (1, 4)

The rules also give evidence of the confusion of relations with which slavery ended and that laid the base for the "melodrama" of black life for the next fifty years.[26]

That melodrama finds a narrative expression in Charles W. Chesnutt's 1899 collection, *The Wife of His Youth and Other Stories of the Color Line*, and particularly in the title story. In his introduction to the collected stories, William Andrews correctly notes Chesnutt's groundbreaking attention to the "moral conflicts and psychological strains" of the postbellum African American middle class (xiii) but fails to note how concretely those tensions were tied to issues of legal status. In dis-

cussing the title story, he comments only on the triumph of the protagonist over "his class and color prejudices after decades of separation
[from] his dark-skinned plantation wife" (xiv). But "The Wife of His
Youth" particularly illuminates the reality of the putative situations
outlined in the Freedmen's Bureau rules for marriages. For that reason
alone, although it is a brief tale, its historical and legal specificity
deserves a bit of attention.

Mr. Ryder is a prosperous light-skinned man, single and greatly
regarded by his set, the "Blue Veins," in Groveland, Ohio. He is about
to give a ball at which he will announce his engagement to the equally
well regarded young widow, the even fairer Mrs. Molly Dixon. On the
afternoon of the ball, as he sits looking over the poetry of Tennyson, he
has a visitor, an aged black woman, "so black that her toothless gums,
revealed when she opened her mouth to speak, were not red, but blue"
(106). Chesnutt's care at establishing color as the sociohistorical center
of black bourgeois culture in postbellum America is evident in the
story's opening pages, but he takes equal care at establishing the legal
and historical realities that belie the assumption by "Blue Veins"
throughout the country that they represent the ultimate of social and
moral refinement of the race.

Mr. Ryder's visitor has come to Groveland seeking her lost husband, as she assumes he has been seeking her: "I heerd you wuz a big
man an' had libbed heah a long time, an' I 'lowed you wouldn't mind
ef I'd come roun' an' ax you ef you'd ever heerd of a merlatter man by
de name er Sam Taylor 'quirin' roun' in de chu'ches ermongs de people
fer his wife, 'Liza Jane" (107)? 'Liza Jane and Sam had been married on
the farm of her owner, and Sam was to be sold downriver although he
was freeborn and was only apprenticed to "Marse Bob Smif." Sam fled,
and Marse Bob sold 'Liza downriver instead.

> "Den de wah broke out, an' w'en it wuz ober de cullud folks wuz
> scattered. I went back ter de ole home; but Sam wuz n' dere, an' I
> could n' l'arn nuffin' 'bout 'im. But I knowed he'd be'n dere to look
> fer me an' had n' foun' me, an' had gone erway ter hunt fer me.
>
> "I's be'n lookin' fer 'im eber sence," she added simply, as though
> twenty-five years were but a couple of weeks, "an' I knows he's
> be'n lookin' fer me. For he sot a heap er sto' by me, Sam did, an' I
> know he's be'n huntin' fer me all dese years,—less'n he's be'n sick
> er sump'n, so he could n' work, er out'n his head, so he could n'
> 'member his promise." (108)

Ryder's response to this story has the rhetorical effect of distancing him from her and the events, but at the same time signifies to Chesnutt's black readers a history with which they were all too familiar:

> "There used to be many such cases right after the war," he said, "but it has been so long now that I have forgotten them. . . . He may have married another woman. Your slave marriage would not have prevented him, for you never lived with him after the war, and without that your marriage doesn't count." (107, 109)

Chesnutt has Ryder repeat this latter legal opinion when he addresses the guests gathered for the ball. Instead of announcing his engagement, Ryder tells the assembly a version of 'Liza Jane's story and comments that the missing husband was in no way responsible, "that their marriage was a slave marriage, and legally binding only if they chose to make it so after the war" (112). He then asks his guests what they supposed a man in such a situation would do if he were a man who loved honor but had set his heart on another in the intervening years. The entire body, including Mrs. Dixon, agreed such a man must acknowledge the first marriage and the wife. Ryder then introduces 'Liza Jane, "the wife of my youth" (113).

It is clear from the Freedmen's Bureau document that Chesnutt has, while embedding a portion of the hidden history of black life in the story, given a picture of the legal moment but has misdrawn it for literary effect. The document indicates that a man to whom a wife is restored must accept her if he is "living alone." Both conditions describe Ryder's situation. There is no requirement that *both* must *agree* to live as wife and husband after the war. That proviso was written as binding on intact couples who sought to reinscribe a shakily documented marriage. By conflating two sections of the document, Chesnutt makes it appear as though this were not a matter of law. The rules do require some proof of a marriage and in the absence of such require a remarriage, which is not likely to happen if one party disagrees and there are no children, as is the case here.

So Chesnutt has some textual support if we assume that 'Liza Jane has no documentary evidence. But let's see what he writes about the marriage:

> W'en I wuz a gal I wuz married ter a man named Jim. But Jim died, an' after that I married a merlatter man named Sam Taylor. Sam

wuz free-bawn but his mammy and daddy died, an' de w'ite folks 'prenticed him ter my master fer ter work fer 'im 'tel he wuz growed up. (107)

A close reading of this passage suggests that 'Liza Jane's marriage to Sam was supposed to be understood as a legal, binding one. In the first instance, 'Liza Jane reports that as a "gal," implying youth and lack of agency, she "wuz married" to a man, ostensibly an older man, not a boy. This transaction is reported in the passive voice, as an event that happened to her, as if perhaps assigned to him by Marse Bob Smif. But sometime after her first husband died, she "married a merlatter man, Sam Taylor," an event reported in the active voice, as though this were an act of choice and so might have been accompanied by some record of her choice, especially since, as we learn later, she was older than he. Perhaps more suggestive, in the second instance, is the status of Sam Taylor. He is a free person, born free and so not prohibited from marrying formally, not restricted to the noncontractual covenant of the slave marriage. There is a good chance that theirs was recorded.

It is clear that Chesnutt wants to draw on his legal knowledge and satisfy his own deterministic sense of history, but at the same time he seems to want to allow Ryder the moral range of action that makes his choice significant. If, once found by the wife of his youth, Ryder is bound by law, then the only moral choice open to him is a negative one, that is to deny his historic identity and refuse his wife, break the law. But give the problem a framework of legal implication without legal imperative, designed to heighten the redemptive moral power of the right choice by showing the reader that the protagonist chooses that which the law might well have forced him to do (and in fact did require), and you can reunite the past with the imputed future of the race on the bases of mutuality of heritage and moral strength. Such a choice is an authentic act of self-realization.

Denial of the Ironic Romantic Self

As important as the denial of authenticity as a marker of romantic identity, perhaps more so because it has gone unremarked, was the denial to blacks of an ironic stance in the world. Just as whites trivialized black spontaneity in their ascription to them wholesale a "childlike" quality, so too the white insistence in the nineteenth century of black "innocence," as in "the absence of knowledge," denied black Americans the essential quality of irony. Blacks could not be admitted to be noninnocent, to be said to know themselves, to have a reflective capacity, because in the romantic paradigm that capacity is a capacity of the self—a human self. Only humans—real beings, not chattel property—can be reflective, know self, understand the world's limitations, experience irony. Property cannot know its own properties. Dr. Samuel Cartwright observed in 1858, "Africans are endowed with a will so weak, passions so easily subdued, and dispositions so gentle and affectionate that they have an instinctive feeling of obedience to the stronger will of the white man" (W. W. Fisher 1058). The Louisiana Civil Code of 1820 went as far as to proclaim that slaves lacked any will at all. In *Livandac's Heirs v. Fon & al.* (1820), the state supreme court found that a slave can contract no agreement nor bind herself in any respect "because she [is] without will."[27]

But this metaphysical ascription of will-lessness had its basis in the very real effects of slavery, as the slaveholders well knew. The law was designed to protect the slaveholder's right to break the will of any slave, hence Stowe's Simon Legree and Frederick Douglass's encounter with Edward Covey. It was not, however, the specific act of beating that took the greatest toll among most slaves, perhaps, but the simple weight of slavery itself, its omnipresence and the certainty of its consequences. Even if one owned a slave and consented to allow her to do no work, someone else could force her to work because she was a slave:

> The owner of a slave cannot be compelled, even by his consent, to refrain from making him labor, when he is able to do so; there is hardly any difference between an emancipated slave, and a slave which [note this pronoun] cannot be compelled to labor; the obligation to work for a master is the essence of slavery.[28]

Martin Delany observes, through his eponymous hero, Henry Blake,

> The mere slave, as such, was deficient in discipline, except that which unfitted him for self-reliance. That was the curse which blighted his moral prospects, the blow which riveted upon him the links of an unyielding chain; the burden which, with mountain weight, pressed his mind to the earth, only to be thrown off by the force of an extra-

ordinary self-exertion, verified the sentiment that—"the day that makes a man a slave / Takes half his worth away." (239)

Blake was occasionally troubled in recruiting for his rebellion by the lack of "self-reliance" among his brothers and sisters, and he located the source of that weakness in the overwhelming presence of the external authority of slavery. The difference between a slave and a free man lay exactly in the relation of that authority to action. "As the former, you were irresponsible, the latter responsible; that was a life of trouble and sorrow, this of care and pleasure. One shuns adventure, the other seeks it; the slave feels an issue, and the freeman makes it. A slave must have somebody to care for him; a freeman must care for himself and others" (242). What Delany is describing in each case is what Patricia J. Williams calls "being in the subject position" in the law (*Alchemy* 3).

Chesnutt captures the sources of this conditioned failure to occupy the subject position in the reflections of Josh Green, a character in *The Marrow of Tradition*. Advised by the mulatto doctor treating him for injuries that he ought to give up his desire to get revenge on his white enemies, Green responds:

> Yas, suh, I've larn't all dat in Sunday-school, an' I've heared de preachers say it time an' time ag'in. But it 'pears ter me dat dis fergitfulniss and fergivniss is mighty one-sided. De w'ite folks don' fergive nothin de niggers does. Dey got up de Ku-Klux, dey said, on 'count er de kyarpit-baggers. Dey be'n talkin' 'bout de kyarpit-baggers ever sence, an dey 'pears ter fergot all 'bout de Ku-Klux. But I ain' fergot. De niggers is be'n train' ter fergiveniss; an' fer fear dey might fergit how ter fergive, de w'ite folks gives 'em somethin' new ev'y now an' den, ter practice on. A w'ite man kin do w'at he wants ter a nigger, but de minute de nigger gits back at 'im, up goes de nigger, an' don' come down tell somebody cuts 'im down. If a nigger gets a' office, er de race 'pears ter be prosperin' too much, de w'ite folks up an' kills a few, so dat de res' kin keep on fergivin' an' bein' thankful dat dey're lef' alive. (113)

Absence of self-knowledge also implies absence of self-regard and allowed whites to assume that the cost to blacks of the daily indignities of slavery, and later of Jim Crow law, was somehow less than that which would be levied on whites were they to find themselves in similar situations. In a 1849 North Carolina case, for example, the court observed that

> accustomed as [the slave] is to constant humiliation, [a slight blow] would not be calculated to excite such a degree as to "dethrone reason," and [deadly retaliation] must be ascribed to a "wicked heart, regardless of social duty." A blow inflicted upon a white man carries with it a feeling of degradation, as well as bodily pain, and a sense of injustice; all, or either of which, are calculated to excite passion, whereas a blow inflicted upon a slave is not attended with any feeling of degradation, by reason of his lowly condition, and is only calculated to excite passion from bodily pain and a sense of wrong.[29]

In essence, the argument held that because slaves had no honor to uphold, they could not be insulted or demeaned and so had no reason to seek recourse. That such an argument could and would remain dear to the sensibilities of whites, and especially to those of white jurists, is revealed in Gilbert T. Stephenson's 1910 report of a similar argument from a New York state court as it applied to African Americans, some forty-five years after the abolition of slavery:

> A Pullman porter, named Griffin, was arrested in Montreal, charged with stealing a pocket-book, but the charge was not substantiated and he was released. He thereupon brought suit against Daniel F. Brady, who caused his arrest, and obtained a verdict for two thousand five hundred dollars in damages. The Supreme Court of New York reduced the damages from two thousand five hundred dollars to three hundred dollars. Upon an appeal by Griffin, the appellate division of the Supreme Court sustained the order reducing the damages. [Judge Drugo wrote]: "You cannot say the he [Griffin] is just the same as a white man, when you come to say how much his name will suffer. He might suffer more. But after all, what are the probabilities about it? Is it likely that when a colored man is arrested and imprisoned he feels just as much shame as a white man of any circumstance might?
>
> "I think if you were to take the Mayor of the city and arrest him he might feel very much more humiliated than this porter, from the fact that he was the Mayor and not a colored man, for if a colored man he might not feel quite as much humiliation and shame.

"In one sense a colored man is just as good as a white man, for the law says he is, but he has not the same amount of injury under all circumstances that a white man would have. Maybe in a colored community down South, where white men were held in great disfavor, he might be more injured, but after all that is not this sort of community. In this sort of community, I dare say the amount of evil that would flow to the colored man would not be as great as it probably would be to a white man." (276–77)[30]

These white attitudes toward characteristics belonging to the realization of personal identity help us understand why nineteenth-century depictions of blacks, whether in laws or in literature written by whites, are of happy darky children or demonic rapists or kindly uncles or smiling mammies (W. W. Fisher; Andrews, *Literary*; Morrison, *Playing*). African American fiction of the same period, however, presents the reader with black characters of fully developed ironic sensibilities, able to stand back from the world and to see it as it is, and to see their own ironic positions in it. Chesnutt's "The Wife of His Youth," already discussed for its legal implications, contains as well a superb example of his ironic interrogation of the romanticization of color. When Mr. Ryder is visited by 'Liza Jane, he is reading Tennyson, looking for passages to use for a toast to "The Ladies" at his ball. Specifically, he is reading the poem, "A Dream of Fair Women," which Chesnutt takes care to quote selectively:

"At length I saw a lady within call,
Stiller than chisell'd marble, standing there;
A daughter of the gods, divinely tall,
And most divinely fair."

He marked the verse, and turning the page read the stanza beginning,—

"O sweet pale Margaret,
O rare pale Margaret."

He weighed the passage a moment, and decided that it would not do. Mrs. Dixon was the palest lady he expected at the ball, and she was of a rather ruddy complexion, and of lively disposition and buxom build. So he ran over the leaves until his eyes rested on the description of Queen Guinevere. (105–6).

Chesnutt gives us a few more lines of Tennyson and then abruptly introduces 'Liza Jane, the antithesis of the Tennysonian "Fair Woman." Such counterpositioning would be clever enough in a short story of the period, but Chesnutt goes further, further in a way that has implications for the discussion of law and literature in general and African American experience and the law in particular. When Ryder's interview with his lost wife is over, she gives him an address where he can reach her if he ever comes across her missing "Sam Taylor." Chesnutt has not yet revealed to his readers the extent of Ryder's recognition of 'Liza Jane. We do not know how much he understands (although we understand everything by this point), nor can we anticipate his reaction once he does understand fully. What will Ryder do with the address? Crumple and discard it as he had sought to do with his past heretofore? Leave it untouched on his desk? Fold it and place it next to his heart in a vest pocket?

Chesnutt's choice is none of these. He gives Ryder a gesture that sustains our interest and comments ironically on Ryder's life and the times in which he lives: "He wrote the address on the flyleaf of the volume of Tennyson, and, when she had gone, rose to his feet and stood looking after her curiously" (110). This is "signifyin'" as irony or irony as "signifyin'," as you would have it. More specifically, Ryder has created an ironic palimpsest, a directed overwriting of one version of experience by another that comments on it. 'Liza Jane's address, a text of numbers and a name yet the sign for his former life and his former/current wife, is superinscribed on the imagined, poetic perfection of a life yet to be lived. Tennyson's evocations of the great white beauties of myth and history are overlaid with the reality of the history of black men and women under slavery. The palimpsestic text instructs Ryder, and the reader, that one must live the history one is dealt, not that of an already imaginary community, his/your membership in which will be even more fictional than its fair exemplars in Tennyson's poetry.

In effect, law and literature generally overwrite each other as competing yet complementary texts of the same order of existence. And specifically, African American literature and American law overwrite ironically the stories each seeks to tell. The history of the division of the races in this country makes such irony inevitable and irreducible. The law writes manacles around every free hand raised in African American narrative, no matter how utopian; African American narrative writes betrayal and oppression across every statute, every case in the canon.

Consider how Paul Lawrence Dunbar's 1902 novel, *The Sport of the Gods*, replicates white attitudes and black irony in the context of African American "crime." Berry Hamilton, a black man, is unjustly accused of stealing from the brother of his white employer, Maurice Oakley, and convicted and sentenced to ten years at hard labor. Oakley forces Berry's wife, Fannie, and their two adult children off the property. They cannot find work in the town and move to New York, where Berry's son, Joe, finds work as a barber but falls in with a fast, indolent crowd and sinks into what Dunbar calls depravity. Young Kitty is her mother's only hope, but she is lured by fashion and beset by circumstance. With the help of Joe's "girl," she gets into the chorus of a "revue." Fannie and the children lose contact with Berry for over two years, and finally she "remarries," to a man who abuses her. Kitty becomes a star, but Joe becomes a drunken hanger-on to his sister's fame and his girlfriend's career. Joe kills Hattie, his girl, in a drunken rage and is sentenced to life in prison.

Skaggs, a white reporter in with the "fast" black crowd, hears the story of Berry and suspects Joe had told the truth when he earlier claimed his father was innocent. A cynical Skaggs gets his editor to let him go down south on a "fishing expedition," and there he uncovers the truth that Oakley's brother, Frank, had lost the money gambling and blamed the loss on a theft. Oakley had wrongly accused Berry, and the biased southern legal system had rolled over the obvious exonerating evidence, to reach a false conviction. Skaggs's scoop becomes a cause célèbre in the North, and the paper forces the governor of the unnamed southern state to pardon Berry.

Skaggs takes Berry to New York for a round of exploitation for the paper but never tells him about Joe or Kitty or Fannie. After a few days, he gives Berry Fannie's address and says goodbye. Berry soon discovers he has lost his family and returns to the newspaper to take a job as a subjanitor, vowing to kill the man who married and abused Fannie. One night he goes to the apartment and finds a wake in progress. The "husband" has died, and Fannie is free to rejoin Berry. Mrs. Oakley, to make amends for her husband's wrong, asks the pair to come back south and live in their old cottage, which they do. At night they can hear the insane ravings of Maurice Oakley, driven mad by the revelation of his and his brother's dishonesty.

Dunbar's usual reliance on sentiment and melodrama is mitigated in this novel by his ironic portrayal of southern whites and their attitude toward blacks.[31] When Oakley discovers the "theft" from his brother, he immediately suspects his servants:

> The negroes are becoming less faithful and less contented, and more's the pity, and a deal more ambitious.... [A]s soon as a negro like Hamilton learns the value of money and begins to earn it, at the same time he begins to covet some easy and rapid way of securing it. The old negro knew nothing of the value of money. When he stole, he stole hams and bacon and chickens. These were his immediate necessities and the things he valued. The present [age] laughs at this tendency without knowing the cause. The present negro resents the laugh, and he has learned to value other things than those which satisfy his belly. (25–26)

Among Oakley's friends, old Horace Talbot thought that blacks were unsuited for freedom and were not so much criminals as innocent primitives with little appreciation of private property:

> But I maintain that they [the North] were all wrong, now, in turning these people loose upon the country the way they did, without knowing what the first principle of liberty was.... Why, gentlemen, I maintain that that man took that money with the same innocence of purpose with which one of our servants a few years ago would have appropriated a stray ham. (53–54)

For Talbot, of course, the first principle of liberty is property, as he exhibits by his nostalgia for slavery, a nostalgia he is certain is shared by emancipated blacks: "'Why, gentleman, I foresee the day when these people themselves shall come to us Southerners of their own accord and ask to be re-enslaved until such time as they shall be fit for freedom.' Old Horace was nothing if not logical" (56).[32]

Beachfield Davis—Dunbar's hilarious parody of a white southern sportsman, a "mighty hunter"—claims the problem is depravity—and the proof is that one of his servants has abused one of Davis's finest hunting dogs:

> When a nigger and a dog go out together at night, one draws certain conclusions.... In about an hour here came Dodson with a

possum hung over his shoulder and my dog trottin' at his heels. He'd been possum huntin' with my hound—with the finest hound in the State, sir. Now, I appeal to you all, gentlemen, if that ain't total depravity, what is total depravity? (55)

Near the end of the novel, when Berry's innocence has been established but the state is resisting his release, Horace Talbot argues it is wrong to

give a nigger a few more years of freedom [at Oakley's expense] when, likely as not, he don't want it; and Berry Hamilton's life in prison has proved nearer the ideal reached by slavery than anything he has found since emancipation. Why, suhs, I fancy I see him leaving his prison with tears of regret in his eyes. (240)

The hidden import of this novel is the incomplete judgment at the end, when Berry can hear Oakley's mad ravings in the night: "[T]hey took the cottage, and many a night they sat together with clasped hands listening to the shrieks of the madman across the yard and thinking of what he had brought to them and to himself" (255). What is unsaid here is how he had brought on their agonies—first theirs, then his own—through the twin agencies of property (whiteness/wealth) and the law. It was whiteness as property that gave Oakley the status to destroy a black man, and it was the law as the extension of his propertiedness that did it. The total inability of any of the white characters to understand black "agency" is based on their assumptions of the law's ability to suppress it. That is, both slavery and the tradition of Black Codes and Jim Crow encapsulated a definition of black life that denied all will, agency, and desire and sought to incarcerate it where it dared emerge. Through Dunbar's controlled irony, this slight, sentimental tale becomes a transparent indictment of both property and law.

All of the African American narratives discussed to this point assume a perspective on the law that may obscure a part of the historical position of black Americans under the law. Whatever the specific issues represented in the text, the narratives represent an African American quest for an idealized "justice" and therefore neglect a central problematic in African American legal status. If we consider for a moment that the "American" system of adjudication based on common law is predicated on the pursuit of dispute resolution rather than on the pursuit of justice, the condition of blacks in the antebellum period takes on another dimension—that is, the laws that reinforced local practices of slavery denied persons of African descent access to and status under the laws that resolved disputes among parties. A full analysis of this problematic is beyond the scope of this book, but we ought to consider that both the criminal and civil laws of the antebellum South, and the post-Reconstruction laws that circumvented the postwar amendments, basically excluded blacks from the status necessary to any resolution in their favor by denying them access to a nonviolent resolution process.

Consider this construction of the situation: laws exist to resolve disputes without violence, violence being too costly a solution in an increasingly complex society because it often removes one of the disputants from the field permanently, perhaps to the detriment of a society that might have need for his services at some later date. As costly would be the permanent alienation of groups of disputants from each other because of the violence of the resolution; such alienation would prove too costly to capitalist cultures, whose economic well-being depend on commercial intercourse if not on amity. Whether the resolutions provided by the processes of law were just would not be the issue when evaluating their function in the society, since the costs of an "unjust" decision would be amortized throughout the society over an indeterminate period and would be far outweighed by the benefits of a resolution that cost nothing to repair since nothing had been ripped asunder.

Enter now the enslaved body, the "person who is not a person" under these laws. He is denied access to the "legal" mechanisms of dispute resolution and so, if he is to resolve any dispute, with state or private citizen, he has only violence at his disposal. Unfortunately for him, he is outgunned from the start; his capacity to inflict violence is always less than that of his opponent, his master.[33] And so he loses most "disputes." While this is undoubtedly "unjust" in most cases in that the merits of his "cause" might have prevailed for him in court, the functional problem defines the injustice differently: he is denied justice because he is denied access to the machinery for dispute resolution available to white disputants and so must operate only in a field in which he is overmatched by virtue of other constraints settled on him by other sections of the law, such as the prohibition against owning property, having control over his own children, owning weapons.

Consequently, acts of violence by whites against enslaved persons are not punished as similar acts by whites against other whites would be since the violent acts in the first instance are recognized as elements of a kind of dispute resolution set aside for the legal relationship between master and slave. But since the prohibition against attacks on whites by blacks is part of the disabling mechanism operating against blacks even in the field of violence-as-dispute-resolution, such attacks fall under an extralegal local scrutiny of workplace-centered judgment in which the master is himself often victim, judge, and agent of punishment. A final irony emerges when we realize that enslaved blacks have status as property in nonviolent dispute resolution. That is, they can be the objects of the lawsuit but not its subject; their bodies can be evidence of the crime, but, in most instances, they cannot be the victims of the crime. I do not need to extrapolate these conditions to the post-Reconstruction period for the attentive reader.

This is why the idealization of "justice" in African American narrative addresses only a part of the problem of life under law. Within the discourse about law just posited, justice is not denied; while the rhetorical goal of the system might be some such abstraction, the operational goal is not justice but efficacy. We see attention to the kind of detail required to explicate the differentiated problem of justice versus efficacy in only a few narratives, such as *The Garies and Their Friends* and *Blake.* The reason for this, I think, is that while the attention of black commentators on legal status shifts from the Declaration of Independence to the Constitution after the Civil War, black Americans never give up their devotion to the *natural law* principles of the Declaration. Even *Justice and Jurisprudence,* for all its devotion to the postwar amendments, cannot abandon the rhetorical allegiance to the grand principles of equality and autonomy under God promised by the Declaration. It is as if African Americans were saying, to the nation but certainly to themselves, that if white folks would just embrace the principles of the Founders wholeheartedly, with black folks as part of the definitions that framed the Constitution, all would be well. They were forgetting that God is in the details, not in the statement of purpose.

CHAPTER 4

Privacy, Property, and Self

> Thus again a patriot was mistaken for a chicken thief; and in the
> South to-day a race that dreams of freedom, equality, and empire,
> far more than is imagined, is put down as a race of chicken
> thieves.
>
> Sutton Griggs, *Imperium in Imperio*

It seems clear now that any African American critique of the law in the
nineteenth century would have to be cognizant of the fact that most
whites, perhaps even those most inclined to sympathize with the historic oppression of Negro opportunity, could scarcely overcome the
equally historic romantic paradigms of identity and authenticity that
had privileged their own positions and limited those of African Americans. While the limitations of *contractual* capacity assumed to be inherent in enslaved persons, for example, were clearly codified in the slaveholding South (i.e., not "legal" persons but with some "moral"
position), whether or not "moral" allowed the enslaved or free-black
identity a capacity for authenticity and irony is a difficult question to
resolve. The evidence of the law seems inconclusive.

On the one hand, laws governing the conduct of free people of
color in the antebellum period generally restricted their rights to
engage in certain activities or to own certain kinds of properties, while
most contractual, and many civil, rights other than citizenship were
recognized. Most tellingly, anti-miscegenation/cohabitation/amalga-
mation laws abounded. These laws suggest that the old patterns of
demonization, trivialization, and deformation of the sense of self were
imposed on free blacks as well as on slaves, denying them access to the
public parameters of self-realization.

On the other hand, there were, late in the period in most jurisdictions, laws that required manumitted slaves to leave the jurisdiction
and other laws that prevented free people of color from entering it. The
laws were passed for fear of the impact of a population of free blacks on
the enslaved population, a fear that could emerge, perhaps, only if one
assumed both that free blacks would suddenly exhibit all the characteristics of selfhood that slavery sought to deny and that slaves had the

imagination to see themselves as free and self-constructed. It seems likely that prohibitions on literacy and the expulsion of free blacks from the community served the same purpose, to control the exercise of imagination among slaves, and were based on the assumption, unspoken but feared, that Africans in America could and would possess an authentic sense of self and would experience that self in an ironically imagined society.

A brief look at how the romantic self was imagined in nineteenth-century African American novels is informative because it shows how little, in some ways, the imagined self differed from the conventional romantic personality in white fiction. That this would be so can be understood if we consider a different perspective for a moment. What if not just white imaginative literature but also the texts of American law and of African American fiction reflected a response to romanticism? On the most superficial level, despite the less technical language of early American law, its texts, like all texts, are shaped by conventions of grammar and syntax as well as of vocabulary, conventions that are reinforced by tradition and imitation. But beyond those visible conventions of linguistic construction, we might not at first see direct evidence of the impact of romanticism on the text of the law, even though, as Robert Ferguson has pointed out, "manuals" of legal education of the early nineteenth century encouraged law students to seek "that comprehension of expression peculiar to the poet" (29). The "poet" so invoked was more likely to be an Enlightenment figure than a romantic one, but Ferguson argues that training for the law in the early years of the Republic was subject to the influences of a "jumble of neoclassical traditions and romantic impulses in eighteenth- and nineteenth-century Anglo-American literature" (9). What I have in earlier chapters described as romantic attitudes and premises common to American political and social philosophy, affecting American law in practice, may also have had some support and even origins in legal education of the day. Whatever the degree of that influence, it is reasonable to assume that the expression and the premises of American law in the nineteenth century were as likely to reflect the romantic impulses of the period as were poetry or the novel or the romance itself.

The influence of any "romanticism" in fiction is easier to observe because the principle of play with and within/against convention *is* the tradition of literature. For that reason, we can, in an investigation of African American literature in the nineteenth century, seek out both strategies of resistance to romantic marginalization in African American texts of the period and some sense of the extent to which those texts may replicate and adapt attitudes, imagery, and narrative practices of the dominant literature. William Andrews suggests, for example, that the representation of slavery in sixty-five published antebellum slave narratives seem to have been informed by romanticism, but after the war the portrayal of slavery in slave narratives (fifty over the next thirty-five years) was more realistic. By romantic, Andrews seems to mean an undocumentable level of idealization in the depiction of relationships and daily life ("Representation" 63).

Toni Morrison (*Playing*, preface) examines specifically the problem presented for African American writers by romanticism. Addressing the problem of "struggling with and through a language that can powerfully evoke and enforce hidden signs of racial superiority, cultural hegemony, and dismissive 'othering' of people and language" (x), Morrison worries, "My vulnerability would lie in romanticizing blackness rather than demonizing it" (xi). Although Morrison opposes romanticization to demonization, demonization is more properly understood as a form of romanticization, and it is necessary to untangle the implications of her fear in order to see its relevance to the overall problem of romanticization in nineteenth-century African American fiction.

Morrison seems to fear something like the idealization Andrews argues is observable in antebellum slave narratives. In those texts, the institution of slavery is presented absent its most salient material characteristics, presumably those of its specific physical, economic, and psychological relationships. In Morrison's case, the problem would be not the idealization of an institution like slavery, or even the idealization of the reaction to such an institution, but of the race itself in reaction to the history of its demonization in the "othering" texts of white culture. Setting aside the immediate political question of the desirability of such idealization, I would ask if African American fiction writers in the nineteenth century idealized the race as Andrews suggests the authors of antebellum slave narratives had done the institution of slavery and in the manner Morrison implies should be resisted. My assumption would be that if they did so, then the representation of matters with which we are engaged, resistance to law, privacy matters, and attitudes toward "liberty" as a condition of romantic identity, would be better read with that idealization in mind.

Three nineteenth-century African American novels I have already mentioned contain elements of both romanticism and resistance: Martin Delany's *Blake, or The Huts of America* (1859–61); F. E. W. Harper's *Iola Leroy* (1892); and Sutton Griggs's *Imperium in Imperio* (1899). Delany's novel, serialized in the *Anglo-African* and in the *Anglo-African Weekly*, is set prior to the Civil War and has to do with resistance to slavery. Harper's is set during the last moments of slavery, during the war itself, and during Reconstruction and is about the resistance of freed African Americans to conditions of life in postwar America. Griggs's book is set during Reconstruction and its aftermath, the counter-Reconstruction and creation of Jim Crow, and is about resistance to the emerging system of legal oppression in an increasingly segregated South. Such resistance called for heroic measures and perhaps for romantic gestures, if not always for romantic heroes.

To understand the role of romantic self-fashioning in these texts, it is useful to look at their depictions of character. Each author has at hand the conventions of Eurocentric romantic literature, the realities of African American life, and the political imperatives of her or his personal historical moment. How character is drawn, then, depends on the weight given each of these factors. Here are descriptions of the protagonists from each of the books:

> Henry was a black—a pure Negro—handsome, manly and intelligent, in size comparing well with his master, but neither so fleshy nor heavy built in person. A man of good literary attainments— unknown to Colonel Franks, though he was aware he could read and write—having been educated in the West Indies, and decoyed away when young. His affection for wife and child was not excelled by Colonel Frank's for his. He was bold, determined and courageous, but always mild gentle and courteous, though impulsive when an occasion demanded his opposition. (*Blake* 16–17)

Delany was a Black nationalist and had little use for whites, even less for mulattoes. His heroes were paragons of unmixed Negro identity.

> Iola, freed from her master's clutches, applied herself readily to her appointed tasks. The beautiful, girlish face was full of tender earnestness. The fresh, young voice was strangely sympathetic, as if some great sorrow had bound her heart in loving compassion to every sufferer who needed her gentle ministrations. (*Iola Leroy* 39–40)

Dr. Frank Latimer was the natural grandson of a Southern lady, in whose family his mother had been a slave. The blood of a proud aristocratic ancestry was flowing through his veins, and generations of blood admixture had effaced all trace of his negro lineage. His complexion was blonde; his eye bright and piercing; his lips firm and well moulded; his manner very affable; his intellect active and well stored with information. He was a man capable of winning in life through his rich gifts of inheritance and acquirements. (*Iola Leroy* 239)

Harper's color bias seems the opposite of Delany's (Iola was as fair as Dr. Latimer) though she did pay him homage by having *one* educated "dark" character in the book, a young woman activist she named "Miss Lucille Delany."

Bernard, handsome, brilliant, eloquent, the grandson of a governor, the son of a senator, a man of wealth, to whom defeat was a word unknown, steps out to battle for the freedom of his race; urged to put his whole soul into the fight because of his own burning desire for glory, and because out of the gloom of night he heard his grief stricken parents bidding him to climb where the cruel world would be compelled to give its sanction to the union that had produced such a man as he. (*Imperium in Imperio* 93–94)

"Cum er long hunny an' let yer mammy fix yer 'spectabul, so yer ken go ter skule. Yer mammy is 'tarmined ter gib yer all de book larning dar is ter be had eben ef she has ter lib on bred an' herrin's an' die en de a'ms house."

These words came from the lips of a poor, ignorant negro woman, and yet the determined course of action which they reveal vitally affected the destiny of a nation and saved the sun of the Nineteenth Century, proud and glorious, from passing through, near its setting, the blackest and thickest clouds of all its journey; saved it from ending the most brilliant of brilliant careers by setting, with a shudder, in a sea of human blood. (*Imperium in Imperio* 3)

These passages introduce us to Bernard Belgrave as he enters adulthood and to young Belton Piedmont on his first day of school. Belton Piedmont is a "pure" black whose mother hopes will be lifted to glory by Emancipation. He is matched in honor, intelligence, and courage only by his mulatto classmate and best friend, Bernard. Taken together they exhibit the best characteristics of innate romantic heroism, each nurtured by a different aspect of African American experience. Unlike Delany, Griggs is evenhanded in his portrayal of his African American characters, favoring neither "pure" blacks nor mulattoes and giving each hero a wife or lover of a different degree of darkness of skin, but of equally prepossessing personal qualities.

The characters in each of these books are exceptional people, fully endowed with humanity, sensitivity, intelligence, beauty, and high political purpose. Each lives a life of adventure and sacrifice in the pursuit of equality of treatment for his or her race under the law. Each finds his and her identity in that struggle, and each places the focus of that struggle squarely on the white man in his role as he who betrays or corrupts the promise of the law. In these books the white man is the "other" in no uncertain terms. In *Blake,* whites are unsalvageable as human beings for the most part, and their appetites for evil are almost incomprehensible. In *Iola Leroy,* some well-intentioned whites are given their due, but they are clearly a separate order of creation, so morally different that Iola twice refuses the honorable suit of a white doctor who has loved her for years. She does so on the grounds that she would have to pass for white (she could do so), and she could never live that life. There is never any suggestion that he live among blacks. In *Imperium,* the ultimate romantic rejection of whites occurs when Viola, beloved of Bernard, commits suicide rather than marry him (see chapter 3).

The romanticization of women's condition in these African American novels is worth a study of its own. In each of the novels, women's moral superiority is generally assumed, and an essentialized woman figure can put every issue in context for the heroic males struggling for solutions to the condition of the race. But there are limits to the evenhandedness of the male writers on this score. Delany, for example, creates in Blake's wife a woman the hero loves dearly but who seems incapable of understanding the moral imperative behind his revolutionary romanticism. Interestingly, and perhaps awkwardly for Delany the separatist, Delany the romantic does fall prey to the idealization of women in the creation of a white woman character whose moral strength and vision changes a vicious slaver into a docile abolitionist. In the main, though, his African American women characters are more richly drawn and less conventional than are the African American men he presents.

Blake is a hero in the mold of Frederick Douglass's Madison Washington, the paragon of unmixed racial virtue in "The Heroic Slave" (1853). Douglass gives full rein to his romantic tendencies in the following description of the almost preternatural emergence of his hero:

> Glimpses of this great character are all that can now be presented. He is brought to view only by a few transient incidents, and these afford but partial satisfaction. Like a guiding star on a stormy night, he is seen through the parted clouds and the howling tempests; or, like the gray peak of a menacing rock on a perilous coast, he is seen by the quivering flash of angry lightning, and he again disappears, covered with mystery. (38)

The figure, a slave contemplating liberty and manhood, is overheard by a white traveler as he yearns for freedom and yet refuses to neglect his responsibilities to his wife. The traveler is taken by the slave's appearance:

> Madison was of manly form. Tall symmetrical, round and strong. In his movements, he seemed to combine, with the strength of a lion, a lion's elasticity. His torn sleeves disclosed arms like polished iron. His face was "black, but comely." His eyes, lit with emotion, kept guard under a brow as dark and as glossy as a raven's wing. . . . He was just the man you would choose when hardships were to be endured, or danger to be encountered—intelligent and brave. He had the head to conceive, and the heart to execute. In a word, he was one to be sought as a friend and dreaded as an enemy. (40)[1]

Douglass's story is too slight to reward too much scrutiny here, but I want to point out that for the purposes of the story, the romantic characteristics of Madison Washington as we see them here are all the character development needed to drive the meager plot, and they are given entirely to a male character; there are virtually no female characters whose actions are consequential to the story, either in plot or ethos. Washington's courage, intelligence, and bravery stem from natural resources that he, as a man, possesses in greater abundance than any other man he encounters. The story itself, lacking any dramatic tension, exposes the dominance, in Douglass's configuration of a just world, of some form of "natural" law based on essential qualities over any positivist legal system based on stipulation and legislation.

It is this point, developed much more concretely and with greater sophistication, that lies at the center of Delany's novel. Just as his plot and his analysis of American law are far more complex than Douglass's, so his character has levels of complexity not available to Madison Washington. Nevertheless, both Henry Blake and Madison Washington are romantic brothers under the skin.

In *Imperium*, no matter how refined the moral sensibility of women and despite their intelligence, attested to in the novel itself, women are excluded from every moment of counsel, every plan to action. When Belton goes off to college, only men act, while women, though present in the student body in greater numbers than men and clearly able and determined to uplift the race, seem only to attend. Later, both Belton and Bernard fall in love with exceptional women who are excluded from any significant action in the plot. One kills herself after reading a book, and the other is simply relegated to the sidelines for the duration of the climax of the book by a rather mechanical plot device having to do with motherhood. Although Griggs grants women a nominal status "higher" than does Delany, it is not clear that the realities of African American life at the time, that is, women attending college, reading, getting involved in the affairs of the world, superseded his romantic ambivalence about their place in the scheme of things.

Only in *Iola Leroy*, written by a woman, are conventions of representation combined with appropriation such that Iola is recognizable as both a conventional woman character and a romantic hero. Iola's willingness to sacrifice herself for the well-being of others never obscures her even greater willingness and ability to do something with her life for her race. In Harper's novel men are romanticized through convention as well as are women, but she clearly has her text focused on the questions of nineteenth-century life as they speak to talented black women. That focus leads Harper to a greater range of representation and a greater depth of care in presentation with Iola Leroy than she employs with any other character.

Playing across these stratagems of idealization and realism in all three novels are some recurring concerns. Not surprisingly, one of these is a concern for family. In each novel men and women seek their families, seek to create new families, fight to free their families, resist falling into, identifying with, or entering into the wrong families. All are faced with the task of constantly redefining and reinventing the family in the face of the heritage of two hundred and more years of having been property first and beloved human beings second. As a romantic problem, the issue of love and community is unavoidable in the sentimental romances and comedies written by whites in the nineteenth century. But it is as a problem of law that the issue of love and community is raised almost universally in narratives written by African Americans both before and after Emancipation.

Another problem in each of the three novels might best be called that of "confederation." Each novel presents a superstructural problem to the protagonists and, by extrapolation, to the race. The superstructural problem is stated most simply as "How are we to come together as a people to survive the presence of white people in the world and the laws they have written to sustain themselves?" In each case, quite specifically in *Blake* and *Imperium* and more generally but no less effectively in *Iola Leroy*, the protagonists devise complex social organizations to support activity that will free them from slavery or Jim Crow. The creation of these organizations constitutes the first resistance to white authority, which action defines the characters in a paradigmatic romantic dialectic. The organizations themselves, an international syndication of slave "cells" dedicated to a general strike throughout the South and in Cuba, a revolutionary cadre planning to seize Texas and proclaim a black nation, and an extended family of African American intellectuals committed to slow but steady betterment of the race, frame the subsequent resistance that will liberate the oppressed. These confederations can be seen as forms of the communities of action to which black Americans have historically turned, from churches to state congresses to "brotherhoods" to national federations to clubs for men and women to national associations to leagues and to coalitions.

Both of these concerns, for family and for organized resistance to the innate inhumanity of the "white" view of African Americans, have at their base complex legal antecedents and, as we have seen historically, were destined to be played out in courts, legislatures, and polling places as well as in fiction over the 150 years after Emancipation. Those relationships are the stuff of further study. But the bulk of the talk and the action in these books is directed at the legal structure that surrounds the characters and of which they are so aware. In *Blake*, not only is the entire legal structure of slavery the villain, but the relationships among law, the institution of slavery in its various local manifestations, and the allure of property are shown to be symbiotic, so that even for a man in a position of trust, the inevitability of profit overrides integrity. Here for example, Judge Ballard, the northern judge who keeps slaves at his "winter" home in Cuba, explains how it is that he has come to invest in the illegal slave trade proposed by Colonel Franks:

> "It is true that I have not been before engaged in the slave trade, because until recently I had conscientious scruples about the thing—and I suppose I'm allowed the right of conscience as well as other folks," smilingly said the Judge, "never having purchased but for peopling my own plantation. But a little sober reflection set me right on that point. It is plain that the right to buy implies the right to hold, also to sell; and if there be right in the one, there is in the other; the premise being right, the conclusion follows as a matter of course. I have therefore determined, not only to buy and hold, but buy and sell also. As I have heretofore been interested for the trade I will become interested in it." (60)

Ballard eventually buys Henry's wife, takes her to Cuba, and resells her to a brutal mistress. Henry himself is a free Negro put at risk by Ballard's reasoning. He plans a massive, international slave rebellion to overturn the law and free his people. Every step of the way Delany has his character circumvent a specific law or ordinance. Henry is as much a picaro as a Byron, and his travels expose the levels of legal force applied to slave and "free negro" alike, north and south.

If Iola Leroy's friends are not revolutionaries, neither are they accommodationists. Throughout the novel, Harper's version of the "Talented Tenth" struggles with its own desire to find a way to be in the world with whites and white self-revelation of racism and greed. The white southerner, Dr. Latrobe, points out to the friends as he argues for the total disenfranchisement of black Americans,

> I think that we are right in suppressing the negro's vote. This is a white man's government, and a white man's country. We own nineteen-twentieths of the land, and have about the same ratio of intelligence. I am a white man, and, right or wrong, I go with my race. (223)

The group's response to Latrobe is to denounce his insistence on the centrality of property and intelligence and to turn once again to the natural-law guarantees of the Declaration of Independence. No matter what you own or the degree of your talents, if you are a citizen you are entitled to the rights of life and liberty. Iola's comrades place a great deal of store in the ineffable sense of being American, in its intangible pleasures beyond the practical and material. Miss Delany, the idealistic young teacher, would have her people remember when they had longed for a common past:

> Hitherto we have never had a country with tender, precious memories to fill our eyes with tears, or glad reminiscences to thrill our hearts with pride and joy. We have been aliens and outcasts in the land of our birth. But I want my pupils to do all in their power to make this country worthy of their deepest devotion and loftiest patriotism. I want them to feel that its glory is their glory, its dishonor their shame. (251)

In *Imperium in Imperio,* Bernard and Belton, too, give us a picaresque view of life in America, this time over a period of thirty years, through Reconstruction and well into Jim Crow. Bernard becomes famous and wealthy in Reconstruction Virginia and defends the more ill-starred Belton in a case that seems to bypass every local and state jurisdiction and arrives directly at the Supreme Court. Taken together, the men represent two kinds of heroes, the man who suffers great loss and the man who seeks to perform great service. They merge in the Imperium, a secret council of black Americans dedicated to the true emancipation of their race, but they differ on means. Bernard plots armed rebellion and secession, while Belton argues for reasoned separation under the law. Here Bernard gives his critique of the law:

> Colored men are excluded from the jury box; colored lawyers are discriminated against at the bar; and negroes with the highest legal attainments are not allowed to even dream of mounting the seat of a judge.
>
> Before a court that has been lifted into power by the very hands of prejudice, justice need not be expected. The creature will, presumably, serve its creator; this much the creator demands. . . .
>
> If a negro murders an Anglo-Saxon, however justifiably, let him tremble for his life if he is to be tried in our courts. On the other hand, if an Anglo-Saxon murders a negro in cold blood, without the slightest provocation, he will, if left to the pleasure of

our courts, die of old age and go down to his grave in perfect peace. . . .

The courts of the land are the facile instruments of the Anglo-Saxon race. They register its will as faithfully as the thermometer does the slightest caprice of the weather. (215)

When Belton rises to address the Imperium with hopes of swaying them from revolution, even he cannot bring himself to defend the legal system:

As for the courts of justice, I have not one word to say in palliation of the way in which they pander to the prejudices of the people. If the courts be corrupt; if the arbitrator between man and man be unjust; if the wretched victim of persecution is to be stabbed to death in the house of refuge; then indeed, has moral man sunk to the lowest level. . . .

. . . The Supreme Court of the United States, it seems, may be relied upon to sustain any law born of prejudice against the negro, and to demolish any law constructed in his interest. Witness the Dred Scott decision, and, in keeping with this, the decision on the Civil Rights Bill and Separate Coach Law.

If this court, commonly accepted as being constituted with our friends, sets such a terrible example of injustice, it is not surprising that its filthy waters corrupt the various streams of justice in all their ramifications. (236–37)[2]

Although he carries that day, Belton's oratory fails in the long run to convince the Imperium, and a plan for treasonous rebellion is laid. The book ends with a premature revelation of the plan by one of the members as an attempt to forestall it. We do not know what happens then. Similarly, we have no idea what happens to Henry Blake's massive slave revolt because the last six chapters of *Blake* are presumed missing. Both Delany's and Griggs's novels end much like the anticipatory fiction of white American proletarian novelists of the 1930s. Having lined out their grievances and proposed a militant solution that calls for a radical revisioning of the legal, social, and economic orders, the texts stop short, unable or unwilling to create a utopian aftermath to the revolutionary moment.[3] Only *Iola Leroy* has some real teleology; it drives toward closure, a domestic comedy in the most social sense of that genre, with all the signs of a legally reconstituted American identity: weddings and reunions and the hope for a better future.

These novels are congruent in their bewildered despair over the ways of white people. Each novel expresses clearly that somehow the great promise of America has been aborted by these evil whites who have corrupted the law, that great civilizing force, into a tool of oppression. What that law actually holds for African Americans in these nineteenth-century novels is determined only by the efficacy of black resistance to its impact on their everyday lives.

Much that passes for common knowledge among the characters in these novels is actually rooted in complex legal genealogies or in brutal state and local ordinances whose purposes were quite clear to all concerned. Black readers of the novels would recognize the daily imperatives enforced by such laws. Evidence of the law as a *romantic* as well as "local" text may be found in assumptions that parallel romantic assumptions about privacy, community, individuality, and freedom, all terms fundamental to the concerns of these novels. In the works of Douglass, Delany, Harper, and Griggs, the problematics of rights, needs, and romantic imperatives can be at least partially appropriated in African American texts to idealize black desires for freedom, privacy, family, community, individuality, and justice and to demonize white hegemony.

African American fictional narratives of idealized desire notwithstanding, however, the pursuit of "rights" by African Americans throughout the nineteenth century and much of the twentieth emerges as a hopeless enterprise. This is so, it appears, because the legal status of whites was based entirely on the original genius of writing their own pretextual needs into the law such that they become the "rights" every other claimant must argue for. No black person's right, observed by law, could ever be as powerful as the white person's need of which that law itself is the reification. Whether the history of the last half of the twentieth century will record the redistribution of the power of legalized desire is an open question.

In antebellum America, the laws and institutions of slavery had rendered the human life of Africans textually irrelevant. As we have seen, Mary Shelley's romantic paradigm in *Frankenstein* was both realized in the personification of corporate identity[4] and demonically inverted, as the necessity for slavery increasingly after 1830 was argued on the basis that what appeared human, the black body in America, was actually less than human.[5] But after the Civil War, the Fourteenth Amendment was added to the Constitution to affirm African American humanity legally by drawing that population into the community of citizenship. In point of historical fact, however, African Americans have had to argue the applicability of that amendment time and again as citizenship slips in and out of their grasp. If Mary Shelley's gothic dream had been inverted by slavery, the Fourteenth Amendment had failed to right it.

Why that was the case is a question with its own shelf of books, but one contributing factor was the influence of romanticism over questions of authenticity in postwar American life. As before the Civil War, romantic paradigms influenced the texts of civic and economic life. The relationships among questions of privacy, property, individuality, and community were sketched in the national consciousness through what Kenneth Burke has called "terministic screens," of which romanticism is only one. In postwar America the hidden ground of struggle for status and substance by African Americans was the refusal of white America to allow them to participate in the most romantic, and the most realized, dream in white American life: the desire of the individual for property and privacy, whether corporate or personal.

The struggle to liberate desire was complicated for black Americans by the assumption by most whites that color was the key to proof of personhood and to the security of any rights, especially those of privacy and property, accruing to the citizen. And the problem of color was complicated by the effects of racial mixing. In an early Louisiana case, for example, the court, while requiring that Beauregard, as defendant, must present his proof that he owned Adelle, a woman of color, added:

> We do not say that it would be so if the plaintiff were a Negro, who perhaps would be required to establish his right by such evidence, as would destroy the force of the presumption arising from color; Negroes brought to this country being generally slaves, their descendants may perhaps fairly be presumed to have continued so, till they show the contrary.[6]

The presumption based on color in *Adelle v. Beauregard* led a later Louisiana court to posit that the condition of slavery was not imposed but was somehow inherent in the condition of being a Negro, such that Forsyth, wishing to claim Nash as his slave, was required to show that slavery "resided in" Nash.[7] "The plaintiffs in this case claim the defendant, a Negro man, as their slave. It therefore behooves them to show slavery *in him*, and property *in them*" (385 [180]). What strikes me about the language here is another apparently "romantic" notion embedded in the presuppositions of the court. Although the court was ultimately sympathetic to Nash's argument, primarily because he was "purchased" in Detroit, where slavery was forbidden by law, it makes its original charge, based on *Adelle v. Beauregard,* from the assumption of inherent characteristics of personhood. In this case, enslavement is not something that happens to you, but it is a condition "in" you, slavery. Similarly, the right to own property, or to have this individual piece of property, is an inherent quality "in" the plaintiff rather than a right or privilege extended by an external body such as the government (Radin 959–61). Even more specifically problematic here is that these dispensations of internal qualities are distributed by race, and race is established by color; that is, under no stretch of the imagination, romantic or not, could the legal roles in this case be reversed. Even though the court found for Nash because, as with Adelle, no legal papers of sale could be produced, it is important not to lose sight of the court's own compelling dictum, that is, that the law, when complied with, allows for a finding of inherent enslavement based on race as understood by color. Adelle and Nash go free not because they were not enslaveable by nature but because the law's needs were not met. Even these restrictions were removed by Justice Taney's decision in *Scott v. Sandford* thirty-five years later.

Fifty years after *Scott v. Sandford* and almost a century after *Forsyth v. Nash, et al,* another Louisiana case provided an almost statistical account of the problem of color before the law. In 1910, the Supreme Court of Louisiana heard an appeal by the state from an acquittal for violation of an act of 1908 forbidding miscegenation. The statute provided that "concubinage between a member of the white race and a person of the negro or black race" was a felony. Octave Treadaway and another person were acquitted on the basis that Treadaway was an octoroon and therefore not a Negro or black person. Treadaway's lawyer provided the court with six pages of citations before he began his argument, which was simply that the framers of the act, being from Louisiana, knew the exactitude with which language in the state differentiated among blacks or negroes and "mulattoes," "quadroons," "octaroons," and "griffs." The court upheld the acquittal, but not unanimously.[8]

What are useful to this discussion from the case are the six pages of citations. The weight of the case law itself, running from the first decade of the nineteenth century to the first decade of the twentieth, shows that rights under the law were apportioned, nationally, and not just regionally, by race. Race in every case was shown to be a function of color as an index of lineage, despite several quasi-mathematical formulas written into legislation in various jurisdictions. In addition, the citations make clear that "color" always referred (with the possible exception of what Treadaway's lawyer called the "Pacific slope") to people whose parents or further antecedents were Africans.[9] It seems clear enough from the records of this case that national citizenship as late as 1910 was proportional to the perception of one's skin color as that color was perceived to represent some locally understandable system of quantifying degrees of racial identity, specifically "negro."[10]

These matters of the nature of the authentic self and the rights that inhere in it appear also in the continuing debate over corporate identity that frames our contemplation of the forces that tended to suppress African American citizenship in the nineteenth century. After *Dartmouth v. Woodward*, much space was given over in courts, law offices, and committee chambers to the problem of the naturalness or artificiality of the person that the corporation might become. Ultimately, the corporation came to be understood to be "a real person . . . an autonomous, self-directed entity in which rights inhered" (Mark 1442). In other words, a citizen of a romantic republic. This status emerged from *Santa Clara* essentially because Chief Justice Waite, before hearing oral argument, ruled that the Court would accept a reading that extended Fourteenth Amendment protection to corporations. He did so because one of the railroad's lawyers in a previous but linked case, former congressman Roscoe Conkling, had sat on the committee that drafted the Fourteenth Amendment and had argued before the Court that the Joint Congressional Committee had used "persons" consciously to cover "corporations." Conkling's claim turned out later to be unverifiable; the manuscript journal of the committee's deliberations does not support Conkling's assertion.[11]

While the granting of Fourteenth Amendment protection against denial of due process to corporations because they are persons was an act of creation at least metaphorically Frankensteinian in its effect, unlike the distraught doctor of Mary Shelley's novel the courts did not desert their creation, hearing more Fourteenth Amendment cases involving corporations than they heard cases involving African Americans until the modern civil rights era. And on balance, it would seem, corporations have been more successful than have African Americans in preserving their status intact. Between 1890 and 1910 only 19 of the 528 cases involving the Fourteenth Amendment before the Court involved Negroes' rights, while 288 of these cases referred to corporations that were considered "persons" under the language of the amendment (Logan 100).

Even more striking is that never again had an American corporation to reargue either its person-ness and the concomitant freedom to act as a social and economic person or its right to protection under the law of the land. This is in no large measure due to the fact that after 1883, American courts abandoned a rights-based jurisprudence to such an extent that "the legal faith of the Gilded Age rested primarily on contract and its formal assumptions about free will" (Soifer 1947).[12]

The emerging power of corporations did not escape the notice of black Baltimorean lawyer F. J. Waring, however:

> Corporations have come to exert a secret yet potent influence over American courts. It is said of a great State that its courts are practically owned by a rich railroad corporation, while it is boldly charged that millionaire interests have dictated appointments to the Supreme Bench of America. Under our elective system, judicial candidates are assessed enormously, and rumor says corporation clients often pay these assessments. Naturally such a pernicious practice makes judges the tools of corporations and disregardful of individual rights. Our courts may be said to be a veto upon public opinion and legislation, and courts and lawyers an organized bulwark impeding reformation. We stand in mute admiration before the common law, that grand fabric which is a lasting monument to Anglo-Saxon brain and genius, but the common law tendency to protect corporate as against individual and private rights has no place in American institutions, We need a change in our system and rules of law interpretation. Judges must no longer sit, Gamaliel-like, at the feet of the common law, but rather mid the glorious radiance of our new civilization and in the fulsome light of modern jurisprudence. In the inevitable conflict between the people and aggregated wealth and power, the courts will experience a purification. (437)

This grounding in contract was further complicated by the passing away of equity action in the law early in the nineteenth century. By the end of the second decade, white Americans had already begun dealing with "property futures" (moving away from exchange of property as the base of contract to "expectation of return on investment") and investment such that a whole new system of expectations and fluctuating values began to undergird public, that is, commercial life. Thus even the contract relationships of corporate economics and law were different from the peculiar equity-like property-in-contract of slavery with which most African Americans first had experience (Thomas, *American* 25–52).

As Wilfred M. McClay argues, in postbellum America "incorporation" was the fundamental dynamic of the refashioning of the nation (27). Incorporation as the merging of disparate elements into a whole, as the absorption of something into a larger entity, and as the formation of a legal corpus with rights, privileges, and liabilities are all applicable to postwar American social reorganization (27; Trachtenberg 3–10). And participation in the ethos of incorporation in all three of these senses was denied to African Americans, effectively excluding them from any active role as citizens. While economic incorporation rolled on inexorably across the postwar republic, there were counteractive social attitudes at work as well. If we were to see Reconstruction as an attempt to meld black Americans into the emerging American corporate state, then we must understand the period of counter-Reconstruction as an attempt to roll back the full tide of incorporation from a centralized federal nation-state to an earlier, more fluid, decentralized, romantic community of self-identified individuals, one that could and would exclude blacks from membership. To draw on a phrase much in use in the 1990s, the "politics of identity" were invented in the counter-Reconstruction of the 1880s to resist the incorporative impulse of postwar technological capitalism. In that case, however, the politics and the identity were forced on black Americans, who preferred to see themselves as citizens indistinguishable from their similarly incorporated white brethren.

The interrelationships of law, contract, and slavery are complex but worth looking into for some understanding of the position of black Americans in relationship to the law as a narrative of their lives. Early on, and steadfastly until the Civil War, as we have noted, slavery was held out as a local matter in the South and not a national one.

On November 30, 1791, Massachussetts congressman Fisher Ames wrote to an unknown correspondent:

> "To the northward," Ames said with characteristic Yankee self-righteousness, "we see how necessary it is to defend property by steady laws," and "the same system of strict law, which has done wonders for us," would promote the advantages of southerners as well. But in the South there was no steady law, only the commands of the gentry. Many among the gentry had favored ratification of the Constitution "because they needed some remedy to evils which they saw and felt, but mistook, in their view of it, the remedy. A debt-compelling government is no remedy to men who have lands and negroes, and debts and luxury, but neither trade nor credit, nor cash, nor the execution of law." (McDonald 213, qtd. in Aschen 143)

The passing of equity law in the nineteenth century, however, changed property and contract law in America, made capitalistic risk acceptable, and changed slavery, by impressing it upon the nation in a new manifestation, into one among other methods for the production of capital. When Powell's *Essay Upon the Law of Contracts and Agreements* (1790) set the grounds for the denunciation of equity as undermining the rule of law because it relied on the individual conscience of judges, it also provided a de facto argument for not just the owning of slaves but for commerce in enslaved people. Martin Horwitz cites Powell to the effect that equity

> "must be arbitrary and uncertain" [because] there could be no principles of substantive justice. A court of equity, for example, should not be permitted to refuse to enforce an agreement for simple "exorbitancy of price" because "it is the consent of parties alone, that fixes the just price of any thing, without reference to the nature of things themselves, or to their intrinsic value. . . . Therefore" he concluded, "a man is obliged in conscience to perform a contract which he has entered into, although it be a hard one." The entire conceptual apparatus of modern contract doctrine—rules dealing with offer and acceptance, the evidentiary function of consideration, and especially canons of interpretation—arose to express this will theory of contract. (160–61)[13]

It is this notion of agreement on price by the parties alone absent any consideration of the nature of things or of their intrinsic value that makes commerce in slaves possible, because profitable, since it makes commodification of anything, regardless of its nature or intrinsic value, possible. Obviously there is a problem in this reading of the development of notions of property and law in the slaveholding South because we have already seen that the moral ecology of individual judges in the antebellum South had a great deal to do with their rulings in cases involving slaves and free people of color, causing them to rule much as though equity had not been supplanted by a new order of thought. Nevertheless, I would consider it possible that a contract-based general notion of "property" and value had suffused the legal infrastructure of the nation by the 1830s, by which time "Planter" society had stopped apologizing for slavery as a system forced on it by circumstance, such that traffic in human beings could be understood as a part of a capitalizing economic practice, while the local experience of actual enslavement and the conflicts of property and obligation emerging from that experience could be grasped by local magistrates by the conceptual machinery of equity.

But the macroconceptual understanding of the centrality of contract is equally undeniable. The net effect was to leave slavery a localized institution in practice, with the locus of power shifted from the court of equity to the lawyer who drew up the contract, or most usually, to the contract itself, however it was arrived at. This power of the contract to define itself in terms of existential value lies at the heart of the need to deny access to it to slaves and free persons of color. That the realization of the power of contract was almost universal is seen in the uniform practice of such denial.

And from what, then, were slaves excluded when they were excluded from contract? From the very essence of American process, for one. For another, from the right to make an advantageous, even excessive bargain for themselves. From the right to capitalize. From the right to compete, obviously, not only as labor but as entrepreneur or capitalist. The inability to enter into these kinds of agreements meant one had no option but to be a laborer, and not even a free competitor in the labor market (or a wife, as was the case with women—and for black women, as a mistress, not even as a wife).

What is obvious is that no principle of natural law or natural rights applies here. The natural-law arguments in the Declaration of Independence were the bases of that document's appeal to antebellum blacks.

Its echoes can be seen, for example, in the words of Madison Washington, "If I get clear, (as something tells me I shall,) liberty, the inalienable birth-right of every man, precious and priceless, will be mine" (Douglass, "Heroic" 39–40). Washington is expressing what McClay calls "the promptings of the boundless self" (41), the hallmark of antebellum expectations for the individual. McClay argues that the ante- and postbellum years are mirrored inversions of each other: if the postbellum American future was integrated, incorporated, consolidated, and committed to principles of national institutionalism, the antebellum period, exemplified by the Jacksonian era, "was marked by . . . a restless, individualistic, egalitarian, wide-open, romantic, liberatory, antinomian, and antiauthoritarian spirit" (42).

The ascendancy of the Constitution and of the promise of the specific protection of positivist law in the esteem of black activists in the latter half of the nineteenth century seems to reflect that community's awareness that the demise of equity created a specific need for the structure of something like contract law. Specific local protection was needed, as well as a system of appeal from a too idiosyncratic local judiciary. Positive law seemed to promise that. It was not until the failure of constitutional guarantees by the end of the century, when the forces of white reaction that looked back to the Jacksonian past had successfully written black Americans out of any incorporated America, that black nationalism arose to reiterate the claims of natural law for America's African population.

The exclusion of people of color from full participation in public life on the basis that they lacked the capacity for a kind of Jacksonian "boundless possibility" is easily seen in the way in which black Americans appeared in courts of law. While antebellum cases such as *Adelle* and *Nash* differ from those over the subsequent postwar and post-Reconstruction decades in terms of cause, matters of race, color, identity, and standing persevere. Moreover, testimony by African Americans was forbidden, de jure or de facto, in most cases throughout the century, as was almost all other black participation except as defendant. In the first decade of the twentieth century, African Americans were excluded either from jury pools or actual juries by common practice throughout the states of the Old South (Stephenson 242–72).[14] There were exceptions, of a sort, as in Louisiana: "Negroes serve as jurors in this parish to a limited extent. The jury commissioners, when they know of an exceptionally good, honest, sober and industrious Negro, have no objection to placing his name in the jury box" (261).

Even in New York City, blacks rarely served on juries. On April 25, 1912, the *New York Age,* a black newspaper, reported briefly on a case that was unique in two respects. Although the charge that Leroy Poindexter had murdered Thomas Brown in a crap game was not an unusual one, the conduct of Mr. Poindexter's defense was. In the first place, Poindexter's lawyer was a woman, a young North Carolina lawyer named Lucille Pugh. In the second place, Pugh's argument was that her client had been deprived of his Fourteenth Amendment rights because there had not been a single Negro on either the grand jury that indicted him or on the special jury impaneled to try him. The *Age* editorialized, "Perhaps the fact that, although there are 85,000 Negroes in the county, it is rare that one gets on any of the juries is evidence of the discrimination in drawing juries" (n.p.). The Poindexter case was carried over to a second trial when the first jury "disagreed" and came to no verdict.[15] It was not until twenty-three years after the Poindexter case, in *Hollins v. Oklahoma* (295 U.S. 394 [1935]), argued by Charles Houston, that there was a reversal of a conviction of a black man for murder because blacks were excluded from jury service.

While Pugh could not forgo the white practice of occasional patronization of one's client because of race ("when I look upon him it brings back to my mind the days when I was a little girl myself, when I was nursed by a loyal colored mammy whose own little children, pickininnies [*sic*], played around a back door") (*State v. Leroy Poindexter* 123), she was committed to the defense and did attempt to move the case to the federal courts and then to set both trials aside for reasons of jury pool demographics. Failing both, she and her cocounsel, James D. McClelland, ran a thorough defense. The result, nevertheless, was conviction on a charge of manslaughter in the second degree, the least of the charges against him. The trial judge sentenced Poindexter to seven and one-half to fifteen years in the state penitentiary (*State v. Baby Poindexter* 543).[16]

Although challenges to such practices date back at least to the federal indictments of fourteen local judges for keeping blacks out of jury pools, events that produced *Ex Parte Virginia* (100 U.S. 339 [1879]), federal actions such as these had little effect on local practices in courts of original, nonfederal jurisdiction. There had been, under slavery, however, a very real exception to these rules and practices that excluded the black presence from the court, an exception that underscores the ironic quality of African American life at the intersection of law, property, romanticism, and self as it appears in a courtroom context in the presentation of the black body. Although specific texts of the law varied from jurisdiction to jurisdiction, the antebellum prohibition in the South generally was against any testimony by slaves and against testimony by free persons of color against whites or in cases in which all parties were whites. In effect, "white" words given under oath were true, while "black" words were not true or were not discourse. There was no such event as testimony of the enslaved voice in a slave state. Such appellate records as we have allow us only the voices of white lawyers on behalf of their black clients in civil matters.[17] Criminal cases involving slaves in most states were relegated to a separate judicial system, one that often worked casually and locally, with judgment and punishment meted out on the slaveholder's property.

Such punishment itself often resulted in civil cases. Then the testimony of the slave was heard, not from her mouth, but read as a deposition of the flesh. The appearance of an enslaved person in court brought evidence as to damage to property (the enslaved body) or could represent the silent, metaphoric presence of a "cause" at law, when a white person could be found to bring suit for and give evidence or testimony for the enslaved person bringing suit for freedom. But not one word of testimony in accusation or defense could pass the black person's lips.

Thus, it was not the *inherent person* of the slave (the enslaved person) that appeared in court but the body of the slave, as property, in almost every instance. Serving as object, as evidence, the slave's body, because it could be seen and not heard, became the story, became the text. It follows, then, that who owned the body, owned the text, owned the right to exhibit the story, the history written on the body. For these reasons, American writers from Melville to Morrison have been fascinated with the objectified, scarred body of the person of color. The scars on Sethe's back in *Beloved*, on Dessa Rose's thighs in Sherley Anne Williams's eponymous novel, on Melville's Queequeg are the manuscripts of the race: history, law, genealogy, poem, and novel. As the ex-slave William Grimes wrote in the narrative of his life by way of celebrating his ownership of his own physical self,

> If it were not for the stripes on my back which were made while I was a slave, I would in my will leave my skin as a legacy to the government, desiring that it might be taken off and made into

parchment, and then bind the constitution of glorious, happy, free, America. Let the skin of an American slave bind the charter of American liberty! (120)

But in the antebellum world of the South, to own the body was to own the right to write and read the history of the race. As the epigraph to this book observes, the story of black lives throughout the nineteenth century, not only under slavery, lies in the whispered consolations offered over their broken bodies, prostrate before the law. Metaphorically and legally, ownership of the body was the key to creation of the self as subject-actor in a personal and collective history. The acting-romantic-creating self was at the center of black silence in the court under slavery, and the reemergence of racial restrictions on voting, jury service, testimony, and property suits during the last two decades of the nineteenth century and the first half of the twentieth century as effectively silenced the African American voice in every court, leaving only its body as victim (and so unable to testify to the reality of lynch law) or as defendant.

The conceptual barriers created by cultural ideograms of privacy, difference, and liberty have remained virtually impermeable by African Americans, and yet it is easy to overlook the constrictive power of the ideology they undergird. It is the complex relationship between the conditions and terms of enslavement and property that made the determination of self for blacks and people of color in the nineteenth century so problematic. Even as postwar constitutional amendments sought to clarify the position of the emancipated Negro "self," attacks on the enabling legislation surrounding the amendments eroded their ability to shield black Americans from the consequences of their previous status. Meanwhile, what rights remained for African Americans were eroding under the weight of an emerging body of Jim Crow laws designed to re-enslave them and to force them into the social and economic margins of American society, where they would be easy prey for rapacious whites and malleable instruments for the enforcement of labor discipline on the white working class by the very corporations who had won so much from the amendment written to liberate them.

In the light of these conditions, the concerns of the Brotherhood of Liberty and its magnum opus, *Justice and Jurisprudence,* take on a more national significance. Excluded from the labor market by a whites-only guild system, excluded from juries, from bar associations, from judgeships, kept off the voting rolls and held in economic bondage through-

out the Old South, and in danger of losing the constitutional protections on which they premised their place in American civil life, both
north and south of the Mason-Dixon Line, black Americans had every
reason to fear for their future as citizens with equity. They understood
that the battle was over their own humanity, the argument drawn in
terms of their basic fitness to share the American experience. For all
that the law could promise as protection, they saw that an activist court
in ideological bondage to a set of assumptions that excluded them from
participation in the discourse over their own freedom could not be
relied upon to read the text of the Constitution in any way that would
ensure them the status written into, so they read the documents, the
Thirteenth, Fourteenth, and Fifteenth Amendments. Consequently, the
closing paragraph of *Justice and Jurisprudence* is not about the majesty of
the law. It is instead an appeal to history and to "first principles":

> The principles of equality before the law, by due process of law,
> occupy great historical places in the arena of the world's history.
> They cannot be interpreted by mere legal fiction, generated by par-
> tisan passion. Their sap is not derived from the scholastic tree of
> technical jurisprudence. In their political and constitutional inter-
> pretation, these venerable provisions touch the life of humanity.
> Their historical, Christian significance means "the unity of the
> human in the divine Fatherhood." The noble lineage of these great
> legal phrases is to be traced through all those proverbs and axioms
> of freedom and liberty, which represent the coined wisdom and
> humanity of past ages. In whatever language they are written, by
> whatever tongue they are spoken, their true interpretation and
> mission is: "Justice against violence"; "Law against anarchy";
> "Freedom against oppression." (Brotherhood of Liberty 504)[18]

The distance between the Brotherhood's assumptions and the true efficacy of man's law and God's justice was exemplified in the failure of
both in Charles W. Chesnutt's 1905 novel, *The Colonel's Dream*. The publication date of the novel notwithstanding, the story is rooted in the
same conditions to which the Brotherhood was responding as the century entered its last decade.[19] But while the Brotherhood saw the primary threat to African American life under law to come from the federal courts, Chesnutt situates his account of the failure of American law
to frame African American life with the same prerogatives and privileges as those owned by whites in the localized refusal of ordinary

white Americans to grant full participation in the life of the community to blacks (Greenfield). Chesnutt's novel is a good illustration of how a black writer creates an ironic vision of the attempt to fashion an authentic American life.

In the early 1890s, Henry French, a man in his early fifties, sells his business in the North for a considerable fortune and returns to his hometown in the South for a visit. A widower, he takes his young son with him. French decides to stay in Clarendon, where he is known as "Colonel" French by virtue of his brevet rank in the Confederate Army, and bring it into the modern world by investing his money and his now-northern sensibilities. Part of this project involves addressing the problem of the races. That the central character in this novel of the color line is white is part of Chesnutt's ironic perspective.

French's nemesis is William Fetters, a "convict labor contractor" who has amassed wealth and political power and who bears French a boyhood grudge. French admires and proposes to Laura Treadwell, a Clarendon lady of good breeding but genteel poverty. Except in his relationship with her, French is defeated at every turn. He champions Bud Johnson, a black convict/peonage laborer who, once free, attacks two bad whites and is lynched; his plan for a new mill is never realized; he alienates the white working class by hiring blacks as workers and supervisors; his son and his faithful black servant are killed in an accident; and his attempt to honor his son's dying wish to have the servant buried next to him in the family plot is stymied when white ruffians dig up the black man's casket and leave it on French's porch. In the end he succeeds only in freeing Laura from poverty by accidentally discovering a way to make Fetters pay an old note owed her father's estate. French leaves Clarendon without Laura and without realizing any of his dream.

Throughout the novel Chesnutt's commentary, whether as a narratorial voice or through the speeches of various characters, returns again and again to the consequences of history as felt in legal contexts, from the rise of some freedmen to the propertied class to the effects of "freedom" on the general population of former slaves:

> What good had freedom done for Peter? In the colonel's childhood his father's butler, old Madison, had lived a life which, compared to that of Peter at the same age, was one of ease and luxury. How easy the conclusion that the slave's lot had been the more fortu-

nate! But no, Peter had been better free. There were plenty of poor white men, and no one had suggested slavery as an improvement of their condition. Had Peter remained a slave, then the colonel would have remained a master, which was only another form of slavery. The colonel had been emancipated by the same token that had made Peter free. Peter had returned home poor and broken, not because he had been free, but because nature first, and society next, in distributing their gifts, had been niggardly with old Peter. . . . He would set his own success against Peter's failure; and he would take off his hat to the memory of the immortal statesman, who in freeing one race had emancipated another and struck the shackles from a Nation's mind. (29–30)

Chesnutt was a lawyer and a court stenographer, and in this novel he examines the criminal-justice system and the legally buttressed economic system it served. Here, at the depth of "the Nadir," Chesnutt finds the banal center of white exploitation of the African American, the criminalization of everyday life and the use of the law to force economic servitude on an entire people. The linchpin of the system was the "vagrancy" law. Originally enacted in many Southern states in the months immediately following the Civil War, such laws provided for the imprisonment of anyone found unemployed after a certain date. After arrest and conviction, the vagrant was liable to work out his or her sentence under any citizen who could claim access to the state's fund of convict labor. Many schemes for distribution existed, but Chesnutt's description is illustrative of the basic principle:

> Stopping, he [French] looked with some curiosity into the door, over which there was a faded sign to indicate that it was the office of a Justice of the Peace—a pleasing collocation of words, to those who could divorce it from any technical significance—Justice, Peace—the seed and the flower of civilisation. . . .
> "Now, gentlemen, here's Lot Number Three, a likely young nigger who answers to the name of Sam Brown. Not much to look at but will make a good field hand, if looked after right and kept away from liquor; used to workin', when in the chain gang, where he's been, off and on, since he was ten years old. Amount of fine an' costs thirty-seven dollars and a half. A musical nigger, too, who plays the banjo, and sings just like a—like a blackbird. What

am I bid for this prime lot?" [The process is to bid the lowest amount of time in service, for the costs. This is, in theory, to protect the convict]

"One year," answered a voice.

"Nine months," said a second.

"Six months," came a third bid, from a tall man with a buggy whip under his arm.

"Are you all through, gentlemen? Six months' labour for thirty-seven fifty is mighty cheap, and you know the law allows you to keep the labourer up to the mark. Are you all done? Sold to Mr. Turner, for Mr. Fetters, for six months." (62–63)

At this sale, French recognizes an old family servant among the prisoners and asks the justice what he had done to warrant the twenty-five-dollar fine posted by his name:

"Peter has not been able," replied the magistrate, "to show this co't that he has reg'lar employment, or means of suppo't, and he was therefore tried and convicted yesterday evenin' of vagrancy, under our State law. The fine is intended to discourage laziness and to promote industry. Do you want to bid, suh? I'm offered two years, gentlemen, for old Peter French? Does anybody wish to make it less?"

"I'll pay the fine," said the colonel, "let him go."

"I beg yo' pahdon, suh, but that wouldn't fulfill the requi'ments of the law. He'd be subject to arrest again immediately. Somebody must take the responsibility for his keep."

French agrees to take Peter under those terms, to free him from the law, but the magistrate insists on recording a bid of time in the record.

"As long as you please," said the colonel impatiently.

"Sold," said the justice, bringing down his gavel, "for life, to— what name, suh?"

"French—Henry French." (67–68)

As French discovers, economic exploitation is not enough to allow whites to sleep easily with blacks among them. They must also find a way to deny them the vote. Over the course of several pages, Chesnutt reveals the white position on voting laws:

If the new franchise amendment went through, said the major, the Negro would be eliminated from politics, and the people of the South, relieved of the fear of 'nigger domination,' could give their attention to better things, and their section would move forward along the path of progress by leaps and bounds. . . .

"Yes, sir," said Mr. Blake, taking the colonel's hand, "I believe in white supremacy, and the elimination of the nigger vote. If the National Republican Party would only ignore the coloured politicians, and give all the offices to white men, we'll soon build up a strong white Republican party." (73–74)

The colonel shook hands with the editor, who had come with a two-fold intent—to make the visitor's acquaintance and to interview him upon his impressions of the South. Incidentally he gave the colonel a great deal of information about local conditions. These were not, he admitted, ideal. The town was backward. It needed capital to develop its resources, and it needed to be rid of the fear of Negro domination. The suffrage in the hands of the Negroes had proved a ghastly and expensive joke for all concerned, and the public welfare absolutely demanded that it be taken away. Even the white republicans were coming around to the same point of view. The new franchise amendment to the State constitution was receiving their unqualified support. (75)

The connection between the franchise and the economic system based on vagrancy law was obvious. A voting black citizenry could repeal the penology laws that governed the correctional system.

"Well," admitted the editor, "I suppose it might seem harsh, in comparison with your milder penal systems up North. But you must consider the circumstances, and make allowances for us. We have so many idle, ignorant Negroes that something must be done to make them work, or else they'll steal, and to keep them in their place, or they would run over us. The law [allowing convict labor] has been in operation only a year or two, and is already having its effect. I'll be glad to introduce a bill for its repeal, as soon as it is no longer needed.

"You must bear in mind, too, colonel, that niggers don't look at imprisonment and enforced labour in the same way white people do—they are not conscious of any disgrace attending stripes or the ball and chain. The State is poor; our white children are suffering for lack of education, and yet we have to spend a large amount of money on the Negro schools. These convict labor contracts are a source of considerable revenue to the State; they make up, in fact, for most of the outlay for Negro education—which I approve of, though I'm frank to say that so far I don't see much good that's come from it." (75–76)

Throughout the novel, Chesnutt undercuts southern arguments by having French observe on his own the opposite truths: Negroes working while whites lie about, squalid conditions of black schools, profits to contractors but not to the state. But the system is too entrenched for him to defeat:

An ambitious politician in a neighbouring State had led a successful campaign on the issue of Negro disenfranchisement. Plainly unconstitutional, it was declared to be as plainly necessary for the preservation of the white race and white civilisation. The example had proved contagious, and Fetters and his crowd, who dominated their State, had raised the issue there. At first the pronouncement met with slight response. The sister State had possessed a Negro majority, which, in view of reconstruction history was theoretically capable of injuring the State. Such was not the case here. The State had survived reconstruction with small injury. . . . No Negro had held a State office for twenty years. In Clarendon they had even ceased to be summoned as jurors, and when a Negro met a white man, he gave him the wall, even if it were necessary to take the gutter to do so. But this was not enough; this supremacy must be made permanent. Negroes must be taught that they need never look for any different state of things. New definitions were given to old words, new pictures set in old frames, new wine poured into old bottles. (192–93)

A politician says that

so long as one Negro votes in the State, so long are we face to face with the nightmare of Negro domination. . . . Our duty to ourselves, to our children, and their unborn descendants, and to our great and favoured race, impels us to protest, by word, by vote, by arms if need be, against the enforced equality of an inferior race. Equality anywhere means, ultimately, equality everywhere.

Equality at the polls means social equality; social equality means intermarriage and corruption of blood, and degeneration and decay. What gentleman here would want his daughter to marry a blubber-lipped, cocoanut-headed, kidney-footed, etc., etc., nigger? (193–94)

Chesnutt's indictment of the legal system courses through the book:

When [the train] came, it brought a gang of convicts, consigned to Fetters. They had been brought down in the regular "Jim Crow" car, for the colonel saw coloured women and children come out ahead of them. The colonel watched the wretches, in coarse striped garments, with chains on their legs and shackles on their hands, unloaded from the train and into the waiting wagons. There were burly Negroes and flat-shanked, scrawny Negroes. Some wore the ashen hue of long confinement. Some were shame-faced, some reckless, some sullen. . . . The scene was not edifying. There were criminals in New York, he knew very well, but he had never seen one. They were not marched down Broadway in stripes and chains. There were certain functions of society, as of the body, which were more decently performed in retirement. There was work in the State for the social reformer, and the colonel, undismayed by his temporary defeat, metaphorically girded up his loins, went home, and, still metaphorically, set out to put a spoke in Fetters's wheel. . . .
[The criminal laws] were bad enough, in all conscience. Men could be tried without jury and condemned to infamous punish-ments, involving stripes and chains, for misdemeanours which in more enlightened States were punished with a small fine or brief detention. There were, for instance, no degrees of larceny, and the heaviest punishment might be inflicted, at the discretion of the judge, for the least offense. . . .
Convict labour was contracted out to private parties, with little or no effective State supervision, on terms which, though exceed-ingly profitable to the State, were disastrous to free competitive labour. More than one lawmaker besides Fetters was numbered among these contractors.
Leaving the realm of crime, they found that on hundreds of farms, ignorant Negroes, and sometimes poor whites, were held in

bondage under claims of debt, or under contracts of exclusive employment for long terms of years—contracts extorted from ignorance by craft, aided by State laws which made it a misdemeanour to employ such persons elsewhere. Free men were worked side by side with convicts from the penitentiary, and women and children herded with the most depraved criminals, thus breeding a criminal class to prey upon the State. (226–29)

"We coloured folks, sir, are often accused of trying to shield criminals of our own race, or of not helping the officers of the law to catch them. Maybe we does, suh," he said, lapsing in his earnestness, into bad grammar, "maybe we does sometimes, but not without reason."

"What reason?" asked the colonel.

"Well, sir, fer the reason that we ain't always shore that a coloured man will get a fair trial, or any trial at all, or that he'll get a jail sentence after he's been tried. We have no hand in makin' the laws, or in enforcin' them; we are not summoned on jury; and yet we're asked to do the work of constables and sheriffs, who are paid for arrestin' criminals, an' for protectin' 'em from mobs, which they don't do." (243–44)

The Colonel's Dream is an ironic title, probably painfully so for Chesnutt. If the colonel's intentions were his own, Chesnutt could not have made them more idealistic:

His aim was to bring about, by better laws and more liberal ideas, peace, harmony, and universal good will. There was a colossal work for him to do, and for all whom he could enlist with him to this cause. The very standards of right and wrong had been confused by the race issue, and must be set right by the patient appeal to reason and humanity. Primitive passions and private vengeance must be subordinated to law and order and the common good. (247)

But Chesnutt knew better than to hope for too much too soon, if ever:

That it might take some time to set in motion the machinery necessary to reach the evil, the colonel knew very well, and hence was not impatient at any reasonable delay. Had he known that his presentation had created a sensation in the highest quarter, but that owing to the exigencies of national politics it was not deemed wise, at that time, to do anything which seemed like an invasion of State rights or savoured of sectionalism, he would not have been so serenely confident of the outcome. (231)

Chesnutt was not at all sanguine that he would soon see the demise of the system he was describing:

> Cherishing their theoretical equality of citizenship, which they could neither enforce or forget, the Negroes resented, nosily or silently, as prudence dictated, its contemptuous denial by the whites; and these, viewing this shadowy equality as an insult to themselves, had sought by all the machinery of local law to emphasize and perpetuate their own superiority. The very word "equality" was an offense. Society went back to Egypt and India for its models; to break caste was a greater sin than to break any or all of the ten commandments. White and coloured children studied the same books in different schools. White and black people rode on the same trains in separate cars. Living side by side, and meeting day by day, the law, made and administered by white men, had built a wall between them. (263)

As basically unromantic as his novel is, as deconstructive of the idealism based on trust in law, even Chesnutt could not foresee how that wall would continue to rise and extend itself into the North. Throughout the nineteenth century these matters had been fought out in the narratives of a rural America and a land-bound peasantry that served it. In the next half-century those narratives would be adapted to meet the realities of an urbanized America. Just as the vagrancy laws had created a "criminal" class out of the rural poor, the urbanization of Jim Crow would create a segregated population of the racialized poor whose lives would come to stand as images of crime and violence. Despite his own ironic critique of southern law, however, Chesnutt seemed to cling to as idealized a vision of American potentiality under law as did the Brotherhood of Liberty. He ends *The Colonel's Dream* with this panegyric to the annealing power of law:

> The seed which the colonel sowed seemed to fall by the wayside, it is true; but other eyes have seen with the same light, and while Fet-

ters and his kind still dominate their section, other hands have taken up the fight which the colonel dropped. In manufactures the South has gone forward by leaps and bounds. The strong arm of the Government, guided by a wise and just executive, has been reached out to crush the poisonous growth of peonage, and men hitherto silent have raised their voices to commend. Here and there a brave judge has condemned the infamy of the chain-gang and convict lease systems. Good men, North and South, have banded themselves together to promote the cause of popular education. Slowly, like all great social changes, but visibly, to the eye of faith, is growing up a new body of thought, favorable to just laws and their orderly administration. In this changed attitude of mind lies the hope of the future, the hope of the Republic. . . .

. . . there are those who hope, and those who pray, . . . that some day our whole land will be truly free, and the strong will cheerfully help to bear the burdens of the weak, and Justice, the seed, and Peace, the flower, of Liberty, will prevail throughout all our borders. (293–94)

While African Americans waited for the colonel's dream to materialize, life had to be lived. During the next two decades, an emerging black press would encourage the African American bourgeoisie to pursue lives like those enjoyed by the white middle class. Messages of uplift and civil rectitude mixed with images of conspicuous consumption, and class pride would compete with the more negative portrayals of the effects of urbanization. Black reading societies and journals such as the *Colored American* magazine of the new century's first decade would present a paradigm of racial and class advancement that, while existing more in the imagination of authors and editors than in the statistics of the Census Bureau, served to create a field in which the imagination of a new African American could range, one in which black citizenship was an integral part of a new national identity. This imaginative potentiality, the same capacity of language that made it dangerous to the system of slavery, promised a reformulation of black life in the face of the growing strength of Jim Crow and national segregation.

CHAPTER 5

Law and the Urbanization of Narrative in "Postproperty" African American Life

> But, ah! Manhattan's sights and sounds, her smells,
>   Her crowds, her throbbing force, the thrill that comes
> From being of her a part, her subtile spells,
>   Her shining towers, her avenues, her slums—
>   O God! The stark, unutterable pity,
> To be dead, and never again behold my city!
>
> James Weldon Johnson, "My City"

The argument for the centrality of law in classical African American narrative has been syllogistic in its simplicity to this point. It is premised on the centrality of romanticized property in capitalist thought and develops through the primacy of capitalism as the economic base of a system of government defined by white property owners.[1] Those owners encase their property interests, and the romantic presuppositions about identity that allow them ownership of those interests as a class, in laws written by and enforced through that government. The identity of African Americans has, consequently, been the most legislated and litigated field in the creation of the "American" self. While white (male) Americans are presumed to exist "in nature" as realized entities, prior to any text or representation of them, African Americans exist only in the written text of their encounters with the paradigms of social force derived by white Americans to manage the state. As such, while white (male) Americans are unabridgeable entities, African Americans are/have been always extant only as they were last defined. The "who" or "what-ness" of self of African America has always been what literary theory calls "contested terrain."

After Reconstruction, the suppression of African American desire was accompanied by the criminalization of it, so that where it might escape the restraints of convention it would meet the irons of the law. Actually, the law moved against black desire as part of an "intricate apparatus," made up also of custom and brute force, designed to redefine African Americans, even before the end of the Civil War. If they were no longer not human and not citizens, they and their every attempt to live authentic lives would be rewritten as criminal.

The argument thus illuminates the condition of African Americans first *as* property under American law historically and then as narrators of stories *about* their property-ness and about their struggles to escape the physical and conceptual effects of the legal system that had defined the life of the race-as-property even as they stepped outside the previous categories of property that had contained them. The stories of "post-property-ness" are both necessary and complex because the reconfiguration of law to accommodate new property relations that recognized the dismantling of black status-as-property gradually reinscribed race as the basis for property by protecting the status of whiteness itself as property (C. I. Harris; Ignatiev; Garvey and Ignatiev; Roediger). Once again romantic identity was tied to property under law in order to exclude the "other." In this version of the text of American social reality, identity has become the property of an ironic version of the legal tradition in which the racial "identity" of blacks had been proof of their property-ness.

"Post-property" narratives of the turn of the century gradually give over to narratives of "post-authenticity" in which traditional and romantic notions of identity are challenged by the increasing urbanization of African American life. Between 1890 and 1900, African Americans moved to cities. Not in overwhelming numbers, but enough so that by 1900 approximately 10 percent of black Americans (seven hundred thousand) lived in fifteen urban areas.[2] New York City was fifth ranked among those cities, with a black population of sixty-one thousand. New Orleans, where *Plessy v. Ferguson* originated, was third, with seventy-eight thousand. This means that 90 percent of the black population lived lives that were residentially and occupationally rural and in fact were still in "the South"; 47 percent of America's black population lived in five states of the Old South.[3] The impact of this early migration and the later, more massive migrations of the first half of the century on African American cultural production has been increasingly the object of study (Griffin; Rodgers; Scruggs; Willis; Carby; Harrison; Trotter).

At the same time, realism in African American narrative began to appear alongside the genteel romanticism of manners and morals, and the complex mix of irony and authenticity that marked the expression of black American experience continued to evolve and change. I have

already noted that in *Sport of the Gods* Paul Laurence Dunbar abandoned the sentimentality and romance of his dialect poetry and short
fiction. But realistic tendencies in black narrative had actually begun to
appear in antebellum fugitive slave accounts. Just as realism in canonical white American fiction is said to have gradually emerged out of
regional romantic literature after the Civil War, something similar was
happening in African American narrative. In this latter case, however,
the stimulus was less geographic regionalism than the movement of the
center of consciousness of black experience from the rural South to both
southern and northern cities.[4]

Narrative representations of black urban life appear first in peri-
odical accounts, and when we look at representations of black life from
newspapers of the nineteenth century, prior to this first migration
toward urban centers, the pictures that emerge depend on which newspapers we read. For instance, white newspapers published before the
Civil War tended to report on sensational aspects of black life, if they
noticed blacks at all. Northern abolitionist papers reported escapes,
recaptures under the Fugitive Slave Act, and anecdotes of bravery,
while southern newspapers ran advertisements for the recapture of
runaway slaves, offers to sell slaves or rent out labor, and news stories.
One analysis of newspapers in antebellum New Orleans finds that the
white press there used fifty-one distinct terms for black Americans, all
of them derogatory. These terms, such as *cuffee, Sambo, free buck,* and
wooly heads appeared in news stories and advertisements. Of the 7,624
items about Negroes between 1850 and 1860, a little over 47 percent
were given over to stories of crime and the law, a bit under 30 percent
to advertisements, and 23 percent to such matters as the free Negro,
colonization, slavery, the slave trade, and the abolition movement.
Only a smattering of space was given at all to the "accidents and incidents" of everyday Negro life in the last decade of slavery (Reddick
2–3).

Forty years later, in the 1890s, the white press nationwide read
more like the proslavery New Orleans papers of 1850–60 than like the
abolitionist papers of the North from that same period. Slavery had
vanished as a topic, and there were no more advertisements for slave
sales or rewards for fugitives, but northern papers, Rayford Logan
reported, had "a tendency to play up crimes in which Negroes were
involved. . . . [T]he papers that seemed most preoccupied with crimes
involving Negroes were those published in the cities that had a rela-
tively high ratio in the population, St. Louis, Philadelphia, Cincinnati,

and Washington" (217).[5] What had changed in black experience with the law was at least partly geographical. Law in the rural South was designed, implemented, and manipulated to control the social and economic activities of blacks, not to regulate their extralegal or "criminal" activities. A black man or woman was more likely to be jailed or given some form of corporal punishment for overstepping social boundaries or for exercising economic independence than for theft or murder (as long as the victim was not white).[6] Such an emphasis, as W. E. B. Du Bois reported in *The Souls of Black Folk* (1903), had

> resulted in the refusal of whole [white] communities to recognize the right of a Negro to change his habitation and to be master of his own fortunes. A black stranger in Baker County, Georgia, for instance, is liable to be stopped anywhere on the public highway and made to state his business to the satisfaction of any white interrogator. If he fails to give a suitable answer, or seems too independent or "sassy," he may be arrested or summarily driven away. (115–16)

In cities however, where "the chance for lawless oppression and illegal exactions" are far less than in the country where most serious encounters of blacks with the law arise out of what Du Bois calls "disputes between master and man," the legal history of black life becomes a narrative of strangers, property, and violence (116). In 1903, Du Bois explains, "Daily the Negro is coming more and more to look upon law and justice, not as protecting safeguards, but as sources of humiliation and oppression. The laws are made by men who have absolutely no motive for treating the black people with courtesy or consideration; and finally, the accused is tried, not by his peers, but too often by men who would rather punish ten innocent Negroes than let one guilty one escape" (131–32).[7]

As Logan noted,

> Such words as "colored" and "negro"—the latter was not capitalized until the *Transcript* did so in 1900[8]— . . . helped [by repetition] to build up the stereotype of the Criminal Negro, a stereotype that was hardened by the use of pejorative adjectives. . . . [T]he following terms were used by one or more papers: "burly negro," "negro ruffian," "African Annie," "a Wild Western Negro," and "colored cannibal" in news stories while "coon," "darky," "pickaninny,"

"uncle," "nigger," "niggah" did not appear in news stories but in anecdotes, jokes, and cartoons throughout the papers. (217–18)

Headlines in the *St. Louis Globe Democrat* from September 18 to September 30, 1895 (Logan 218), were particularly reflective of the treatment:

Negroes Sentenced for Twenty-one Years

Held up by Masked Negroes

Six Negroes Die of Poison

She Killed Her Lover—Minnie Hall, A Negress

Killed at a Negro Fair

Drunken Farmer Killed by a Negro

St. Louis Negro Sentenced

Killed a Negro

Negro Miner Murdered

Colored Dynamiter Convicted

Stabbed a Negro

Death of a Man Shot by a Dissolute Negress

Negro's Horse Stealing Methods

The "Dissolute Negress" article of September 28, 1895, reports on page 3 that the subject of the story lived in a "neighborhood inhabited only by negroes and which has become notorious by reason of the large number of robberies and murders which have occurred there" (218).

It may have been the case that these perceptions were influenced by the shock of the new. Du Bois notes that urban crime had increased immediately after the Civil War as white soldiers flocked to the cities instead of back to the farms and hamlets from which they had come. By the 1880s, however, when the first of the black migrations to the cities began, those rowdy white boys and men had been assimilated, and the level of physicality of city life had adjusted itself upward, but more or less comfortably. The influx of black newcomers with no urban socialization caused a new wave of extralegality and illegality perhaps no greater than that caused by the white veterans and their younger brothers of twenty years previously, but certainly as remarkable as that had been, and now with the appearance of a singularity and a causality that could be attributed to racial difference (*Philadelphia* 238–40).

Du Bois argued that black Americans, because of their experiences with southern police and legal infrastructures designed in the first instance to control and even reenslave Negroes, had an unexpected, or as he put it, "curious," response to white obsession with black crime. "Negroes refused to believe the evidence of white witnesses or the fairness of white juries, so that the greatest deterrent to crime, the public opinion of one's own social caste, was lost, and the criminal was looked upon as crucified rather than hanged" (*Souls* 133). Whites, on the other hand, "used to being careless as to the guilt or innocence of accused Negroes, were swept in moments of passion beyond law, reason, and decency" (133–34). Du Bois's own short story of black frustration in the face of white racism, "Of the Coming of John," ends in such a moment of white passion beyond the law, albeit, as Du Bois makes clear, a passion in response to the equal passion for retribution felt by his protagonist (166–80).[9]

The African American press of the period, however, tells a different story. Stories in the *Baltimore Afro-American*, the *Richmond Planet*, the *Littleton True Reformer* (North Carolina), and the *Colored American Magazine* from 1889 to 1900, for example, deal with temperance matters, regional church conferences, African American citizenship, national and local "race leaders," the performance of black schoolchildren, wedding anniversaries, the John J. Waller case, laws limiting Negro action, local crimes (and the reporting here is somewhat less sensational than in the white press; for example the *Afro-American* reported the case of Mr. Bowers who killed a man named Green for ruining his daughter and refusing to marry her; Bowers was acquitted, and the news story applauded his black lawyer while noting with something like a tone of pride that it was the only case in the state of a man indicted for killing his daughter's seducer),[10] lynching (the *Richmond Planet* ran a weekly column of lynching data giving numbers and names of victims nationwide), literary and cultural events (the *Planet* reported an 1895 lecture to the Acme Literary Association by Dr. D. N. Vassar on communism; discussion followed), college life, segregation laws around the country, grand opera, dental hygiene, penal reform, and suffrage reform.[11]

These newspapers and journals, and others like them across the country, spoke of a black community of hardworking citizens with civic concerns and personal triumphs and sorrows that had nothing to do with their intersections with the lives of whites. Yet these papers were at the same time their links to the broader world of "the Race" and its legal tribulations. Here black "crime" issues meant not the sensation of a Negro mistress shooting her faithless white lover but the realities of penal policies that governed the lives of so many young black men already incarcerated and zoning efforts to protect local schools from being crowded by the houses of prostitution forced into black neighborhoods by white politicians.

Just as the urbanization of African American life at the end of the century made travel between country and city and among urban centers necessary and so made *Plessy v. Ferguson* inevitable, many other forces were at work at the end of the century to promote a decision like *Plessy* and to stimulate the spread of Jim Crow, while at the same time those same forces served to stimulate the emergence of a more realistic narrative style in African American writing. One was the emergence of an ultimately unsuccessful class-based movement of poor white and black farmers throughout the South in opposition to large landowners and unfair financial policies. Economic upheavals at national and local levels kept whites in urban areas of the South uneasy about having to compete with industrious blacks for jobs and customers, and so state legislatures sought ways of keeping blacks and whites apart, to protect the jobs of urban whites and prevent rural blacks and whites from easily finding common ground on which to meet. The fact that 90 percent of black Americans lived in rural settings hamstrung their abilities to organize in any numbers to resist statewide actions against them, and the resultant oppression in turn stimulated emigration to urban centers. Finally, the failure of Reconstruction policies to allow black Americans any indemnification or reparations from slavery meant that blacks could not accumulate a sufficient economic base to create a class identity that would or could transcend local issues.

While *Plessy* arose out of a complex of contradictory impulses centered on the changing economy and demographics of the South, its impact was not immediately obvious.[12] In the Wilmington, North Carolina, episode discussed in the previous chapter, for example, although the forces that drove that 1898 conflict were essentially those described just above, no reference was made by any of the participants of either the "factual" or "fictional" accounts of the "riot" to the *Plessy* case. Nevertheless, the years following *Plessy* were times of severe economic hardship and political powerlessness for African Americans. Literacy tests and poll taxes effectively disfranchised blacks. For example, black voter registration in Louisiana declined from 130,334 in 1896 to only 5,320 in 1900. Blacks who dared to object, and even many who did not, often fell victim to Ku Klux Klan or other racial terrorism. Indeed, at least thirty-five hundred lynchings of black people occurred between 1882 and 1925.[13] This terror, too, propelled some blacks to the relative safety of cities.

Even in cities, however, the day-to-day implications of Jim Crow laws and practices were inescapable. The nation seemed racked by race, often to the point of absurdity. There were segregated pet cemeteries, for example, and prohibitions against mixed domino games. In Atlanta in 1904 a brother and sister sued the local streetcar company because the conductor had made them move to the rear of the car with the challenge, "Haven't I seen you in colored company?" They won, and the court stated that "the wilful assertion or intimation embodied in the declaration now before us constitutes an actionable wrong. . . . It is a matter of common knowledge that, viewed from a social standpoint, the negro race is in mind and morals inferior to the Caucasian," and so the insulting assignment of race was an actionable affront.[14] On the other hand, in Asheville, North Carolina, in 1906, it was reported, without irony, that a black man was about to sue the city directory for not indicating in its listings that he was indeed a Negro. Although a white man had sued because his name had been marked with an asterisk, the traditional local method for designating a black person, the black gentleman wanted to sue for the absence of such a designation by his name. He feared that as a hotelier catering to blacks, he would lose customers if his trade thought him to be a white man. The commentator of the report wrote, "But save in such a case as above, it would be hard to imagine a circumstance in which a court would hold that it is injurious to a Negro in his trade, business, office, profession, or in his social relations to be called a white man" (Stephenson 33).[15]

These reports, from southern towns and cities, exist in court records and newspaper files. But by the 1900s, African American migration to northern cities had brought a different tone to African American narrative itself, although hints of what was to come had been audible a decade and more earlier. In 1902, Paul Laurence Dunbar straightforwardly decried the urbanization of black life:

To the provincial coming to New York for the first time, ignorant and unknown, the city presents a notable mingling of the qualities of cheeriness and gloom. If he have any eye at all for the beautiful, he cannot help experiencing a thrill as he crosses the ferry over the river filled with plying craft and catches the first sight of the spires and buildings of New York. If he have the right stuff in him, a something will take possession of him that will grip him again every time he returns to the scene and will make him long and hunger for the place when he is away from it. Later, the lights in the busy streets will bewilder and entice him. He will feel shy and help-less amid the hurrying crowds. A new emotion will take his heart as the people hasten by him,—a feeling of loneliness, almost of grief, that with all of those souls about him he knows not one and not one of them cares for him. After a while he will find a place and give a sigh of relief as he settles away from the city's sights behind his cosey blinds. It is better here, and the city is cruel and cold and unfeeling. This he will feel, perhaps, for the first half-hour, and then he will be out in it again. He will be glad to strike elbows with the bustling mob and be happy at their indifference to him, so that he may look at them and study them. After it is all over, after he has passed through the first pangs of strangeness and homesickness, yes, even after he has got beyond the stranger's enthusiasm for the metropolis, the real fever of love for the place will begin to take hold upon him. The subtle, insidious wine of New York will begin to intoxicate him. Then, if he be wise, he will go away, anyplace—yes, he will even go over to Jersey. But if he be a fool, he will stay and stay on until the town becomes all in all to him; until the very streets are his chums and certain buildings and corners his best friends. Then he is hopeless, and to live elsewhere would be death. The Bowery will be his romance, Broadway his lyric, and the Park his pastoral, the river and the glory of it all his epic, and he will look down pityingly on all the rest of humanity. (81–83)

Whom the Gods wish to destroy they first make mad. The first sign of the demoralisation of the provincial who comes to New York is his pride at his insensibility to certain impressions which used to influence him at home. First, he begins to scoff, and there is no truth in his views nor depth in his laugh. But by and by, from mere pretending, it becomes real. He becomes callous. After that he goes to the devil very cheerfully. (88)[16]

Nor was Dunbar's vision of the city unique. Ten years later, in *The Autobiography of an Ex-Coloured Man,* James Weldon Johnson reflected on New York:

> We steamed up into New York harbour late one afternoon in spring. The last efforts of the sun were being put forth in turning the waters of the bay to glistening gold; the green islands on either side, in spite of their warlike mountings, looked calm and peaceful; the buildings of the town shone out in a reflected light which gave the city an air of enchantment; and truly, it is an enchanted spot. New York City is the most fatally fascinating thing in America. She sits like a great witch at the gate of the country, showing her alluring white face and hiding her crooked hands and feet under the folds of her wide garments—constantly enticing thousands from far within, and tempting those who come from across the seas to go no farther. And all these become the victims of her caprice. Some she at once crushes beneath her cruel feet; others she condemns to a fate like that of galley-slaves; a few she favours and fondles, riding them high on the bubbles of fortune; then with a sudden breath she blows the bubbles out and laughs mockingly as she watches them fall. (441–42)

After one of his characters describes the criminal careers of several denizens of a low dive in Manhattan, Dunbar comments:

> There was not a lie in all that Sadness had said either as to their crime or their condition. He belonged to a peculiar class,—one that grows larger and larger each year in New York and which has imitators in every large city in this country. It is a set which lives, like the leech, upon the blood of others,—that draws its life from the veins of foolish men and immoral women, that prides itself upon its well-dressed idleness and has no shame in its voluntary pauperism. Each member of the class knows every other, his methods and his limitations, and their loyalty one to another makes of them a great hulking, fashionably uniformed fraternity of indolence. (150)

> Here is another example of the pernicious influence of the city on untrained negroes. Oh, is there no way to keep these people from rushing away from the small villages and country districts of

the South up to the cities, where they cannot battle with the terrible force of a strange and unusual environment? Is there no way to prove to them that woolen-shirted, brown-jeaned simplicity is infinitely better than broad-clothed degradation? . . . that the stream of young negro life would continue to flow up from the South, dashing itself against the hard necessities of the city, and breaking like waves against a rock,—that, until the gods grew tired of their cruel sport, there must still be sacrifices to false ideals and unreal ambitions. (212–13)

Dunbar even reached back to Mary Shelley's *Frankenstein* for an object lesson on the perils of the city. I suggested in chapter 2 some analogues between her romance and the condition of black Americans in the nineteenth century. Dunbar gives us yet another in his tale of urban dissipation. Joe, a young man up from the South, is "enslaved" by liquor. The themes of liquor and oppression had been linked in black narrative in the nineteenth century by the shared advocacies of abolition and temperance on the part of white and black northerners. The hundreds of pieces of short fiction written by blacks in abolitionist papers were divided between moral tales of flight from the South and moral tales of flight from alcohol, both seen as the sites of black enslavement.

Dunbar evokes the horror of drink in the chapter he devotes to Joe's murder of Hattie, his "girl." The chapter is entitled simply, "Frankenstein." In the murder scene, Joe comes to Hattie's apartment in a drunken rage, and stalks into her bedroom, his hands held out before him, twitching and involuntarily grasping:

> "You put me out—you—you, and you made me what I am." The realisation of what he was, of his foulness and degradation, seemed just to have come to him fully. "You made me what I am, and then you sent me away. You let me come back, and now you put me out."
>
> She gazed at him fascinated. She tried to scream and she could not. This was not Joe. This was not the boy that she had turned and twisted about her little finger. This was a terrible, terrible man or a monster.
>
> He moved a step nearer her. His eyes fell to her throat. For an instant she lost their steady glare and then she found her voice. The scream was checked as it began. His fingers had closed over

her throat just where the gown had left it temptingly bare. They gave it the caress of death. She struggled. They held her. Her eyes prayed to his. But his were the fire of hell. She fell back upon her pillow in silence. He had not uttered a word. He held her. Finally he flung her from him like a rag and sank into a chair. (208–9)[17]

This episode, and the closing episode of the novel, discussed briefly in the previous chapter, give to this transitional period of African American narrative a gothic tone, a hint of decayed romance. It is possible to sense some of the same tone in Chesnutt's *The Marrow of Tradition* and *The House Behind the Cedars*, as well as in Pauline Hopkins's *Of One Blood.* In these novels the gothic secret, miscegenation, incest, murder, madness, coexists with complex social relationships of race and class depicted, for the most part, realistically. The gothic tone continued in African American fiction well into the century, as can be seen in Oscar Micheaux's 1925 film, *Body and Soul,* starring Paul Robeson,[18] and Rudolph Fisher's 1932 novel, *The Conjure Man Dies,* considered the first African American detective novel.[19] As late as 1936, George Schuyler's serialized novel, *Black Empire,* reads like a mixture of Poe and H. G. Wells.[20]

The process of urbanization had not always been seen as destructive to black character. Frederick Douglass's life apotheosized the understood effect of escape to the urban North. The move to the city in Douglass's case is the opposite of the traditional literary trope of the loss of rural innocence to urban vice; for Douglass the only loss was of isolation and the profit was a new world of urban alternatives and self-knowledge; not loss of soul but the capture of self and of the possibilities of freedom.

One could even anticipate prosperity in the city, although riches were relative to some alternative fate. Two late-nineteenth-century African American narratives of urban life exemplify the relative perception of status, legal and economic, that was possible in the North. The first of these, *Appointed,* is a pseudonymous novel published in Detroit in 1894. Its authors, writing under the name Sanda, were Walter H. Stowers and W. H. Anderson, Detroit newspapermen.[21]

Appointed is an awkward novel, but it is too often neglected in discussions that center on Pauline Hopkins and Frances Harper. Stowers and Anderson, like Harper and Hopkins, have written a novel in which who marries whom is very important, yet, like Harper and Hopkins, they have written a purposefully political novel. In it, Detroit is a paradise of the northwest, and its heroic protagonists, John Saunders and Seth Stanley, are paragons in search of the right and/or opportunity to marry the female paragons set up for them.[22]

The novel, which is full of Christian didacticism, tells the story of John Saunders, a black civil engineering graduate of the University of Michigan, and his friendship with Seth Stanley, the white scion of a wealthy Detroit family. Stanley's task is to grow into fitness as a man, and his model is John Saunders, who works as a menial for his father's business. As their friendship grows, so does Seth, morally and intellectually, and the gauge of that growth is his ability to comprehend the depth of America's race problem. The price of his education, however, is John's life, in a lynching during a "fact-finding" trip they both take to the South.

Discussion of *Appointed* could easily be fit in previous chapters, since its use of the black "other" against whom a white hero defines himself and its sentimental plot focusing on marriage are versions of issues raised in relationship to the impact of law and romantic attitudes on African American narrative at the end of the nineteenth century. In fact, the first half of the book is almost a textbook exercise in writing a "white" novel of sentiment; John Saunders makes only a token appearance in the first 175 pages of the novel, most of the space being taken up by the preliminary education of Seth and his beloved Marjorie in the subjugation of passion and desire. It is in book 2 that we discover John and his fiancée, Edith, as models of that restraint. At story's end, with John's death, Seth's loss earns him Marjorie's vows, while Edith is left to rechannel her desire into efforts to advance the race. Whites enjoy the familial rewards of moral earnestness, while the black characters struggle further with programs for elevation and uplift.

Nevertheless, *Appointed* stands as one of the earliest of the urban black novels because of its vision of the urban North as a site of freedom and equality in contradistinction to the rural and oppressive South. For example, even though it follows *Appointed* by eleven years, Chesnutt's *Colonel's Dream* is clearly still rooted in the agrarian past. When the colonel fails in his attempt to reform his ancestral hometown because he cannot counter the force of economic oppression based on law, he retreats to the North and leaves the South to grind out its own agrarian destiny on the backs of its black population. Throughout their story, however, Stowers and Anderson hold to the argument that emigration to the North is the surest route to equality and freedom. Even when Seth, like the colonel, tries to apply the economic leverage of his northern wealth to the conditions of the South, his point is clear: change or he will take his business elsewhere. The immediate refusal of the whites with whom he is dealing to consider abandoning the advantages of a contract/shares economy driven by vagrancy laws, and Seth's disinclination to bother further with them, are indicators of the authors' attitude toward the South. The final piece of evidence is John's death at the hands of a white mob for being an educated northern "nigger."[23]

The novel ends, as I have noted, with Edith Darrow's desire for husband, family, love reconstituted into determination to educate the next generation of African Americans. Meanwhile, Seth and his bride convince Seth's father to open even more opportunities for blacks in his many business enterprises in the North, and Detroit is seen as a city blessed with an enlightened white patriarchy and a solid black middle class.

Another version of urban life at the end of the century is presented in James David Corrothers's *Black Cat Club*. Although its publication date is the same as that of Dunbar's *Sport of the Gods* (1902), its basic material comes from columns written in the *Chicago Tribune* a decade earlier. The urban life of African Americans as Corrothers described it is quite a different existence than the refined sorrow and Christian forbearance depicted in *Appointed*. Corrothers's characters inhabit a satirical underworld of lowlife, razors, and indelible flights of linguistic play and fancy.

Sandy (Doc) Jenkins presides over the Black Cat Club, a "literary" group the motto of which is "Death to eavesdroppers, policemen, and reporters" (19). The club is literary because its sole purpose is to meet, drink, and engage in competitive storytelling; Jenkins keeps a black cat with which to "hoo-doo" his literary rivals in these contests. The members are bound by two articles of faith: they do not believe in women's rights, and none is allowed to marry. What little narrative tension there is in the frame story of the club lies in the epistolary love story between Sandy Jenkins and a young admirer Corrothers lays over the collected columns to give some shape to his book; will he marry and thus bring an end to the Black Cat Club?

The stories collected by Corrothers and the characters he creates to tell them represent a complex tradition of urban and rural, ante- and postbellum African American folk narrative (8). Among the tale-tellers are Bad Bob Thompson, a former policeman "dishonorably discharged from 'the force' for his association with levee highwaymen," Professor

Lightfoot Johnsing, the con man, and Saskatchewan Jones, a man "possessed of a consuming desire to mutilate human countenances with his razor" (29). Other members were sinners, ex-slaves, layabouts, and former preachers.

In his study of black folk culture, Lawrence Levine argues that black folklore has no noble bad men, no Robin Hoods who stole from the rich to give to the poor:

> [B]lack bandits . . . were never pictured as either innocent or good. . . . The brutality of Negro bad men was allowed to speak for itself without attenuation. Their badness was described without the excuse of socially redeeming qualities. . . . They killed not merely in self-defense but from sadistic need and sheer joy. (417–18)

The urban folk character of the 1890s, Stagolee, is one of these bad men:

> Stagolee, he went a-walkin' with his .40 gun in his hand;
> He said, "I feel mistreated this mornin', I could kill most any
>   man."
>
> (Levine 414 n. 26)

Certainly urban black narrative at the turn of the century had to express that demonic presence; it did so, however, in narratives that were contained within the community. The stories told by the members of the Black Cat Club were cleaned-up versions of the legends of Stagolee and his avatars, suitable for sale to the white community through Corrothers's newspaper columns and his book:

> Jim Johnson lubbed a yallah girl
> Until his brain began to whirl;
> But Sambo Brown he lubbed huh, too,
> An' out o' dat a quarrel grew.
> So Jimmy Johnson comes to town
> A-purpose to cahve Sambo Brown.
> Along about de hour ob noon,
> He fines him down in Smiff's saloon;
> 'Fo' Sambo knowed whut he wuz 'bout,
> Jim Johnson drawed him razah out
> An' cut him all around de face—
> All up de back, an' evah place!,

He cut him low, he cut him high—
Cleah f'om his ankle to his eye—
He clipped bofe ears off f'om Sam's head—
It was a sin how po' Sam bled!

(Corrothers 23–24)

Sambo Brown gets his own carves in, nevertheless, and at the end of the epic struggle, their pieces are swept out of the room.

However cleaned-up the stories are, there is little gentility evident in them, in contrast to that found in *Appointed* and other novels of the Talented Tenth. No college men are allowed in the society of the cat, and college education itself is always demeaned and mocked by the members whose own skills, developed outside the law, seemed more relevant to urban life. Chapter 4, for example, is devoted to a satirical "take" on the Du Bois–Washington controversy over education versus training:

De cullud graddiate is ag'in' Bookah T. Washin'ton. But I tell you dat man's doin' a heap mo' good in de Souf den all de graddiates whut's a-slanderin' uv 'im an' writin' resolutions. . . . We ain't got much book l'arnin', but we has lit'a'ly cahved ouh way to fame an' fortune. (59–60).

Issues of class and race coincide with matters of law and property in the story:

"You kin allus tell 'at feller when you sees 'm. He's dressed lak a *genamun!*. He looks 'po'tant, an' he's allus hol'in indignation meetin's an' resolutin' 'gin' de lynchin'. An evah time he resolutes, dey's ten mo' niggahs killed. But de eddicated shade is a-makin' a repertation outen it, an' putty soon he'll be wantin' to run foh Congress, an' boss his white imployah. Dat feller is a fool, an' ef 'twusn't foh *him* de cullud race 'ud hab mo' peace ob' mine. It don't do no good foh to 'buse de Southern white folks; an' to tell 'em whut God's gin' to do to 'em ef dey don't stop lynchin' de niggahs. Dat only makes 'em mad. De thaing foh to do is to be a *genamun* an' git yo' pocket full o' check books, fust mo'gages an' cash.

"Now, s'posen dey was a lynchin' 'bout to take place, an de curly-headed brunette whut was to be de pahty acted upon hel' a fust mo'gage on de home uv evah man in de lynchin' pahty. An'

s'posen mose o' dem mo'gages wuz 'bout due er ovah due; an'
s'pozen jes' 'fo' dey lit de fiah er strung 'im up, de cullud man wuz
to say: 'Genamuns, ef you lynches *me*, ma *son*'ll fo'close all ma
mo'gages t'morrer! *Dis am ma ultimatum!*' Do you think dey would
have any lynchin'-bee 'at day? No sah! Now, whut could de college dahkey do?—Nothin' but say his prayers. All de big wo'ds in
de dictionary couldn't save 'im!" *(Thunderous applause by the club)*.
(57–58)

Corrothers's stories generally value experience over theory and
the flesh over the soul; topics range from the "best good thing I ever
did" and "good things to eat" to a tale of city con and country bumpkin
and an episode in which a great debate over common sense and
courage leads to a razor fight. With the exception of one or two visits to
local churches and a trip to Terre Haute, Indiana, to meet up with Sibyll
Underwood, Sandy's bride-in-waiting, the club convenes in the lowest
dives, white and black, in Chicago. Vast amounts of alcohol and food
are consumed, great brags are made, and urban life among the working
poor is given a richness and complexity missing from the Edenic
Detroit of *Appointed*.

The ironic consciousness of such a community is summed up by
the distinction made between local and national politics. The members
of the Black Cat Club are, like most black citizens of the day, true to the
Republican Party in national elections, but locally they always vote the
Democratic ticket, " 'c'ase dey'll let evahthaing run wide open, an' po'
cullud folks gits a chance to earn a dollah to buy po'k chops wid"
(110).24

"Let de Dimocrats git in, an dey opens up evahthaing, an' hun-
duds o' 'spectable cullud people kin git hones' wo'k to do, as po'-
tahs, cooks, an' waiters, in de gamblin' houses an' saloons. An' den
dey can provide fer dey famblies, an' donate money to de chu'ch.
An' nobody don' hab to gamble lessun he *want* to. De gamblahs
don' stan' outside wid hog hooks, pullin' people in! Now, let de
'Publicans git control uv de city gov'ament, an' thaings shets down
tighter'n a retired glue factory. An' dahkies has to lib on livah an'
co'n meal—an' don' git a drink o' liquor once a mon't!" *("Cries of:
Ain't it so?")* "Jes' let de 'Publicans git in an' stop gamblin', an'
whut does de gambler do?—Gits 'im a san'bag an' goes to hol'in'
up Christ'uns! Dat's whut he does! Dat chap won't wo'k—hit's

'gi'nst his principles. He'll resk his life to git a dollah druther'n to wo'k. An' when he gits it, he'll spen' it lak a prince, while a hones' man'll go to law wid you about a penny. But comin' down to natchul facks, I hates a Dimocrat wo'se'n I hates a snake!" (*Cries of "Dat's right, too!"*) "I'm a *'Publican!* 'Publican bred an' 'Publican bo'n!—'Publican clean th'u'—'speck to lib an' die a 'Publican! Ma father wuz a 'Publican! Ma mammy wuz a 'Publican! Didn't de 'Publicans free us, an' gib us our vote? An' whut have de Dimocrats done? Nothin' but beat our fo'-parents, lynch our people, an' teach dey chillun to holler *'nigger!'* " (110–11)

Corrothers's Chicago, in which police are on the take, story lines are resolved by razor strokes, men live by their wits if they have them, and women are distant and mysterious beings if they are "good" and mere objects if they are bad, is not unlike Dunbar's, Johnson's, and much later, Claude McKay's New York. Jacob Riis's account of black life in New York City, contained in his study of urban poverty, *How the Other Half Lives* (1890), notes that left to "himself," the Negro in New York "is [in personal habits] immensely superior to the lowest of the whites, the Italians and Polish Jews, below whom he has been classed in the past in the tenant scale" (150), but at the intersection of black and immigrant lives, at the "border-land where the black and white races meet in common debauch," all that is sacred is abandoned and of "this commingling of the utterly depraved of both sexes, black and white, there can be no greater abomination" (156). In all of these cities, fictional and "real," the law circumscribes the black community, walling it off from a presumably less anarchic "native" white urban existence. And in all of these urban sites, black Americans' stories are circumscribed by the same question of law that drove black narrative for the previous three generations, the question of legal status, local and national.

However, the urbanization of African American life did not isolate the fictional urban black man and woman from their rural families, friends, or pasts. The rural South is ever present in the minds and hearts of urban characters, but as a site of oppression and death as well as the homeland from which they are in exile. In *Appointed*, John Saunders ventures south with his white friend only to die at the hands of a white mob; in *Sport of the Gods*, Berry Hamilton languishes in a southern prison while Fannie takes their children north to New York in search of work; in Dunbar's short story "One Man's Fortunes" (*Gideon*

131–61), the South is the only place an educated black man, in this case a man trying to practice law, can get a job; and in Otis Shackelford's *Lillian Simmons* the southern Negro's mistrust of whites and belief in a separate world of Negro life is the norm against which the protagonist measures the dangers of life in the North.[25]

An urban black world somewhat more realistic and less fancied as well as less anarchic, and more ironic, at the turn of the century can be found in the collected shorter pieces of Jack Thorne.[26] Thorne was a native of Fayetteville, North Carolina, lived as a young man in Wilmington, and left there for a life as a Pullman porter and then, in New York, as an employee of the YMCA, a music company, and Sears, Roebuck. Informed by his own experience and through his contacts in Wilmington, he wrote his novelistic treatment of the 1898 "riot," *Hanover; or the Prosecution of the Lowly* (1900). In it he creates a context for the coup that is far less sentimental than Charles W. Chesnutt's *(Marrow)* and far more naturalistic, even documentary, than any fiction by his contemporaries.[27]

But the bulk of Thorne's urban writing was done in New York, published as *Eagle Clippings* because many of the short pieces in which he depicted the intersections of law and life as black Americans were experiencing them were first published in the *Brooklyn Eagle.* One of the more sensational episodes on which he reported was the case of Hannah Elias. The Elias case can be read as a previously unknown narrative of African American life intersecting the law.

Apparently, Mrs. Elias, a "Negro" woman, had somehow got from Mr. John R. Platt, a wealthy white man, the sum of $685,000 over a period of time. In his declining years, Platt sought to recover the money, claiming he was blackmailed. Mrs. Elias denied the charge.[28] Thorne's attention to these intersections was more often than not ironic, and this case delighted him. While noting that Platt met Mrs. Elias, then about sixteen years old, in an establishment in the Tenderloin section of Manhattan, he pointed out that over a period of time she plied her trade with such skill that Platt was cured of rheumatism and lived to be quite an old man. Thorne pointed out as well that specialists are usually highly paid for their services in the medical field, and it seemed obvious to the observer that Platt "returned frequently for treatment lest the malady return," causing Thorne to ask, "Is not such a man an ingrate who would seek to beat a poor woman out of the paltry sum of $685,000, which she had earned by performing such a miraculous cure?" Finally Thorne reminded his readers that there were many among them in the city worth tens of millions who had stolen from the poor yet were not being served papers. "Are there howling mobs standing night and day about their premises? For Christian shame! Now Mrs. Elias, who is a wealthy taxpayer, is entitled to police protection, and should have it" ("Hannah Elias" 26).

Thorne's mockingly ironic tone is not overdone, in light of the apparent facts of the case. Crowds of people were indeed outside Mrs. Elias's house at 236 Central Park West in the summer of 1904. Many wanted a glimpse of the charming octaroon who had garnered nearly seven hundred thousand dollars from an elderly lover. Others were waiting to see the police come to arrest her for extortion. Platt had charged in a civil suit that Elias had extorted sums of money from him, and pressure had been brought on the district attorney to consider criminal charges. In early June Elias was arrested after police forced their way past Kato, her Japanese houseboy, and she was held for trial on "Coon Row" in New York's infamous "Tombs." By the time of her arrest, tour buses with megaphoned guides were making hourly stops at the house.

In court, however, the state's case proved nonexistent, and Elias was freed when Platt refused to testify against her. The civil trial went the same way, particularly after Platt testified that his family had forced him to bring suit against Elias and he had nothing to hold against her. It was a sad case and in many ways striking for the apparent evenhandedness of the treatment afforded Elias. The relationship between her and Platt had only come to light because a deranged man had shot a visitor to 234 Central Park West, thinking the victim was Platt. The police's inquiries into the shooting had revealed to Platt's family the twenty-year relationship with Elias, and his adult children had insisted that he recover the money they stood to inherit.

As a bittersweet love story, the Elias-Platt episode has all the trappings of melodrama. In addition to the deranged shooter and the accidental discovery of the affair were the May-December difference in their ages, race (although Mrs. Elias maintained that she had always lived among whites and scarcely knew any Negroes), an arranged divorce paid for by Platt, real estate investments, prostitution and the Tenderloin, an infant child of the liaison prematurely dead, even visiting firemen from San Francisco out on the town. The story itself was carried on the front pages of the *New York Times* from June 1904 through May 1905. The *Times* even saw fit to editorialize on the occasion of Mrs. Elias's acquittal that the Negroes of the city had insulted the whites of the town by rallying to her defense as though they thought she might not get a fair trial.[29]

Thorne's New York provided him with quite a storehouse of material. By far the most striking of his published pieces suggests Thorne's familiarity with the practices of the contemporary criminal-justice system and with criminological theory. The article, originally published in the *Voice of the Negro* sometime in 1905–6, is an attack on the white racist writer Thomas Dixon Jr. Thorne was responding to Dixon's defense of the Ku Klux Klan, that such noble-looking men as the white aristocrats who both founded and supported the Klan could not be evil while the "bestial looking" Negro of the "lowest type" clearly waited and lusted to prey on white women. Here is Thorne's opening to his attack on Dixon:

> The most interesting and fascinating report of murder trials nowadays is that of the alienist who is generally the prosecuting attorney's most valuable adjunct when circumstantial evidence is the main channel by which conviction is hoped to be secured. While the average newspaper reporter follows closely the proceedings of a trial, notes the evidence of the witnesses, the quarrels of lawyers in their efforts to convict or acquit, the alienist sits by and attempts to open up to the world's gaze the soul of the accused. Every lineament of the features comes under the scrutinizing gaze of the alienist; the eyes, the forehead, the mouth, the chin, the ears, the hands—all of these members are closely studied by this wonderful reader of character and generally arrayed on the side of conviction. For the alienist will show that these carefully studied lineaments evidence weakness—the murder mania, that the crime for which the prisoner stands charged was inevitable. But what a saving it would be for the State and society if such devils could be singled out and incarcerated before they do incalculable harm. (Thorne, "Alienist" 33–34)

Thorne goes on to argue that this is pretty shaky business, yet Dixon wants Americans to accept the patriotism of the Klan on the evidence of the width of its founders' brows. Thorne was evidently widely read and used his access to the *Eagle* and other papers to expose legal and social injustice as well as cant and white hypocrisy. Among issues raised in *Eagle Clippings* are the burning of a black newspaper in Memphis, the Wilmington riot, racist legislation in Virginia, the slave trade and its forty million fatalities, miscegenation laws, white judges with mulatto mistresses, lynchings in 1898 in Palmetto, Georgia, the New Orleans race riot of 1899, the 1904 Statesboro, Georgia, lynchings, and the murder of a black postmaster and his child in South Carolina.

The piece Thorne never published suggests that Dreiser was not the only novelist at the time thinking about crime and naturalism. A planned novel, "A Twentieth Century Episode," was to be the story of Maggie Tiller, a schoolmate of Thorne in Wilmington. As a teenager, Tiller traveled North with Sam T. Jack's Creole Company of actors and singers in the 1890s. Sometime after the turn of the century, Tiller was sentenced to death, for murder, in Chicago. Thorne planned the novel as based on his interview with her in Chicago while he was on a Pullman layover. She had changed from the innocent girl he had known "to a heartless wanton, boastful of her shady career." How she had become such a person was to have been Thorne's big story.[30]

The period 1910–26 is a period of essentially lost African American writers, like Jack Thorne a decade earlier, caught up in the transition from rural to urban, romanticism to realism. The northward migration of black Americans continued, accelerating with the coming of the war in Europe and stimulated by the unceasing hostility of white southerners to black self-determination. One black novelist noted,

> The Negro, long silent through necessity under the regime of lynching, disenfranchisement, court injustice, economic exploitation, inadequate school facilities, and other dehumanizing manifestations of race prejudice in the South, eagerly and promptly took advantage of [the war] and swept towards the North and greater justice, freedom, and opportunity. (Walter White, letter to Henry Goddard Leach, September 27, 1924, NAACP Papers, reel 8)

Increasingly the Negro came not just to New York but to Harlem, but the impact on the new arrival was not so different from that of a decade earlier. Writing in the mid-1920s, Rudolph Fisher recorded the shock of the new, the modernity of the place, in his short stories:

> The railroad station, the long, white-walled corridor, the impassable slot-machine, the terrifying subway train—he felt as if he had been caught in the jaws of a steam-shovel, jammed together with other helpless lumps of dirt, swept blindly along for a time, and at last abruptly dumped. ("City of Refuge" 3)

It was Harlem that had changed Jutie—this great, noisy, heart-less, crowded place where you lived under the same roof with a hundred people you never knew; where night was alive and morning dead. It was Harlem—those brazen women with whom Jutie sewed, who swore and shimmied and laughed at the suggestion of going to church. ("South Lingers" 36)

For Fisher, the city was a frontier between civilization and wilderness, one requiring the ameliorating hand of tradition to make it liberating or enlightening. When tradition was missing, as in the truly dispiriting story "Fire by Night," urban energy is simply violence. Or it is betrayal, as in "City of Refuge" from 1925. King Solomon Gillis arrives in Harlem fresh from the South, where he had shot a white man and escaped a lynching. Gillis is a country boy, a naïf, not a "bad man." He is bowled over by the reversal of authority he finds in Harlem: a "cullud policeman." To Gillis it was proof that "[i]n Harlem, black was white. You had rights that could not be denied you; you had privileges, protected by law" (4). In fact, the vision awakes in him an ironic ambition to be a policeman, "so I kin police all the white folks right plumb in jail" (9).

But the role of law is not what Gillis thinks it is. Things are reversed in Harlem for sure, but not just as he supposes. The real switch is that your enemies are not the southern crackers who drove you out of town but your own kind. Black folks prey on black folks in Harlem, and the role of the police is simply to "police" the secondary economy that drives the ghetto: drugs, liquor, theft, prostitution. Gillis falls into the economy and falls prey to the invisible structures of greed and betrayal that shape it. Confronted at the end of the story by white detectives, Gillis fights their color, as though he were down South, not just their authority. As he fights he reprises memories of legal and economic injustice and realizes how ironic it was to hope that Harlem would be a city of refuge. But when a uniformed black policeman arrives, Gillis drops his arms and recalls that this is, after all, not the South. He grins and surrenders, as Fisher suggests, exultantly.[31]

Aside from James Weldon Johnson's *Autobiography of an Ex-Coloured Man* and, perhaps, Walter White's *Fire in the Flint* (1924), names and titles from the period between Chesnutt's new realism and the Negro or Harlem Renaissance are scarcely recognizable, even to most scholars. Yet these books were written and read, and like their nineteenth-century counterparts in the classical African American narrative tradition, most of them had agendas of law and legal status at their centers: (1) to prevent race prejudice and its illegal intrusion into the lives of black people by exposing it more fully; (2) to represent the educational, social, economic, and legal progress of the Negro; and (3) to suggest ways black Americans could contend for their rights (G. E. Walker).[32] Those narratives and their successors, produced between 1925 and 1940, unlike the earlier classical texts, had far less to do with the Constitution and the effort to secure the blessings of liberty and much more to do with surviving the legal and extralegal violence of life as an African American living Jim Crow, as is given voice in this excerpt from a 1926 letter that opened with a reference to the hung jury outcome of the first Sweet case trial in Detroit[33] and moved on to reflections on the law:

> It is written in the Constitution that a Negro is a citizen and equal before the law; there is lip acknowledgment too, that the Negro is a man and brother. But in practice this is a white man's country. the Negro is a "nigger," who must keep his place; and niggers are socially unknown. The constitutional dictum and the legislative decrees for enforcement do not correspond with fact; that is all. "Law," grows out common customs and usages, and the tacit understandings in the minds of people concerning customs and usages. A "Law" is a fact, it exists by and of itself, and because of the essential ingredients of which it is composed—a fact is a thing existent, a legislative body may recognize it, but it is impossible a legislature should declare it. . . .
>
> The negro has a hard, long and wearying road to travel in this country, but there is no escape. The white man is in the saddle, fully determined to forcibly maintain his supremacy and perpetuate his dominion. It is for the Negro to endure injustice and remain patient. (A. W. Wright, letter to "Lewis," January 3, 1926, NAACP Papers, reel 9)

Cases such as those of Pink Franklin in South Carolina, Steve Greene in Arkansas, and Thomas Williams in New Jersey (1910), *Guinn v. U.S.* (1915), *Buchanan v. Warley* (1917), the 1917 Brownsville Massacre case, *Moore v. Dempsey* (1923), the Sweet case in Chicago (1925), *Corrigan v. Bulkley* (1926), and *Nixon v. Herndon* and *Harmon v. Taylor* (1927), all handled to one degree or another by the NAACP or lawyers it had hired, were well known in black communities around the country

(Goings 9–17). Black newspapers and NAACP chapters as well as women's clubs and fraternal organizations were media through which legal resistance to race baiting and Jim Crow were publicized. These "factual" narratives of black life were as available in the black community as were the latest song sheets, "Victrola" records, and movies.[34]

This makes more understandable the single most pervasive fact of black narrative literature of the period; that is, it is without exception premised on the existence of laws that circumscribe black existence, so that the stories to be told are stories of lives lived in response to those laws, to that circumscription. The second most pervasive fact about this literature is that it is about the legal sanction for violence afforded whites in the climate created by the existence of Jim Crow laws and the cases that validated them. From these premises come two dominant types of narrative at the end of the classical period: (1) the narrative of white violence as an expression of Jim Crow and its obligations, on whites and black people; (2) the narrative of segregated black life. Of these the first to consider is the lynching narrative.

CHAPTER 6

Lynchings and Passing

Hair—braided chestnut,
    coiled like a lyncher's rope,
Eyes—fagots,
Lips—old scars, or the first red blisters,
Breath—the last sweet scent of cane,
And her slim body, white as the ash
    of black flesh after flame.

> Jean Toomer, "Portrait in Georgia," from *Cane*

Walter White's *Fire in the Flint*[1] was published in 1924, six years after he arrived in New York from Atlanta to be James Weldon Johnson's assistant at the national headquarters of the NAACP, and two years before the publication of Alain Locke's *New Negro*, the public launching of what has come to be called the Harlem Renaissance. In 1912 the Association had published *Notes on Lynching in the United States* and had followed it in 1919 with *Thirty Years of Lynching in the United States, 1889–1919*.[2] In 1918 it gave its support to the federal antilynching bill proposed by Leonidas Dyer (R-Mo.).[3] Roughly, between 1889 and 1926 thirty-two hundred black Americans were lynched, and lynching as a form of American "justice" was known around the world.[4]

Flint is a novel of the political awakening and subsequent death by lynching of a young black doctor. White modeled the character after a friend of his, a Harvard graduate who had tried to establish a practice in Georgia, had failed, and gone to New York where he was successful (White, letter to Eugene Saxton, August 23, 1923, NAACP Papers, reel 7). When White's protagonist, Kenneth Harper, returns to his hometown in Georgia to establish a practice after years in the North and service in the world war, he exemplifies the Washingtonian approach to the problem of the color line. Jim Crow life was "unfortunate, mighty unpleasant and uncomfortable at times. . . . Lynching, too, was bad. But only bad Negroes got lynched. And, after all, those things weren't all of life" (17). His plan is to cast his diploma down in his old home town, prosper, and gain the respect of all the good people, black and white.

By the end of the novel, and of his life, after the death of his brother and the rape of his sister, Harper is a model of Du Boisean activism.

White's plot is strongly influenced by Chesnutt's *Marrow of Tradition* in its last half, and the book draws on Chesnutt's *Colonel's Dream* for its economic analysis of racial injustice. But perhaps as strong an influence as either of these was White's own experience growing up in Georgia and as a field investigator of lynchings throughout the South and Midwest (letter to Claude McKay, August 15, 1924, letter to Eugene Saxton, August 19, 1923, NAACP Papers, reel 7).[5] Because White was fair-haired, blue-eyed, and light-complexioned, he was able to travel south to sites of reported lynchings, strike up conversations with local whites, and attend meetings where Klan activities were discussed.[6] White's exploits were known in the black community, especially among his colleagues at the NAACP.

Even as *Fire in the Flint* was at the printers, *There Is Confusion* was published. Written by Jessie Fauset, literary editor of the NAACP's magazine, *Crisis*, from 1919 to 1926, it presented the character Vera Manning, modeled on White, as a black woman already passing for white who decides to go south as a reporter and expose KKK complicity in the wave of lynchings that followed the First World War and the return of Negro veterans. Manning expresses a genteel version of the ultimate horror Harper finds when Fauset has her say that "those white bullies, thinking I was one of *them*, told me the most bloodcurdling, fiendish tales. I really got an investigation started. Mr. Kirchner has taken it up. Oh, Joanna, I'm glad I'm colored—there's something terrible, terrible about white people" (270). Fauset's novel of coming of age amid the black bourgeoisie of the early twentieth century includes the inescapable reality of lynchings in the South, but lynching itself is not at the center of her attention.

White claimed that he wrote the original draft of *Flint* in twelve days, then spent considerable time revising it.[7] Apparently driven by what he had seen firsthand, and challenged to make it somehow more visible to the American public, he wrote with considerable ardor. But he was not without some sense of the necessity to control the subjective nature of his responses to what he had seen. From the first, he claimed,

> I tried, with the same scientific objectivity of the chemist in the laboratory, to place Kenneth Harper with certain ideas and ideals in the midst of a definite environment and then to present as fairly as I could his reactions to the environment and the environment's

reaction towards him, letting the story work itself out along those lines.

There are some people who say that in writing about the Negro, one should leave out the racial and interracial conflict. I most passionately do not believe in that school of thought. If one is going to write realistically about the Negro or Negro characters, he cannot leave out this phase of the Negro's life in America[,] for no Negro, intelligent or non-intelligent, illiterate or educated, rich or poor, ever passes a day but that, directly or indirectly, this thing called the race problem creeps into his life. (White, letter to Edgar H. Webster, April 14, 1925, NAACP Papers, reel 8; letter to Claude McKay, August 15, 1924, NAACP Papers, reel 7)[8]

One of his revisions underlines how substantially the novel is grounded in considerations of law. Responding to suggestions that he not demonize whites in the narrative, White created a white judge with enlightened attitudes toward race to whom Harper would go to sound out the legal implications of the problems the black community was facing. The character, Judge Stevenson, was, White wrote, developed "to the point where I almost idealized him—made him, in fact, a higher type than an environment like Central City would produce." Even so, the legal position that Stevenson could sketch out for Harper was anything but hopeful, based as it was on his decades of observation of party politics, the economics of sharecropping and contract labor, and the class divisions that set poor whites against all blacks (*Flint* 150–65). White described how he constructed one conversation between Stevenson and Harper out of his own experience: "[I]t is almost verbatim one I had two or three years ago with E. L. Wharton, Vice-President of the Greensboro National bank at Greensboro, N.C., and, mind you, Greensboro is infinitely more liberal than Central City" (White to Saxton, August 23, 1923). White's transformation of the banker to a judge not only reinforces the legal context in which he sought to cast the problems of his protagonists but reinforces the intertextual relationship between property and law in the lives of black Americans that had been established in the previous century.

His re-creation of his southern observations, his evocation of the "race problem," and his descriptions of lynchings in the novel eventually put him at odds with his first publisher, Doran. Doran wanted White to tone down his depiction of white racism and duplicity, as well as his representations of the grosser physical aspects of lynching. Actually, the depiction of virulent white racism and White's implication of most southern whites in a concerted program of intimidation through legal and illegal attacks on black self-sufficiency bothered Doran more than the violence. After attempts to negotiate satisfactory revisions with White failed, Doran withdrew from its agreement to publish the novel (Saxton to White, August 16 and October 8, 1923, NAACP Papers, reel 7).[9]

At one point in his discussions with Doran, White wrote the following in a letter to Eugene Saxton at the firm:

> You state in your letter that my "documentation is exclusively on one side of the case. . . . [T]here is nobody in court but the attorney for the prosecution." Granting this for the sake of argument, is it not about time that the prosecution should be heard? For fifty years or more the argument has been all on one side, i.e., for the defense. Thomas Nelson Page, George W. Cable, Thomas Dixon, Hugh Wiley, Octavus Roy Cohen, T. S. Stribling, H. S. Shands, Irvin Cobb—all have painted the Negro as a vicious brute, a rapist, a "good old nigger," or as a happy-go-lucky, irresponsible and shiftless type. . . . But that point is minor when compared with the larger question of what will be the ultimate effect on white America and civilisation by perpetuation of the system of which the Negro is the victim in America. (August 19, 1923)

Appealing to his sometime mentor H. L. Mencken, White got an introduction to the Knopfs, Alfred and Blanche, and eventually placed the novel with them.[10] The publication of the book brought fundamentally approving reviews and many letters of approval personally to White, as well as the kinds of responses Doran perhaps anticipated. White's response to criticism of his portrayals of white violence toward blacks was always straightforward, as in this excerpt:

> My dear Mr. Frissel, I could furnish you with hundreds, even thousands, of cases far more terrible than anything that is pictured in my novel. . . . Only yesterday I received a letter from Wrens, Georgia, of a colored woman, the mother of eight children and a widow, who was beaten by a white employer, her daughter kicked in the stomach, and beaten because the mother refused to allow the white man to send her boy to a logging camp. The employer went away, returned with a shotgun and shot two of her daughters and

the mother. The woman is appealing to us [the NAACP] for help saying that she cannot even have the man arrested. . . . It is true that lynchings are decreasing but the only reason they are decreasing is not because of any growing love for the Negro on the part of the whites but because Negroes have migrated from the South, leaving fewer Negroes there to be lynched and hurting the South economically, and because organizations like the N. A. A. C. P. have dared to expose, perhaps in untimely fashion and manner, the barbarisms which are taking place every day. (Walter White, letter to A. S. Frissel, September 20, 1924, NAACP Papers, reel 8)[11]

In his novel, White sought to expose both the legal constraints on southern Negroes and the economic as well as social bases of lynching. From the beginning White provides Harper with opportunities to understand how the legal system underwrites oppression for his people. From the economic oppression of the country sharecroppers to the bootlegging and sex industries of the city, the legal and illegal economies of Jim Crow endanger black men and women. The Klan may move at will to intimidate farmers, and white men may rape black women with impunity. The illegal sex industry that forced some black women into prostitution also spread venereal disease.[12]

Harper gradually awakens to the fragility of his class position under the weight of custom and law and after an unsuccessful attempt to report the murder of a black man by a white man, joins a plan to form a sharecroppers' cooperative. Here Harper learns how lynching operates as the enforcement arm of cropping shares. Stimulated by the ideas of his fiancée, whose insight into the system exceeds his own, he steps forward as a leader of the black community, now placing his faith in the law, assuming that if blacks do everything legally, they will avoid angering whites. Despite what he has learned about lynching, he still has no experience with it and sees it as secondary in importance to the farm problem.

This line of argument is problematic because it is reinforced by a characterization White deliberately places in the narrative. He not only has Harper say, "Lynching is mighty bad, but after all only a few negroes are lynched a year, while thousands are robbed [by sharecropping] every year of their lives" (158), but his narratorial voice tells the reader, "Where stark terror followed in the wake of the Klan rides in the seventies, the net result of similar rides today is a more determined union of Negroes against all that the Klan stands for, tinctured with a mild amusement at the Klan's grotesque antics" (173–74). The effect for the moment in the text is to posit that for blacks in the South economic oppression was worse than extralegal violence. White's own experience in the South must have led him to some position like this. In a 1924 letter White writes of the Negro's perseverance "despite the burning of a million fiery crosses and other silly attempts of the Ku Klux Klan to intimidate him" (White to Henry Goddard Leach, September 27, 1924, NAACP Papers, reel 8). But White was writing of life for blacks in the *North* when he made that observation. In the same letter he speaks with equal concern for the economic and physical oppression of the South. Still, the melodramatic ending of the novel obscures any earlier centrality of White's economic argument in the novel, as we will see.

Harper so relies on the law that he makes provisions not only to resist the system of credit sales to poor farmers through cooperative buying power (a strategy he cheerfully equates with the experiments going on in Russia after the revolution) but sets aside reserves of money "to be used as the nucleus of a defense fund with which a test case might be made in the courts when any member was unable to secure a fair settlement with his landlord" (175). But money was not all that stood between the sharecroppers and their day in court. His brother, Bob, tells Harper,

> "There isn't a white lawyer in Georgia who'd take a case like this. In the first place, the courts would be against him because his client's a Negro, and in the second place, he'd have to buck this combination of landlords, storekeepers, and bankers who are getting rich robbing Negroes. If a white lawyer took a case of a Negro sharecropper, he'd either sell out to the landlord or be scared to death before he ever got to court. And as for a Negro lawyer," here Bob laughed sardonically, "he'd be run out of town by the Ku Klux Klan or lynched almost before he took the case." (29–30)

In a rapid series of developments, White presses home the importance of law: a black woman is tarred and feathered, whipped and dropped in the street by the Klan; Harper cannot go to the law because the sheriff is a Klansman; Harper's brother decides to go to Harvard Law School and come back to fight for his people; the black community arms itself, "feeling there was no help they could expect from the law, felt that their backs were being slowly pressed to the wall" (195); a decision is made to pursue a test case to put an end to the shares' credit system.[13]

To this point in the novel, the general pattern has been similar to that of Chesnutt's *Colonel's Dream*; a man returns home and by force of will and intelligence seeks to reform an unjust economic system by operating through and with the law. But from here to the end, White follows Chesnutt's *Marrow of Tradition*; powerful white businessmen use newspapers to stir up white citizens against all Negroes, while a black doctor is called on to treat a member of one of the city's "first" families because no white doctor has the skill; the white patient is saved, but the black doctor loses a member of his family to racial violence. In White's version, the defeat is even more complete than in Chesnutt's. Chesnutt's doctor survived and left town, but Harper not only loses his brother to a lynch mob; his sister is raped and he himself is lynched.[14] Harper's death is not described in any detail, but White's prose takes on a much more urgent tone than any he uses elsewhere when he describes Bob's death:

> The mob dragged the body hastily into the open. The roof of the old barn was about to fall in. Before dragging it forth, they had taken no chances. A hundred shots were poured into the dead body. Partly in anger at being cheated of the joy of killing him themselves. They tied it to the rear axle of a Ford. Howling, shouting gleefully, the voice of the pack after the kill, they drove rapidly back to town, the dead body, riddled and torn, bumping grotesquely over the holes in the road. . . .
>
> Back to the pubic square. In the open space before the Confederate Monument, wood and excelsior had been piled. Near by stood cans of kerosene. On the crude pyre they threw the body. Saturated it and the wood with oil. A match applied. In the early morning sunlight the fire leaped higher and higher. Mingled with the flames and smoke the exulting cries of those who had done their duty—they had avenged and upheld white civilization. . . .
>
> The flames died down. Women, tiny boys and girls, old men and young stood by, a strange light on their faces. They sniffed eagerly the odour of burning human flesh which was becoming more and more faint.
>
> . . . Into the dying flames darted a boy of twelve. Out he came, laughing hoarsely, triumphantly exhibiting a charred bone he had

secured, blackened and crisp. . . . Another rushed in. . . . Another.
. . . Another. . . . Here a rib. . . . There an armbone. . . . A louder cry.
. . . The skull. . . . Good boy! Johnny! . . . We'll put that on the man-
telpiece at home. . . . Five dollars for it, Johnny! . . . Nothin' doin'!
. . . Goin' to keep it myself! . . .

The show ended. The crowd dispersed. Home to breakfast.
(236–37)

In a manuscript labeled "The Technique of Lynching Mailed to
H. L. Mencken 12–20–29" (NAACP Papers, reel 11), White continued
his discussion of lynching. The manuscript first covers the history of
lynching in America and then White asks the readers' permission to
give samples from the available accounts of lynchings as responses to
black autonomy after Reconstruction. From his examples we see the
sources of some of the scene of Bob's lynching in *Fire in the Flint*. White
cites newspaper accounts of bodies burned, body parts amputated or
snatched from the fire and sold to onlookers. What strikes a reader is
the lengths to which whites went. Mobs broke into jails and hospitals,
pursued numbers of victims for hours and even days, and concocted
punishments for which there could not possibly exist any equivalent
crime: fingers cut off sequentially, ears cut off, and noses, eyes plucked
out. In one lynching a corkscrew was bored repeatedly into the living
bodies and limbs of a man and his wife and slowly pulled out, bringing
great pieces of raw flesh with it (6).[15] Women and children were
lynched, and women were often raped before being hanged or burned.
In 1918 a pregnant woman was suspended by her ankles from a tree,
doused with gasoline and set on fire. When her clothing had burned
away, the mob cut open her womb, and the eighth-month fetus was
stomped to a pulp while men with guns riddled the woman's body
with bullets (7–8). White investigated this last lynching personally and
sent a detailed account to Hugh M. Dorsey, then governor of Georgia,
where the crime occurred (White, letter to Charles P. Fagnani, February
10, 1925, NAACP Papers, reel 8).

Far from exaggerating the actions of whites in violence against
blacks, as Eugene Saxton and Doran and Company feared, White
could not put in a novel for general circulation the true extent of lynching's bestiality. The most vivid fictional portrayal of a lynching in
African American fiction prior to 1924 had been in a venue almost
invisible to whites, black film. In 1919, black filmmaker and novelist
Oscar Micheaux released a feature film that contained many of the

issues emerging in black print fiction: miscegenation, urban crime, southern poverty, sharecropping and peonage, and lynch law. *Within Our Gates* is the story of Sylvia Landry and her attempt to save a country school in Mississippi.[16] As light-skinned Sylvia travels north and south, falling in love, being hit by a car, escaping the affections of criminals, suffering from betrayal by a trusted cousin, and encountering her white father, Micheaux gives the viewer a unique look at African America at the beginning of the modern era. Micheaux's narrative style owes more to Pauline Hopkins and Sutton Griggs than to any contemporary black novelists, but his decision to portray a lynching as vividly as possible commensurate with the technology available to him breaks with tradition.

The basic elements we have seen in White's fictional and nonfictional accounts of lynching appear in Micheaux's film. In a flashback, Sylvia's cousin tells Doctor Vivian, Sylvia's suitor, the story of the lynching of Jasper Landry. Jasper and his wife were Sylvia's adoptive parents, darker and less refined than she. A sharecropper, Landry was cheated year in and year out by the white plantation owner whose land he worked. But when Sylvia arrived, adopted as a young woman with an education, things changed. Because she could read and write and do mathematics, Sylvia took charge of the Landry accounts and showed her father how he had been cheated.[17] Landry went to the plantation with a proper account and presented it to Gridlestone, the planter.

As Gridlestone threatened Landry with legal and illegal retaliation if he tried to stay free from debt, a white sharecropper whom Gridlestone had offended by calling him "no better than a Negro," fired through the window. In the confusion that followed, Gridlestone was killed and a house servant, seeing Landry but not the white man, thought Landry had done it. When the inevitable lynch mob had killed the servant and found the Landries, the major lynching scene was set. Micheaux included white women and children in his lynch mob and armed them with guns and sticks. Jasper Landry and his wife were beaten and hanged and the crowd tried to shoot their young son, who escaped. Sylvia had gone to a relative's house for food and was tracked there by the brother of the dead white man. He attempts to rape her and the scenes of their struggle are intercut with scenes from the lynching, including the burning of the bodies of the Landries and the general glee around the fires of the white mob. While it appears as though Micheaux may have used stock bonfire footage for the pyre scenes, the editing is skillful enough to produce a sense of terror and outrage in the context

of the narrative to that point. The crowd scenes in which the Landries
are beaten and hanged are powerful in part because of the presence of
women and children as participants rather than as observers. The
episode ends ironically as well as pathetically when we learn that the
white rapist is stopped in his attack by a tell-tale scar on Sylvia's breast
which indicates to him that she is his own daughter from a legal marriage to a black woman.[18] It is he who has paid for her education and
sent her to the Landries' to be raised.

The film ends with Sylvia married to her doctor and the message
proclaimed that blacks should be proud to be Americans. In a line the
origins of which in Micheaux's mind must remain mysterious, Dr.
Vivian predicts to Sylvia that despite the fact that her mind has been
warped and "in spite of your misfortunes, you will always be a
patriot—and a tender wife."[19]

White's novel ends with no solution for any of the black characters
or the black community. Law has failed to protect them. As one of the
white plotters points out, "Under the laws of Georgy, [the governor]
can't even sen' a man down here to investigate unless he's officially
asked by citizens of th' county! And who's goin' t' ask him?" (240). Just
before his death Harper had consulted lawyers in Atlanta, including a
Harvard Law graduate, and even the most liberal of them, while dis-
mayed over the violence, could not begin to entertain such structural
changes as giving blacks the vote or improving the schools. Left without hope for structural relief, we find economic injustice has faded from
our consciousness and lynching is suddenly the center of our attention.
In Micheaux's film, the economic and legal issues, including the lynching, are subsumed in the marriage of Sylvia and Vivian. Just as the genteel conventions of the 1890s had driven black women writers to cast
their stories along the plot lines that concentrated on questions of family and respectability, particularly the question of who will marry
whom, so Micheaux's early film posits the answer to contract fraud,
peonage farm labor, urban crime, white on black rape, and lynching as
marriage and middle-class patriotism. In this representation, Micheaux
follows the practices of the black genteel press of representing a new
American nationalism with middle-class black Americans safely incorporated.[20]

Incorporated perhaps, but within certain limits. Explicit in
Micheaux's film and in White's novel is the complete absence of any
desire on the part of any of the black characters for what whites of the
period called "social equality." Charles Chesnutt had illuminated the

term a decade and a half earlier, as we have seen, when he had a white politician tell Colonel French that

> "so long as one Negro votes in the State, so long are we face to face with the nightmare of Negro domination. . . . Our duty to ourselves, to our children, and their unborn descendants, and to our great and favoured race, impels us to protest, by word, by vote, by arms if need be, against the enforced equality of an inferior race. Equality anywhere means, ultimately, equality everywhere. Equality at the polls means social equality; social equality means intermarriage and corruption of blood, and degeneration and decay. What gentleman here would want his daughter to marry a blubber-lipped, cocoanut-headed, kidney-footed, etc., etc., nigger?" (*Colonel's Dream* 193–94)

Social equality was the issue used by whites at the end of Reconstruction to obscure the issue of social justice for black Americans. Arguments for Jim Crow were usually couched in terms of the threat of social equality, and white fiction through the 1920s reflected the spurious threat of intermarriage and "corruption of blood." At the end of the nineteenth century, the term had come to dominate the matter of the color line in the discourse of most southern whites, replacing any language that spoke to matters of justice under the law for blacks.[21] At the base of the white pretense of the danger of forced association with African Americans lay the sexual issue that was also at the center of lynching as a means of social control. While most lynchings of black men were not related to sexual encounters between those men and white women, such encounters were posited as the reasons for mob action. White men so controlled the image of the white woman that they could with startling consistency turn that ownership into the platform from which black men were lynched. In reality, many if not most victims of white-on-black lynchings were outspoken or independent men, and occasionally women, who came to the attention of the white community; they died for their autonomy. The issue of white-black sexuality did have its element of reality, it is true, but it was not that which white men promulgated. It was rather that the presence of independent and autonomous black men and white women in the same culture would in the nature of things liberate both even further from the economic and social control of white men. Loss of ownership of the black body had endangered white financial security until Jim Crow and lynch law could be rigged in place to reenslave it. Loss of ownership of the white female body could do as much, if not more damage, particularly if that loss meant that white men would have to dismantle the platform on which all arguments for lynching were erected and from which the practice depended (Carby 309).

And perhaps as complex in its consequences would be the loss of control over the black female body that the weakening of Jim Crow might provoke. The black female body had, under slavery, been part of the slaveholding white male's economic base. After Emancipation the black female body lost its direct economic value to white men but became a valued signifier in the struggle to establish a public policy of race useful to whites. The abandonment in that struggle of black men and women by white women seeking suffrage alienated many black women from the early first stage of the women's movement. Black women found their own club movement as a confederation of efforts to further the fortunes of the race and to rehabilitate the image of the black woman in public discourse.

This process of alienation and confederation explains why a reader can search African American fiction in vain for the novel or short story in which the desire for the kind of social equality fabricated by whites is expressed. In the classical African American novel, the dismay of the black hero or heroine over an inability to live with, bond to, eat with, or even sit next to white people does not exist. But the dismay over the forced encounter with whites engendered by white male rapaciousness is a familiar theme. Walter White, a man who in his own life practiced more "social equality" than the most rabid segregationist could dream up, had Kenneth Harper mystified by the currency of the term:

> He thought again of his conversation with Roy Ewing. What was the elusive solution to this problem of race in America? Why couldn't the white people of the South see where their course was leading them? . . . Kenneth saw his people kept in the bondage of ignorance. Why? Because it was to the economic advantage of the white South to have it so. Why was a man like Reverend Wilson patted on the back and every Negro told that men of his kind were "safe and sane leaders"? Why was every Negro who too audibly or visibly resented the brutalities and proscriptions of race prejudice instantly labeled as a radical—a dangerous character—as one seeking "social equality"? What was this thing called "social equality" anyhow? That was an easy question to answer. It was about the

only one he could answer with any completeness. White folks didn't really believe that Negroes sought to force themselves in places where they weren't wanted, any more than decent white people wanted to force themselves where they were not invited. No, that was the smoke-screen to hide something more sinister. Social equality would lead to intermarriage, they thought, and the legitimizing of the countless half-coloured sons and daughters of these white people. Why, if every child in the South were a legitimate one, more than half the property in the South would belong to coloured owners.

Did the white people who were always talking about "social equality" think they really were fooling anybody with their constant denunciation of it? Twenty-nine States of America had laws against intermarriage. All these laws were passed by white legislators. Were all these laws passed to keep Negroes from seizing some white woman and forcing her to marry him against her will? Or were these laws unconscious admissions by these white men that they didn't trust their women or their men to keep from marrying Negroes? Any fool knew that if two people didn't want to marry each other, there was no law of God or man to make them marry. No, the laws were passed because white men wanted to have their own women and use coloured women too without any law interfering with their affairs or making them responsible for the consequences. (91–93)

What was clear to Harper was that the point of all the talk was to keep white men from having to marry black women and legitimize their children. The issue was property, as it had been in the nineteenth century, even before the Civil War, and life under post-Reconstruction white law carried the same burdens as pre-Emancipation life had done for women and children particularly. The status of children still followed the mother's condition, even in the twentieth century, especially if the father were white.

"Social equality"'s focus on autonomy and self-definition among black men and women and the power of lynch law to levy the most horrible consequences on them for the exercise of either reiterated in no uncertain terms that the program of suppression of authentic human life, including the open acceptance of human desire, among black Americans was still uppermost in white thoughts along the color line. And all of this was all too clear to African Americans as well. Kenneth

Harper had thought he could escape the power of whites to control the inmost qualities of his private life, but that was because as a young man, away at school, "he had seen little of the windings and turnings, the tortuous paths the Negro must follow to avoid giving offense to the dominant white sentiment. As he saw each day more and more of the evasions, the repressions, the choking back of natural impulses the Negro practised to avoid trouble" (73), Harper realized his life was not his own.

White's second and last published novel, *Flight*, was a study of the phenomenon of passing. While White and the other authors who treated the subject[22] saw it as a social issue, it has a legal component that harkens back to Albion Tourgee's failed strategy in *Plessy v. Ferguson*, whiteness as property. In a very real sense, "passing" was the practice of trading on a social asset, a property, in what might be recognized as a secondary or "underground" market. White skin and "good" hair in children born into African American families of record constituted social assets that could be turned into economic assets, either through marriage for women or jobs and professions for men. In addition, "whiteness" as *a* property or as property could be used to protect oneself from legal circumscriptions levied on black folks generally, such as prohibitions against certain marriages or more informal relationships.[23]

But what made "passing" a phenomenon of some frequency was the fact that although in 1896, in *Plessy*, the United States Supreme Court had severely limited the legal argument that race constituted property that could be held by an individual and traded on outside the police powers of the law, the increasing social and economic pressures of de jure segregation and Jim Crow made it profitable enough for some African Americans to pay the social costs necessary to be admitted as whites in the everyday world of commerce and social intercourse from which they were usually excluded.

While it was not illegal to pass for white, or for black, for that matter, a person so passing who violated any Jim Crow or segregation ordinance usually also violated the criminal code in the jurisdiction of the ordinance.[24] In some cases, however, issues of race or color as property reemerged, and the outcome was not always foreordained. Such a case was *State v. Treadaway et al.* (1910),[25] introduced briefly in chapter 5. This is one of those cases one chooses to treat as an African American narrative because the story would not exist without the specific identity of the defendant and the relationships he chose as he "wrote" the text of his life.

Legal definitions of "white" and "Negro" at the beginning of the twentieth century varied from jurisdiction to jurisdiction, and for most casual purposes local custom allowed most people to know where they and others stood. Sometimes local custom influenced legal definitions, as in North Carolina, where in 1892 the state supreme court held that associating with Negroes was proper evidence to a jury that one *is* a Negro[26] or in Texas, where in 1894 the court found that if a woman's first husband was a white man, that was admissible evidence that she is a white woman.[27] But most states followed some formulaic program of generational inheritance of "blood" to determine race. By 1910, every state held that if one of your parents was black, you were a Negro; if only one of your grandparents was black, you were a Negro in every state but Ohio. Beyond the one-quarter (grandparents) level, states began to vary widely. While many held you to be black if one of your great-grandparents (one-eighth) was black, and some held you to be black if one of your great-great grandparents (one-sixteenth) was black, only Alabama, in 1903, found you a Negro if one of your great-great-great grandparents (one-thirty-second) was black.

What strikes a reader in search of some understanding of how these rules might be applied is how the narratives admitted as evidence in specific cases are the raw materials of popular narrative art. In *State v. Chavers,* a North Carolina antebellum case,[28] the applicable statute defining "free persons descended from negroes" called for scrutiny to the fourth generation inclusive. But the evidence presented at the trial of Chavers, charged with carrying about his person a shotgun, contrary to law forbidding free persons of color from doing so, as to his race was "to show the color of his father—the kind of hair which he and his father both had," and his own color. From this the jury was allowed to decide. In another North Carolina case, the court found that "it does not require any peculiar scientific knowledge to be able to detect the presence of African blood by the color and other physical qualities of the person."[29] Both of these were cited in a 1944 North Carolina case, *State v. Miller et al.,* in which the court accepted testimony of a Dr. Fred Long, who had known the defendant all his life, that "when he was born he had certain definite physical characteristics of the colored race. That in his opinion he was of mixed blood. His mother is of the whole white blood. 'I know these negroes and I did not consider his grandmother a full negro. . . . I think he is . . . about 3/8 negro; I think his people on the other side had some white blood in them.'" The court also noted that by reputation in his community, Miller was a colored man.[30]

The issue in *Treadaway* was doubly inscribed with matters of race. In the first instance, Octave Treadaway was accused of violating section 1 of Act No. 87 of 1908, as a person of the "negro" or black race committing concubinage with a white person. In the second instance, Treadaway's defense claimed the law did not refer to him in that, while he was not white, neither was he a "person of the negro or black race." Instead, Treadaway argued, he was an octaroon, a person one-eighth colored, and so not covered by the law since an octaroon would not be a negro within the meaning of the statute. Treadaway won his appeal. As Justice Provosty concluded for the court, after citing seven closely printed pages of precedent, "These decisions are authority that a negro is necessarily a person of color; but not that a person of color is necessarily a negro. There are no negroes who are not persons of color; but there are persons of color who are not negroes" (508). Justice Provosty then enumerated the various divisions of personhood based on color recognized by the state of Louisiana. As an octaroon, Treadaway fell into one of those categories of colored person who is not a Negro by definition of law and therefore was not prohibited from concubinage with a white woman.[31]

What becomes obvious in the decision and the accompanying dissent is that while Treadaway was not white, he was free because of the property of whiteness he owned that distinguished him from Negroes. It is that whiteness and nothing else that established his standing before the law, and it was his particularly, a condition that he could, in practice, endow to his heirs. It is also clear that this property is good in this instance only in the state of Louisiana. In some other state, Treadaway might have been clearly a Negro and apt to be in violation of some statute or another.

What, then, is "passing"? Treadaway did not seek to be white; he only sought to be not a Negro. In New Orleans, perhaps to be an octaroon was sufficient to protect one from Jim Crow. It is interesting that none of the major novels of passing consider it a legal question, nor does any present a story of the challenge of racial identity in court. The power of "passing" as an element of black and white social mythology is that it is one pathway to desire. To be white, after all, is to be free of proscription, to be allowed to want and to pursue. James Weldon Johnson's *Autobiography of an Ex-Coloured Man* (1912) and Nella Larsen's *Passing* (1929) are cases in point (Marren).

Johnson's novel, published anonymously, turns on class as well as color. Having grown up more or less unscathed by racism or Jim Crow proscription in New England, the virtually white unnamed protagonist makes his way through late Victorian and Edwardian America sampling white and black life. After the vagaries, none too unpleasant, of the Deep South and the excesses, none too debilitating, of New York have made their mark on him, he leaves for Europe with his white patron, a man with whom he travels as an equal (of sorts, given that he has no money of his own). In time, the protagonist decides to return to America and use his musical gift and his new knowledge of European culture to make a career as a black composer. Traveling south, he picks up the "native" folk material he needs, but at the last moment encounters a lynching that frightens him so much that he flees to the North and resumes life as a white man. Successful in business, he falls in love and tells the woman of his racial past. She, a white woman, accepts him, but he continues to live as a white man. His wife dies in childbirth, and he lives on with his children, sometimes taking out his old manuscripts and wondering at what price he has bought his current life.

The protagonist gently floats through this narrative, never really wanting anything badly, except to please his mother, until the end of the book. Desire, here, is only curiosity and an occasional appetite, and there are only three things in the novel the protagonist truly wants. Two of them are denied him. One is some relationship with his father, a white man who, his mother assures him, is as much to them as "law and custom" will allow. The other is to be someone who will bring honor to the black race. The thought comes to him as a boy and returns to him in Europe. This is what has brought him south, and it is what the lynching he witnesses places forever beyond his reach. Here Johnson describes an effect of the law that would seem never to be visited on whites: the shaming effect of becoming both a status criminal and a status victim at the same time. The protagonist's response to the lynching, after the horror of seeing a man burned alive, is shame:

> A great wave of humiliation and shame swept over me. Shame that I belonged to a race that could be so dealt with; and shame for my country, that it, the great example of democracy in the world, should be the only civilized, if not the only state on earth, where a human being would be burned alive. My heart turned bitter within me. I could understand why Negroes are led to sympathize with even their worst criminals and to protect them when possible.
>
> . . . it was not discouragement or fear or search for a larger field of action and opportunity that was driving me out of the Negro

race. I knew that it was shame, unbearable shame. Shame at being identified with a people that could with impunity be treated worse than animals. For certainly the law would restrain and punish the burning alive of animals. (497–99)

As Johnson, a lawyer for fifteen years by the time of the composition of the novel, would have been aware, black Americans were, by virtue of custom and law, the only people condemned to violation of the law by the very fact of their existence. The status of "Negro" was a sentence to contract labor and peonage in the South and disenfranchisement in the North. To attempt, as a citizen, to do what a white person could do would be to break the law were one a Negro. No wonder the protagonist flees from his previous decision.

That flight allows him to attain his last true desire, the love of a good woman who will, eventually and after some soul searching, accept his love. The protagonist fears he will be rejected, and at his beloved's tears when she learns his secret he feels himself "becoming" black, physically, feels his hair and skin and bone structure change. It is the only time in his life, he reports, that he really wished to be white. But she does love him, and they marry, illegally, of course, and she dies a few years later, because deception cannot go wholly rewarded in the late Victorian novel. So even the last desire is granted but taken away by the narrative. There is irony, of course, of a predictable sort. The protagonist has some self-awareness and realizes he gave up race building for personal happiness. He sees himself a smaller man than he might have been, and he makes no larger analysis of how he came to be there. But we can see from Johnson's argument that American law forces black people into the most impossible compromises, brutal in their ultimate irony. The law, in effect forces the protagonist to become white in order to become American. In few other metaphors than "passing" do we see the extent to which citizenship is consequential to color.

The great difference between the novels of Brown, Webb, Delany, Hopkins, Harper, and Griggs and the classical African American novels of the twentieth century is that identity as romantic essentialism functioning as a marker of property or of being propertied, central in the earlier texts, fades in the later novels, and questions of identity as authenticity take its place. One novel sits astride both paradigms and exemplifies each. Set in the immediate post–Civil War decade, it looks back at the badges and indices of slavery in the reactionary South, but by raising the question of distinctions without differences it anticipates the novels of Johnson, White, Larsen, and Schuyler in which issues of personal authenticity, while still romantic questions, are cut loose from issues of property.

Charles W. Chesnutt's *The House Behind the Cedars* (1900), is perhaps the first African American novel to have as its primary subject the conscious effort to pass out of the role of the "other" by claiming whiteness and to implicate color in discussions of property and propertiedness.[32] It is in this novel, for example, that we get the first expression of passing as a metaphoric prerequisite to citizenship, when the mulatto John Warwick, born Walden, passing for white, reflects, "For he had always been, in a figurative sense, a naturalized foreigner in the world of wide opportunity, and Rena was one of his old compatriots, whom he was glad to welcome into the populous loneliness of his adopted country" (61).

Warwick had come upon his "naturalized" status simply by moving from North Carolina to South Carolina and changing his name. In a scene infused with irony, Chesnutt drew on his legal training to invent a conversation between young John, the illegitimate son of a deceased white father and a free black woman, and a learned and kindly white lawyer who had been a friend of his father's in the small North Carolina town in which they all lived. It is in this conversation, after announcing his intention of becoming a lawyer, that young John understands both his status and the implications of his skin color:

> "I am white," replied the lad, turning back his sleeve and holding out his arm, "and I am free, as all my people were before me."
>
> The old lawyer shook his head, and fixed his eyes upon the lad with a quizzical smile. "You are Black," he said, "and you are not free. You cannot travel without papers; you cannot secure accommodations at an inn; you could not vote, if you were of age; you cannot be out after nine o'clock without a permit. If a white man struck you, you could not return the blow, and you could not testify before him in a court of justice. You are Black, my lad, and you are not free. Did you ever hear of the Dred Scott decision, delivered by the great, wise, and learned Judge Taney?" (152)

John has not, and even when Judge Straight informs him of the scope of Taney's opinion, he rejects the notion that it would apply to

him, since he is obviously white. If, he reasons, white blood were superior, as whites claimed it to be, then surely it would outweigh the small
amount of black blood his personage contained. No, the judge replies,
because it is more profitable to whites for the reverse to be true.

> "Lawyers go by the laws—they abide by the accomplished fact,"
> admonishes the judge, "to them, whatever is, is right. The laws do
> not permit men of color to practice law, and public sentiment
> would not allow one of them to study it."
> "I had thought," said the lad, "that I might pass for white. There
> are white people darker than me." (153)

The judge's response is a lawyerly one. He notes that John has begun
life in North Carolina as a black person and must remain one there, but
were he to move far enough away, anything might be possible. Then he
turns to the law itself, pointing out that even in passing it might be
good to have the law on your side, if possible. While North Carolina
had adjudicated blackness to the fourth generation, South Carolina was
a different matter:

> "The term mulatto," he read, "is not invariably applicable to every
> admixture of African blood with the European, nor is one having
> all the features of a white to be ranked with the degraded class des-
> ignated by the laws of this State as persons of color, because of
> some remote taint of the Negro race. Juries would probably be jus-
> tified in holding a person to be white in whom the admixture of
> African blood did not exceed one eighth. And even where color or
> feature are doubtful, it is a question for the jury to decide by repu-
> tation, by reception into society, and by their exercise of the privi-
> leges of the white man, as well as by admixture of blood."
> "Then I need not be Black?" the boy cried, with sparkling eyes.
> "No," replied the lawyer, "you need not be Black, away from
> Patesville. . . . As you have all the features of a white man, you
> would, at least in South Carolina, have simply to assume the place
> and exercise the privileges of a white man. You might, of course,
> do the same thing anywhere, as long as no one knew your origin.
> But the matter has been adjudicated there in several cases, and on
> the whole I think South Carolina is the place for you. They're more
> liberal there, perhaps because they have many more blacks than
> whites, and would like to lessen the disproportion." (154–55)

Chesnutt's irony does not obscure the relationship between matters of color, citizenship, and property here. The novel itself turns on matters of property quite eponymously, and whiteness is not the least of the properties under scrutiny in it, while gender as property and in terms of having properties that deny one agency is implicated as well. When John's sister is discovered by her white fiancé to be black and poor, she is rejected by him; nevertheless, John himself, a man of position and property, is still acceptable to the white fiancé, and is told he will never be thought of as anything but white (138). John's "citizenship" in his adopted world is a function of property and gender, we feel sure, given his ability to actively display a "post-property" persona, a skin that will pass for white.

Much is made in the novel of romantic ideals of race and desire, color and property, even through literary allusion. Chesnutt seems to have the most fun with Scott's *Ivanhoe*.[33] There is a mock tilting event at a chivalric revel at which John's sister Rena, short for Rowena, is first noticed by her white suitor. Chesnutt plays with the name Rowena and suggests parallels between Rena's story and Rebecca's in Scott's novel. He clearly enjoys giving his black heroine the name of Ivanhoe's Saxon beloved. And Rena expresses the romantic sentiments of the day when she considers her condition long before her secret is found out:

> But would her lover still love her, if he knew all? She had read some of the novels in the bookcase in her mother's hall, and others at boarding school. She had read that love was a conqueror, that neither life nor death, nor creed nor caste, could stay his triumphant course. Her secret was no legal bar to their union. If Rena could forget the secret, and Tryon should never know it, it would be no obstacle to their happiness. But Rena felt, with a sinking of the heart, that happiness was not a matter of law or of fact, but lay entirely within the domain of sentiment. (69)

Writing in the last decade of the century on the manuscript that was to become the novel, Chesnutt had to reach back two decades at least to recover a moment in southern American legal history to make this conflict more complex than a mere conflict with oppressive legality. When Rena says there is no legal bar to her marriage to Tryon, that fact is no guarantee of happiness. The fact itself places the novel's events between 1865 and 1873, when North Carolina had no law forbidding miscegenation; postwar South Carolina had no such law until

1895.[34] Were Rena not passing for white, there would be no law to prevent her marriage to Tryon. The barrier here is custom, not law. The further irony is that two romantic constructs are confronting one another. The general cultural romanticism that privileges the story of the beloved collides with the typological romantic image of the despised other. Tryon and Rowena share citizenship in a romantic kingdom of the heart but can share no such identity in the romantic American republic of property, custom, and law.

Ultimately, these conflicts between desire and the overwhelming power of law are expressed through the burden of caste. While statutory law itself does not prohibit any action taken or proposed in the book, it is the weight of law applied to race to produce the heritage of caste that dooms Rena and Tryon. Again and again Chesnutt has either Rowena or her lover declare that love should be stronger than, or independent of, law. "The law, you said, made us white," Rena complains to her brother, "but not the law, nor even love, can conquer prejudice" (161). And yet Tryon "was now driven by an aching heart toward the same woman stripped of every adventitious advantage and placed, by custom, beyond the pale of marriage with men of his own race. Custom was tyranny. Love was the only law" (263).

Tryon and Rena live too soon after slavery to be free of the weight of its former legal power to define social reality. The power of romance, of the novels in Rena's mother's hallway, of the chivalric pageants of old Charleston, of the culture of the beloved as story are as nothing beside the power of the image of the despised as legal narrative, even when that narrative has been formally superseded:

> A Negro Girl had been foisted upon him for a white woman, and he had almost committed the unpardonable sin against his race of marrying her. Such a step, he felt, would have been criminal at any time; it would have been the most odious treachery at this epoch, when his people had been subjugated and humiliated by the Northern invaders, who had preached Negro equality and abolished the wholesome laws decreeing the separation of the races. (130)

The father of this girl had been guilty of a sin against society for which others—for which he, George Tryon—must pay the penalty. As slaves, Negroes were tolerable. As freemen, they were an excrescence, an alien element incapable of absorption into the body politic of white men (227).[35]

Tryon's imagined nation of white men exists only, but vitally, in memory. It is a nation whose "wholesome" laws have not been repealed, a nation in which Rena's story could be only one more narrative of property—of *being* property. Her postproperty narrative, an obscene story of excrescence, can never be published in Tryon's nation.

Rena's death, the ultimate denial of incorporation, and Tryon's belated self-admission of his true love for her are melodramatic to our tastes but no more so than the treatment of other themes of the violation of custom and the African American subgenre of the tragic mulatto, into which *Cedars* also falls. This is a good place to recall Vladimir Nabokov's observation that a happy ending of an interracial love affair, with marriage and children unto the generations, is one of the three most unlikely plots in American literature (314).[36]

Three decades later, prohibited and prohibitive desire plus a minor, mordant irony sit at the apex of Larsen's *Passing* (1929), almost literally, when in the novel's final scene a woman passing for white falls or is pushed to her death from a penthouse balcony. Clare Kendry is married to a white man and is passing for white. A chance encounter with an old school chum, Irene Redfield, allows her to reveal that she wants to find a way back to the black community without necessarily giving up her assumed racial status. Irene is not sympathetic but through a sequence of initiatives by Clare becomes the agent of her reintroduction to a world she had abandoned. Unfortunately, Clare and Irene's husband fall in love, but before any consequence can ensue, Clare's deception is discovered by her husband, a racist, who confronts her at a party to which he has tracked her. It is there that she falls to her death.

Larsen's story is very much about law and the conflict between illicit and domesticated desire. Jim Crow practices in Chicago have driven Clare into a white world made available to her by her genetic history. Orphaned and without resources except her beauty, she hides her origins. Irene, on the other hand, in the face of the same Jim Crow practices in Chicago, turns to the comfort of nuclear family, hers of birth and that which she creates with her doctor-husband Brian and their two sons. Irene argues to herself and to Clare throughout the novel that honest desire is that expressed within the black community for husband, family, home, and even material comfort. Clare, it is clear, even seeking the same comforts of husband, family, and home, pursues illicit desire because she can only attain it through the denial of some portion of her true self: her father had been the illegitimate son of a white man, but that relationship had not been enough to make him, let alone her, "white." Consequently, her marriage was illegal, as was her desire. Even Clare's later love for a black man is illicit, since he is Irene's husband. *Passing* is a slender book, and is not complex in either its "sociological" or its psychological aspects, but it does expose some of the desperation of middle-class desire that even the most fortunate African Americans of the early century felt.[37] It also provides the reader with one brief ironic moment at the very end of the story. The irony is in the "legal" judgment passed on Clare's death: had she fallen, jumped, or been pushed to her death? The decision of the investigating officer is also a judgment of Clare's life: "Death by misadventure, I'm inclined to believe" (189).

In October 1925, Walter White wrote to Heywood Broun about a fascinating episode in the representation of passing and the problem of lynch law. White reported that he had just seen a performance of *Appearances*, a play written by Garland Anderson, a thirty-eight-year old African American bellhop from San Francisco. Anderson's play, largely self-promoted and self-produced, was something of a cause célèbre among New York literati for the moment. The play's story, of a young black bellhop unjustly accused of rape by a white woman, is at once an indictment of the lynch mob mentality and a celebration of the "power of positive thinking." The defendant refuses an attorney and in the play's climactic scene argues his own case so effectively that the true villains, a corrupt district attorney and an immoral white woman, reveal themselves in court. White tells Broun, "The court room scene in the second act is one of the most effective and moving spectacles I have ever seen in the theatre" (NAACP Papers, reel 9).[38] What White does not reveal to Broun is that the acquittal of the defendants (another man is also accused) is based not so much on the evidence of their innocence, although they are innocent, as on the revelation that their accuser is not a white woman at all but a "Negress" passing for white.

Anderson's reason for indicting his own race in this tale of personal responsibility for one's own fate is not clear. His intended audience was almost certainly white once he got to New York, and there was surely some question of presenting a play on Broadway in 1925 in which the black protagonist was of higher moral stature than his white female antagonist. The title itself is suggestive; billed as *Appearances*, the play's original title was "Don't Judge by Appearances" and it was copyrighted as "Judge Not According to Appearances." The implication of the title might as easily be "don't assume a white woman is white" as "don't assume a black man is guilty." The matter was complicated even more in production by the casting of Lionel Monagas as the protagonist Carl. Monagas was a fair-skinned black Venezuelan actor assumed by most people at the time to be white. A black actor who passed for white played a black man falsely accused of a stereotypically "black" crime by a black woman passing for white. To add to the ironic complexities of the moment, Anderson's first entrée to New York Theatre came when, on the advice of a friend, he sent the manuscript of his play to Al Jolson, the white vaudevillian who had premised his career on performing in blackface. In the revised New York production of 1929 the woman's role in the deception is downplayed and the prosecutor is the sole villain.[39]

Passing as a phenomenon of black life deserves scrutiny also as an early-twentieth-century response to the romantic notion of "authenticity" that had borne so heavily on nineteenth-century efforts to define the individual. While the obvious fact is that blacks had passed permanently over the color line for three hundred years, the emergence of the act as a matter to be discussed in fiction for its qualities as an act rather than for its positive consequences marks its modernity. If *Plessy* rejects the idea that property to whiteness is possible to find in any person with black "blood," the Court is seemingly ignoring one aspect of the complex consideration of property under the law, the notion that property is alienable. That is, the ability to assign a property from oneself to another other than through inheritance marks the condition of property interest. Nevertheless, there are properties that are not alienable but retain such characteristics of property as having value, use and enjoyment benefit, expectation, reputation and status, and so on. For example, one could not sell to another one's gender or one's measurable IQ or one's citizenship or one's law degree, yet these are considered property and may not be taken or rescinded without due process of law. Neither, by extension, could the law transfer whiteness to anyone who had not held it as a supposedly intrinsic property already, since whiteness is inalienable property to all previously defined whites. Thus, no one who was not white could ever become white; in an era of legal preference for the property of whiteness, then, non-white people labored under real disadvantages, for while one might, in America, change classes if one were white, the application of class to race produced only caste, in which one enjoyed or suffered a relative position of privilege in a "parallel" social universe, parallel to that of the dominant social universe in which whiteness was an essential and protected form of property privilege.

The decision to pass, therefore, came to be experienced as a metaphysical act as well as an existential one. That is, while the value of the material consequences of the act were demonstrable, the meaning of the act was not clear. Under the law as it had evolved, one could never, if one were black, become simply an "American" after *Plessy* because one could never become white; the legal divide between whiteness as property and all other conditions had become a chasm. As *Treadaway* suggests, one could be recognized as not-black without becoming white. In the passing novels of the early twentieth century it is the ontological question that dominates the narrative. While Chesnutt argues in *The House Behind the Cedars* that passing is desirable and that negative consequences derive from being unable to pass successfully, Johnson, Walter White, and Larsen probe the meaning of the act itself and weight the relative costs with an emphasis on blackness as a property to be valued over and above its worth in terms of use value.

This argument, at base, is an argument over authenticity. Chesnutt's generation, including the Brotherhood of Liberty, had hoped, in the last shade of Reconstruction memories, for an American life, free of the vicissitudes of race. But race was already a complex mix of metaphysics and existential practice, and the determination of "authenticity," as a Negro, a white, and eventually as a citizen, resembled an exercise in scholasticism. That this is so can be seen in a Chesnutt article written seven years before *Plessy* was handed down. In the article Chesnutt is considering a South Carolina case involving the right of access to schools. He quotes from the court's decision:

> The definition of the term mulatto, as understood in this state, seems to be vague, signifying generally a person of mixed white or European and Negro parentage, in whatever proportion the blood of the two races may be mingled in the individual. But it is not invariably applicable to every admixture of African blood with the European, nor is one having all the features of a white to be ranked with the degraded class designated by the laws of this state as persons of color, because of some remote taint of the Negro race. The line of distinction, however, is not ascertained by any rule of law.
> . . . Juries would probably be justified in holding a person to be white in whom the admixture of African blood did not exceed the

proportion of one-eighth. But it is in all cases a question for the jury, to be determined by them upon the evidence of features and complexion, afforded by inspection, and the evidence of the rank and station in society occupied by the party. The only rule which can be laid down by the courts is that where there is a distinct admixture of Negro blood, the individual is to be denominated a mulatto or person of color.

Chesnutt then cites a later case:

The question whether persons are colored or white, where color or features are doubtful, is for the jury to decide by reputation, by reception into society, and by their exercise of the privileges of the white man, as well as by the admixture of blood. ("What" 5–6)[40]

An attentive reader will recognize these citations as virtually identical to speeches assigned to Judge Straight in Chesnutt's *House Behind the Cedars*, written a decade later. Their appeal to Chesnutt must have been the evidence they provide for the subtext of the judge's advice and of the body of Chesnutt's later fiction, namely that race, including whiteness, is a socially constructed phenomenon, not an essential characteristic of groups or of individuals. They also serve Chesnutt as examples of the lengths to which whites would go to establish distinctions where there were no differences, as in the peculiar effect of such laws on reputation. He notes as his closing observation in the piece that the lines drawn in different jurisdictions, arbitrary as they were revealed to be as he surveyed them in the article, had one common effect—they made mixed blood a prima facie proof of illegitimacy, the "offspring of a union not sanctified by law"—but that for some reason the reputations of these technical bastards did not suffer as much as those of whites under similar charges. The reason, he implies, is that class is the hidden factor; persons of color suffer from imputations of illegitimacy as they rise in wealth and social standing. As long, however, as a person of mixed blood remains embedded in the socioeconomic class where whites are used to finding black Americans, then the occasion of mixed-race bastardy is hardly worth commenting on.[41] To whites, Chesnutt noted, it was beside the point that, in fact, mixed-blood people were, by 1889, more likely to be the children of married mixed-blood parents than of poor black girls victimized by foolish or venal white men. The reader can further note that the possession of "white blood" by a person of color had been often a protection against "illegal" enslavement in the antebellum South, where appellate courts often found that while being a "negro" was prima facie evidence of being a slave, being of mixed heritage was likely proof of being a free person of color, even without documentation.

However much Chesnutt might have wished in 1889 that the "good citizen" turn his mind to the question of whether such laws and policies were "wise," *Plessy* shut the door on any hope that such logic chopping would eventually fade into irrelevancy, and by the 1920s it became clear that, social construction or no, as far as most whites were concerned, there were black Americans and there were white Americans. Consequently, when we look at the caste system at work among blacks at the beginning of this century, we realize that for some, at least, the question of the nature of one's civic life was essentially reducible to the question of whether one ought to be a true black person or a faux white. Given the presence of White and Larsen, for example, at the "white" end of the caste spectrum, the immediacy of the question is obvious. In each case, the argument of the narrative produced by these light-skinned black writers suggests that the authentic life of the race, however the individual author experienced it, was rejected only at great, perhaps unacceptable costs.

In the summer of 1919, George Schuyler, a young black veteran, was chief clerk in the executive office of the Atlantic Branch United States Disciplinary Barracks on Governors Island in New York Harbor, working at his duties recording the vicissitudes of liberty on the same day that Rudolph Fisher, another young black man, was presenting his hope for the future in his Class Day oration on graduation from Brown University: "Devoutly revering its supreme ruler, which is law; persistently upholding the principles of its savior, which is evolution; and constantly comforted by its holy spirit, which is truth, science is at last free to serve mankind. Is there any finer liberty than that?"[42]

One can only speculate what resonance these words, spoken at the end of a great war, on the brink of a new paradigm, modernism, carried for Fisher on his way to medical school dreaming of being free at last, protected by law, natural process, and truth. But twelve years later, in 1931, Schuyler, by then the most famous black newspaperman in America, was ready to take Fisher's faith in science and the intervening decade's experience with law, truth, and evolution and stand them on their collective ears while he punctured the hyperbole he felt existed on both sides of the issue of the color line.

Schuyler's 1931 satiric novel, *Black No More: Being an Account of the Strange and Wonderful Workings of Science in the Land of the Free, A. D. 1933–1940,* tells the tale of a medical treatment to make Negroes white and the consequences of its widespread application. While Schuyler has sacred cows he wants to skewer, such as the NAACP, and obvious villains he wants to mock, such as southern senators, passing itself is at the center of his sights. Perhaps because Schuyler is not as good a novelist as he is a newspaperman, he has trouble holding on to narrative tone in his satire. For this reason, and perhaps because of some genuine ambivalence, his story both attacks the desire of blacks to be white and produces some rather realistic reasons for the existence of such desire, the legal constraints against full citizenship for African Americans.

Having had his black hero Max Dishman meet a beautiful white woman in a Harlem nightclub and thereby set his tale in motion, Schuyler brings Max up short against her ignorant and automatic retreat behind race prejudice and white privilege. Later, Max dreams of her, and the dream becomes a "nightmare of grim, gray men with shotguns, baying hounds, a heap of gasoline-soaked faggots and a screaming, fanatical mob" (24). Soon thereafter, on learning of Dr. Junius Crookman's ability to turn black folks white, Max's first fantasy is of

[n]o more jim crow. . . . As a white man he could go anywhere, be anything he wanted to be, do most anything he wanted to do, be a free man at last . . . and probably be able to meet the [white] girl from Atlanta. . . . What a treat it would be to mingle with white people in places where as a youth he had never dared to enter. At last he felt like an American citizen. (26, 48)

Schuyler's ploy of tying Max's desire for freedom to his desire for the woman runs the risk of trivializing the issue of the color line for the reader but suits Schuyler's intent well enough and prevents the novel from becoming a lecture disguised as a novel. Max's picaresque pursuit leads him, as a newly minted white man, to the very bowels of white racism, a center of ignorance and greed that Schuyler determinedly makes as ludicrous as it is distasteful.

In the world in which every black American can pass for white, the role of legal segregation as a bulwark against miscegenation and "social equality" is severely diminished. *Plessy* is, in effect, reversed. As Schuyler writes of Crookman's discovery: "It looked as though science was to succeed where the Civil War had failed. . . . Through his efforts and the activities of Black-No-More, Incorporated, it would be possible to do what agitation, education, and legislation had failed to do," that is, solve the "Negro Problem" (25, 54–55). Schuyler shows the NAACP (the National Social Equality League in the novel) little mercy for its failure, as he saw it, based largely on his disdain for their bureaucratic approach to race relations. To his mind, blacks had good reason to be "more or less skeptical about [its] program for liberty and freedom" because it was largely reactive rather than innovative. "While the large staff of officials was eager to end all oppression and persecution of the Negro, they were never so happy and excited as when a Negro was barred from a theater or fried to a crisp" (88). Then they would spring into action with telephone calls and stenographers. The countless polls and surveys taken by the NSEL and similar groups produced only the obvious reports, "revealing that amazing fact that poor people went to jail oftener than rich ones; that most of the people were not getting enough money for their work; that strangely enough there was some connection between poverty, disease, and crime" (97).

What is hidden behind the sarcasm here is the key to the novel's purposeful attitude toward human failings and the law. The assumed logic of Schuyler's remarks suggests that class differences produce social dysfunction in America. The reader, as Schuyler knows well enough, will recognize that in the context of his novel and the world it represents, class has been racialized such that the distribution of the consequences of class is skewed by racial identity. Consequently, should we be able to affect the distribution of those consequences by removing the ability to skew it by race, either *(a)* much social dysfunction would disappear, or *(b)* we would be able finally to see the inequalities of class-based distribution of the society's wealth, goods, and services and act to correct them, so ending much social dysfunction.

What actually happens is quite different. First of all, whites are dumbfounded that there is no way to stop African Americans from becoming white if they want to. There is no law that protects whiteness as property; no law against passing exists. Whites take to the streets in some places to shut down "Black-No-More, Inc." clinics. This vigilantism is countered by the law occasionally, but sentiment among whites soon embraces extralegal responses, as this editorial from the *Oklahoma City Hatchet:*

There are times when the welfare of our race must take precedence over law. Opposed as we always have been to mob violence as the worst enemy of democratic government, we cannot help but feel that the intelligent white men and women of New York City who are interested in the purity and preservation of their race should not permit the challenge of Crookmanism to go unanswered, even though these black scoundrels may be within the law. There are too many criminals in the country already hiding behind the skirts of the law. (50)

Even the esteemed black intellectual Dr. Shakespeare Agamemnon Beard (W. E. B. Du Bois) sends a telegram to the attorney general of the United States insisting that Crookman and his associates be arrested for the good of both races. And while Dr. Beard and the *Oklahoma City Hatchet* have reasons for fearing "Crookmanism," the ordinary black man on the street is having his own reaction, basically being "too busy getting white to bother reading about lynching, crime, and peonage" (119). What becomes clear in the novel is that the law will deserve no special status from Schuyler as a repository of national identity or as a barrier against injustice. Law is simply a mechanism through which special interests inscribe their programs on the national agenda. As such, law is for sale to the highest bidder—sought after when it can be used to reinforce the status of the powerful and ignored when it contradicts or is useless to respond to the desires of that same class.

Eventually, law reinscribes foolish bigotry, as distinctions among degrees of whiteness are written as differences in privilege. Now Negroes who have become white will be set aside by the fact that theirs is a whiter whiteness than that of genetic whites and so to *have* color becomes a marker of privilege. Genetic whites flock to the tropics as suntans become popular; skin darkeners hit the market. In the end, both science and law fail to resist the human capacity for self-deception. America remains a nation divided along newly artificial racial lines. The light of science has forced nothing but the composition of new legal fictions.

CHAPTER 7

Resistance in Renascence

> Matthew gripped the table. All that cold rage which still lay like
> lead beneath his heart began again to glow and burn. Action,
> Action, it screamed—no running and sulking now—action! There
> was murder in his mind—murder, riot, and arson. He wanted just
> once to hit this white American in the jaw—to see him spinning
> over the tables, and then to walk out with his arm about the
> princess, through the midst of a gaping, scurrying white throng.
> He started to rise, and nearly upset his coffee cup.
>
> W. E. B. Du Bois, *Dark Princess*

George Schuyler was a proponent of individual self-determinism, of
the power of the singular personality to shape the world to his own lik-
ing. Although he flirted with leftist ideals in the 1920s and early 1930s,
he was caught at times between some collective sensibility tying him to
all black people and a generally consistent refusal to be bound by pre-
dictive assumptions based on race. W. E. B. Du Bois struggled with just
these issues in his 1928 novel, *Dark Princess*.[1] The political purposive-
ness of the novel is unmistakable, and it is clearly a fictional working
out of themes Du Bois presented in his 1926 essay "Criteria of Negro
Art": political and social propaganda presented through an aesthetic
romanticism.

Du Bois's is a complicated novel of many voices and competing
sensibilities, not all of which Du Bois controlled to the same degree of
success. In some ways this is a very romantic, fin de siècle, fiction. In
part it seems even older than that. The protagonist, Matthew Towns, is
described very much as Henry Blake is described by Martin Delany
seventy years earlier in *Blake, or The Huts of America*—noble in
physique, mind, and character, a "high mimetic" picaro, a man on a
noble quest who is at every moment ethically "greater than" his sur-
roundings. While Du Bois's romantic longings in the book will go unremarked here so that I can concentrate on his approach to law in the
novel, his roots in a nineteenth-century literary tradition need to be recognized.

Like Sutton Griggs's *Imperium in Imperio* at the turn of the century and George Schuyler's serialized romances from the early 1930s of a black African empire, *Dark Princess* is about a movement by people of color to replace the hegemonic presence of European politics and culture with a new world order based on the historic superiority of the ethical vision of people of color. Actually, the presence of such a movement is the frame for the real business of the novel, which is taking Matthew Towns on a Faustian tour of life's vicissitudes through the medium of an old-fashioned bildungsroman, or novel of development of a young consciousness. This makes for a confusing read along the way because, as I noted above, Du Bois has already assigned a set of romance hero characteristics to Towns, characteristics that he is nevertheless quite willing to set aside to allow Towns to develop as he needs him to. It is along the paths of the world's ways that Du Bois embeds his critiques of the color line, how the law creates and maintains it and what is to be done to eradicate it.

In the main, Du Bois's is an economic critique, in which economic interests determine the forms of culture and shape the law to their own ends. The forms of culture control the ability of various segments of the society to choose among levels of quality in their lives. This is where black Americans feel on a daily basis the impact of racism: as a form of cultural control. As Towns says to a visiting friend after being forced to take "Jim Crow" seats in a New York theater:

> [I]n a great modern city like New York men and women sell their bodies, souls, and thoughts for luxury and beauty and the joy of life. They sell their silences and dumb submissions. They are content to let things be done; they promise not to ask just what they are doing, or for whom, or what it costs, or who pays. That explains our slavery. . . . [L]ook around. How many Negroes are enjoying this? How many can afford to be here at the wages with which they must be satisfied if these white folks are to be rich? (63)

As Du Bois sees it, the wealthy white world deprives the mass of whites, and that mass, particularly the white middle class, proposes the legislation, passes the laws, invokes the practices that oppress Negroes and ensures the wealthy their necessities and luxuries. In that way the responsibility of the upper class of whites is hidden since they have not directly asked for such laws and practices. Ironically, of course, the very presence of black workers is used to manage labor discipline, "colored labor" acting, in Du Bois's view, as "the wage-hammering adjunct of white capital" (58). And whoever is ultimately responsible, both classes of whites are complicit in ignoring the consequences of their legal acts on the mass of black Americans. Particularly in their cultural repro- duction of these relationships, whites ignore the presence of people of color and ignore their true stories. As Towns and his guest leave the the- ater where they have just seen a play in which a husband kills his wife's lover, Towns remarks how inadequate a representation of social rela- tionships such stories are: "Why can't they try other themes—ours for instance; our search for dinner and our reasons for the first balcony. Good dinner and good seats—but with subtle touches, hesitancies, grop- ings, and refusals that would be interesting" (64). The everyday lives of African Americans are "interestingly" circumscribed by law in ways invisible to and unexperienced by whites.

Towns only gradually becomes aware of how deeply seated these conditions are. Once a promising medical student, now driven from his study by racial barriers, Towns flees to Europe and is enlisted by the Dark Princess to evaluate the revolutionary potential of the black peo- ple in America. His first report to her notes that while one can still find caste and discrimination, oppression, insult, and lynchings, and "while he [the Negro] knows that he is not treated quite as a man and lacks the full freedom of a white man, he believes he is daily approaching this goal" (57). Towns believes that the moment for violent revolution is past. But after the lynching of a friend on a train filled with Klansmen, Towns bitterly embraces terrorism and revenge, imagining that "[a]ll the enslaved, all the raped, all the lynched, all the 'jim-crowed' marched in ranks behind him, bloody with rope and club and iron, crimson with stars and nights. He was going to fight and die for vengeance and freedom" (85–86).

This episode is framed by a Klan convention that intends to call for new legal restrictions on blacks, including the repeal of the Fifteenth Amendment, a cry of white reaction from the 1880s. At this point in the novel, Towns's (or Du Bois's) bleak vision is of an extralegal nation of sanctioned violence, an outlaw nation the resistance to which can only be *un*sanctioned violence. Because there is no protection under the law, freedom can be won only by the overthrow of law. Towns agrees to help in a plot to blow up a train and distributes posters declaring revenge on the men "who seek our disenfranchisement and slavery. . . . Here was the challenge. An atrocious lynching; an open, publicly advertised movement to take the first step back to Negro slavery. Kill the men who led it" (87).

At this point, I want to step back from the narrative to comment on one of its practices. When Towns is arrested after the aborted plot on the train (Towns himself prevents the destruction when pleaded with by the princess), Du Bois moves the story to a courtroom, and the story is essentially retold, in miniature, as legal narrative. That version differs from our experience of the story, although it is not factually incorrect. Judge Windom declares that the purpose of the court is to get at the truth. But we as readers already know the truth; will the law uncover it as well? This double narrative needs to be examined if only because it offers us a chance to look directly at the difference in narrativization in law and fiction. (In chapter 8 I examine the same practice in novels by Richard Wright and Willard Motley.)

When Towns, at this juncture described once again as every inch the noble, romantic hero, pleads guilty to a charge of conspiracy but refuses to name anyone else involved, claiming to have acted alone, the discussion moves to the judge's chambers. Windom's *in camera* accusation against Towns is interesting. He does not believe Towns acted alone and says he is guilty of refusing to name others. Obviously, Towns has decided to protect the conspirator Perigua, a revolutionary West Indian against whose plans Towns eventually acted, even at the cost of his own freedom, so his admission of guilt is designed to prevent the introduction of evidence that would expose the extent of the conspiracy to blow up the train. Since Perigua is dead, however, Towns is not protecting his person as much as he is protecting his black world from white interrogation.

Windom has no inkling of the nature or depth of Towns's alienation from the process in which they are both involved and in sentencing him to ten years in Joliet Prison delivers a judgment that could have been written just as easily by Dreiser or Wright or Motley: no external pressure excuses crime. Crime in every case is no more than the failure to rise above circumstance. Windom tells Towns, "I know that you have suffered injustice and perhaps insult and that your soul is bitter. But you are to blame if you have let this drown the heart of your manhood" (101). Du Bois reveals with this speech how inadequate he finds the law as a way of knowing black experience. His fiction has told us all we need to know about Matthew Towns's manhood and the degree of his culpability. The law can only repeat its own platitudes about responsibility.

Windom's preachments actually reflect a common attitude in the criminal law and in penology at the time, one that had begun to emerge in the last quarter of the nineteenth century at the same time that constitutional protections for blacks were eroding and as black migration to urban centers was increasing. From this perspective, one that Craig Haney calls "psychological individualism," the American legal system argued that most social conflict, including criminal and other antisocial behavior, was a matter of personal aspiration, personal ability, and personal deviance (479). The influence of a free-will doctrine of law had been in evidence throughout the nineteenth century and by the end of the 1890s prisons had evolved as sites of cultural refashioning, institutions where medical models of social and psychological intervention were practiced on deviant yet morally responsible criminals, creatures whose individual defects had caused them to commit crimes and against whom almost any reconstitutive act could be justified. Based as most of these interventions were on the premise that the absence of "order" was at the root of moral decay, it is not surprising that black Americans suffered the most from the institutionalization of these correctives, given the history of white attitudes toward the characteristics of black life. Whatever rehabilitative promise a prison science of moral refashioning might offer to the white criminal, only the most brutal treatment by the state might reach the black offender's moral center.

Given these positions, it is not surprising that Du Bois levels the following critique of the impact of imprisonment on men when it is suggested that after his imprisonment Towns will be ready to take up the struggle once again: "No, I shall be old and weak. My spirit will be broken and any hope and aspirations gone. I know what jail does to men, especially black men—my father" (104). Towns's intimation of his response to prison is not, however, based solely on the general debilitating effects of incarceration. In Towns, Du Bois has created a character who, however implausible to a modern reader in his heroic nobility, is a prototype for the protagonists in almost every one of Chester Himes's novels of the 1940s: the sensitive, vulnerable black man who looks strong on the outside but experiences himself as without emotional stamina. When asked if he does not consider the possibility that the good he can do in the future outweighs any mistakes of judgment he has made in the past, Towns replies:

> I have thought much of this, and I much doubt my fitness. I know and feel too much. Dear Jimmie saw no problem that he could not

laugh off—he was valuable; indispensable in this stage of our development. He should be living now, but I who am a mass of quivering nerves and all too delicate sensibility—I am liable to be a Perigua, or a hesitating, complaining fool—untrained or half-trained, fitted for nothing but—jail. (104)

Du Bois's antitheses to Town's personification of the romantic sensibility made almost too pure for this world by his sensitivity are found in his portrayals of Sammy Scott and Sara Andrews, the two major characters in the novel most closely tied to the law. Scott is a black Chicago ward heeler and alderman, an "attorney-at-law" whose politically amoral assistant, Sara Andrews, is the real architect of his South Side political machine. Andrews, who is light enough to pass but chooses not to except when it advances her immediate plans, sees in Scott, and later in Towns, instruments with which to build personal power through the judicious application of the law. Here law is the frame that shapes political power and the fulcrum for the levers of the money and influence that move the city, the state, and the nation.

Andrews realizes that Scott is clever but at heart "small-time" in his understanding of "legal graft":

> She recognized politics as a means of private income, and her shrewd advice not only increased the office income but slowly changed it to safer and surer forms. "Colored cabarets are all right," said Sara, "but white railroads pay better."
>
> She pointed out that not only would the World-at-Play pay for privilege and protection, but the World-at-Work would pay even more. Retail merchants, public service corporations, financial exploiters, all wanted either to break the law or to secure more pliable laws; and with post war inflation, they would set no limit of largesse for the persons who could deliver the goods. . . . Sammy was skeptical. He still placed his chief reliance on drunkards, gamblers, and prostitutes. "Moreover," he said, "all that calls not only for more aldermen but members of the legislature and more Negroes on the bench." (112–13)

Sara sets out to make Sammy the indispensable black broker of law and politics in Chicago. In an improbable set of machinations and circumstance (Du Bois was irrepressible in his plot construction), Sara arranges for Towns's pardon with the cooperation of the Ku Klux Klan and uses him to front for Scott's political machine. Towns's experience with the law has made him both cynical and nihilistic, and his outlook makes him Andrews's and Scott's near-perfect foil:

> He had no illusions as to American democracy. He had learned in jail how America was ruled. He knew the power of organized crime, of self-indulgence, of industry, business, corporations, finance, commerce. They all paid for what they wanted the government to do for them—for their immunity, their appetites; for their incomes, for justice and the police. (126)

Towns's political career in Chicago and then in Springfield as a state legislator is choreographed by Andrews, and Du Bois picks his way through the intricacies of finance and regulatory law as he moves the story along. Du Bois is intent on casting this minor exposé of the interrelatedness of corporate greed with national policies[2] in the frame of the story of race and poverty politics in the urban North, but the novel he is writing and the sensibility he brings to it work against him. In particular, Du Bois's affection for his hero as a romantic figure, and his own rather genteel Edwardianism, keep interrupting the "realism" of his muckraking.

In a curious way, the tensions in the text caused by these interruptions mark its modernism. Du Bois seems to recognize the modern condition and at the same time exhibits a quite visible remorse for the passing of the older verities and order. The novel has characters that speak in the idiom of the moment and others, including the narratorial voice, that prate on and on in what approach parodic forms of Victorian circumlocution. Du Bois is capable of romanticizing nature through his description of Towns's relation to the black earth of his mother's farm in Virginia and of apotheosizing labor in his description of the construction of the subways with images that remind the reader of Hart Crane's in *The Bridge*.

While Sammy Scott is truly a modern man bereft of ideology or principles and so willing to be guided by Sara Andrews's ambitions, Matthew Towns is a nineteenth-century man trapped in the modern world by Sara Andrews, a thoroughly modern woman. The Dark Princess and her vision of a new world order based on an ethos of color has receded into a romantic haze of memory:

Chicago is the American world and the modern world and the worst of it. We Americans are caught in here in our own machinery; our machines make things and compel us to sell them. We are rich in food and clothes and starved in culture. . . .

Courtesy is dead—and Justice? We strike, steal, curse, mob, and murder, all in the day's work. (284)

Towns learns in the Illinois assembly that "legislating was not passing laws; it was mainly keeping laws from being passed" (146). Initiatives for birth control, mothers' pensions, and labor legislation protecting women and children go nowhere, but the interests of the big utilities are served by the successful efforts of lobbyists to prevent regulatory laws from emerging. Towns sees that all power is in corporate hands; meaningful legislation, legislation that would transfer power from them to elected representatives of the common people, would never see the light of day (147).[3]

Eventually, Sara arranges sufficient backing to ensure Towns's election to Congress, the first black elected to national office from the North since Reconstruction. She also arranges their marriage. Both of her victories are to be cemented at that most rare of events, a black-white dinner party. Towns is to assure Sara's white allies that he will protect their interests, and Sara will announce their engagement. But the Dark Princess, who has been secretly living at the small farm of Towns's own mother in the South, appears at the last moment to save Towns's soul and his talents for the true revolution, the gradual cultural ascendancy of the dark races over the light. Towns rejects his nomination and Sara before the gathered wealth and power in Sara's drawing room, and he and the Dark Princess return to his mother's farm in Virginia, where their son is born and is presented to the reader as the hope of the future.[4]

In this novel Du Bois rejects the Western metanarrative of the law as the medium through which history moves in favor of a more mystical metanarrative of family, and more specifically of matrilineality. Power flows through women, as fertility and as culture. The bankrupt power of the white West is confronted by the potential reforming grace of Asian/African culture. America has power but no culture; Asia/Africa has culture that is weakening for lack of access to the power to reproduce itself. Du Bois's symbolic answer is to embody the hope of America in its black population, posit the Black Belt of the agricultural South as the American equivalent of the international world of color, and through the marriage of Towns and the princess, and the birth of their son, prophesy a new age.

In 1928, Du Bois's mysticism, which can be seen quite early in the century in his romantic faith in an African American version of *die Volk* in *The Souls of Black Folk* (1903), has not yet given way to a full commitment to Marxian teleology, although he does have the princess study in the Soviet Union before she sets out to create a racial reordering of the geopolitical map. But Du Bois's mysticism notwithstanding, his critique of American law at various levels stands today as trenchant and prescient. And his (inadvertent?) blend of modernist and Edwardian voices is more likely an accurate representation of how the modern moment actually struck most Americans than the avant-garde voices of Paris and the symbolic "Harlem" of the Harlem Renaissance provided.[5]

At the same time that Du Bois was writing, modernism's interrogation of the very bases of terms like *authenticity* was under way. As a collection of responses to the fragmentation of believable systems of authentication since the 1880s, literary modernism required at once a recognition of that fragmentation in the narrative practices of the text and a position vis-à-vis the permanence, desirability, and danger of that fragmentation in the content framed by those practices, in the "story." The appropriation of black American experience as part of a cultural response to fragmentation by whites notwithstanding, black literature in the 1920s had its own responses to the question of authenticity. One of these was the turn from historicity, as if it were no longer possible for black Americans to define themselves in relationship to a series of historical misadventures among white folks and their laws. Instead, the black protagonist turned to self-experience, a romantic practice. These responses usually made up the body of works that examined the lives of black Americans as lived away from the intersections of black and white experience.

In part, this turn was an element of the complex relationship of black Americans to the modern moment. It might be possible, for instance, to argue that black life in nineteenth-century America anticipated twentieth-century modernism. In a previous chapter I noted how much of that century's white project of the suppression of black desire depended on the rejection of the capacity for irony in black identity, in this case "irony" defined as the reflexive capacity for unmediated knowledge of the self within the structure of the external (to the self) world. I also argued there that the denial by whites of the ironic in black experience did nothing to mitigate its very real presence, either in the life or in African American narrative.

If we consider that one aspect of modernism was the task of facing an unmediated universe, one in which we were to exist without the mediative effects of cohesive systems of explanation or simplification on which the previous centuries had relied, then the centrality of irony to modern life becomes visible. I would argue here that "American" law's basic antipathy to irony resides in law's identity as a heavily mediated encounter with the past in the moment. That is, American case law filters the past through a dense layer of convention designed to control the effects of the past on the immediate moment and on all subsequent moments like it. By extension, it would seem as though American legislators anticipate that mediation when they draft laws and so are affected by it. Thus part of the tension of modern life derives from the contradiction between the force with which modernity imposes itself on civil life and on the mediating function of the law as both litigation and legislation. In such a time, irony comments on the contradiction between what is and what the mediated moment ought to be. Just when the law fails in its mediating role, irony steps in, insulating us from the full impact of the modern. And when irony fails, we make a virtue out of necessity by embracing the fragmentation of the past and *declare* ourselves immune to the shock of the modern, declare ourselves *post*modern, when we are, in truth, postironic.

But certainly the position of black Americans under the law has been always ironic. Even in the postbellum period, and using the framework of the discussion at this point of the study, the irony is evident. That is, on one hand black Americans sought to see the law, first natural law as limned in the Declaration of Independence and then positive law as structured in the Constitution and its amendments, as a metanarrative, a mediating text between them and the romantic despotism of white Americans. On the other hand, black Americans found over and over again that the law failed to mediate contradictions in their experience and in fact only served that function for whites, serving as well as a mask for the reality of a rapidly expanding and racially differentiated economic and political power in the service of contract and corporatism.[6]

Thus, African Americans had, by the 1920s, already experienced the dismantling of the explanatory power of the law, leaving them, with the exception of religion, without any mediating screens through which to reconcile fundamental contradictions in experience. The turn away in narrative from intersections with the machinery of white cultural hegemony should be seen as a turn toward a world in which the law as mediating system is irrelevant, a world in which the machinery of mediation is personal and immediate, a world in which the law of white folks appears more and more distant from the everyday concerns of the storyteller and her audience.

For these reasons the emblematic conflict between identity and desire acted out in the African American novels of high and low urban life did represent one true thing about black American life: that it was lived for the most part away from white observation, that there was a black American life that was not always and immediately responding to Ol' Massa or Miss Ann, that urban life had moved black life from under the constant scrutiny of white obsession with tradition, place, and the laws and customs that honored and supported both. African Americans in cities no longer were forced to live lives of white design, at least not so directly as they had done.

One narrative practice that affirmed that distance was the story of the all-black community as a site of relationships, crises, and solutions. There were, in fact, several all-black communities in the United States, and almost all of them were in the South or Midwest. While few of their actual stories were historicized for popular consumption, the idea of a community that mirrored white town life in every respect but the color of its inhabitants made some kinds of storytelling easier. For instance, the traditional crime procedural story could be adapted for a black audience if one could posit a community in which all the antagonists were black, including the police and the court system.

Another ploy was to imagine a domestic American community inhabited solely by African Americans in which every aspect of a traditional American town was reproduced and in which the inhabitants were full and active participants in the civic and economic life of the nation as it was experienced locally across the continent in white towns and villages.

One such narrative was the 1939 all-black film *Midnight Shadow*. The premise of the film is set out in the preamble that scrolls down the screen as the opening shot:

> In the southern part of our country, lies that great land of romance and sunshine, known as the Old South. Here amid fertile fields,

vast acres of timber, oil lands and rippling rivers, live millions of black men and women in the most highly concentrated area of Negro population in America.

Here in certain communities the like of which is found no where else in the world, these people of darker hue have demonstrated the abilities of self-government by the orderly processes of law of which they are capable when unhampered by outside influences.

It is in a community such as one of these that the scene of our story is laid and the events which follow are depicted.

The "events which follow" are less significant than the issues raised by their representation. The story is of a pilfered deed to oil property, the apparent violation of trust, and the accidental death of the heroine's father. One issue raised by the representation is that of intent versus effect: is the crime used to set in motion activities intended to show to some assumed audience, perhaps white, the truth of the premise of the preamble, that is, that black Americans "have demonstrated the abilities of self-government by the orderly processes of law of which they are capable when unhampered by outside influences," or is the preamble used to create a somewhat plausible context in which black Americans can see other black Americans owning oil lands and businesses, living in comfortable homes, having professional identities, and occupying positions of authority all in a clearly fictional circumstance, just as poor whites could see their social "superiors" do in films made for them?

That the conditions are fictitious seems clear enough. Oxley, Oklahoma, is presented as an all-black town of wide streets, spacious homes, business-suited patriarchs, dapper young swains, sweetly glamorous heroines, gruff but fair police detectives, and foolish but well-intentioned amateur detectives played by charming juveniles and their even more foolish sidekicks. Such a world was a fiction in white films, and its fictionality in an all-black film was a difference by degree rather than of kind. There were all-black towns in Oklahoma and in Kansas, Mississippi, Georgia, and Florida; there were blacks and American Indians in southeast Oklahoma and northwest Texas who owned land on which oil was found. But the realities of finance, politics, and race prevented the emergence of anything like the idyllic Oxley.[7]

And difference by degree changes to difference of kind when the action of the film moves from fictive Oxley to Shreveport, Louisiana, on the trail of the thief. Shreveport, the hub of business operations governing the development of the East Texas oil fields at the beginning of this century, was one of the most segregated cities in the South. Our amateur detectives track the thief to the Shreveport offices of an all-black oil development company, advise the black executive in the posh head offices, alert the police (all of whom are black), and catch the criminal.

That a film made for distribution to black audiences located primarily in the South would posit a set of social, economic, and legal relationships that could not and did not exist, as its audience well knew, answers a part of the question of intent. Black films made for black audiences did not need to argue the plausibility of black Americans as law-abiding citizens. The audience knew themselves to be lawful people.[8]

The black audience in black movie-houses throughout the South wanted films that would show them as they knew themselves to be and as they knew they would be, given the opportunity. The argument of the preamble, even if it was presented only to allow the reproduction of a rather common script straight out of white movies, suggests a complex continuation of the critique of American law written throughout African American narrative. One version of the critique makes the case that, were the national "law" as embedded in the Constitution to operate as it ought, that is, to allow African Americans the acquisition of property, position, and political power, fictional Oxley would represent a material world more common to black experience. Another version argues that American law operates so unjustly in the lives of black Americans that the only conditions under which they might imagine their active participation in a world of law would be if that world were wholly black, "unhampered by outside influences."

This latter argument is the opposite of the argument for passing into whiteness. *Midnight Shadow* and the movies like it *(Boogie Woogie Blues, Girl in Room 20, Juke Joint, Miracle in Harlem, Murder in Harlem, Harlem Hot Shots)* made in the 1930s and 1940s create communities in which freedom to enjoy the benefits of citizenship (in its broadest terms) comes from immersion in blackness rather than escape into whiteness. *Midnight Shadow* is emblematic in that such citizenship is tied directly to the legal protection that allows the acquisition of both property and capital and, if property or capital is lost, returns that capital to the black citizen in the black community through the lawful exercise of state authority.

Between the totally fictional and hermetic locales of *Midnight Shadow* and the more recognizable though still fictionalized world of black community life of such novels as Walter White's *Fire in the Flint,* into which whites intruded their seemingly never-ending store of race hatred framed in legality, lies the world of Red Brook, New Jersey, the setting for Jessie Fauset's 1931 novel of black "society," *The Chinaberry Tree*. The white world of Red Brook scarcely intrudes directly into the lives of its black citizens, but the indirect effect of its laws cause confusion and pain to Fauset's characters. It is in this semi-isolation that *Chinaberry* differs from Fauset's earlier *Plum Bun* (1928) and *There Is Confusion* (1924). In those novels Fauset's Negro characters negotiate the urban worlds of Philadelphia and New York, worlds in which the presence of whites defines an ever increasing segment of the characters' reality as they mature. The effect on them is, if they are not lucky, the most unacceptable of compromises. As Joanna argues to her lover Peter, in *Confusion:*

> Why, nothing in the world is as hard to face as this problem of being colored in America. See what it does to us—sends Vera Manning South and Harley overseas, away from everybody they've ever known, so that they can live in—in a sort of bitter peace; forces you to consider giving up your wonderful gift as a surgeon to drift into any kind of work; drives me, and the critics call me a really great artist, Peter, to consider ordinary vaudeville. Oh, it takes courage to fight against it, Peter, to keep it from choking us, submerging us. (283)

The problem of *The Chinaberry Tree* appears to be one that would lead an author to the same intersected site of conflict, since the novel tells the story of interracial marriage as a legally forbidden relationship. The inability of a wealthy young white man to marry the black woman he loves sets off two generations of emotional impoverishment, and every complication in the novel proceeds from that impoverishment. Fauset resolutely centers the tension of the novel in the misunderstandings among various subsequent sets of lovers caused by their inability to speak directly to the question of the first, forbidden love. But the almost bucolic setting of Red Brook and its long tradition of the more or less benign separation of the races allows her to situate the direct racial conflict historically rather than immediately. In a wonderfully prescient brief passage, Fauset comments on how the results of that first interracial love came to stand, as do all racially charged relationships, for the whole history of America:

> Gradually, like the old definition of a simile, the case of Sal Strange and her daughter, Laurentine, became confused, the sign was accepted for the thing signified and a coldness and despite toward this unfortunate mother and child became a fetish without any real feeling or indignation on the part of the executioners for the offenses committed. . . . [T]he legend, although still extant and occasionally revived was beginning to be something quite apart and remote from the Mrs. Strange and her daughter whom colored Red Brook observed occasionally at church or community entertainment. (22)

Choosing for a moment to use terms like *executioner* and *offense*, Fauset locates the origin of all the confusion in the black community in laws passed by white men. But these were laws and practices that could and should be located historically and with a clear sense of their relativity to a specific time and place. That this was the case is clear to the doctor-hero of the novel, Stephen Denleigh, as Laurentine reveals her past to him:

> "I don't believe you really know about me after all Stephen. I'm just—nobody, not only illegitimate, Stephen, but the child of a connection that all America frowns on. I'm literally fatherless."
> He frowned, his face almost as pale as her own. "What bosh to talk to a physician! Biology transcends society! Is that over your head darling? I mean to say the facts of life, birth and death are more important than the rules of living, marriage, law, the sanction of the church or of man." (120)[9]

Later, he points out to her: "As I see it, the two of them were defying, not the laws of God, nor the laws of man speaking universally. Simply the laws of a certain section of America" (160). Although Stephen's belief in the transcendent ability of the laws of science to obviate the laws of man replaces Rowena's similar belief in the "laws" of love in Chesnutt's *House Behind the Cedars*, Laurentine recognizes a practical and metaphoric fact of her life that binds her every bit as much as it did Rowena: just as miscegenation in the antebellum period produced what Eva Saks has called the "invisible father," the aporia caused by the law's provision that condition follows the mother, so in the 1920s Laurentine is quite "literally" fatherless, meaning here that there is no story that can be written in which both she and her father appear (Saks; Samuels).

Behind the problem of antebellum miscegenation, however, whether as rape or love, had always lurked the constant possibility of incest. In a nicely conceived legal twist, Fauset updates and separates the traditional story of the "tragic mulatto" from this subtext of incest. In the traditional treatments of the theme, either the white father would rape a second generation of enslaved women, some of whom were his own children, or siblings "passing" for white would marry siblings who "were" white. In *The Chinaberry Tree*, Fauset's incest story is embedded entirely in the black community, occasioned by a simple, if tawdry, tale of adultery and hidden identity. Although she masks the incest-adultery story by framing it in the miscegenation story, it is the consequential separation of the incest theme from that of miscegenation that makes this novel a "post-property" novel of black experience.

By "post-property" I mean simply that issues of race once complicated by antebellum property relationships remain as legal issues in African American narratives but are separated *from* race-as-property dynamics, as incest is contained within the story of the black communities of Philadelphia and Red Brook but is distinct from, and not causally related to, the miscegenation motif. It is with Chesnutt's *House Behind the Cedars* that the possibility of a classical African American novel as a narrative of "post-property" life begins to emerge. In *Cedars* and Fauset's *Chinaberry*, as well as in the rest of her novels, black protagonists have passed beyond the condition of property to the position of being propertied.

Chesnutt does not free his characters from the consequences of having been property, nor does the condition of propertied-ness extend to all his black characters, but in the story of Rowena and Tryon he sets the conditions for such a story. Later, as we can see in Fauset's novels, the law remains a device through which black desire is inhibited, but it operates differentially and almost always in hypothetical communities of hermetic African American–ness that interact to greater or lesser degrees with the subsuming white world and in which black citizens still live out to some degree, however reduced, the implications of past relationships of law and property. Angela Murray's mother in *Plum Bun*, for example, practices a necessarily existential form of passing:

> [I]t amused her when by herself to take lunch at an exclusive restaurant whose patrons would have been panic-stricken if they

had divined the presence of a "coloured" woman no matter how little her appearance differed from theirs. It was with no idea of disclaiming her own that she sat in orchestra seats which Philadelphia denied to coloured patrons. . . . [H]er frequent occupation of [them] was due merely to a mischievous determination to flout a silly and unjust law. (15)

Later, the Murray household experiences more stringent discrimination in the attitude of a Philadelphia hospital on the occasion of Mrs. Murray's illness. This race prejudice is a fatal psychic blow to the Murrays. Soon both parents are dead, not from any physical consequences of the hospital's treatment of Mrs. Murray, but as if they wither and die from the knowledge of racial perfidy. Time and again in these novels Fauset returns to how forcefully, albeit indirectly, custom and law operate to suppress the desires of black folks.

What does not vanish from Fauset's novels anymore than it had from Chesnutt's is some observance of the conventions of romance despite this progression from embedded propertyness to autonomous propertied-ness. In *Cedars*, Chesnutt interrogates the romantic preconceptions of race and love but kills off his heroine nevertheless. Fauset constantly challenges the moral ground of white supremacist attitudes but never gives up her reliance on the saving power of romantic love. Joanna in *There Is Confusion* speaks for all of Fauset's heroines, as well as for Rowena in Chesnutt's novel, when she says,

But now that we have love, Peter, we have a pattern to guide us out of the confusion. When you left me for Maggie, I used to lie awake at night and think of all the sweet things I might have said to you. Oh, if you've suffered half as much as I have, you've suffered horribly. I learned that nothing in the world is worth as much as love. For people like us, people who can and must suffer—*Love* is our refuge and strength. (283–84)

These "sweet homes"[10] are all crucibles of romantic resolution, of love, renunciation, or death, to the problems of the post-propertied African American living in a world of laws made to reinscribe her and him as property. *Plum Bun*'s Angela Murray "possessed an undeniable air, and she dressed well, even superlatively. Her parents' death had meant the possession of half the house and half the three thousand dollars worth of insurance. Her salary was adequate, her expenses light"

(64). But Philadelphia was no haven for a young woman of color who wanted more out of life. She found it unbearable, "with its traditions of liberty and its actual economic and social slavery, its iniquitous school system, its prejudiced theatres, its limited offerings of occupation! . . . So hidebound were its habits that deliberate insult could be offered to coloured people without causing the smallest ripple of condemnation or even consternation in the complacent commonwealth" (261).

As another hypothetical community, "Harlem" is a complex site for the representation of law and romanticism in African American life. A black world unto its own by the 1920s, it lay somewhere between Oxley and Red Brook. More immune than Red Brook from even the collateral effects of the legal complexities of the nineteenth century, Harlem was still no Oxley if only because as either a real or fictional space, it was not impervious to white interference, day or night.[11]

Criminality, for instance, as well as color preoccupy the popular black fiction of the period, the fiction we generally include when we think of the Harlem Renaissance.[12] The major novels continue the delineation of African American urban life begun by Dunbar, Johnson, and Corrothers and essentially record the criminalization of that life. By criminalization I mean the creation of a public consciousness of African American life the primary characteristics of which suggested to white Americans a life lived outside the limits of legally acceptable behavior. Claude McKay's *Home to Harlem* (1928), Wallace Thurman's *The Blacker the Berry* (1929), and Rudolph Fisher's two novels, *The Walls of Jericho* (1928) and *The Conjure Man Dies* (1932), all reproduce a Harlem in which most black men and women work day jobs of unbearable pettiness and thrive at night on the extralegal excitement of equally petty crime: numbers, local bootlegging, and prostitution.

Fisher's 1928 novel, *The Walls of Jericho*, is a slight story of class and caste in Harlem. In its marginalized world of prohibition Harlem, with its after-hours clubs and numbers rackets, working-class, darker characters comment on lighter-skinned "dickty" Negroes of the emerging upper-middle professional class. As a part of the expansion of physical Harlem to the West Side by this professional class, Fred Merrit, a *very* light black lawyer who could "pass" and is bitter at whites, buys a house on a white block. But Merrit's real enemy in this case is not his white neighbor but another black Harlemite, Henry Patmore—a tavern owner, bootlegger, and all-around hard case—whom he has defeated in a civil suit.

This general satire on whites and gentle depiction of extralegal Negro life assumes a community in which whites are represented by their ignorance of black life, and the law is a somewhat distant set of rules into which a black man or woman can become enmeshed. If we eliminate the working-class "boy-meets-girl" plot of Joshua Jones and Linda Young, where most of the charm of the book is displayed, we are left with the problem of residential segregation (see the Sweet case in Chicago for an actual example of the consequences incurred by a black professional moving into an urban white neighborhood in the 1920s) and the desire for revenge on the part of Henry Patmore—both issues involving Fred Merrit.

Fisher is obviously playing off his audience's knowledge of the Sweet case, although no black person in a northern city in the 1920s needed any special instruction in the vagaries of residential segregation. The reader anticipates neighborhood reaction to Merrit's arrival, once his secret is known, and sure enough, his house is burned to the ground. The gimmick to the plot, however, is that the arsonist in this case is not a white racist but Henry Patmore, who saw Merrit's "block-busting" as an opportunity for revenge. Patmore assumed, and rightly so, that any act of violence against Merrit in or around his new home would be taken as white resistance to Merrit's presence. But Patmore is found out easily enough, and not a lot is made of the ironic implications of his plotting. Since Patmore is also a rival of Joshua Jones for the hand of Linda Young, Jones is happy to clear the whole thing up and get rid of Patmore.

Fisher's other novel, *The Conjure Man Dies: A Mystery Tale of Dark Harlem* (1932), is generally accepted as the first detective novel written by an African American.[13] It, too, is set in the all-black world of Harlem, and this time the law itself is represented not as the web of hegemony supporting white racism but as the distant voice of white authority filtered through the agency of a black policeman:

> Of the ten Negro members of Harlem's police force to be promoted from the rank of patrolman to that of detective, Perry Dart was one of the first. As if the city administration had wished to leave no doubt in the public mind as to its intentions in the matter, they had chosen, in him, a man who could not have been under any circumstances mistaken for aught but a Negro; or perhaps, as Dart's intimates insisted, they had chosen him because his generously pigmented skin rendered him invisible in the dark, a conceivably

great advantage to a detective who did most of his work at night.
In any case, the somber hue of his integument in no wise reflected
the complexion of his brain, which was bright, alert, and practical
within such territory as it embraced. He was a Manhattanite by
birth, had come up through the public schools, distinguished himself in athletics at the high school he attended, and, having himself
grown up in the black colony, knew Harlem from lowest dive to
loftiest temple. (14)

But Dart is only a foil for the real center of the action, Dr. John
Archer,[14] a Harlem doctor whose forensic curiosity involves him in a
murder case and whose Holmesian powers of deduction lead the law
to closure in the episode.[15] Archer's use of the "scientific method"
guides him and Dart through a welter of suspects, the foremost of
whom is an African, Frimbo, an educated man who seems the antithesis of Archer in some ways, in that he is that most unscientific, at first
blush, of practitioners, a social scientist. And he is a witch doctor as
well. But the murder is actually quite quotidian in motivation, and a
spurned lover is uncovered in due time.

However much the substance of the novel is made up of the search
through false assumptions to the ordinary squalor of love and death,
the conflict that Fisher saw fit to inject into it via the circumstance of
Frimbo, is other matter, the matter of modernism. I would enter the
argument over our various "modernisms" only this far, to suggest that
insofar as modernism in the American twentieth century was a turning
away from, as a response to the impossibility of, all previous metanarratives, and a fear that none would come to take the place of those frag-
mented husks of belief clinging to the edges of modern sensibilities,
then it was also a *conscious* identification of that turn and the simulta-
neous elevation of that response to a principle of thought and action.

That being the case, then John Archer and Sam Dart represent
modernism as creatures of skepticism in the service of knowledge,
while Frimbo, the educated African, represents the crumbling fragility
of the metanarrative impulse, whether of "social" science or of superstition. As we have seen above, in Fisher's Class Day oration at Brown
University, Fisher himself is not immune to the appeal of the overarching design, invoking three possibly totalizing schema to take the place
of traditional religion-as-superstition: law, evolution, truth. And it
would be hard to argue that these are not metanarratives in their own
right. Certainly law, as it was seen by African Americans fighting for

civil identity in the nineteenth century in the forms of the Declaration of Independence and the Constitution, was the text that both explained and controlled their destinies.

By the 1920s, however, the grand scheme of the law had become the petty diagram of everyday denial, and perhaps only in the executive offices of the NAACP was it still the field on which great battles would be won. As Fisher's short stories, and the stories and novels of McKay and Thurman and Hughes, showed, life in Harlem was not lived in the sweep of those grand texts. Du Bois, in *Dark Princess,* was busy constructing his own great narrative of the "Race," and Fisher himself could not completely resist the notion that there might be something out there beyond Archer's skeptical science and Dart's law of the "Colony," but modernism was seeping into black narrative and sketching out the changing role of law in African American life.

Another protomodern novel from 1932 is Wallace Thurman's roman à clef, *Infants of the Spring.* In Thurman's account of life among Harlem's own "lost generation" of aesthetes, drunks, and serious artists, law is clearly, at least for a while, something outside the world of the novel, or outside the world of art. It comes, when it comes at all at first, as a report from another world. Thurman introduces the theme not through his black characters, but through the "liberal" sensibilities of Samuel Carter, white habitué of the Harlem scene and frequent visitor to "Niggerati Manor," the rooming house that shelter's Thurman's cast of characters:

> News of a lynching upset him for days. He would excitedly buttonhole everyone with whom he came into contact, and be apoplectic in his denunciation of lawless southern mobs. Apprised of isolated cases of racial discrimination in restaurants and theaters, Samuel would go into a rage, write letters to all the daily newspapers and to city officials, excoriating the offending management, asking for a general boycott, and demanding police and legislative action. (30)

Lynching itself is far from the door of "Niggerati Manor," but it is in the personal past of some of its visitors. Bull, for instance, is the nephew of a man who was lynched somewhere in the South on the mere suspicion of having raped a white woman. The brutal but ironically sensitive Bull takes his revenge on whites by "[h]avin' ev'ry white woman I kin get, an' by hurtin' any white man I kin. I hates the bastards. I gets drunk so's I kin beat 'em up an' I likes to make their women suffer" (69). Euphoria Blake was a backwoods teenager in Georgia when her mother shipped her off to the state normal school to learn to be a teacher. When she got off the train at the shanty that passed for a station, she looked around for the school bus:

> Maybe the bus was late and would be coming down the road. Well, I looked around. And for looking: Right there on the side of the road near the shanty was a telegraph pole. And dangling from that telegraph pole was the body of a Negro man. He had been lynched. (79)

After three years of nightmares she left school and came to New York City, determined to be a Joan of Arc to her people, to lead them against whites.

But the lives of Euphoria and Bull and the others do not add up to a threat against the control whites have over black experience. At one point Thurman has Ray, his protagonist, argue that communism is the theoretical answer to the problem of the color line, *if* blacks could get angry enough at white capital to pick up the gun (218). But this answer goes nowhere in the novel, no further than the analysis with which it competes, that Negroes should simply intermarry or pass or find some way to give up whatever being black has meant. Unlike communism, amalgamation requires no change on the part of whites, no necessity for them to face up to their evil.

Even the law, when it does appear finally to take one of the tenants of Niggerati Manor away, fails to measure up to its reputation as an instrument of white racism; it is merely the accidental operation of a system of impersonal destruction: "The machinery of justice was a depressing contraption and the spectacle of the moronic Pelham helpless in its impersonal maw was certainly not an edifying performance" (246). Courts of justice were such sadistic organizations. They seemed to gloat and thrive over the writhings of their victims. The more meager the offense, the more simple the individual, the less pity and leniency he merited (248).

Arnold Rampersad has written that Negro artists of the 1920s "were as aware as anyone else about the pressure of the modern on their lives and their art" ("Approaches" 50). Thurman goes him one better, it seems, when he gives the following observation to Steve: "There's really very little to revolt against since the Victorians have been so thoroughly demolished. And it's too soon to rebel against the present regime of demolition" (220). Left without any formalisms to oppose, no legal metanarrative to resist (that having been left behind in the South), the black artist in Thurman's novel has only "futile intro-spection, desperate flagellations of self which still left him in darkness and despair" (147). These hallmarks of the narrative of the anxiety of the modern artist are inscribable on black as well as white artists. Euphoria Blake is modeled on Zora Neale Hurston, who will be no Joan of Arc but will be accused of abandoning any progressive project for her people and be reviled by black cultural historians for half a century. Bull's sexual violence will spill out all the way forward through the work of Richard Wright and Chester Himes to the career of Eldridge Cleaver, where it will finally become a political agenda.

Thurman and Fisher were the only African American "modernist" prose fiction writers prior to Ralph Ellison. They had short careers and died young. Their contemporary, Langston Hughes, was a modern man and a realist in the practice of his fiction but, because of his attrac-tion to a Marxian metanarrative of history, he was less devastated by the impact of modernism. His fiction, as seen in his 1933 collection, *The Ways of White Folks*, is located at the intersection of black and white America. Unlike Thurman and Fisher, Hughes sees the law as one of the primary texts of social life, one that permeates existence. In the story "Home," for example, when Hughes writes, "Ma never had any money. Her kids had barely managed to get through the grade school. There was no higher school for Negroes in Hopkinsville," he embeds the entire history of the legal deprivation of black America since Eman-cipation, the conscious efforts of white America to suppress African American desire, in his story. He throws American use of segregated schools and differentiated funding—legal instruments of cultural and economic oppression—into relief against the opening scenes of the story, scenes of the use of police to victimize the poor in Berlin and of the "Army of the Unemployed" encamped in Washington, and has his protagonist, Roy, understand that although in Europe the power of the state is used against class instead of against caste, as it is in America, the effect is the same.

Roy's return home after a career in Europe as a musician is awk-ward for Hopkinsville. He is black in the white South. He is a man but not enmeshed in the subtle regulations of black male life spun by white custom or law. While law does not overtly oppress him here at home, neither does it protect him, and custom, with the finality of law, catches him at last. He is left to hang "all night, like a violin for the wind to play" (49). If art is not Thurman's "useless flagellation of self," neither is it a haven in Hopkinsville at night when the law vanishes: "[A]s for the cultured Negroes who were always saying art would break down color lines, art could save the race and prevent lynchings," responds Oceola in "The Blues I'm Playing," "Bunk! . . . My ma and pa were both artists when it came to making music, and the white folks ran them out of town for being dressed up in Alabama" (113).

Law and custom operate at the intersections in most of Hughes's stories in this collection. In stories of interracial sex, law and custom blend into one practice. A woman cannot protect her children from the law's inequity:

> Gee, Ma, when I think how papa left everything to his white fam-
> ily, and you couldn't legally do anything for us kids, my blood
> boils. You wouldn't have had a chance in a Kentucky court, I
> know, but maybe if you'd tried anyway, his white children would
> have paid you something to shut up. ("Passing" 54)

Nor can she protect herself from her son's betrayal as he trades on that same father's color and asks her not to visit him while he abandons his own dark-skinned children. In yet another town, an interracial love affair brings no lynching, just economic reprisal by whites against every black person in town and the total segregation of the black community from civic life, including the schools ("Mother and Child" 189–97).

"Father and Son" is the story in this collection in which the law is most directly implicated in the situation of the characters. Colonel Tom is aging and has no legal heir, although he has several children by his Negro housekeeper/mistress. One of these children, a boy, has been sent away to school and returns, a young man set on challenging the system that circumscribes him and the father who refuses to recognize him. Caught up in this story are issues of property, white political power, custom as law and law as custom, marriage law, the Scottsboro case, and lynching. At its melodramatic end, the boy and his brother are lynched and the old man is dead at the hand of his son. Hughes does not alter any of the formulaic tensions of race and property inherited from Hopkins, Harper, and Chesnutt, but by the 1930s the melodrama has taken on a tragic inevitability, here influenced and shaded by Hughes's Marxian sensibility.

The Great Depression reinforced the realistic and naturalistic elements of the classical African American narrative and its critique of American law without replacing or displacing the remnants of romanticism that had survived the urbanization of black life. As I have been trying to show, it also retarded the development of a modernist narrative of African American life under the law. Both of these effects can be seen at the end of the 1930s in the work of Zora Neale Hurston, although her fictional milieu was not the urbanized North but the rural South.

Hurston's development as a writer also involves a shift from classical conventions in the African American novel, and in the treatment of law the shift is perceptible, even though direct encounters with the world of law are only a small part of the two novels that deal with black experience. Hurston, the renewed interest in the career of Dorothy West notwithstanding, was the only woman writer of the Harlem Renaissance to write significantly into the 1930s and early 1940s. A southerner, an anthropologist, a wit, and a novelist, Hurston wrote several works of fiction, drama, and anthropological folklore before edging into obscurity and poverty.

In the two novels of southern black life she produced in the mid-1930s, *Jonah's Gourd Vine* (1934) and *Their Eyes Were Watching God* (1937), Hurston frames events in a Jim Crow universe; as in previous novels of the century, the legal construction of reality emerges out of *Plessy*, and black life is represented as a hermetic experience.[16] In *Jonah's Gourd Vine*, the law is represented as a counternarrative to the vernacular tale being experienced by the reader and the characters. That is, when John Pearson refuses to testify in his own defense and refuses to call his friend Hambro to the stand as well, he does so to prevent the story of the community's domestic entanglements from becoming a part of the white counternarrative of black life. Pearson tells Hambro:

> Ah didn't want de white folks tuh hear 'bout nothin' lak dat. Dey knows too much 'bout us as it is, but dey some things dey ain't tuh know. Dey's some strings on our harp fuh us to play on and sing all tuh ourselves. Dey thinks wese all ignorant as it is, and dey thinks wese all alike, and dat dey knows us inside and out, but you know better. Dey wouldn't make no great 'miration if you had uh tole 'em Hattie had all dem mens. Dey wouldn't zarn 'tween uh woman lak Hattie and one lak Lucy, uh yo' wife befo' she died. Dey thinks all colored folks is de same dat way. (261–62)

Just as Jim Crow circumscribes the physical reality of a day-to-day black life, white control of legal narrativity, of the spaces, voices, and materials of the production of legal stories, threatens the validity of the vernacular narrative. This was especially true in the nineteenth century, before and after Reconstruction. By the 1930s, however, there was less and less of a reason for the legal narrative to wield such a power. The counternarrativity continued to exist, but its threat to the validity of any other narrative of black experience had decreased in proportion to the rise of black cultural production. African American literature that examined the same conflicts that appear before the law became a formal counternarrative to the law's own contradistinctive storytelling. Thus, ironic as it may seem, the increasing power of black narrative contradicts the power of legal narrative even as, with the advent of the depression, Jim Crow as a social practice seemed ever more deeply entrenched. This parity proved to be temporary, however, as black literary production also sank beneath the weight of capitalism's woes in the 1930s.

The function of counternarratives in Hurston's fiction does not remain as straightforward as any zero-sum model might suggest, however. In *Their Eyes Were Watching God*, Hurston trades on counternarrativity as she had before, but reverses the direction of its value to the protagonist. When Janie is brought to trial for the death of Tea Cake, the fact that white law privileges some narratives and not others saves her life, for it is clear that the vernacular tale of the death of Tea Cake as told by his male friends would convict her:

> Then she saw all of the colored people standing up in the back of the courtroom. . . . So many were there against her that a light slap from each one of them would have beat her to death. She felt them pelting her with dirty thoughts. They were there with their tongues cocked and loaded, the only real weapon left to weak folks. The only killing tool they are allowed to use in the presence of white folks.
>
> So it was all ready after a while and they wanted people to talk so that they could know what was right to do about Janie Woods the relic of Tea Cake's Janie. The white part of the room got calmer the more serious it got, but a tongue storm struck the Negroes like wind among palm trees. They talked all of a sudden and all together like a choir and the top parts of their bodies moved on the rhythm of it. They sent word by the bailiff to Mr. Prescott they

wanted to testify in the case. Tea Cake was a good boy. He had been good to that woman. No nigger woman ain't never been treated no better. Naw suh! He worked like a dog for her and nearly killed himself saving her in the storm, then soon as he got a little fever from the water, she had took up with another man. Sent for him to come there from way off. Hanging was too good. All they wanted was a chance to testify. (153)

And later, after the prosecution presents its case, the community is intent on having its voice: "The palm tree dance began again among the Negroes in the back. They had come to talk. The State couldn't rest until it heard" (154). The ensuing scene, in which the judge threatens the black audience with jail and refuses to hear them, would be just another example of the oppressive weight of white power in the courtroom in a narrative from any earlier period. But here the silencing of black voices is essential to Janie's vindication. Hurston's text suggests that the misogyny of the black community prevents its several members from accepting even the evidence of their own personal histories with the deceased and the defendant. Janie's only hope is that a white lawyer can tell her story, a white judge can distill it, and a white jury can hear it as it happened.

As Hurston constructs the rest of the trial, we are to accept that Janie's story told in her own words saves her. Some commentators on the novel have expressed their discomfort with this scene because we never hear Janie's testimony; a third-person omniscient narratorial voice summarizes her telling of the story.[17] But I think two things are clear enough. One is that we have just been treated to seventy-four pages of the story as Janie has told it through the frame story to her friend Pheoby. Hurston leaves the job of constructing the testimony to the reader by providing a metanarrative frame within which one can imagine what must be said:

She had to go way back to let them know how she and Tea Cake had been with one another so they could see she could never shoot Tea Cake out of malice.

She tried to make them see how terrible it was that things were fixed so that Tea Cake couldn't come back to himself until he had got rid of that mad dog that was in him and he couldn't get rid of that dog and live. He had to die to get rid of the dog. But she hadn't wanted to kill him. A man is up against a hard game when

he must die to beat it. She made them see how she couldn't ever
want to be rid of him. (154–55)

Hurston has not written the words Janie actually spoke, but the
truths she intended to have her words say. When Hurston wrote, "She
made them see," she is in effect leaving the job of the creation of that
speech to the reader.

Another matter is that Hurston here pits one narrative system
against another and for reasons critics are still arguing over intends for
white legal discourse to prevail over vernacular storytelling. While she
will not write Janie's testimony, because it can only be told in vernacular conventions if she is to deliver it, she does give you the judge's dis-
tillation in his instructions to the jury:

> Gentlemen of the jury, it is for you to decide whether the defen-
> dant has committed a cold blooded murder or whether she is a
> poor broken creature, a devoted wife trapped by unfortunate cir-
> cumstances who really in firing a rifle bullet into the heart of her
> late husband did a great act of mercy. (155)

The jury remains out for only five minutes and returns with a verdict of acquittal. Janie is immediately surrounded by a protective wall
of white women while the judge, jury, and both lawyers congratulate
her. The black community leaves the courtroom, heads down, defeated.
The effect of this representation is that Janie's is experienced entirely in
terms of white hegemony. While it is possible to argue that Hurston
could not afford to let Janie's vernacular testimony carry the day, that
the reader had to hear only white voices tell the story of Tea Cake's
death and what it meant because white narrative is privileged here, as
it always is in the law, it is also possible that Hurston was representing
another version of the relationship of law to power.

In the law, the question is of standing: who is entitled to speak?
From the professional certification of judges, lawyers, and other officers of the court, through the less "official" vetting of expert witnesses,
to the basic question of whether a plaintiff has standing before the law
to bring her story to the bar, narrators are narrators only if they are recognized to be so. But once authorized to speak, is the narrator's voice
unassailable? Literature has had its problems with the unreliable narrator, from the Bible and Homer to Browning to Conrad to F. Scott

Fitzgerald, with Borges and John Barth at the extreme end of the scale. In literature the reader makes do with what she is given. In court, the perjured witness is jailed or fined, the discredited witness is sent down from the stand, testimony is sometimes stricken. Similarly, lawyers and judges are bound by rules of accountability to protect their auditors and the later readers of the text of the case from unreliability. Reversals can be built on the unreliability of judges, mistrials granted on the unreliability of advocates.

However, Hurston as an anthropologist writing fiction, and as a student of the most famous male anthropologist of her day, Franz Boas, may have been reconstructing the narrative relationship of the court to conform to the model of ethnography she had learned from Boas. In this reading, the power of the anthropologist resides in his role as mediating site between his informant and the culture desiring to receive her information. Janie, as informant, cannot tell her tale directly to her actual audience, at least as the scene is represented to us. There are two mediating sites between her and the recipients of the information she has. One of these is the anthropologist/novelist herself, who, having given you her "field notes" in the form of the previous seventy-odd pages, now summarizes and rationalizes Janie's testimony, so that we, the recipients, have a précis of her argument. As in *Jonah's Gourd Vine*, Hurston places law as a counternarrative against *volksprache*. Whether this reflects an ambivalent relationship between Hurston's own rationality, her rural Florida roots, and her anthropologist's systemic vision of the organicism of folk institutions deserves further reflection. But it is clear in this narrative that the conflict is between the law, which is represented by white speech and demands closure, and folklife, represented by the indigenous speech of the black audience at the trial, whose ethos is open-ended, processional, transcendent, and ambiguous.

But the other audience for Janie as informant is the jury, and the mediating site between her and it is the judge. Janie's story is redacted through him even more concisely than it is through Hurston's authorial voice, and this time the frame is not the storyteller's narrative sense but the judge's knowledge of, and theory of, legal social relationships. The judge reports to the jury his reading of Janie's experience and situates it within a possible grammar of the law; he suggests to them how her story can be read. Thus the effect of the court scene can be to reinforce our awareness of law's mediating role, particularly as Hurston forces us to see it operating against an unmediated discourse of the death of Tea Cake as represented by the community's insistence on Janie's culpability.[18]

The courtroom scene is actually the second trial in the story and is embedded in the first. The first begins on the opening page of the novel when Janie returns home and is confronted by a jury of her peers, arrayed on the porch waiting for something to happen: "It was time for sitting on porches beside the road. It was the time to hear things and talk. . . . They became lords of sounds and lesser things. They passed nations through their mouths. They sat in judgment" (5). In Hurston's frame story, Pheoby represents the court that must decide what Janie has done with her life, and her "assignment" to hear Janie's story is the excuse for the overall narrative. As such, the story told to Pheoby is the testimony Hurston does not write for the embedded trial scene. But Pheoby is more, or other, than that legal analogue; she, too, is anthropologist to Janie's informant:

> "Most of dese zigaboos is so het up over yo' business till they liable to hurry theyself to Judgment to find out about you if they don't soon know. You better make haste and tell 'em 'bout you and Tea cake. . . ."
>
> "Ah don't mean to bother wid tellin' 'em nothin', Pheoby. 'Tain't worth de trouble. You can tell 'em what Ah say if you wants to. Dat's just de same as me 'cause mah tongue is in mah friend's mouf." (9)

In this case, however, the outcome is irrelevant to the text as Hurston has built it. By the time Janie returns home to this judgment, she is free of its consequences. It matters not at all to her what the jury on the porch decides. In fact, the greatest effect of the narrative is not to liberate Janie, but to stimulate growth in Pheoby, who grows "ten feet higher" just from listening to the story (158). Unlike the "scientist" anthropologist, Pheoby forgets her objectivity and promises to be Janie's advocate in the community. Then she hurries home, not to report to her colleagues, but to be with her husband, so infused is she with the essence of true devotion revealed through Janie's narrative.[19]

Why, ultimately, is the counternarrative of the law used in reverse by Hurston in her second novel? At the end, the only liberating narrative has been that constructed within the conventions dictated by the law white men make and operate. The narrative Janie tells Pheoby is

not necessary to Janie's own freedom. She is free on the first page of the
novel. And on its penultimate page she tells Pheoby, "'Course, talkin'
don't amount tuh uh hill uh beans when yuh can't do nothin' else. And
listenin' tuh that kind uh talk is jus' lak openin' yo' mouth and lettin' de
moon shine down yo' throat" (158). I don't know what drove Hurston,
but the very presence of the text itself, a kind of permanent talking,
makes me wonder at what we are being warned against. In the confines
of this novel, white legal discourse is a very narrow, blessedly narrow,
thing. Then again, it bursts its own confines and operates not only positivistically, driving to some formal closure, but affectively as well,
leading to waves of emotion from the whites who have heard the story
in the court, not unlike the effect Janie's direct account produces in
Pheoby. Vernacular black narrative, on the other hand, overflows its
banks from the start of the novel and only at the end hardens into a narrow tool for killing. There is likely no resolution in the text; it frames the
narrative and a counternarrative, celebrates one and allows the other a
specific liberating force. It disavows storytelling and tells a story about
the disavowal. It insists that doing is better than talking, but talks all the
way through and at the end stands alone in a room, pulling the world
in around it, removing itself from the field of action. By the novel's end,
the room could be anywhere, the time could be any time, and language
is abandoned:

> The kiss of his memory made pictures of love and light against the
> wall. Here was peace. She pulled in her horizon like a great fish-
> net. Pulled it from around the waist of the world and draped it
> over her shoulder. So much of life in its meshes! She called in her
> soul to come and see. (159)

In the world of light, image, and memory that Janie inhabits at the end
of the novel there is no room, no need, for either law or literature, both
systems of social realization. There is no need for any narrative in her
life.

Hurston's work, especially its folk realism, may have influenced
other writers of her period. The work of Richard Wright, Willard Motley, and Chester Himes draws on the strengths of the realistic tradition
of the novel, and Wright and Himes in particular reach into the same
sources of narrative strength, local particularity and black isolation
from white systems of social control, that Hurston taps. The naturalism
that is a part of her contemporaries' commitment to the social novel

produces stories considerably less romantic in their resolutions, and the ever-present threat of the failure of narrative to sustain life under the burden of American law contradicts the mediating role Hurston allows that same law. To understand how the African American modernist narrative of status and destiny under the law finally emerges in Ralph Ellison's *Invisible Man*, we will have to work through the problems presented by that commitment.

CHAPTER 8

At the End of Histories

> What did they think of us transitory ones? Ones such as I had
> been before I found Brotherhood—birds of passage who were too
> obscure for learned classification, too silent for the most sensitive
> recorders of sound; of natures too ambiguous for the most
> ambiguous words, and too distant from the centers of historical
> decision to sign or even to applaud the signers of historical
> documents? We who write no novels, histories or other books.
>
> Ralph Ellison, Invisible Man

Black and white narratives and counternarratives compete openly in
the field of major fiction throughout the 1940s. In the fiction of Richard
Wright, Willard Motley, Chester Himes, and Ralph Ellison, white law
and black life begin to write different stories. The extent to which, by
this point, modernism had really seized the black narrative as it had
other Western narratives is a debated question (Michaels; Lauter;
Baker, *Modernism*; duCille; Douglas; Hutchinson; North). In that
debate, it is sometimes seen as dismissive to exclude black writers from
discussions of "high" modernism. I would not like to be tarred with
that brush, but I do want to suggest that within the limits I have set and
will set on my on reading of this period, the "features" we identify with
canonical modernism—the sense of fragmentation, loss, cultural
anomie, recentering of the narrative consciousness in the mind of the
artist—none of these seemed to speak strongly to the conditions out of
which most black writers wrote prior to 1950. Either most of these
impressions were too late, historically, to be new to African Americans,
or they were irrelevant to the artistic lives of black fiction writers. Even
Wallace Thurman's depiction of what passed for Harlem modernism
was closer to the Bohemia of Floyd Dell, John Reed, and Louise Bryant
than to the stripped-down, rearticulated, elliptical, well-lighted waste-
lands of Eliot, Woolf, Hemingway, and Stein. White modernism of the
first half of the twentieth century exposed the dismantling of the major
metanarratives of Western culture and lamented that loss while
attempting to capture its consequences stylistically. If there was a par-

allel African American modernism of the same period, it had its emphases elsewhere.[1]

Motley's *Knock on Any Door* and Wright's *Native Son* are substantial novels of the period in which the critique of American law is framed through a premodernist literary naturalism.[2] They can be read comparatively because they share characteristics of surface structure. Each presents an economically powerless young protagonist whose fate is shaped by the implacable mechanisms of society, presented naturalistically. Each protagonist lives a violent life, commits at least one murder, is captured after an extensive manhunt, tortured by the police, tried in the press, defended by a "liberal" attorney whose argument is based on sociological determinism, prosecuted by an offensive, opportunistic district attorney, and is convicted and executed. In addition, each protagonist "comes to terms" with his identity as killer in a dramatic scene.

Each writer, after the success of these major novels, eventually left America to live and write abroad, joining a long list of expatriate black American writers, musicians, artists, and performers. In expatriation, the social marginalization of black Americans in the United States was consciously seized by its victims and wrung into a deliberate existence outside those margins. A sense of marginalization is powerful, in terms of race and class, in both of the novels under consideration here, and this sense, while superficially similar to the alienation of the white modernist artist, is even more isolative of the writer's sensibility. The white modernist artist erases or otherwise makes society irrelevant or reinvents it with his or her consciousness at the center of its self-narrative. The black writer of the same period writes over the society's self-narrative and in its margins and endpapers.

Reading *Native Son* and *Knock on Any Door* intertextually, that is, both together and against one another, shows, for example, that in each of the texts, despite their differences, "the law" is either argued to be or revealed to be inadequate as a way of knowing the identities and lives of those who live marginally. The argumentation or revelation tactics fall generally into two categories: (1) the limits lawyers establish for the range of admissible data and the assumptions they make about how "knowing" is constituted are either argued against or shown in juxtaposition to other ways of knowing; (2) the broad epistemological questions raised by the substance of the issues under consideration reveal significant areas of indeterminacy when "the law" is brought to bear on them. In fact, those who seek to read the lives of marginalized litigants and criminal defendants through the epistemological screen of the law are doomed to misread those lives. That is the impact of each of the novels because such misreading costs the protagonists their lives: judge and jury each send young men to death on the bases of what each thinks it knows and understands of the lives in question, while the reader sees through another screen and acquits or shows mercy.[3]

The texts clearly invite us to these readings since, in each case, the defense lawyers are given opportunities to make arguments from the lives of the defendants as the reader has experienced them, but they are constrained by the epistemological requirements of the court. The care with which Motley worked on the trial section of *Knock on Any Door* is instructive. In preparation, Motley attended the 1941 trial for murder of a nineteen-year-old named Sawicki, took copious notes, and spent considerable time with the public defender, Morton Anderson ("Andrew Morton," for the defense, in the novel). Anderson's answers to Motley's questions about how to set up a defense and his permission to use part of the "Sawicki" closing argument for the novel shape Motley's approach to the final courtroom scenes. In an apparent attempt to be certain that he did not overstep the limits of his naturalistic approach, having fixed the portrayal of an unsuccessful defense, Motley took the chapter in which Nicky is sentenced to a Chicago judge to be checked for accuracy.

The published account of Morton's defense of Nicky clearly reflects this care, but there are limits to what the conventions of judicial proof will allow. While Motley has gone to great length (436 pages in the Signet edition) to put us inside the life of Nicky Romano so that we understand and accept his killing of Officer Dennis Riley, Morton must attempt, in the twenty-odd pages given to him, to circumvent Nicky's confession on the witness stand by convicting society of a greater crime, two murders—that of Nicky Romano years ago and consequentially of Dennis Riley at the hands of the soul-dead Romano:

> Then, standing erect—looking straight into the jury box—Morton said, "Nick Romano was murdered seven years ago! I so charge! I accuse—Society!—of the murder of Nick Romano! And I tell you, too, to leave without illusion. . . ." He went on slowly. "Society . . . you and I . . . all of us . . . we . . . the *good* people!—murdered!— Nick Romano! Why is he here before us? *We ordered him here!* We brutalized and murdered him and we made this rendezvous with him seven years ago. . . . I say that my client is innocent. Your only

duty is to consider whether or not the State has *proved* beyond a reasonable doubt that he—and no one else—caused the death of Dennis Riley. Before God—I submit that it hasn't been proved." (Motley 459–60, chap. 85)

Motley's problem is that his lawyer cannot do to the jury what the novel can do for its reader, that is, create the "reality" of Nicky Romano's life. Here is Morton's attempt to do the job:

Come inside the beautiful walls of the reform school with me, where he was incarcerated long months, where he was stripped of his clothes and beaten, where he obeyed a gangster rule—ate, worked, slept, rose, lived by whistles! and curses! and fists! See, with us, the whip of these—men, they call themselves—as they administer their form of police rule. Hear the curses of the keepers in *your* eardrums. Feel the lash of the whip in *your* flesh. Leave, like Nick, without illusions as to how we reform our youth. . . . Come with us along Maxwell Street where the fences buy anything from a boy—no question asked. Listen, with him, to the thieves. Look, with him, at the corner prostitutes. (458–59, chap. 85)

These commands go on through evocations of crap games, pool halls, jackrolling, and death. But Motley cannot assign to Morton any of the novelist's skill; the jury is ultimately unmoved. Nothing Morton can say can validate Nick Romano's life for those who formally sit in judgment:

"Well, let's look at it this way—" said one of the housewives [on the jury], the one with the boy Nick's age. "Ever since he was nothing but a boy he's been a criminal and none of *our* children would have done the things he did. I know my boy wouldn't." (471, chap. 87)

The problem here is basically epistemological. Morton chooses a phenomenological approach to knowing; he implores his audience to create, or re-create, sensations, the assumptions being that knowledge is the sum of phenomenal experience. If only the jury could see, feel, hear enough, they would *know*. Unfortunately for his case, he cannot do to them what has been done to Nicky; he can only ask them to imagine or recall similar sensations. Plato had argued in his dialogue *Phaedo* that all experience belongs to the immortal soul and is accumulated as the soul cycles through the physical and "formal" worlds; it needs only the proper stimulus to be recalled as knowledge. But then Plato had never met a Chicago jury, and Morton is no Socrates; these folks are having none of it. Morton's problem can be restated in the terms of this discussion. His arguments from the streets, from the margins of social life, must penetrate both formal and experiential barriers to knowledge. His jury of housewives lives at the experiential center of ideologized American life. That is, their lives, however similar to that of the Romanos of the city, can rarely find adequately clear expression in their own judgment since the ideologically correct version of their lives is that their children are happy, they are secure, they are self-sufficient, and they are all morally intact.

The unresolved contradiction between what their lives are supposed to be and what they are leads them to the harshest judgments of the boy who acted because he could not sustain that contradiction and his identity any longer. The judgments of these women are further circumscribed by the legal positivism of the task they face in rendering judgment. They must assume, says the law, that there is a demarcation between that which is permissible and that which is not, a demarcation by definition impervious to amendment or contradiction. That is how one tells what is legal from what is not. When the jury sees its collective experience as both legal by the law and justified by ideology, Morton and Romano lose any chance they ever had. Nicky's acts can be showed to be *not* legal, and there can be no justification for that condition in his life according to the ideology that is the text of reality for the jury. Morton's argument simply cannot hold; Nicky has no claim to the role of victim because the jury must believe the legal to be the just and Nicky is so clearly not legal by his actions.

It makes no difference that the judge and both lawyers know that there is no necessary identity between the legal and the just; the judgment is the jury's. Morton's only chance to secure justice for his client is to decenter the position of society, in this case the jury and its sons, from legality. That is why he charged them all with the larger crime and insists that they indict themselves; he must separate the notion of the legal from that of the just. He fails, I would argue, because a court of law cannot formally frame such an approach. It is that disparity between the legal and the just, and its protected status and substance, that reverberate through these texts and, as we have already seen, through the texts of much African American narrative. Fiction, not the legal brief, is the discursive frame through which African American narratives as ironic texts may best reconcile, or at least recognize, those contradictions.

Ultimately, it is not necessary to impute to Motley some elaborate philosophical agenda to conclude that the text suggests, through our very experience of it, that the basis of argument in criminal court is rooted in an assumption that knowledge is phenomenal, is approachable through fact displayed as evidence and testimony, and is quantifiable and thus cumulative in its effect. This is, after all, the text "edited" by Mr. Anderson and vetted by a criminal-court judge. The text also suggests that such an approach fails to represent the real lives of the participants, since those are seen more authentically through the associative screen of representational fiction. Finally, this text calls the very positivism of legal epistemology into question.

Pursuit of an African American critique of American law has, as we have seen, many surprises and a few "required" texts. Richard Wright's *Native Son* is both required and surprising. I have no desire or need to replicate the body of criticism of this novel that the last six decades have produced; I do want to make some comments on issues that may not have been obvious to previous readers. A close reader of this book will by now have a pretty good idea of how to raise her own questions about *Native Son* and American law, but I want to continue the epistemological discussion begun with the consideration of how knowing is represented in *Knock on Any Door*. For me, *Native Son* raises the last (but is not the last to raise it) of the epistemological issues central to a late classical African American critique of American law, the drive to self-knowledge and the problem that drive presents for the law. Let's skip to the third section of the novel, where Boris Max's defense of Bigger Thomas is, like Morton's of Romano, deterministic. Bigger must be understood by the judge to be the product of a system that is designed to destroy the lives of the poor and the dispossessed.[4] But unlike Nicky Romano, who throughout the progress of his trial never knew what hit him and who could only say, over and over again, "I'm Nicky Romano and I want to live!" Bigger Thomas is driven by the need to know what it *meant* to be someone, anyone, in such a universe as he could discern. His ontological questions are best approached epistemologically.

When we are invited to say, "I think, therefore I am," how are we allowed to extend that statement? Does Descartes mean to imply that I also know that I am? Probably. But if that is so, then here is something

I cannot say: "I think, therefore I am innocent." If we take *innocent* to mean a condition of being without knowledge, as do most first-listed dictionary entries, no person who knows that she is, can be innocent. This is why Bigger and Max are working at cross-purposes to each other in the last section of *Native Son*. We all know that Bigger is going to be convicted and killed; Wright has been setting us up through two-thirds of the book just for that denouement. But the third section is clearly the section of the book he reserved for himself to work out his own position. That working out is displayed as the dialogue between Max's arguments, addressed to the court and to Bigger, and Bigger's self-construction as he talks to himself and to Max. I call your attention to only two problems within that exercise. The first is implicit in the earlier reference to Descartes. Once Bigger Thomas knows who he is, he is no longer innocent of the crimes of which he is accused. What Wright posits is that in order for Bigger to survive psychically, he must choose to be "he who has committed those crimes" because he has no other place to stand that is not premised on that acceptance. Wright and history have shorn him of every possible support; every privileged stance that a white defendant could give away has been denied Bigger, and he must either be chattel to the strangers who claim to own him or stranger to their strangeness. He must choose not to be owned in order to be. So it does Max no good to plead Bigger innocent; the price to Bigger is too great. To be authentic, to be romantic, to be real, to be a citizen, Bigger must be guilty.

The second problem is that Bigger and Max occupy radically different ground when they argue responsibility. To return to a Cartesian construct for a moment, let's ask this question: how can you tell the taster from the soup, the dancer from the dance? Do I taste the soup or am I of the soup? Do I think myself or am I thought? Bigger insists that he thinks himself; Max argues that he is thought. Bigger is willing to rewrite his own history to apprehend his own life; Max is willing to deny Bigger's soul to authenticate his history. Wright's text of Bigger's struggle provides a countertext to Motley's. Bigger's self-insistence can be read as an argument to render moot the judgment of the court. He insists on the right to be the contractor of, not the contracted for. His lust was not for white women; it was for the redefinition of the rights to property, a term to be understood metaphysically as well as materially.[5] Thus, for Bigger Thomas, there can be no willingness to play the hand dealt, to honor one's promise to see things through to some pre-ordained end. Once again we are in the presence of a text in which it is argued that "the law" cannot be the instrument through which I am known; its proofs are insufficient. This brief redaction of a complex argument is not meant to obscure the very real problems this segment of the book gave later black readers nor to gloss over the complexities of what critic Caesar R. Blake has called "the tangled relation the novel posits among law, morality, justice, and the exigencies of social fact and social reality" (188).

Wright's reliance on something like the "naturalistic" method to produce his vision of that relation is documented in his essay "How Bigger Was Born." As Walter White had done in his composition of *Fire in the Flint* fifteen years earlier, Wright sought to use the page as his laboratory: "Why should I not, like a scientist. . . , use my imagination and invent test-tube situations, place Bigger in them. . . , and work out in fictional form an emotional statement and resolution to this problem" (867)? At the heart of the experiment would be the "conditions of life under which Negroes are forced to live in America" (867). In this desire to document the conditions of Negro life he was not unlike White, or Chesnutt, or Delany and certainly directly influential on Motley, Chester Himes, and Ralph Ellison.[6]

Wright's essay also documents how thoroughly he had thought through the history of the legal suppression of the very sense of American-ness that was in the heart of every black American. As he saw it,

> There was in the back of [Negro] minds . . . a wild and intense longing (wild and intense because it was suppressed!) to belong, to be identified, to feel they were alive as other people were, to be caught up forgetfully and exultantly in the swing of events, to feel the clean, deep, organic satisfaction of doing a job in common with others. (860)

It is the ability to imagine this kind of connection and to feel that same imagination at work in the lives of his people that is at the center of Wright's, and the Negro people's, romantic capacity for nationhood. Ultimately, for all the horror of urban blight and violence and murder, the great crime in *Native Son* is the denial of human community to an entire race of people imprisoned in the white bosom of the nation. Even Bigger, "hovering unwanted between two worlds—between powerful America and his own stunted place in life" (871), sensed himself somehow tied to the nation, to the promises of its Declaration and the protections of its Constitution. Wright says of Bigger:

I don't say that Bigger knew this in the terms in which I'm speaking of it; I don't say that any such thought ever entered his head. His emotional and intellectual life was never that articulate. But he knew it emotionally, intuitively, for his emotions and his desires were developed, and he caught it, as most of us do, from the mental and emotional climate of our time. (871)

His conclusion was that his character had to be seen in revolt against this legal history in the most immediate sense, and the consequences would be played out not in some abstract discussion of rights and justice but first in terms of flesh and death, and then in the abstractions of self and society.

From *Native Son* to Ellison's *Invisible Man* is the usual jump-cut in African American literary histories of this period, but in this case I want to stop off along the way. About a year before Ellison's novel came out in 1952, a black writer named Edgar Rogie Clark published a prose poem in *Masses and Mainstream,* a Marxist journal. Here are some lines from "Psalmnettes for the Dark Seraph":

How can I keep silent in these days? for a government based on Democracy is formed, yet crafty counsel is taken to exclude my people: second rate citizens must wear a color badge and Black Laws are printed in pocket editions. . . .

"Where is the Land of Democracy?" someone asked, "where is this land of Burning Desire?" Yes, tell me, too, tell me more about this soulstirring vision of the new-freedom land: one day perhaps I'll get a ride to this Land of Liberty. . . .

They that make the laws mock us: we have been made into a farce: they that wait at the polls laugh at us: and we are the joke of drunkards.

Other fiction in the intervening decade asked the same questions, detailed the same inequities under the law. What some of them share that has not been evident outside of the work of Wright, and Hughes to a lesser extent, is an engagement with the matter of class as it relates to the legal status of African Americans. In 1937, for an issue of Dorothy West's *New Challenge,* Wright had written "Blueprint for Negro Writing," in which he attempted to lay out the desired class dimension of African American literature as he saw it as a black writer and as a communist. Noting the tendency of the petit bourgeoisie of any oppressed minority to assume the values of the dominant class, he pointed out, however, "The workers of a minority people, chafing under exploitation, forge organizational forms of struggle to better their lot. Lacking the handicaps of false ambition and property, they have access to a wide social vision and a deep social consciousness" (54). His concern was that black literature, when it was not merely aping white literary fashion as an adornment for the race, had not reflected that consciousness but had instead appealed to white audiences for acceptance of, and justice for, black Americans as citizens just like themselves. His corrective to this mistaken focus was to urge the black writer to write for the masses of black working people, drawing on, but somehow transcending, the influences of black nationalism, black folk tradition, and the black church. The key to that transcendence was a class perspective based on a Marxist analysis of American society: "It creates a picture which, when placed before the eyes of the writer, should unify his personality, organize his emotions, buttress him with a tense and obdurate will to change the world" (59–60).

Wright went on to argue that such an analysis was only a starting point, and he disavowed any slavish adherence to an "ism" approach to writing. Nevertheless, his own commitment to a Marxist perspective led him to a specific description of the problem black Americans had with the law, the exclusion of Negroes from the institutions of American life through a legal infrastructure built on "a plantation-feudal economy" (58). Contrary to Wright's reading of previous African American literature, such a perspective had been addressed at least once before, by Charles W. Chesnutt in *The Colonel's Dream* (1905), but without the class-based perspective that Marxism attaches to economic analysis. Still, Chesnutt's depiction of the relationship between southern law and its economy could have been sketched as an illustration of the classic Marxist base-superstructure paradigm.

Wright's failure to recognize the early relevance of Chesnutt's work notwithstanding, his argument did point to the condition of black writing at the moment. The "so-called Harlem school of expression" (63) had led Negro letters nowhere. Wright's unstated assumption was that literary art had to be useful to its audience, and if that were to be the case for black literature, then a new kind of discipline and perspective was necessary. The goal, after all, was social, not aesthetic. Wright would not publicly state, as Du Bois had done in the 1920s, that Negro art needed to be propaganda, and he did disdain in the essay any subjugation of the "craft" of writing to "the social office of other professions" (63), but the message of the essay is clear: Negro writers should consciously address the historical class position of African Americans and with an interiorized perspective of class-based realism write to the Negro people with the goal of raising them to a greater level of consciousness of the origins of their condition. Only from there could any change in that condition proceed.

William Attaway's *Blood on the Forge* (1941) attempts to meet Wright's challenge with a combination of Negro folk culture, classical European mythic motifs, and the principles of proletarian fiction as laid down in disputes on the literary Left in the late 1920s and early 1930s. His analysis of the position of the black masses at the onset of modern America is portrayed through the lives of three half brothers, each associated with a dominant theme of the African American past: Mat, the representative of the power of the Christian mythos and its sacred texts; Chinatown, the representative of the hedonistic legacy of the slave system; Melody, the folk artist. Defeated by the share system, peonage, and Jim Crow life in the South, the three brothers flee their serfdom and are recruited to a life of industrial labor in the steel mills of Pennsylvania. There they encounter alienation from their pasts and the emptiness of their wage-slave present and future. At the end of their story, Mat is dead, Chinatown blinded, and Melody the guitarist is hobbled with a mangled left hand with which he must learn to make a new, modern, industrial music to replace the folk music that no longer tells the story of their lives.

Attaway's novel takes advantage of one of Wright's observations in building its argument. Wright had written that the use of literary craft to propel the development of a new world need not obscure reality: "No theory of life can take the place of life. . . . [The writer] may, with disgust and revulsion, say *no* and depict the horrors of capitalism encroaching upon the human being. Or he may, with hope and passion, say *yes* and depict the faint stirrings of a new and emerging life" (60). Attaway chooses the path of disgust, and when he does so utilizes the characteristics of proletarian literature in an inverted, even demonic, fashion. The result is a harrowing depiction of a system of legal industrial slavery from which there is no escape for black Americans and perhaps not for working-class whites.

Four fundamental principles of the depiction of modern life in the strain of proletarianism emerged out of Soviet practices in the 1920s and were debated through the infrastructure of left literary culture in the United States in the 1930s: (1) a purposeful attitude to the outside world; (2) the apotheosis of labor; (3) a spirit of collectivism; (4) a celebratory theme of metal and machines (Suggs, *Proletarian*). Attaway denies the validity of each of these foci in the lives of his black protagonists. He shows the impossibility of having a purposeful attitude toward the outside world when the lives of black Americans are excluded from that world and its institutions by law and custom buttressed by law. Neither has he much to say toward apotheosizing labor. The labor to which his protagonists are relegated is destructive of their lives, their psyches, and of the land itself, both as agriculture and as industry. What Attaway shows is that this work to which men are forced by laws that curtail their full participation in the economy is not "labor" in any humane sense of the word. The spirit of collectivism appears in the novel only in the conflict between the mill owners and the attempts of the mill workers to unionize. Using "deputies" in a perversion of the law, the mill owners attack the workers who are engaged in lawful organizing activities. Caught between the two forces, Mat signs on as a "deputy" and is killed in the battle for the factory. At the moment of his death, Mat realizes that he has become what he has struggled against for his entire life, but his collectivist epiphany comes too late to save him or the strike. Finally, Attaway presents a picture of metal and machines that could have come from Hieronymus Bosch. The factory and the machines that gouge the earth to feed it also consume the men who tend them and by extension their families. Men lose limbs and organs, develop cancers; women die in childbirth or suffer sterility; children grow stunted and twisted, morally as well as physically. The machines that run both day and night soon rob the men of their very identities, as the characteristics that define them spiritually are obliterated and replaced by sheer physicality. Mat loses his personal integrity, his memories of his wife, and his devotion to his mother's religion; Chinatown loses the ability to perceive the sources of pleasure that he sucked up from life; Melody loses all sense of the rhythms of natural life from which he created a world he and his brothers could safely inhabit even as he loses the use of the hand that shaped those rhythms into song.

While *Blood on the Forge* is clearly sympathetic to the general plight of all workers, the weight of the novel lies on the specific alienation from life of its black protagonists as a consequence of racism in the context of human alienation under industrial capitalism. Here there are no reactionary white men betraying the Constitution or the Declaration of Independence; there are virtually no whites who carry that discussion.

When whites appear, they are agents of a mindless but systemic oppression that quite clearly serves an economic order that knows nothing of constitutional issues. Yet everything that has been done to the brothers is "legal." The legal subtext of the novel is so fundamental it is almost undetectable. In it, the natural law of agrarian life, built on the foundation of seasonal growth and encompassing the equality and dignity of humans, is subverted time and again by a positivist legal system, built on economic advantage and supporting relationships of exploitation that are *de*natured and unnatural in their effects on humans. This is true of the peonage system under which the brothers first work and of the industrial system under which they witness the degradation of all life around them.

Attaway renders two judgments at the end of his book. One is a sweeping vision of the ability of industrial capital to delude the very senses of its victims. In it, blind Chinatown talks with a blind veteran on the train. The vet had been a steelworker, too, escaping the mill only to be maimed by its products. He hears still the echoes of the big guns of the western front, and he tells Chinatown to listen. Chinatown believes he hears and gets caught up in the romance of war, the image of the guns superimposed on that of the big smokestacks of the mills. "[Melody] looked at the two blind men closely. Their heads cocked to one side, listening for sounds that didn't exist. They were twins" (237).

But Mat had been a victim of his own special blindness, one that was more immediate and more closely linked to his status as a black man in a white world. When he died during the assault on the workers, he had done so at the hands of a young white man. A terrible force during the melee, Mat had crushed and beaten down everyone before him. Then, looking into the face of his next victim, Mat saw the same rage he had felt when he confronted the authority of the overseer in the fields of his youth. Mat realized at that moment that some force larger than he had made him into what he had despised, an agent of oppressive authority. With that realization he hesitated, and the young man killed him. Attaway didactically points up the larger lesson of Mat's ironic realization by letting the white "deputies" who had hired Mat comment on the way black men serve the "legal" purposes of capital:

> Sure is a shame that big nigger had to go and get himself killed. But I don't reckon he can pin it on nobody. Just accidental in the line o' duty, that's all. He was game, all right, but crazier 'n hell. That's the thing 'bout nigger deputies—they're fightin' the race war

'stead of a labor strike. Always be like that, I guess, as long as they come from the South. There'll be somebody to take his place, an' that there's one reason why the union ain't gonna win. They didn't figure on the South when they started this here. (233–34)

Attaway's text argues the interrelatedness of economic structure and law in the maintenance of a system that transcends race but exploits it. The text also implicates the history of American domestic geopolitics. It is not "race" that the union organizers do not anticipate, it is the historical reality of the "South" and all that it stands for in the legal relationships between whites and blacks, between free labor and peonage.

Attaway's answer to the indenture that characterizes this interrelatedness is "art." At the novel's close, Melody is regaining his ability to capture the moment in his music. Even as he and Chinatown ride the workers' train to the next mill, his deformed hand shapes the new sounds into new songs, songs that had seemed deformed themselves when he tried to make them for his brothers but now seem to make sense. There is no programmatic solution, yet there is endurance. How one reads the ending is probably the ideological question. Is it escapism? What of us who are not artists? Are we doomed to destruction? Or is it enough that we can read this book and recognize the danger we are all in? Might we then begin to organize our lives differently? Does Attaway, by the dismantling of all other accessible paradigms, force us to confront the systematic prison in which we are all held? Historically, the answer is that Attaway's vision had almost no influence one way or the other. The book as a depiction of labor came out in direct competition with John Steinbeck's *Grapes of Wrath* and scarcely made a ripple in the universe of possible readers. And unlike Wright's own *Native Son*, *Blood on the Forge* imprinted no startling new picture of black sensibility on the consciousness of black or white readers.

The prison of class and race in industrial America is just as impregnable one war later, in Chester Himes's *If He Hollers Let Him Go* (1945) and *Lonely Crusade* (1947). Bob Jones has a couple of years of college under his belt and works in a shipyard. His social worker girlfriend, the daughter of a doctor, sees him as a lawyer. In *If He Hollers Let Him Go*, Himes catches his nigger by the toe and never lets go, sending Jones spiraling into self-doubt, indecision, and paranoia. From Presidential Executive Order 8802, which makes his job possible in the first place, to the Los Angeles County Court that in effect sentences him to the army, the delicate equilibrium Jones tries to maintain as he walks the color line is framed by the law and by the history of black men as objects under that law. Himes's determinism is powerful because he grounds the force of society's blind disregard for Jones in a legal system that has both current operatives and a history, the dimensions of which even the law's minions do not fully know but that Himes insists works psychologically on Bob Jones because he knows it as part of the cultural knowledge all black men have.

The history that weighs the most heavily is that of miscegenation, from the various intraracial color references throughout the novel to the looming presence of Madge, the white woman whose rape charge sends Jones to his impotent encounter with the court. Jones is vulnerable because of his sexual desire for Madge, but vulnerable in a way no white character could ever be. Himes takes care to show the various levels of sexual tension in the shipyard among workers who are integrated not only by race but by gender. And he shows how that tension works within prescribed limits to break the monotony of industrial work. But he also shows how race and class operate to establish even narrower limits within the space where gender and "work" overlap. In the shipyard, men direct the work at all levels, and some black men direct some work in order to keep misunderstandings between managers and workers at a minimum. But by custom, black men cannot direct the work of white women, although white men can direct the work of black women. So when Jones, a leaderman, encounters Madge while he is looking for a "tacker" to do some work in his section, he anticipates trouble. The relationship is compounded by class. Bob Jones is smarter, better educated, and knows a wider world than most of the workers in the shipyard, particularly more than the white "Okie" refugees of the rural South. Madge is a "cracker" of the type young black men are told by their mothers to avoid. For those mothers, the history of their lynched male children is written in the lipstick of blonde cracker women: "She was a peroxide blonde with a large-featured, overly made-up face, and she had a large, bright-painted, fleshy mouth, kidney-shaped. . . . Her big blue babyish eyes were mascaraed like a burlesque queen's. . . . She looked thirty and well sexed, rife but not quite rotten" (19).

Jones's girlfriend, Alice Harrison, on the other hand, "fell into the living-room like Bette Davis, big-eyed and calisthenical and strictly sharp" (53). Alice is a princess of the race, and Bob, for all his natural

endowments and his own sense of his status above Madge, feels inse-
cure in the presence of the proof of Alice's class position. Even Alice,
however, is susceptible to the vicissitudes of racism, and she prefers the
social company of colleagues and contemporaries her own "color" and
of her own class. Much of the tension between her and Bob Jones
emanates from the inability of either to formulate a shared position
from which to confront a racist world. Ultimately, the plot tension of
the novel is generated by these various conflicts of class, race, and gender.

Himes's critique of the legal status of African Americans is made
explicit, however, in two distinct sections of the book. In one eight-page
segment that opens chapter 18, Himes has Jones dissect the very notion
of citizenship for African Americans from the perspective of a people
who are and have been trying to see themselves as Americans and not
as Africans since Emancipation. Himes is clearly not a "nationalist" in
these passages. For example:

> That was the hell of it: the white folks had drummed more into me
> than they had been able to scare out.
>
> I knew the average overpatriotic American would have said a
> leaderman was justified in cursing out a white woman worker for
> refusing to do a job of work in a war industry in time of war—so
> long as the leaderman was white. Might even have called her a
> traitor and wanted her tried for sabotage.
>
> It was just that they didn't think I ought to have those feelings.
> They kept thinking about me in connection with Africa. But I
> wasn't born in Africa. I didn't know anybody who was. I learned
> in history that my ancestors were slaves brought over from Africa.
> But I'd forgotten that, just like the aristocratic blue bloods of Amer-
> ica have forgotten what they learned in history—that most of their
> ancestors were the riffraff of Europe—thieves, jailbirds, beggars,
> and outcasts. (152)

Later Jones mused: "That's all I'd ever wanted—just to be accepted
as a man—without ambition, without distinction, either of race, creed,
or colour; just a simple Joe walking down an American street" (153).
But in his second direct critique, Himes has Jones explain why he felt
this was impossible: "Sometimes I get to feeling that I don't have anything at all to say about what's happening to me. I'm just like some sort
of machine being run by white people pushing buttons. Every white

person who comes along pushes some button on me and I react accordingly" (166). Jones explains this loss of agency as his awareness that every white person in the world has "got the power of some kind of control" over him (167), can tell him where to sit on the streetcar, what tickets he can buy at the movies, how to direct his own workers. The power he is describing is the power whites have toward Negroes in 1945: to act without fear of let or hindrance. Jones knows that no act of aggression short of direct assault by a white toward a black can be challenged under the law. And he knows, as the story bears out, that if direct assault comes from the state, he has no appeal. It is this powerlessness under the law that ultimately destroys Bob Jones.

There is a desperate attachment to the idea of an American identity in the classical African American narrative and Himes's writing during the 1940s is not only in the tradition but echoes its earlier manifestations and exemplifies it uniquely within the context of his own time. Nevertheless, what we begin to see in *If He Hollers Let Him Go* is even more realized in the later novel: the nexus of identity as a function of the plot begins to shift from the determination of legal/social status—including the question of one's racial status as a function of law—to psychological self-identification. You might want to argue that this shift is a matter of degree rather than kind, but with Himes some provocative problems begin to emerge in African American fiction.

African American literature of the nineteenth and early twentieth centuries abounds with expressions of devotion to the ideal of a nation "conceived in liberty" to which people of African descent yearned to belong. At the same time, the reality of the neverending betrayal of those desires etched a measure of desperation under or through each declaration. The novels of F. E. W. Harper, Pauline Hopkins, Sutton Griggs, and their contemporaries at the end of the nineteenth century are congruent in their despair over the ways of white people. Each expresses clearly that somehow the great promise of America has been aborted by these whites who have corrupted the law, that great civilizing force, into a tool of oppression. In most cases however, as in this observation by Belton Piedmont in Sutton Griggs's *Imperium in Imperio* (1899), black love for the American promise was almost blind in its steadfastness:

> The Anglo-Saxon has seen the eyes of the Negro following the American eagle in its glorious flight. The eagle has alighted on some mountain top and the poor Negro has been seen climbing up

the rugged mountain side, eager to caress the eagle. When he has attempted to do this, the eagle has clawed at his eyes and dug his beak into his heart and has flown away in disdain; and yet, so majestic was its flight, that the Negro, with tears in his eyes, and blood dripping from his heart has smiled and shouted: "God save the eagle." (243)

Forty years later, the onset of the Second World War afforded African Americans a reason to consider just how devoted to the American eagle they cared to be. Could this "desperate Americanism," this implacable desire to be *of* America without condition—but an America free at last of the bretrayals of its fundamental ethos by whites—remains unrealizable but no less deeply held while the ultimate sacrifice is asked again as it was in World War I? In a 1943 editorial in *Negro Quarterly*, Ralph Ellison argued that there were three possible Negro responses to the war: a black militant rejection of a white man's war; a sycophantic unqualified acceptance of the war aims of the allied nations; or dual attention to the goals of victory over fascist enemies abroad and over fascist racism at home. Adam Clayton Powell Jr., put it succinctly as a struggle for democracy "on a world basis" and a "bloodless revolution within these shores against a bastard democracy" (125).

Anticipating the last of Ellison's points by almost a year, and claiming to speak with a racial voice "that comes out of a bruised and beaten past, out of a confused and shadowed present, an obscure future," Himes opens his 1942 essay "Now is the Time! Here is the Place!" with this "clarion" call to combat with native American fascism: *"Now, in the year 1942, is the time; here, in the United States of America, is the place for 13,000,000 Negro Americans to make their fight for freedom in the land in which they were born and where they will die"* (214). For Himes, this fight must be a "second front," a domestic struggle against white oppression that echoes the rhetoric and resolve of the war against international tyranny, a war he also feels must be prosecuted by black Americans as a part of their American identity.

For Himes, there is no Negro past that is not American, and no Negro future, however international the struggle of the united democracies might be, that does not lie in America: "We Negro Americans do not have a choice. We have to win on *both* fronts—and at the same time" (217). And to claim the integrity of the domestic struggle within the context of a wider war is easy for Himes. His America is a Negro America:

> Here, in the land of our fathers, we fight for what is ours. Democracy is the Negroes'. Is not the blood of Crispus Attucks, who fired the first shot and gave the first life for its creation inalienable proof of this? Did not the red blood of black soldiers which has colored every American battlefield win us this democracy? Was the blood of the American heroes of other races a different blood? Did they spill more of it? Did they all die twice?
>
> Does not, also, the nation of the United States of America, in a comparable degree, belong to the Negro American by right of creation, by right of development, by right of occupation? Are not these the inalienable rights by which people claim nations? . . . This is our native land, our country; our participation in the war effort is a fight for what is ours. Our fight at home is simply for the possession of it. . . .
>
> In the broader view, the Negro Americans' fight for freedom is more than racial. It is a fight for justice, for an ideal, for a form of government in which people will be bound together, neither by race, nor creed, nor descent, but by common objectives and aims for the benefit of all. It is a fight to preserve in living force the spirit of the Declaration of Independence; a fight for the effective administration of the rights, privileges, and regulations of the Constitution of the United States. No American of any race, true to the ideals of Americanism, can refuse to participate in the Negro Americans' fight and on their side, for that which we fight is the only true Americanism. (217–18)

But these ideas did not originate with Himes. On January 31, 1942, James G. Thompson had written to the *Pittsburgh Courier* urging some sort of public campaign to establish the black American viewpoint on being half-free in a war for democracy. As a consequence, the *Courier* began the "Double V" campaign calling for two victories, at home and abroad, over forces of oppression. A crest made of interlocking Vs and the word "Double Victory" and "AT HOME—ABROAD" symbolized the campaign. An American eagle perched atop the crest. On February 14, 1942, the *Courier* wrote above its masthead: "We, as colored Americans, are determined to protect our country, our form of government and the freedoms which we cherish for ourselves and the rest of the world, therefore we have adopted the Double 'V' war cry—victory over our enemies in the battlefields abroad. Thus in our fight for freedom we wage a two-pronged attack against our enslavers at home and those abroad who would enslave us. WE HAVE A STAKE IN THIS FIGHT. . . . WE ARE AMERICANS TOO!" Around the country Double V clubs sprang up, other black newspapers joined the campaign, pins and memorabilia were produced, and Double V girls were featured in weekly photo layouts. The campaign lasted until September 1945.[7]

For Himes, one complication within the problem of African American Americanism and antifascism in the context of the war is predicated not on common cultural memory but on class. Throughout *If He Hollers Let Him Go*, Himes allows Alice the argument befitting her class status, that amelioration lies in self-improvement. Alice and her father are Booker T. Washington avatars, with all the insensitivity to class context that Washington's publicly advanced panacea implied. Another more complex and more systemic response is predicated on class as well, class conflict. While there are Communists among the workers at the shipyard, nothing they offer is allowed to have a bearing on Bob Jones' problems as Himes constructs them. The CPUSA had not embraced the Double V campaign for fear it would hamper the American war effort and reduce the usefulness of that effort to the Soviet Union's resistance to German aggression. Himes approached the problem of the Communist argument in his 1942 essay. The halting, almost obscurantist, prose style of the following passage suggests just how uncomfortable Himes might have been sorting through the politics of his own brand of Double V desperate Americanism in the face of an internationalist argument:

> Or is it presumed . . . that this present conflict is only the beginning of some world-wide social upheaval in which all the impurities of society will be purged and the world emerge in a new splendor of equality of mankind? The latter is a precept difficult of normal rationalization. . . . [T]he self-application required to imbue the average person with the ardor to fight to preserve and make strong a form of government which will never serve the purpose for which one fights, and as a consequence, after the victory for its continuance is attained, must be overthrown and replaced by another form of government—the utter acceptance of this line of progression—is well-nigh impossible for average intelligence.

There is no question concerning the reality of this precept. . . .
Not that the objectives are actually conflicting; nor that the logic is
false. Simply *that at this time it is not the point.*

The point is the Negro Americans' fight for freedom and equality in this present structure of American Democracy. (218–19)

It is in *Lonely Crusade,* written in 1945 and revised throughout 1946,
that Himes takes a closer look at class politics rather than cultural continuity. In the novel Himes's fundamental critique remains that of *If He
Hollers:* the ultimate suppression of blacks in America is the suppression of black desire *for* America into impotency under the psychic
weight of legal power, specifically the suppression by the manipulation
of law of black's most basic desires for work and home in the context of
an American history and an American reality.[8]

As the effect of the suppression of basic human desires is even
more realized in the later novel, its significance as a transitional African
American narrative emerges. In it, the nexus of African American identity begins to shift from the determination of legal/social status—
including the desperate question of one's status as an American
citizen—as a function of racial identity under the law to psychological
integrity and the maintenance of an American *self* as a part, a major
part, of ego-identity. With this, the question of how to realize desperate
Americanism transmutes in the novel into something pathological and
new to African American fiction.

Half a century earlier, in the novels of Griggs, Hopkins, Harper,
and Chesnutt the moral superiority of Negroes was a given. It was presumed by the authors, enacted as though endowed by the characters,
and embraced by the black bourgeois reading public. Even Bigger
Thomas can be understood to have chosen the existential "high
ground."[9] In the novels of Hopkins and her contemporaries, the perspective on the world provided by the tradition of the "talented tenth"
sought to sustain a solid front to the white forces arrayed against the
race. But by 1947, Himes could write of a black community no more
sure of where it stood or what, if anything, it might want to believe or
stand for than any other random collection of individuals.

Given such superiority, the denial of an American identity to
Negroes by white America was seen by blacks, and particularly by
black writers, as an aberrant practice. But in Himes's novels of the mid-
1940s, it appears as though the denial of American-ness is but one term
in a tautology of frustration. In other words, blacks were not American

because they were inferior and the sign of their inferiority was their "insanity" and their insanity was the product of centuries of denial of their American-ness. Himes argues that the product of this epistemological trap is that desperate Americanism finally gives way to the psychosis of desperation. The true issues in the dilemma of African American identity are no longer legal but are to be found instead within the psyches of Himes's characters and in the fragmentation of black communal life.

In the novel, Ray McKinley, an older black man, began fantasizing killing whites after he saw a lynching. Disturbed by his fantasies, McKinley sought professional help. But the result was only that the old man's need for revenge became more deeply imbedded:

> He became certain that the analyst had known beyond all doubt that over the centuries of oppression—an oppression of body, spirit, and soul so complete that no one before had ever plumbed its depths; an oppression composed of abuses that had completely destroyed the moral fiber of an entire people, abuses to the innate structure and character and spirit so brutal that their effect was inheritable like syphilis—the Negroes of America had actually become an inferior people. (70)

Moreover, McKinley's fantasies suggest, for Himes's fiction at least, that the shift from the earlier generation of writers was really one of kind rather than of degree. McKinley's plan is to kill a white man and plead temporary insanity, although McKinley believes himself to be truly permanently insane, not just temporarily so. And he believes all Negroes are insane with him:

> Finally he convinced himself that there were many people in the world—perhaps all intelligent people—who, like the analyst, knew beyond all doubt that the Negroes were mentally ill from this oppression—ill beyond the circumstances of their present lives. (71)

Even the protagonist, Lee Gordon, was a victim:

> Insanity? Of course it was insanity, McKinley told himself, looking at the tired, dull hurt in Lee Gordon's eyes. This thin, too intense, tightly hurting boy across from him was also insane, but did not know it yet, as were all Negroes, he told himself. (75)

The shift, for Himes, is away from the formulation "all Negroes are legally people and so legally Americans" as a proposition to put case for and to defend. In a 1944 essay, "If You're Scared, Go Home!," Himes had argued that "it was by the calm and considered acts of the voters of the United States who ratified the Thirteenth, Fourteenth, and Fifteenth Amendments to the Constitution that Negroes were made equal. They were made equal . . . by the will of the majority of the people." (233) This reliance on the word of the people made law changes to a recognition of the implacable consequence of the willed hatred of blacks by whites in another formulation, "all Negroes are legally inferior and insane." Thus the struggle for some sort of realizable "American" identity in Himes's version of the African American narrative is no longer solely with an external normative structure called "the law" but with an internalized nomos, to be wrestled with in the dark. And in this novel by Himes, the struggle is almost equally divided between the external and the internal forces.[10] *Lonely Crusade* is, in this respect, a progenitor of Ellison's *Invisible Man,* for Ellison, too, divides the agon between the internal and external forces that shape his protagonist and locates the external forces as Himes does, in the complex welter of sociopolitical relationships that are shaping American character at large. Like Himes, Ellison critiques the impact of those forces by laying them out against the topography of an imagined African American psyche.

Ellison differs from Himes, however, in that the basis for our understanding of the imagined psyche is deeply historical rather than psychosexual. For Ellison the landscape of African American identity against which the American mythos is played out is actually historiographic rather than topographic. Even the recurring motif of insanity is sited in the historic record rather than in the synapses of the protagonist. The confusion felt by Ellison's hero/narrator is not located as close to the center of his organ of psychic pain as is that felt by Himes's Bob Jones and Lee Gordon. Himes's books are examples of psychological realism bordering on naturalism, of the failure of a man's identity to withstand the shocks of an inimical system. Ellison's novel is the story of the madness of history, of the failure of the meta-narrative of American history to adequately account for the protagonist's condition.

Given his psychological, even psychosexual, focus, Himes is as willing and as able as any previous American writer to confront the structural reality of legal oppression and the denial of an American identity as an objective reality. His characters have histories, almost all of which have at their center some encounter with the law, some experience with the law as a frame within which a carefully circumscribed life must be lived. And it is in Himes, I think, more than any other African American writer, that you see so clearly the difference between white and black life. Every one of his black characters must first consider the law's response to his or her every desire, or risk failure, loss of freedom, loss of life. I think that it is because of this intimate relationship with the law that Himes's black male characters are so devastated by its betrayal of them. In a May, 1944, *Crisis* essay, "Negro Martyrs are Needed," Himes contemplates revolutionary change as a solution to this betrayal. He is absolutely clear about just how central the rule of law under the Constitution is to African American life:

> There can be only one (I repeat: *Only one*) aim of a revolution by Negro Americans: That is *The enforcement of the Constitution of the United States.* At this writing no one has yet devised a better way of existence than contained in the Constitution. *Therefore Negro Americans could not revolt for any other reason.* This is what a Negro American revolution will be: A revolution by a racial minority for the enforcement of the democratic laws already in existence. (231)

Only a writer who believes that defense of the Constitution is sufficient cause for a revolution in the twentieth century could create characters like Bob Jones and Lee Gordon, men as wounded by the violence done to the law as by the violence done to them under the law.

In *Lonely Crusade*, Himes threads the law as an organizing principle through the lives of all the characters. He does this historically by having the men reflect constantly on the history of lynching. He does it immediately through the efforts of the union and the Communist Party to organize defense workers under the new labor relations laws and the executive orders with the force of law that were governing the defense industries. He does it contextually through constant references to the enabling legislation of the New Deal. Most obviously he governs Lee Gordon's moral development through his constant confrontations with a legal system that both promises fulfillment of and frustrates his potentialities as a man and as an American. Himes ties Gordon's psychic state to the larger fate of black Americans by having him constantly interrogate his own understanding of black history in America under the law. He easily realizes that the law is powerless to enforce equality and in fact enshrines discrimination. This contradiction is the fact of life in America under which blacks have labored:

It was this acceptance of theirs that kept them living, Lee Gordon contended. This state of believing that they must stay in their place, expecting only a Negro's due. It was this that kept them alive in a nation where equal opportunity was a hallowed legend and civil equality the law. For whenever a Negro came to believe that full equality was his just due, he would have to die for it, as would any other man. (139)

While ultimately Himes allows his protagonist just such a culminating act of existential heroism through which he can define himself finally as not cowardly, not insane, not less than any other American, he carefully circumscribes the conditions under which that heroism would be expressed by explicitly eliminating the black man—white woman sexual trauma that was at the heart of *If He Hollers Let him Go*.

For Himes, the reality of sexuality as a dynamic between black men and white women is given. And the consequences of that dynamic for the black man are historically fixed, as far as he is concerned: violence, betrayal, jail, or death. In fact, this complex of cause and effect is so common that it is the rule rather than the exception. For this reason alone, Himes cannot afford to omit it from the novel. But its very quotidian nature also eliminates it from the list of precipitating events that could lead Gordon to the moment of existential sacrifice in which he realizes himself in terms of class and nation. As Himes writes in "Negro Martyrs are Needed," a true revolutionary moment for Negro Americans can only coalesce around an "incident" in which a strong Negro man publicly reacts to a serious betrayal of his rights as an American:

> The incident, of course, must be a denial of some rights guaranteed to every citizen of the United States by the Constitution, such as the right of any decent, honest person to live wherever he chooses, or the right of a citizen to vote or serve on juries. *Incidents such as an unjust accusation of rape serve no primary purpose* other than to agitate or inflame and fix no constructive precedent for progress. (234–35, emphasis mine)

Himes follows this blueprint exactly in *Lonely Crusade*, so that it is Lee Gordon's desperate American-ness, not his desperate maleness, that drives him to confront authority.

In Himes's plot, the Communist Party has assigned a young white woman to bring Gordon closer to its own vision of his potential. To the minds of the party functionaries who design this assignation, this means convincing Gordon how the institutions of American life under capitalism have denied him and all black males full agency in their own lives, even targeting them for legalized assault from which there is no escape given the power of the system of American law. The young woman is to seduce Gordon and then give him a document that shows him the possible consequences of their affair. The document contains excerpts from the transcript of the trial of a young black man accused of rape by white army officers. In its introductory remarks it declares that the excerpts will show the prejudice of the judge, the contradictions and improbabilities of the prosecution's case, the defendant's true story, the inadequacies of the defense attorney, the biased instructions to the jury, and "[t]he mockery of justice when a Negro is tried in any American court on the charge of raping a white woman" (*Crusade* 10–11).

Although Himes posits the case as a parallel to Gordon's recent attempt to have sex with Jackie, the party's young "agent," there are actually no correspondences between the two. What the case does offer, however, is an example of another kind of encounter with the law, one in which he cannot embroil Gordon directly without violating his own revolutionary premises. Himes could not afford and probably would not have wanted to write a novel about black manhood and America without involving sexuality and lynching, legal or otherwise. But the text as it develops draws Gordon finally to an understanding of himself not solely as a man driven toward a preextant gendered racial destiny but as a black man within two different contexts, class and nationhood, that transcend his gendered racial identity. Gordon accepts an essentialist identity "a Negro" but also posits himself as a worker and a citizen, with rights that can be protected. Himes's argument for Gordon here should be contrasted to similar issues in Richard Wright's *Native Son*. Himes has Gordon reject the argument that the history of black oppression can be a precedental excuse for criminal acts; in other words, there is no absolution in that history, even if one defines the Negro's essential identity as the victim of oppression entitled to act against the society that underwrites such oppression. This is a version of the position taken by Bigger Thomas in *Native Son*. That is, Bigger rejects Boris Max's argument from environmental causes in favor of his own essentialist argument. Gordon rejects both totalizing environmental and essentialist arguments, opting instead for some sense of "normal" versus "subnormal," in which to excuse crime by essence or environment is to accept subnormality in the subject, reducing him to an object at the end. Gordon wants to be "normal." The suppression of this desire in black Americans, to be just an average Joe, by their American experience is one of the great "crimes" against them and Himes tries to chart its psychic cost (*Crusade* 361 ff.).

At the novel's end, it is the denial by the police, as agents of both government and capital, of the constitutionally guaranteed right of assembly, that catapults Gordon into action for himself and for his fellow workers, black and white. In the final scene of the novel, Gordon's self-realization momentarily transcends his racial and gendered identity and locates itself in class and American citizenship, a new American possibility, a new American identity for Godon.

As he had argued in his 1944 essay, Himes shows that no such vision would be possible if the precipitating "incident" were a case of rape. The Johnson trial transcript stands in for the obligatory black male rape case Himes felt he could not avoid but it is placed not to propel his hero but to show how deeply ingrained racial antipathy contaminates what is supposed to be reasoned discourse under the law. Even the issues of class that accompany the Johnson incident are blanked out by the "noise" of race and sexuality. For these reasons Himes simply could not let Gordon get involved in a direct public encounter over race and sex. But he could not be true to his vision of black male experience if he left such an episode out of the mix that would shape Gordon's development.

The final scene of the novel is the fulfillment of Himes's 1944 requirement for a public reaction to the denial of a basic right. In the scene, a mass rally of workers is confronted by armed police and industry goons. Just as the intimidating show of force is about to fracture the solidarity of the workers, Gordon dashes to the side of a wounded white comrade despite the danger of physical violence from the police.

> But he did not look around. He pushed with all of his might into the chest of the deputy in his path, saw him fall away. Ducking beneath the blackjack of another, he was through the [police] line. Out of the corner of his vision he saw the gun of Walter come leveling down on him. And from the parking lot he heard a worker cry: "Don't shoot that boy!"
>
> He reached Joe Ptak, snatched up the union banner, and holding it high above his head, began marching down the street. (398)

This moment of proletarian splendor, as fleeting as it is, signals Himes's truly revolutionary desire: to transcend not only race but history as well, to eradicate the precedent of African Americans' history under American law, particularly the history of the loss of constitutional standing and protection, by telling a story of how one man might reapprehend it. Taken as a piece as they should be, Himes's texts of the war years of the 1940s try to explicate the tensions of desperate Americanism. With history, both private and public, at his back and little but promises before him, Himes seems to stand astride a defining moment, a war to be won on two fronts for the public life of black America and a private struggle for manhood, citizenship, and even sanity for himself. Himes's text of history as precedent should be read not in comparison to his later genre novels, in which he loses faith in the revolutionary ethos and in history generally, but in comparison to *Invisible Man*.

Ellison's novel is, in fact, a meditation on history as a metanarrative rather than as precedent, and the key question of the novel read in this way is whether one is to live inside history's narrative or to step outside it. This is the problem for the narrator and for his alter ego, Tod Clifton. And it is the problem, by extension and design in the novel, for all American blacks. The question is problematic, rather than self-evident, because, as the epigraph to this chapter suggests, black Americans had not, so Ellison felt, written history or novels that contained the record of their existence. This is, of course, the import of the epigraph of this book, taken from a text that antedates Ellison's by half a century. The argument of each is that if black hands have not held the pens, then the text is not representative of the experience of black people in America. Consequently, especially for Ellison, what it can possibly mean to live the history of such an encounter is excruciatingly difficult to comprehend, for blacks and for whites but for black people particularly. That both Mrs. Mossell and Ellison place their observations about the absence of fiction and history from black writers in the context of African American experience with American law at least helps us locate the epicenter of that complexity.

Issues of the law begin to appear in my edition of *Invisible Man* with the 1981 introduction that precedes the novel. Ellison's account of the composition of the novel is told almost entirely in images and metaphors of legality and illegality, citizenship and rights. His neighbors question the legality of his wherewithal while he is writing, and he checks off for us the possibilities of gainful employment they would recognize: thug, numbers-runner, pusher, "sweetback" as well as barber, postal worker, lawyer, tailor, and so on (ix). He emphasizes that he has "fifty legally earned dollars" in his pocket one day (x). His account of the "war" novel he was writing at the time focuses on the contradiction between the Negro's acceptance of his duty as a citizen to protect the country of his birth and the failure of that country to protect either his freedoms or his personal safety. As he feels the new novel begin to impose itself on him, it does so through the agency of his activism in causes at the centers of which sat the law: reporting the 1943 New York City riot for the *New York Post*, agitating for the release of Angelo Herndon and the Scottsboro Boys, marching to desegregate Harlem stores. All of these seem to be "grist for [his] fictional mill. Some speaking up clearly, saying, 'Use me right here,' while others were disturbingly mysterious" (xvii).[11] At a deeper level, law intrudes on Ellison's plans for his novel when he tries to find the story and the voice he is going to write. He wants to avoid writing another "protest" novel, and he wants the story told in an ironic rather than an angry voice (xviii). The story, as he begins to see it, is of the "ongoing conflicts, tragic and comic, that had claimed [his] group's energies since the abandonment of the [*sic*] Reconstruction" (xviii) and had forced black experience to the margins and to the underground of American life. He associates this existence with the experience of the narrator of Dostoyevsky's *Notes from Underground*, effectively establishing the narratorial voice for his own novel as that of the outlaw (xix).

Ellison's peculiarly astigmatic judgment of previous African American narratives at this point complicates his account of the genesis of the book. He wants to argue that "most protagonists of Afro-American fiction . . . were without intellectual depth. Too often they were figures caught up in the most intense forms of social struggle, subject to the most extreme forms of the human predicament but yet seldom able to articulate the issues which tortured them" (xix). That these judgments will not stand is clear enough from the record of African American literary scholarship of the last twenty years, and was probably clear enough in 1981 when Ellison wrote this introduction. There is little ironic detachment in his account of his own struggle with the composition of the novel, no understanding that his wish that his outlaw narrator not be seen as "not American" has precedents in African American narrative. Ellison wants very much, if his introduction is to be taken at

face value, for his novel to read as a pursuit of full, formal, legal American-ness for black folks. His goal is to represent that pursuit and create
a fiction of its accomplishment:

> So if the ideal of achieving a true political equality eludes us in
> reality—as it continues to do—there still is available that fictional
> *vision* of an ideal democracy. . . . Which suggested to me that a
> novel could be fashioned as a raft of hope, perception and enter-
> tainment that might keep us afloat as we tried to negotiate the
> snags and whirlpools that mark our nation's vacillating course
> toward and away from the democratic ideal. (xx–xxi)

That democratic ideal had been the visionary goal of every black
writer from Douglass to Chester Himes, and the history of the nation as
far as those fictions were concerned was the story of its failure to realize the vision. So as a meditation on history via African American experience, Ellison's novel lacks a sense of its own tradition. Nevertheless,
what we can see from his text is that African American encounters with
American law *are* the history that must be meditated on.

Ellison conducts his meditation inside a philosophical frame that
can be summed up by this epistemological question: Does reality reside
in a material fact to be observed (or overlooked), or does it reside in the
observer and her/his faculties? Put another way: Is there a "real" me or
an observed and recorded me? This was the question put, with greater
existential immediacy, to Bigger Thomas, as we have seen. In Ellison's
text of the question, one's answer constructs the rules for one's meditation on history. If there is a reality independent of observation, then any
narrative record of it, history or law included, ought properly try to "get
it right." If there is no reality independent of observation, then "history"
needs to be encountered as the observation and not as the fact.

Ellison lets us know early on where he stands when he reveals in
the prologue that his narrator is invisible "because of a peculiar disposition of the eyes of those with whom I come in contact" (3). He exists
in some corporeal sense but not to most people in any way that has any
impact on the historical moment because they do not record his presence. The novel proper will be the history of this invisible man and of
how he learns that he is not seen and can therefore step out of history.

I am arguing that these histories, his personal history and that larger
one out of which he will step, are basically legal histories, or at least histories of the moments of intersection between black people and Ameri-

can law. I try not to be reductionist because even a fool can see how much else Ellison's text is, but Ellison can no more escape the "reality" that to think about African American history is to think about American law than he can escape the necessity of language itself in narration. And if he is going to write a meditation on history via a novel about African Americans, then he must have the law in the center of his text.

If we jump to the center of the book (there are twenty-seven chapters, counting the prologue and epilogue, and chapter 13 is where we are headed), we find the central speech of the novel. It is about law. The narrator has just emerged from Hades (Ellison very early on invokes the great medieval lawyer-poet, Dante) as represented by a factory hospital where a series of electroshock treatments have shorn him of his youthful illusions and of his previous identity. He is a new man.[12] And he is innocent, with the innocence of Adam:

> Things whirled too fast around me. My mind went alternately bright and blank in slow rolling waves. We, he, him—my mind and I—were no longer getting around in the same circles. Nor my body either. Across the aisle a young platinum blonde nibbled at a red Delicious apple as station lights rippled past behind her. (249–50)

And with the innocence of childhood he is thrust guileless into the world: "When I came out of the subway, Lenox Avenue seemed to career away from me at a drunken angle, and I focused on the teetering scene with wild, infant's eyes, my head throbbing" (251).

He is, in fact, a New Adam, a version of Mary Shelley's creature. In this passage, for example, Ellison captures the tone of Shelley's novel. The narrator has, like the creature, been educating himself, laying up in a safe place and reading books, "countless" books:

> I had no doubt I could do something, but what, and how? I had no contacts and I believed in nothing. And the obsession with my identity which I had developed in the factory hospital returned with a vengeance. Who was I, how had I come to be? Certainly I couldn't help being different from when I left the campus; but now a new, painful, contradictory voice had grown up within me, and between its demands for revengeful action and Mary's silent pressure I throbbed with guilt and puzzlement. I wanted peace and quiet, tranquillity, but was too much aboil inside. Somewhere

beneath the load of the emotion-freezing ice which my life had conditioned my brain to produce, a spot of black anger glowed and threw off a hot red light of such intensity that had Lord Kelvin known of its existence, he would have had to revise his measurements. (259)

It is this New Adam who takes to the streets in the winter of chapter 13 and comes upon the eviction of an elderly couple from their tenement flat. Among their belongings is the material history of a people, and the last three items Ellison catalogs are tied to matters of law: a packet of lapsed insurance policies (contracts), a newspaper clipping about the deportation of Marcus Garvey (criminal law), and the manumission papers of the old man, Primus Provo, dated 1859 (slave law). From that point on, the encounter is presented as an encounter with the idea of the law, from the evicting marshal's insistence that the old couple was "legally evicted" to the narrator's speech to the crowd.

The speech is an ironic turn on what it means to be law-abiding. The old couple want to go in the house one more time to pray. The marshal says no. The crowd gets angry and the narrator, up to this moment a spectator, steps up and says, yells to the crowd: "No, No! . . . Black men! Brothers! Black Brothers! That's not the way. We're law-abiding. We're a law-abiding people and a slow-to-anger people" (275). And with every example he gives, he drives the crowd to the realization that every time black folks try to act within the law they are punished for that trust. At first he is unaware of his effect, since he is trying to calm them. But his message overrides his intent; to be black and to abide in the law, says the narrator, is to ask for punishment. And he drives his slow-to-anger audience to ever-increasing levels of indignation, turning them from a crowd to a group, an entity that can take action.

At one point he tells the crowd:

Look at [the old couple] but remember that we're a wise law-abiding group of people. And remember it when you look up there in the doorway at that law standing there with his forty-five. Look at him, standing with his blue steel pistol and his blue serge suit. [Look at him! You don't see just one man dressed in one blue serge suit],[13] or one forty-five, you see ten for every one of us, ten guns and ten warm suits and ten fat bellies and ten million laws. *Laws*, that's what we call them down South! Laws! And we're wise, and law-abiding. (278)[14]

A few moments later he reminds them that the old man is eighty-seven years old and has worked all his life and ought to have something to show for that. The theme of the speech is the betrayal of hope by history, in this case of black people's hopes since Emancipation by the very system of laws that they had every right to expect would not only protect but nurture them. In an inspired metaphor, Ellison evokes the systemic failure of the major legal documents and icons of the nation in the image of the "dream book," a collection of explicatory passages on common motifs in dreams used by Harlemites to choose the numbers they would play in the illegal lottery, the "numbers" or "bolito." The book itself stands for the failed explanatory texts of black experience, each of which comes under scrutiny in the novel. Included at the center of the list of those texts, the only one referred to specifically by name, is the Constitution:

> Yes, these old folks had a dream book, but the pages went blank and it failed to give them the number. It was called the Seeing Eye, The Great Constitutional Dream Book, The Secrets of Africa, the Wisdom of Egypt—but the eye was blind, it lost its luster. It's all cataracted like a cross-eyed carpenter and it doesn't saw straight. All we have is the Bible and this Law here rules that out. So where do we go? (279–80)[15]

Where he goes from this speech is to the second half of the novel, where he encounters the Brotherhood and their historical materialism as a challenge to the mythology of white supremacy he has grown up with. When he tries to explain that he spoke up because the old couple reminded him of his past, that he is like them, a Brother explains:

> Oh, no, brother; you're mistaken and you're sentimental. You're not like them. Perhaps you were but you are not any longer. Otherwise, you'd never have made that speech. Perhaps you were, but that's all past, dead. You might not recognize it just now, but that part of you is dead! You have not completely shed that self, that old agrarian self, but it's dead and you will throw it off completely and emerge something new. *History* has been born in your brain. (291)

The advantage, for a while at least, that the narrator finds in his association with the Brotherhood is the control that he believes it gives him over history. When one of his alter egos in the novel, Tod Clifton, first introduces the idea that one might find it absolutely necessary to "plunge" out of history in order to preserve one's own sanity, the narrator reflects, "I didn't answer. Maybe he's right, I thought, and was suddenly very glad I had found Brotherhood" (377). One reason for that gratitude was that he was under the tutelage of Brother Hambro, the Party's chief theoretician and, of course, a lawyer. It was from Hambro he had learned a dictum that explains much about life, and about the law: "Life was all pattern and discipline; and the beauty of discipline is when it works. And it was working very well" (382).

This point is made nowhere better in all of African American fiction than in Lloyd L. Brown's 1951 novel, *Iron City*. Brown, an editor of *Masses and Mainstream,* a Marxist journal, writes a novel of black Communists in prison and uses their presence and the plight of a young black prisoner to exemplify the virtues of intellectual and ideological discipline in the face of oppression. The prison, Iron City, stands for the larger society against which the Communists struggle on behalf of their race and their class, and various elements in the pasts of the prisoners are linked to the larger history of the lives of black Americans. One image is telling for its irony:

> And when a man started to talk that way, the others would caution him, saying: "Look out now, brother, else when the flag comes down you'll go up!" For it was the custom that each morning Old Glory was hauled to the top of the tall white flag-pole . . . and at sundown it was lowered. Every evening when the gang went off they could see the knotted loop at the bottom of the halyard slowly rising on one side of the towering mast as the flag came down in solemn majesty on the other. Never did they watch the descending banner of freedom; their eyes stayed fixed on the inexorable, jerking rise of the rope on the other side. And thus each working day of their lives the railroad's patriotic ceremony came to remind them of the supreme law for the black majority of Mississippi's people. (153–54)

Brown and Ellison intersect at times in their choices of "targets" and even in their selection of scenes. For example, both have implicit and explicit critiques of Marcus Garvey and the Universal Negro Improvement Association, both have an eviction scene with an inven-

tory of the household items on the street that is the catalyst for the protagonist's awakening, both use the term *laws* to mean "policemen."

Nevertheless, Brown and Ellison part company on the degree to
which their texts support the analysis that is the product of personal
and political discipline. While Ellison ultimately abandons the Brotherhood because he cannot stomach the particulars, explicitly the betray-
als, of their local politics and politicians, Brown depicts a "local" politics of integrity and loyalty. Brown ties the larger class analysis
available to the Communist prisoners because of their commitment to
Marxian discipline to their personal qualities of steadfastness and capability, so effectively that when Paul, the cell (literally) leader, points out
that there is no privileged space in prison any more than there is an
unexploited industrial job under capital, the validity of the analogy
seems evident on the authority of his character as a man.

The three black Communists create a committee to reopen the case
of Lonnie, a hapless young man who is sentenced to die for a murder
he did not commit. Guiding the committee in its actions on the outside
through their wives and Party comrades, they find the evidence to
free him. Now solidly accepted by the other prisoners, the Communists
deliver their most complete statement to the other cons about what is to
be done. Asked if the Party isn't going to try to get the Communists out,
too, Paul points out that Lonnie's case was an emergency and took
precedence: "But of course you got to see it another way too. The fight
for Lonnie is part of our fight. . . . [I]t could have been you up there on
Murderers' Row—Merle Gaither, alias Slim" (245). The case gave the
Party the chance to show that instead of being violently opposed to the
state, it was fighting state violence:

> [T]hird degree beatings, legal lynchings. Reminds them of how we
> always have done that, Scottsboro and all the rest, led the fight
> against the Coal and Iron Police terror and the company thugs in
> the steel and mining towns around here. Now it's against the law
> for McGregor Steel to have all the shotguns and tear-gas and clubs
> they used to fight against the men, and people will remember how
> we fought to have that law passed. . . . When you boil it all down
> and whatever the Court decides about Lonnie or us or anything
> else—that won't be the end. The final say comes from the people
> and you can't fool them all the time. No matter if they fill up all the
> jails and all the Holes—somebody is going to stand up and holler

out the truth. It's always been like that. Of course I knew that before I came to jail, but there's something else I found out for sure in here—there will always be other people who will help you spread the word. Regardless of danger, Slim. Regardless of anything. People like you. (246)

Ellison, however, will reject the Marxist metanarrative of history and law and "the people" and choose to step out of history altogether, as Clifton had warned. Since Ellison tells this story in flashback, the first half of the novel opens in that same timeless, lawless underworld where it will end. In the prologue, Ellison introduces the themes of history and law before beginning his flashback narration. He opens straightforwardly enough by explaining his invisibility with an anecdote of violent assault, a crime perpetrated by him on a white man he almost kills. The presenting cause of the assault was the white man's careless insult, but it was his equally careless disregard for the narrator's presence that moved the episode to violence. In this epistemological "moment," the narrator realizes his invisibility, his nonexistence as a material fact: "Something in this man's thick head had sprung out and beaten him within an inch of his life. . . . The next day I saw his picture in the *Daily News*, beneath a caption stating that he had been 'mugged.' Poor fool, poor blind fool, I thought with sincere compassion, mugged by an invisible man" (5).

From the inception of his narration then, the narrator places himself outside the law by virtue of his invisibility, his unreality. For if he exists only in the perception of his antagonists, whites and their institutions, then how can he be understood to be within the jurisdiction of any law of "real" things? One of the subtextual arguments of the novel is that if one is invisible to the law in terms of the extension of its guarantees and protections, then one is invisible to its sanctions as well. Thus, the metaphor of an underground life introduced in the prologue must suggest not only the hidden life of black Americans but the illegal life of the race in America, a life in which it has been necessary to put together out of the detritus of white society the forms of a life and to steal from its sources of power the energies to sustain that life: "Though invisible, I am in the great American tradition of tinkers. That makes me kin to Ford, Edison, and Franklin. Call me, since I have a theory and a concept, a 'thinker-tinker'" (7); "there's always an element of crime in freedom" (155). Ellison's other version of this latter dictum comes later in the novel, from one of the first members of the Brotherhood that he meets: "[S]ometimes the difference between individual and organized indignation is the difference between criminal and political action" (293).

As Ellison has his narrator work through the implications of slavery, miscegenation, slave resistance, and manumission as prolegomena to his formal story, he is both establishing the historical base on which to rest his longer narrative and establishing it as a history of questions of law, of legal and illegal actions and of the authority to describe them as such. As he says of his victim in the assault, as the person, white, who had the power to define reality, he had to accept the responsibility for being attacked. After all, had he called for the police, the narrator would have found his suddenly visible self in a very real jail (14).

For all his invisibility, the narrator insists that he is not an anomaly in nature. Rather he is the end result of a historical process, one he intends to limn in his story. That process begins, as does every slave narrative that preceded Ellison's text, with the legal status of his people, enslavement, and then emancipation. The narrator reads this history of shifting status under the law as a one-sided tale. That is, his grandparents are not presented as having agency, as being in the subject position under the law. They are instead its creations. They are told they are slaves. Then they are told they are free. Only in his grandfather's old age is he allowed to see that the old man has hidden his agency behind a grin of acquiescence, that he has waged a guerrilla war against white people all his free life, has lived, if only in his own perception, as an outlaw.

Ellison sets this deathbed revelation as a puzzle for the narrator to solve, but it doesn't stymie most readers for long. The old man's intention to "overcome 'em with yeses, undermine 'em with grins, agree 'em to death and destruction" (16) is the game of the trickster, a signifying act with significance for those who know the game and rewards for those who can play it. The narrator, throughout his own story, remains unaccountably dense about this. Only at the absolute end of the novel, when he accepts his role as the underground warrior, waiting and gaining strength, using the resources of his antagonists to sustain himself, does he finally understand what kind of struggle his grandfather had tried to wage.

What is not discernable in the early chapter is the implication of that struggle, and the narrator's attempt to understand that and to build some course of action on it is the civic, public heart and soul of the narrative. The passage in which the narrator lays out the acceptable readings of his grandfather's struggle takes up an entire page near the end of the book, but it is worth quoting with some completeness. And it is the severest test of the novel's integrity to measure if the novel has done enough in the intervening pages between the prologue and the epilogue to support the narrator's reading.

Before I quote it, I want to point out that the sentiment behind it should be familiar by now, since it is the theme as well of Frederick Douglass, William Wells Brown, Martin Delany, Pauline Hopkins, Frances E. W. Harper, Sutton Griggs, W. E. B. Du Bois, Walter White, Langston Hughes, Richard Wright, and Chester Himes: that white America had failed to nurture and advance the basic principles upon which the nation had been founded and that it was left to black Americans to rescue the promises of the Declaration and the Constitution:

> Could he have meant—hell, he *must* have meant the principle, that we were to affirm the principle on which the country was built and not the men, or at least not the men who did the violence. Did he mean say "yes" because he knew the principle was greater than the men, greater than the numbers and the vicious power and all the methods used to corrupt its name? Did he mean to affirm the principle, which they themselves had dreamed into being out of the chaos and darkness of the feudal past, and which they had violated and compromised to the point of absurdity even in their own corrupt minds? Or did he mean that we had to take the responsibility for all of it, for the men as well as the principle because we were the heirs who must use the principle because no other fitted our needs? Not for the power or for vindication, but because we, with the given circumstance of our origin, could only thus find transcendence? Was it that we of all, we, most of all, had to affirm the principle, the plan in whose name we had been brutalized and sacrificed—not because we would always be weak nor because we were afraid or opportunistic, but because we were older than they, in the sense of what it took to live in the world with others and because they had exhausted in us, some—not much, but some—of the human greed and smallness, yes, and the fear and superstition that had kept them running. (Oh, yes, they're running too, running all over themselves.) Or was it, did he mean that we should affirm the principle because, we, through no fault of our own, were linked to all the others in the loud, clamoring semi-visible world, that world seen only as a fertile field for exploitation by Jack and

his kind, and with condescension by Norton and his, who were tired of being the mere pawns in the futile game of "making history"? Had he seen that for these too we had to say "yes" to the principle, lest they turn upon us to destroy both it and us? (574–75)

An attentive reader can make her own list of references in the book to matters of historical and legal interest used by Ellison to build the ground on which, or below which, the narrator comes to these final questions that imply their own answers; and I want to avoid that kind of list making here. I only want to put a case that Ellison's narrative is built on the eighty-five-year history of African Americans from the opening of Reconstruction, through Jim Crow and the Great Migrations of the teens and twenties, to black America as an urban phenomenon in the forties. His great scenes, the Battle Royal, Adam Trueblood's cabin, the Golden Day, the college and Bledsoe's office, and the mixing room at Liberty Paints are all evocations of one or another of the confrontations between black people and the larger, normative white world during that period.

Common to all of these, and central to Ellison's apparent understanding of black experience with white law, is the theme of violation. While the Adam Trueblood episode, in which the old black peasant explains his physical violation of his own daughter, is the touchstone for this theme, each of the others, in its own way, represents it, as the violation of specific law (Trueblood), the violation of protocol (the Golden Day), the violation of expectations (Bledsoe; the Battle Royal; Liberty Paints), the violation of codes and mores (the Battle Royal), and the violation of personal sensibility throughout the narrator's residence at and removal from the college. The presence of Mr. Norton at the center of the emotional whirlpool that is the telling of the Trueblood tale gives that story an added dimension of violation and evokes another relationship between men and law.

By playing off Norton and his obsession with both "fate" and the purity of his daughter against Trueblood's existential understanding of his own actions and his lack of illusions about the fundamental purity of any of us, Ellison adds a tragic reference to the narrative. By tragic here I mean that obsessive overvaluing of the destiny of one's own blood and the laws one erects to protect the obsession, laws that in the end can only be violated, never sustained. Ellison reveals his own ironic perspective on the tragic in Western culture by having Norton use as his own touchstone Ralph Waldo Emerson's essay "Self-

Reliance." This association is ironic not only because it underlines the social mythology of nineteenth-century America as it plays itself out in the institutions that persist and influence the twentieth century, even the lives of black Americans whose exercise of self-reliance could never anticipate the restrictions of law and custom imposed by whites, but because it is "self-reliance" that dooms the incestuous Oedipus in our culture's archetypal tragic drama. The social conservatism of tragedy as it derives from Greek myth is specifically targeted at the attempt to create a realm of human agency that might lie beyond the reach of the laws of the gods. So Norton and Trueblood are caught up in a dance of laws with the gods of fate and seem unable, as Norton fears, to avoid violating the laws that govern the dance.

But Ellison abandons fate in this meditation on history early on for an existential path more like that of Trueblood's. By the end of the book, when he reencounters Norton, he is powerless to affect him, and Norton has no idea who he is. Even though Norton had, in the early chapter, linked the narrator's destiny to his own (and that of the one race to the other), Norton has no memory of that moment nor any understanding of the idea. If the narrator is to make some whole out of his experiences, it will be some existential fabrication out of the bits and pieces he has carried around with him: the letter of recommendation, the broken bank, the prison shackles, the doll, the sunglasses, the memories of the college and the factory and the Brotherhood and the riot. Similarly, he abandons the discipline of historical materialism because it fails him as a black man.

When Brother Tarp gives him the shackle from his time on the chain gang, evocative of the slave shackles on Bledsoe's desk back at the college, the narrator doesn't know what to make of it; the Party insisted on the avoidance of race in historical analysis, but it used race when planning political policy. Rightly or wrongly, the narrator cannot reconcile the history of class oppression he has embraced with the fact with which Brother Tarp has confronted him, that the history of his race is the history not just of oppression but of incarceration, and its material component is in his hand at the moment (389). This becomes clear to the reader, if not immediately so to the narrator, when a Party functionary, Brother Westrum, sees the shackle and asks what it is. The narrator tells him and Westrum, a black man, recoils from it.

> "Brother, I don't think we ought to have such things around!"
> "*You* think so," I said. "And why?"

"Because I don't think we ought to dramatize our differences."
(392)

The point here is that the differences being referred to are historical differences. This is the crux of the African American critique of the narrative of American history, especially its legal history: that it has never been made clear that the history of black folks under American law is *different* from that of whites. Brother Westrum is correct, in that if the history of Negroes is too different, that is, if it is a legal history as much as it is an economic history, and if that legal history is too different from that of whites, then there is no historical ground for class solidarity against current oppression. This is bad news for a revolutionary movement whose primary theoretical tool is historical. Brother Westrum, it must be said, does not see all of this himself. He is primarily worried about losing his white folks.

I think that the modernism of Ellison's novel, and what differentiates it from those narratives we have discussed heretofore, lies in the journey the narrator undertakes from the bosom of the metanarratives of history and positivist law to the casual embrace of the existential moment. The extended modern moment in twentieth-century Western culture began with the realization that the hyperelaborated systems of explanation through which Western institutions operated no longer could bear the weight of their task. Religion, history, metaphysics, and law all proceeded from premises unequal to the sheer bulk of the experiences for which they were supposed to account. The cultural response to this failure was complex, but the representation of the consequent fragmentation of systems of explanation and the icons that had represented them, the romantic centering of the artistic persona as the fulcrum for all further attempts to understand the universe, and the lamentation for the unitary past by that romantic persona or some part of his or her voice were widespread exercises in what we have come to call modernism.

All three of these are present in Ellison's novel. Let me point out one small but exemplary node of experience to illustrate their presence. A recurring problematic in the novel is that of the conditions under which one person may touch another, particularly the conditions under which blacks may touch whites. The circumscription that controls this intimacy is, of course, law.

At the Founder's Day celebration at the college, the narrator observes Dr. Bledsoe's familiarity with the white guests of honor, including the fact that he touches them, "as though exercising a powerful magic" (115). The narrator remembers, "I too had touched a white man today and I felt it had been disastrous, and I realized then that he was the only one of us whom I knew—except perhaps a barber or nursemaid—who could touch a white man with impunity" (114). Earlier that day, the narrator had taken Mr. Norton on his ill-fated tour to Adam Trueblood's and to the Golden Day. At the Golden Day, the narrator and Mr. Norton meet the black patients of a mental ward on an afternoon outing, and the narrator overhears a conversation about boxing:

> [A]nd Johnson hit Jeffries at an angle of 45 degrees from his lower left lateral incisor, producing an instantaneous blocking of his entire thalamic rine, frosting it over like the freezing unit of a refrigerator, thus shattering his autonomous nervous system and rocking the big brick-laying creampuff with extreme hyperspasmic muscular tremors which dropped him dead on the extreme tip of his coccyx which, in turn, produced a sharp traumatic reaction to his sphincter nerve and muscle, and then, my dear colleague, they swept him up, sprinkled him with quicklime and rolled him away in a barrow. (75)

Minutes later, Mr. Norton, who has fainted from the impact of Trueblood's story, is slumped over in a chair as the inmates gather to see the narrator resuscitate him:

> And before I could move, a short, pock-marked man appeared and took Mr. Norton's head between his hands, tilting it at arm's length and then, pinching the chin gently like a barber about to apply a razor, gave a sharp, swift movement.
>   "Pow!"
>   Mr. Norton's head jerked like a jabbed punching bag. Five pale red lines bloomed on the white cheek, glowing like fire beneath translucent stone. I could not believe my eyes. I wanted to run. A woman tittered. I saw several men rush for the door. (79)

The use of boxing metaphors and images was widespread among black writers in the first half of the twentieth-century (Early, *Bruising, Tuxedo*; Sammons).[16] The appeal of such images is obvious, since the ring was the only place in most of the United States where a black man could strike a white man and not die for it. As the narrator points out, the only other blacks who regularly touched white people were barbers and nursemaids. At least in polite society. The narrator fails to note, however, what had been obvious enough at the Golden Day: that black prostitutes regularly touched and "serviced" white customers. The narrator alludes, of course, to the sexual prohibitions of his culture in the Battle Royal episode and, in a powerful image that anticipates the outrage of psychic rape in Toni Morrison's 1987 novel, *Beloved*, condemns the theft of nurture through power:

> And I remember too, how we confronted those others . . . who were unfamiliar in their familiarity, who trailed their words to us through blood and violence and ridicule and condescension . . . who, as they talked, aroused furtive visions within me of blood-froth sparkling their chins like their familiar tobacco juice, and upon their lips the curdled milk of a million black slave mammies' withered dugs, a treacherous and fluid knowledge of our being, imbibed at our source and now regurgitated foul upon us. (112)

It is clear that this tangle of physical impulses and prohibitions is a part of the same historical text written by whites that supported and sustained their institutions of oppression. As the narrator observes, "This was our world, they said, as they described it to us, this our horizon and its earth, its seasons and its climate, its spring and its summer" (112). And the students of that text, the black students in "Historically Black Colleges and Universities" throughout the South were supposed to learn these descriptions and accept them, even celebrate them. So when the narrator begins to see the outlines of the text, as when Bledsoe points out to him that "white folk have newspapers, magazines, radios, spokesmen to get their ideas across. If they want to tell the world a lie, they can tell it so well it becomes the truth" (143), he still doesn't quite understand the weakness of it.

Bledsoe has accepted the impregnability of the text and is content to work in the margins, or better yet, as a subtext to the white inscription of reality. Unlike the novels and stories we have looked at in this study, which often function as palimpsests, black overwriting on the texts of white desire, Bledsoe's school, and by extension all black institutions suffered to exist by white benefactors, operate below the white text. As Bledsoe knows so well, "You let the white folk worry about pride and dignity—you learn where you are and get yourself power, influence, contacts with powerful and influential people—and stay in the dark and use it!" (145).

Having begun to realize that reality is only a text written by whites, the narrator must go forth to find the limits of the text, find the aporia, the cracks in the story, where things do not, once set in motion, go as the outline might suggest. As a part of that search through the text of white reality, the novel takes the narrator into increasingly intimate contact with white people, to culminate in not one, but two sexual encounters with white women: with the unnamed temptress whose patronizing lust for his "primitiveness" is barely concealed beneath her facile liberalism and with Sybil, the white dilettante who "assumed [his] lectures on the woman question were based upon a more intimate knowledge than the merely political" (515).

There are in each of these episodes the clearly observable, and probably not so surprising, reversals and transgressions of black-white male-female social/sexual roles. Playacting at rape, the white woman becomes the aggressor. The black man, counter to the stereotypes of him, is hesitant, concerned. When he does give in, after trying to evade or deceive her, it is with personal disgust and a halfhearted attempt at rationalization.

The encounters have none of their expected or intended consequences for the narrator, but they do produce a sudden anger at whites for their intrusive sexuality. It is an example of the narrator's (or Ellison's?) confusion about the question of race as a subsumed category of class in American life that the narrator conflates race and class in the expression of his anger; "whites" and "the Brotherhood" are synonymous in his complaint in this passage:

> I walked in a sweat of agony. Why did they have to mix their women into everything? Between us and everything we wanted to change in the world they placed a woman: socially, politically, economically. Why, godammit, did they insist upon confusing the class struggle with the ass struggle, debasing both us and them— all human motives? (418)

The narrator's charge is flawed because it is historically misleading. He describes his experience as a black man but assigns it to his class position. The "we" who want to change the world could be the proletariat, but the "we" who are blocked from progress by the presence of "their" women are black Americans. For instance, it is not white working men but black boys who are shamed in the presence of the naked white woman with the American flag tattooed just below her navel during the Battle Royal (19). Similarly, the "they" who seek to block change could nominally be the capitalist class, but in this passage it is also the revolutionary cadre of the Brotherhood, whose white women sow confusion. Ultimately, a deep reading of the passage suggests, class cannot subsume race as experience for African Americans because of, or for reasons exemplified by, sex as framed by law.

Ellison's use of women in the novel is limited because his meditation on history is on its maleness. Not only is sexual desire always represented in its most "unacceptable" form, male desire for some forbidden female essence, from the Battle Royal through Adam Trueblood's incest to the "seduction" of the narrator, but women by and large play very limited roles in the book otherwise, and are simply not present as characters whose own desires and aspirations drive the story. They seem to be used by Ellison as signs for the circumscription of African American life.

Women as historical agents seem not to exist. We are given no hint, for instance, as to the content of the narrator's "Woman Question" lectures. More telling, I think, is the exclusion of women from any of Ellison's more direct meditations on history in the text, the places where he seems to be speaking to the reader without the mediation of fictional devices. A good example of this absence is in Ellison's trope on zoot-suiters and history. The monologue itself (440–41) is masterful but centers entirely on the male persona, as though there were no history of women in the universe Ellison inhabits.

Ellison's understanding of these young men, as "men outside of historical time," "untouched," ignorant of the Brotherhood and historical materialism, of the dialectic, leads him to call them "men of transition." They are dangerous because, being outside of time, they are also outside of the law. More specifically, they are outside of the traditional texts of reality and foreshadow, somehow, that which is to come, the new texts, the new laws, the new metanarratives: "For the boys speak a jived-up transitional language full of country glamour, think transitional thoughts, though perhaps they dream the same old ancient dreams" (441).

What is to come is the problem for Ellison. Historical materialism and the dialectic through which revolutionary Marxism transformed it assumed a set of derivable rules, a path that could be anticipated, a telos toward which history, like a good plot, drove. The role of the

Brotherhood, in its truest sense, was to make these rules, that telos, clear, to explicate the laws of history and see to it that they were carried out. But Ellison/the narrator is not so certain that can be done. What if someone, many someones, stepped outside of history, or were placed there, and brought their own imperatives. These zoot-suited boys, for instance:

> [W]ho knew but what they were the saviors, the true leaders, the bearers of something precious? The stewards of something uncomfortable, burdensome, which they hated because, living outside the realm of history, there was no one to applaud their value and they themselves failed to understand it. . . . What if history were a gambler, instead of a force in a laboratory experiment, and the boys his ace in the hole? What if history was not a reasonable citizen, but a madman full of paranoid guile and these boys his agents, his big surprise! His own revenge? For they were outside, in the dark with Sambo, the dancing paper doll; taking it on the lambo with my fallen brother, Tod Clifton (Tod, Tod) running and dodging the forces of history instead of making a dominating stand. (441)[17]

This paean to lumpen culture is prescient in its implication that the new narratives of reality will be written on the lam, outside the rules, beyond the law as we know it. The narrator's argument prefigures all we have come to appreciate about culture and its sources in industrial and postindustrial society, especially our understanding of the formative influence of African American experience on "mainstream" American culture. What Ellison contributes to the development of that appreciation in this passage is the awareness that the "something precious" is created as part of the circumvention of law, the denial of historical imperative, the transgression of hundreds of daily circumscriptions and suppressions of ordinary human desire visited on black Americans by the structures of law and custom that formally define white American identity and its inscribed privileges.

Nevertheless, Ellison's is, as I have suggested, a very "gendered" version of transgression, limited in its vision to the maleness of human experience. Not only can he not imagine the new "saviors" as women, he can give no example or image of women as creators of these new paradigms, as speakers of this jived-up transitional language, as stewards of something uncomfortable. This far he misread the immediate future of American culture, as he lived to realize, I am sure.

Even further, however, the double bind that black women have faced historically under the law seems outside Ellison's experience or imagination. That to be a woman and to be black would entail a concentration of restrictions on one's right to self-definition through history seems not to have occurred to him, and it is this limitation of vision that situates Ellison historically and places his novel at the close of the classical period in African American narrative in its intertextual relationship with American law. The struggle for agency under the law is for Ellison a male struggle; women appear to have no desires that are not equatable to male desires or mirrors of them, and no woman is shown seeking the subject position under any of the rules that shape her life.

When a woman is aggressive, she is sexually aggressive, as a mirror of male fantasies and fears. Similarly, when she is sexually aggressive, she is dangerous to men. Adam Trueblood is the "victim" not only of biology in the person of his adolescent daughter but of his wife's understandable but still uncomprehending anger. When the narrator is seduced in his first sexual encounter with a white woman, the revelation of that relationship could ruin his future in the Brotherhood. In his second sexual encounter, when he attempts to turn the tables on the Brotherhood and use a white woman's sexuality to gain information about his foes, he not only fails to do so, but is degraded by the drunken excesses of the night.

It is an indication of the weight Ellison would want to place on that image of male degradation that the last major episode of the novel, except for the riot that plunges the narrator into the underground, is the scene in which he plunges into drunkenness and sexual abandon. It is as though the opening sexual tension of the novel as depicted in the Battle Royal scene, intensified beyond the pressures of traditional scenes of adolescent initiation by the fact that it proceeds from the suggestion of an act that is legally forbidden, miscegenation, is ultimately resolved in an illegal, adulterous, drunken, miscegenative act conceptual worlds apart from the hotel ballroom where the narrator first encountered a naked white woman.

The other striking aspect of the episode seems to follow from the first, that Ellison does virtually end the novel as a story of the narrator's contact with whites with a sexual encounter, and one entirely devoid of affection, attraction, or concern. From Sybil's body to the riotous streets is just a short bus ride. From the riot to the step out of history is only a plunge down a manhole. After Sybil, time becomes meaningless to the story:

> Sybil, forgive me, I thought. The bus rolled.
> But when I opened my eyes we were turning into Riverside Drive. This too I accepted calmly, the whole night was out of joint. I'd had too many drinks. Time ran fluid, invisible, sad. . . . high above the shoreline, the Palisades, their revolutionary agony lost in the riotous lights of roller coasters. "The Time is Now . . ." the sign across the river began, but with history stomping on me with hobnailed boots, I thought with a laugh, why worry about time? (532–33)

The narrator had hoped to learn from Sybil something he could use against the Brotherhood, but had only encountered wretched excess. From that encounter, there is nowhere to go but out, it seems. Events make it so in any case, as the lumpen class of Harlem takes history into its own hands, just as perhaps the young hipsters had taken their comic books in their hands to read stories that spoke to them (442). When the narrator recalls Tod Clifton's death, he recasts it from any grand, romantic sacrifice to just the kind of death the young men would have absorbed from the dominant texts of their ahistorical lives. At one point he had pleaded with his own understanding as he

> moved with the crowd, the sweat pouring off me, listening to the grinding roar of traffic, the growing sound of a record shop loudspeaker blaring a languid blues. Was this all that would be recorded? Was this the only true history of the times, a mood blared by trumpets, trombones, saxophones and drums, a song with turgid inadequate words? (443)

The question to which Ellison returns again and again is both ontological and epistemological, depending on the form he chooses to use to pose it: what is real? how do we know it? Ellison chooses the most profoundly disturbing images to answer the question, however it is put. When the narrator addresses the crowd that has gathered at Mount Morris Park in Harlem to protest Clifton's death and to celebrate it, the question of reality is at the heart of his own internal dialogue, expressed in a complex image of reality and fantasy. After "reading" the first entries on a fictional death certificate, he comes to the crux of the matter, "Cause of death (be specific): resisting reality in the form of a .38 caliber revolver in the hands of an arresting officer, on Forty-second between the library and the subway in the heat of the afternoon" (458).

The description of how reality intrudes on the body, "one bullet entering the right ventricle of the heart, and lodging there, the other severing the spinal ganglia traveling downward to lodge in the pelvis, the other breaking through the back and traveling God knows where" (458), is clinical in its dispassion, echoing the description of Jack Johnson's knockout heard that long-ago afternoon in the Golden Day. But the world in which this reality works is another matter, somehow. If reality for black men is a .38 caliber police special in the hands of an officer, how is one to live with that oppression? Ellison's answer, the one he gives the narrator, is the one he has been building all along, the one he refers to in the 1981 introduction, the one the hipster boys reach for—fiction, image, turgid words, words of promise, bright colors, constructions made to look like reality: "It was perfectly natural. The blood ran like blood in a comic-book killing, on a comic-book street in a comic-book town on a comic-book day in a comic-book world" (457–58).

Just so, with the death of Tod Clifton, the encounter with Sybil, and the revolt of the lumpen proletariat of Harlem, Ellison is signaling more than the approaching climax of the narrator's story. Ellison's own story, his meditation on the history of his race and its American past under the law, is also coming to a close, but outside of time and history. What are the conclusions to which the text draws us, if this is the end? That the old stories no longer sustain the present? Not southern white supremacy, not back-to-Africa black nationalism, not pie-in-the-sky socialism, not Booker T. Washington accommodationism, not NAACP activism, not the Constitution? That we are left with only pieces of the past? That the present has no real meaning; it is only ragged blues, awful comic books, drunken sensuality, and wildernesses of racial guilt and pain and riotous anger and excess?

The narrator sits underground listening to Louis Armstrong's recording of Andy Razaf's "What Did I Do to Be So Black and Blue."[18] The novel we read is the answer to Razaf's musical question, and the answer is, "Nothing." The answer is that under the system of social control whites have fashioned out of their first revolutionary agony, being black is enough. But, like most modernists, Ellison has not given up his faith in the idea of a metanarrative that can explain it all. For him, it is that first principle after all, that entry in the Constitutional Dream Book, that says men can have freedom and liberty and equality.[19] He still thinks he can find an answer to what ails the body politic and bring it to the people. He can devise a new explanation, a new metanarrative that speaks for everyone:

> In going underground, I whipped it all except the mind, *the mind.* And the mind that has conceived a plan of living must never lose sight of the chaos against which that pattern was conceived. That goes for societies as well as for individuals. Thus, having tried to give pattern to the chaos which lives within the pattern of your certainties, I must come out, I must emerge. . . . Even hibernations can be overdone, come to think of it. Perhaps that's my greatest social crime, I've overstayed my hibernation, since there's a possibility that even an invisible man has a socially responsible role to play.
>
> "Ah," I can hear you say, "so it was all a build-up to bore us with his buggy jiving. He only wanted us to listen to him rave!" But only partially true: Being invisible and without substance, a disembodied voice, as it were, what else could I do? What else but try to tell you what was really happening when your eyes were looking through? And it is this which frightens me:
>
> Who knows but that, on the lower frequencies, I speak for you? (580–81)

To speak for us all, black and white, is not always the metanarrative dream of the "classical" black writer, when she or he has confronted our shared history directly. But it is, strangely and almost contradictorily, the dream of the modernist artist. In his and her romantic isolation, the artist becomes the only "everyman" available. Ellison, with his roots in the South, his exposure to the sociological novel and its theories during his association with the proletarian and Communist movements of the 1930s, and his obvious mastery of European continental literature, brings the classical impulse as far as it can go. The modernist in him shuns the cellblock solidarity of a novel like Brown's *Iron City* and embraces a centripetal descent into artistic solitary confinement. He speaks for the people after fleeing from them for several hundred pages.

The Reemergence of Desire and the Postclassical Narrative, or "Hoo-Doo . . ." and "How-To . . ."

> So it is no accident that the source of Hip is the Negro for he has been living in the margin between totalitarianism and democracy for two centuries.
>
> Norman Mailer, "The White Negro," 1957

> I am a soul in the world: in
> the world of my soul the whirled
> light from the day
> the sacked land of my father.
>
> Amiri Baraka, "The Invention of Comics," 1971

> It's like a jungle sometimes, it makes me wonder
> How I keep from going under
> It's like a jungle sometimes, it makes me wonder
> How I keep from going under
>
> Grandmaster Flash & the Furious Five, "The Message," 1982

After *Invisible Man*, after *Brown v. Board of Education*, a modernist narrative moves resolutely toward the center of African American literary practice. The events of the third quarter of the twentieth century focused the nation's eyes on black experience with an intensity and complexity of purpose that had not been present since Reconstruction. The "classical" African American narrative as a response to American law and life was reshaped by the intensity and complexity of that attention. African American poetry, drama, and much more explicitly modernist fiction gradually took their places alongside the realistic or naturalistic novel in the examination of the legal identity of the black American.

I had wanted to call this last chapter "Hoo-Doo, Neo-Romanticism, and Racial Politics," because that could easily be the title of a tale in which African American desire begins to reemerge in magical visions of nationalisms and aesthetics deeply scored by ironic conflicts between the racialization of pathology and the normative impulses of racial pride during the 1960s and early 1970s. Such a tale would culminate as the reemergence of desire finally manifests itself in the careers of the major black women writers of the final quarter of the century. But there is another tale to be told as well, "How-To: Using the Tools of the Master," the account of African American desire as legal theory, the final rehabilitation of desire. That these formulations of desire appear as part of the corpus of African American legal theory as well as in the traditional genres of storytelling is testamental to the intertextual relationship that has always existed between the two narrative systems.[1]

But I wrote the book to take my understanding of that intertextuality just down to the end of the classical period of African American narrative. The two tales alluded to in the preceding paragraph properly belong to another book. All I can do in this epilogue is to suggest what happens after Ellison, to give a few examples of how African American narrative engages the law and desire once it also begins to engage modernism. For instance, the emergence of the Black Arts (or Black Aesthetic) movement in the 1960s and 1970s should be understood at least in part as a challenge to the modern civil rights movement, which was itself a reemergence of the challenge to the restrictions on black legal status emerging from the principle of white supremacy.[2] The cultural and political challenge thrown up by black nationalism and the Black Arts movement was not a challenge merely to redefine the fundamental assumptions of the civil rights movement, but a challenge to it to confront white epistemological hegemony with a "Black" epistemology based on the power of language to redefine experience. In a way, this was not unlike the calls to action made variously by pre–Civil War black nationalist and abolitionist movements. Unlike them, however, this call emerged from the arts communities. Like some of them, the local abolitionist communities that directly violated the Fugitive Slave Law, for example, the modern movement called for direct confrontation with white authority. In this case, however, the confrontation was to be as much with the language of authority and the authority over language as with the mechanisms of state authority.

These confrontations occurred in the pages of poetry anthologies, on broadsides, in performances, in novels, stories, dramas, and essays of rage and violence. They were produced in cities, on campuses, and in prisons. Inasmuch as they were a challenge to authority, their validity was premised in the experiences and identities of their authors. So the militant images of black male "narrators" of black resistance were placed over and against images of white state authority. The Black Panther Party and the heroes its narratives produced (as well as the cultural copies they stimulated in film and fiction) existed side by side with the Malcolm X–Nation of Islam narratives and the Martin Luther King Jr.–civil rights movement narratives. All of these narratives and the heroes (and a very few "heroines") that populated them had one thing in common; they stood in contravention of one or more actual laws or systems of law authored by whites and administered publicly by whites for whites. If I could characterize one major difference between the public experience of black people between 1955 and 1980 and that of blacks in the analogous period of 1896 to 1940 it would be that in the earlier period black folks, in ever increasing numbers, went to jail for who they were; in the latter period black people in great numbers consciously decided to risk jail for what they were willing to do. This was the new story that needed a new voice.[3]

While the voices were new, the dynamics of the movement as a response to extant authorities were not so.[4] The questions raised by the Black Arts movement about who could speak and in what voices for the black masses were not unlike those raised by white leftist writers and theoreticians three decades earlier during the "proletarian" literary movement. The prolit critics, too, had claimed there was a link between art and the political agenda of an oppressed people. And the Black Arts movement generally privileged the same narrative forms found by prolit writers most congenial to a depiction of that agenda, realistic and naturalistic narrative. So, for example, the writers of the Black Arts movement looked back to Richard Wright and prized his work over that of Ellison and James Baldwin.[5]

The men whose voices and bodies were placed in confrontation with white authority often were martyred to that confrontation in "real" life. The political activists who survived that period are, with a few exceptions, no longer at the center of that national confrontation. Of the male writers whose plays, poetry, fiction, and essays stimulated and recorded those confrontations, only a few have voices that are heard often today. Black women writers have come to represent African American experience to most American readers.

While the presence and popularity of these women is often explained in terms of marketing and white audience rejection of strong black male public identities, it is as likely that there are other, equally complex contributing factors to their successes. After Dorothy West

and Zora Neale Hurston in the 1930s and Ann Petry in the 1940s and
1950s, black women writers of narrative were predominately poets,
Gwendolyn Brooks, June Jordan, Nikki Giovanni, Sonia Sanchez,
Audre Lorde. Some women wrote prose narrative exclusively, such as
Louise Merriwether, Alice Childress, and Margaret Walker, but there
was little general market for fiction written by black women. Outside
the general market, women associated with the Black Arts movement
were restive under the increasing doctrinal rigidity of its most excessive manifestations, but were even more put off by the privileging of a
patriarchal masculinity that was seen as intrinsically necessary to black
cultural nationalism. By the early 1970s, black women writers were
seeking different venues and even different voices for their experience
(Cade; Walker; Jordan; Southerland). Meanwhile, two developments
coincided to create a market for extended black narrative and to produce a cadre of black women ready to write those narratives.

The first of these was the women's movement. While black women
in general often found little in common with the middle-class, white
characteristics of the second wave of feminism that began to emerge in
America alongside the civil rights and antiwar movements of the 1950s
and 1960s, the broader acceptance of women in colleges and universities touched the lives of middle-class black women as well. Of the
group of African American women who emerged as publicly recognizable novelists and short-story writers in the late 1970s, only one did not
have a college degree. And the careers of these women were paralleled
by the careers of other women of color who went on to academic life,
providing the interpretive and authorative voices in English and Black
Studies departments that called for the work their sisters could and
would produce. Meanwhile, black men, whose confrontational personae had driven the early and middle years of the civil rights struggle,
paid the price in public disaffection. Martin Luther King Jr. was probably the only nationally known black man whose public reputation
could shelter a public movement and protect the public identities of
even moderate activists like Andrew Young and Julian Bond. Among
writers, few survived the public antipathy toward a black male presence. Those who did, Amiri Baraka and Ishmael Reed being the best
known of these, did so by finding university jobs.

One complex example of the intersection where law and black
male and female literary authority collide is Ishmael Reed's 1986 novel,
Reckless Eyeballing. Reed's relationship to the movement is important to
understand because his experimentation in prose forms of narrative

were not at all like those usually praised or produced by members of the Black Arts movement. One consequence of its militant opposition to a white aesthetic generally was an increasingly doctrinaire position on artistic matters, such that Reed early on rebelled against the revolution and went his own narrative and figurative way, abandoning the realist or naturalist fiction of his comrades and embracing for his own ends any of the modernist devices that allowed him to deploy his arsenal of Afro-American/Afro-Caribbean voodoo imagery and symbolism. For Reed, the source of reaction to white culture would be the religious and artistic diversity of the African Diaspora.

In *Reckless Eyeballing,* however, we see Reed taking aim at another "threat" to his right to make art as he sees fit, the "new" orthodoxy of feminist anger. Ian Ball, Reed's protagonist, writes a play about a black man lynched for "reckless eyeballing," that is, looking in the wrong manner at a white woman. But instead of being a protest against racist law, the play is a vehicle for radical feminist antimale anger: the "victim," years later, has the black man's corpse dug up and put on trial for visual rape. Ball (on behalf of Reed) turns the racist charge against black males into the radical feminist charge against all men. The "eyeballer," Ham Hill, gets his day in court, but is convicted by an all-woman jury (as opposed to the all-male makeup of the lynch mob twenty years earlier).[6]

The painfully ironic aspect of this internal exile into which the persona of the strong, confrontational, articulate black male slid was that with the Civil Rights and Voting Rights Acts of 1964 and 1965, a brief public climate of racial advance appeared.[7] This was the second development that stimulated a change in the climate of acceptance of narratives of African American experience. The assassinations of Malcolm X and Martin Luther King Jr. notwithstanding, the position of the federal government that the laws of the land would not only protect the civil and political rights of black Americans but that they would punish white Americans who violated those rights had an effect on how white Americans acted. The declaration of programs of redress such as federal contract regulations and more formal affirmative-action legislation and executive dicta met little of the hostility and accusations of reverse racism with which they were to be attacked thirty years later.

The normative function of the law actually seemed to work for a while, and the "Second Reconstruction" was under way. One of its unexpected aspects was the increase in popularity of African American life as a subject for narrative. Blaxploitation films had been made in the

1960s, celebrating the contralegal position of the black male in society, James Baldwin had come back from self-imposed exile to write about black Americans under the law, and television in the early 1970s discovered the black family as a site of situation comedy. Some black male writers were continuing and altering the realist/naturalist tradition and were supported by small but steady readership. These men, among them John A. Williams, Ernest Gaines, Al Young, George Cain, David Bradley, and James Alan McPherson, continued as well the critique of African American interaction with the system and structure of American law. But it was black women fiction writers who were poised to ride the swell of public interest in African American experience.

The careers of Gloria Naylor, Alice Walker, Toni Cade (Bambara), and Toni Morrison flourished in this new climate and led to a second "generation" of black women writers whose careers and reputations, like those of Naylor, Walker, and Morrison (Bambara died in 1997), continue to grow. While the discussion of any essential differences between the narratives of black women and men qua women and men is beyond the scope of this study, the continuity of the centrality of law and legal status in all African American narrative should be apparent. Although the fictions of these women are clearly postclassical, if not always postmodern, essentialist psychology and epistemological fragmentation have not replaced the question of the positioning of the black narrative subject under the law as a subtextual agenda. It still remains the case that African American women writers generally assume the shaping presence of the law as white writers do not.

Let Toni Morrison's *Beloved* (1987) serve as an example. It is important to recognize in the first instance that *Beloved* is an extended meditation on the law, as Ellison's single published novel was on history, and on more than one kind of law. The title page reads "Beloved, A Novel by Toni Morrison." But in fact, *Beloved* is a romance, and as such it is about the contradiction between human desire and natural law.[8] In romance modes, as Northrop Frye has pointed out for us, not only is nature personified and the heroine or hero identified with nature and its processes, but natural *law* is often set aside for the hero, so that he or she can take on forms or perform acts not available to the other humans in the story.

The story Morrison presents is premised, however, on the very unromantic case of Margaret Garner (Sethe), a fugitive slave whose actual infanticide was fruitless, as she and her surviving children were remanded to slavery nevertheless. Framing her story is the formal structure of law, both of criminal law (murder) and federal slave law, the Fugitive Slave Act of 1850 (Middleton). Finally, the legal subtexts for the romance itself are the local laws of slavery in Kentucky that regulate the relationships among the inhabitants of the farm at Sweet Home, the regional legal culture of the Upper South under which Baby Suggs labored bringing forth children to be sold away, and the great national debate over the very legal presence of slavery in the nation.[9]

Within these legal frames and on their bases, Morrison constructs a cradle of desire, represented by the bodies of Sethe and Beloved, the infant/spirit she kills. Morrison shows, through the dialectic of longing, how the laws that surround the cradle seek to smother desire in its bed. At the center of the book is a terrible yearning that is challenged by the law at every turn. The resolution of the dialectic of longing, and of the book, is figured forth at the book's climax in Sethe's second chance to respond to law's ultimate challenge. In her first encounter, Sethe sought to deny the law's agency by removing from its purview the objects of its attention; she intended to kill all her children rather than see them returned to enslavement. Such a choice is to accept the law's definition of her children and her self as objects under the law. Infanticide becomes a tool of slave resistance to the laws of slavery, an act of reaction.

Victoria E. Bynum has noted, apropos slave infanticide, that the scholarship of Angela Davis, Paula Giddings, Deborah Gray White, and Elizabeth Fox-Genovese

> has recorded slave women's propensity for arson, poisoning, the feigning of female illness and pregnancies to escape work, and occasional acts of abortion and infanticide. Because of slave women's responsibilities to children and family, they usually resisted enslavement by engaging in acts of individual rather than collective defiance. (5 n. 11)

In chapter 1 some examples of these acts, such as those of Hannah and of Rev. G. W. Offley's mother either committing or threatening infanticide, were presented. These examples suggest that Sethe's act whispers an unspeakable desperation hidden from whites but part of the memory of the race, a desperation that came from her understanding of the true nature of slavery under law, that her children did not belong to her and would never belong to her (197). It was with that understanding that she made the first plan to flee slavery-as-place

(Sweet Home) and when slavery-as-law (schoolteacher and the local marshal) pursued her even into freedom, death was her only escape from her objectification.

> Let schoolteacher haul us away, I guess, to measure your behind before he tore it up? I have felt what it felt like and nobody walking or stretched out is going to make you feel it too. Not you, not none of mine, and when I tell you mine, I also mean I'm yours. I wouldn't draw breath without my children. I told Baby Suggs that and she got down on her knees to beg God's pardon for me. Still, it's so. My plan was to take us all to the other side where my own ma'am is. They stopped me from getting us there, but they didn't stop you from getting there. Ha ha. (203)[10]

What wants to be hidden, and what Morrison reveals, is the fact of being the people on whom such desperation is visited. James Weldon Johnson, you will remember, had written of this vulnerability:

> All the while I understood that it was not discouragement or fear or search for a larger field of action and opportunity that was driving me out of the Negro race. I knew that it was shame, unbearable shame. Shame at being identified with a people that could with impunity be treated worse than animals. For certainly the law would restrain and punish the malicious burning alive of animals. (499)

This is why Baby Suggs takes to her bed, "just grieving and thinking about colors and how she made a mistake. That what she thought about what the heart and the body could do was wrong. The white-people came anyway. In her yard. She had done everything right and they came in her yard anyway. And she didn't know what to think" (209). The Fugitive Slave Law saw to that. It is this failure of the law to protect its black citizens, familiar enough in these texts to have become a trope, that is the most damning aspect of the African American literary critique of American law. The pain expressed in these narratives of betrayal is almost unbearable by the reader.

But the second time around, as Morrison constructs it, allows Sethe to reconfigure her object identity, to act in her own behalf. Believing that she is once again confronted by the law as an agent of denial of desire when the benevolent Mr. Bodwin drives his cart up to her yard to pick up her living daughter, Denver, Sethe attacks him with an ice pick in order to protect the ghostly Beloved. The effect is to signal her transformation from object to subject. Beloved's re/presence allows Sethe to re-create the moment of her most abject powerlessness under the law and to correct her response to it. As Sethe learns that one must attack the evil and not the victim, the allegorical message is that black folks must learn to turn their anger outward, not inward, away from themselves—and when they do, even "good" white folks may be put at risk.

That Sethe is prevented from killing Mr. Bodwin is testamentary to the law of women with which Morrison infuses the romance she has crafted. While the law of the nation is represented as a male construct and through male bodies, there is a law of women that permeates the relationships surrounding the house at 124 Bluestone Road. This law is fundamentally that of a matrilineal descent system, or Morrison's adaptation of the idea of one. Throughout the novel, property is held almost exclusively by women, and it is the proximity of men to women that gives them status or authority. In the most dire cases, as with Paul D, for example, separation from women renders men without focus or property, without a nexus. Men go to great lengths to be near women, as Sixo does in his relationship to the Thirty-Mile Woman. At their worst, men seek to wrest things from women.

But it is in the area of "crime" that the matrilineality assumes its most significant posture. Morrison puts at the center of the romance the criminal act Sethe commits against the matrilineality, the murder of a woman of her own line of descent. It is crucial to Morrison's design that Sethe not suffer too long for her crime against the state, for the civil murder of a child, and that she not be taken back into slavery; law must not either cancel or compound law lest it obviate Sethe's more deeply situated transgression. It is crucial because the "deeper" crime is against the line of womanhood, and it is from the regulatory mechanisms of that law that her punishment will come.

When Beloved reappears in the family, we see her asleep. Various readings of this appearance make sense, particularly the essence of Beloved as newborn. But I was struck one day by the memory that Aeschylus's *Eumenides,* a play about murder in a matrilineality, opens with a scene of the Furies, the matrilineal instruments of revenge, asleep after a long trip in which they have tracked the killer to his place of sanctuary. I think it makes good sense to read one thread of the romance Morrison has woven as a reworking of the *Eumenides,* or at least of that part of it that describes the acts and fate of the Furies.[11]

Readers will remember that the Furies are the forces of matrifocal rectitude; they protect the presence of women in the world and especially track down and punish those who harm women in intrafamilial conflict. In Aeschylus's play, they have tracked Orestes to Apollo's shrine and are there urged on by the ghost of Clytemnestra, Orestes' mother and victim. Pursuing Orestes to Athens and the court of Athena, the Furies are defeated by "law" and must either destroy Athens or accept a new role in the universe. Rather than flood the city with the poison of their menstrual blood, the Furies adopt the role of goddesses of fecundity and associate themselves with Nature and the seasons, move underground and become beloved rather than feared.

In Morrison's version of this story, the crime is not the murder of the mother by the child, but of the female child by the mother. Within the world of women, this horrific act is shunned, and all womanness at 124 is isolated from the rest of the community. The crime is so horrible and its consequences so uncontrollable that the visible representative of the mother principle, Baby Suggs, sickens and dies, as if under a plague. Then, when the presence of Paul D threatens to recast the matrilineality into a patrifocal household, however benign, the baby Beloved, exorcised as a ghost, returns to exact vengeance and to protect the line of womanhood from which she had emerged and from which she was torn.

In essence, Beloved in her reappearance is a Fury. She ousts Paul D, alienates her sister Denver, and begins the long attritive punishment of her mother. As Beloved grows in strength, Sethe, increasingly mad, sinks toward death. Only after the episode in which she relives the infanticidal act and shows herself willing to kill the man to save the woman is she set free. Beloved vanishes, either satisfied or frustrated; has Sethe set things right or simply escaped Beloved's vengeance? In the *Eumenides,* the Furies are defeated by a legal maneuver: Apollo stipulates a definition of parenthood that excludes women, and Athena's court rules that no crime has been committed since *only* a woman has been killed and not a man, a father, a true parent.[12] In such a conceptual universe, Orestes goes free and there is no role for the Furies other than the total destruction of civil life. But Athena offers them the status described above, and the Furies become the "Eumenides," the good principles of the months and seasons of the year. Meanwhile, Athena

and Apollo have presided over the disestablishment of the matrilineality and laid the legal and relational groundwork for patriarchy while
neutralizing, by denying them any legal status, the "legal" power of
women to protect themselves.

Morrison's version rewrites this misogynistic text. When Sethe
attacks Bodwin, she is prevented from actually harming him by her
daughter Denver and the massed women of the community who have
come to confront the vengeful power that Beloved represents.[13] To
these women, this vengeance was too destructive and endangered all
that was good in the essential relationships among women. In the middle of the excitement of Sethe's attack, Beloved vanishes. Some say she
exploded, others saw her run into the woods. But Morrison tells us, in
effect, that she becomes the Eumenides. She merges with the earth, the
water, and the air and becomes the "genius" of the place.

> Down by the stream in back of 124 her footprints come and go.
> They are so familiar. Should a child, an adult place his feet in them,
> they will fit. Take them out and they disappear again as if nobody
> ever walked there.
>
> By and by all trace is gone, and what is forgotten is not only the
> footprints but the water too and what is down there. The rest is
> weather. Not the breath of the disremembered and unaccounted
> for, but wind in the eaves, or spring ice thawing too quickly. Just
> weather. Certainly no clamor for a kiss.
>
> Beloved. (275)[14]

In the house itself, the hegemony of womanness begins to give
over to the loving presence of Paul D, allowed to return by the absence
of Beloved. Even "Boy," the fittingly named dog, returns. Boy had fled
when Beloved reappeared, his very name too much of a male principle
to be admitted. Is this the desired world? Was the rule of women's
vengeance too severe? What takes its place? The answer is in the telling
of the story, and the law is only one part of the answer. Although the
precipitating cause of the story itself is the law, and the resolution can
be read as a commentary on the conflict between vengeance and resti-
tution, what Morrison makes of the law is hard to read. At the end of
the book, the emphasis has shifted from the law in an interesting way.
It is not just that Beloved has become a natural force, "a naked woman
with fish for hair" (267), but that peace is restored through narrative.

Paul D returns to the house and rouses Sethe from a slumber near death by telling her his story, wanting "to put his story next to hers" (273). Together, their combined narrative ought to stretch into the future, since, as Paul D points out, they "got more yesterday than anybody. We need some kind of tomorrow" (273). Meanwhile, the new household is, like Athens in Aeschylus's play, protected by the benevolent spirit of the transformed fury of woman's vengeance-as-law, terror transformed to weather and woods, to nature, to romance. All law is replaced by narrative and its devices.

In the preface to her novel *Contending Forces,* Pauline Hopkins wrote, as I have already cited in chapter 3 of this study, that "*we must ourselves develop the men and women who will faithfully portray the inmost thoughts and feelings of the Negro with all the fire and romance which lie dormant in our history,* and, as yet, unrecognized by writers of the Anglo-Saxon race" (14–15). Hopkins's prescription was not filled with the writer who could recognize and harness the capabilities of the romance and the romantic until the career of Toni Morrison. More than any other writer since the nineteenth century, Morrison seems able to apprehend the centrality of desire and its suppression to the African American narrative.

Morrison writes from inside Paul D as he reflects on the power of prison guards, white men with guns, men he could break with one hand if they were unarmed:

> And these "men" . . . could, if you let them, stop you from hearing doves or loving moonlight. So you protected yourself and loved small. Picked the tiniest stars out of the sky to own; lay down with head twisted in order to see the loved one over the rim of the trench before you slept. Stole shy glances at her between the trees at chain-up. . . . A woman, a child, a brother—a big love like that would split you wide open in Alfred, Georgia. He knew exactly what she meant: to get to a place where you could love anything you chose—not to need permission for desire—well now, *that* was freedom. (162)

Denver, speculating on her mother's sexuality and her missing father and Paul D, remembers her grandmother's advice: "Slaves not supposed to have pleasurable feelings on their own; their bodies not supposed to be like that, but they have to have as many children as they can to please whoever owned them. Still, they were not supposed to have pleasure deep down" (209).

In Morrison's text, desire is rightfully the possession of every man and woman and is denied only by the ethos of institutionalized racism that slavery had become by the middle of the nineteenth century. After Emancipation and the Civil War amendments, it was the agenda of the counter-Reconstruction and Jim Crow as a way of life in the South to continue that practice of denial. Legal strategies such as those of the NAACP in its struggle to end state-supported segregation and those of the loose confederation of groups that made up the modern civil rights movement were designed to regain lost ground on measurable terrain. But the terrain of desire was terra incognita to the law. Miscegenation laws were not abandoned as part of a strategy, and no one set legal sights on the myriad of locally idiosyncratic rules and practices that limited property, access, pleasure. Since the definer always did the defining, many of these issues could not be understood as "legal" problems, falling as they did outside the purview of any positivist, statutory law.

The more recent implications of these problems are suggested in the collection of essays from the 1994 Amherst College conference "*Brown* at Forty." The papers from the conference show that matters of race and law have become broader cultural texts requiring newer and more provocative reading technologies than had been applied in the past (Sarat). Commentators in the collection fall along a continuum of concern for the interpretive and hermeneutic implications of *Brown* and its aftermath, but it is clear that at the center of their interests are "postmodern" issues of meaning, textuality, essentialism, and the intersection between universals and particulars and the definitions of those. As editor Austin Sarat notes in the introduction, "[T]he significance of *Brown* is that it made it possible to ask new things of law and to tell new stories about what it means to be African American" (8).

On another interpretive front, beginning in the 1980s, the emergence of Critical Race Theory to challenge institutionalized positivism broadened the screen on which we view African American narrative's interrogation of American law. A brief discussion will suggest why the practice of Critical Race Theory is a narrative practice, as suggested by Sarat's observation about the essays in his collection, as well as a legal one and how that narrative practice introduces the subject and subjectivity of desire into some forms of legal discourse. Critical Race Theory here will refer to a body of work by scholars, many of them people of color, most in law schools, and almost always viewing American law from the "left." This work seeks to challenge "the ways in which race and racial power are constructed and represented in American legal culture and, more generally, in American society as a whole" (Crenshaw et al. xiii). Central to its practice has been the development of "counter-accounts of social reality," rereadings and narrativization of the construction of race and racism under American law.

The two pieces I want to look at, Derrick Bell's *And We are Not Saved: The Elusive Quest for Racial Justice* (1987) and Patricia J. Williams's "Alchemical Notes: Reconstructed Ideals from Deconstructed Rights" (1987),[15] are early complementary versions of the Critical Race Theory project of creating "counter-accounts." Bell's book considers the consequences of a century of civil rights litigation and concludes that however ambiguous those consequences might be, African Americans cannot afford to abandon the litigative approach. Williams's article looks at the implications of another emerging narrative model in legal theory, Critical Legal Studies. These texts are specifically concerned with problems of the ironic discrimination between the ideal and the real.

How adequate is the law as a way of knowing, and what is the impact of the answer to that question on the lives of African Americans? As I noted in the introductory chapter, *epistemological* for the purposes of this discussion suggests the problem of the law as a way of knowing or certifying what is. For example, the line of epistemological speculation that leads from critical empiricism to logical positivism also leads to, and through, the positivist construction of the American legal system. Thus it is possible to stipulate for discussion that the rules for what is admissible knowledge among lawyers at the bar constitute an epistemological structure, if not a system in any traditional philosophical sense. That is, when lawyers think, in the process of acting as lawyers, they want to privilege certain proofs and not others. More specifically, the texts by Bell and Williams implicate a specific consequence of this practice of the privileging of proof and argumentation by the law and its agencies, in the manifestation of desire. More generally, they address the question of how African Americans in the last quarter of the twentieth century might find the law as an epistemological window through which their "real" status and substance can be glimpsed.

In both these texts it is the explication of the limits of a legal epistemology operating to reinforce marginality that warrants remarking. Years after the end of the major period of expatriation for black American writers, the discussion of life lived on the edges of American society continues among black Americans. Forty years and more after Motley, Himes, and Wright, Bell and Williams take up a more direct argument about the marginalizing power of American law by looking at the history of constitutionally based theories of civil rights. Both Bell and Williams, mentor and student, acknowledge the other's contribution to the thinking that produced the texts they published. That being so, it is not surprising to find that each deals with the same area of law and that each contains a critique of one aspect of Critical Legal Studies, in which it is argued that the civil rights movement cannot abandon civil rights litigation, however limited an advantage such litigation has historically given its constituency. Finally, each uses fictional devices to present at least some aspect of the critique and to situate the issue of marginality in it.

It is a sign, or perhaps an illusion, of the times that, however much the works of Bell and Williams address the same historical marginality of race and class in America attended to by writers discussed earlier in this book, Bell and Williams are not writing from the margins themselves. Certainly, Bell's previous tenure at Harvard Law School and Williams's degrees from there and Wellesley and her faculty positions at the University of Wisconsin's and Columbia University's law schools contrast strongly with the relative sociopolitical statuslessness of black writers in the 1930s and 1940s. It is interesting to note that the focus on law and the experience of Bell's and Williams's subjects obscures questions of the effect of class while the implications for any consideration of race are quite clear. Nevertheless, central to the argument of both the lawyers' texts is their definition of their positions at "the margins of the center" of the institutional life of the law, of the academy, and even now, of American society.[16]

Although each arrives at different arguments in these published treatments of the question, it is because they privilege that ironically marginalized perspective that they can most profitably be read intertextually with Wright and Motley, as though their pages were interleaved throughout an ongoing examination of what the law can and cannot say about the lives of black Americans.

Derrick Bell's book is a collection of ten discourses on the prospects of the civil rights movement as a function of its legislative and litigative history, from the drafting of the Constitution to 1987. The discourses are set within a multiple-fictional frame that seems most peculiar to our modern tastes for straightforward books about important things; the whole book looks to the reader to be much more "fictional," for instance, than Motley's naturalistic sociological "treatise" on how to destroy a young boy.

The frames work like this: the narrator, a black law professor at a prestigious institution, recalls a black bicentennial convention, in honor of the Constitution, held in a mysterious setting and financed by an anonymous benefactor. The purpose of the meeting was to reconsider the relationship of the Race to the Text. By the second day, the first day's harmony had given way to contention and disaffection, and to escape the all-too-familiar turmoil the narrator fell into a reverie about an old friend, a black woman civil rights lawyer who had vanished from sight. He was roused sometime later by a colleague offering him a packet containing the next day's reading. The packet held nine of the ten discourses Bell presents in the book. On seeing the contents of the packet, the narrator reveals that he is implicated in their production and tells the story of how he had been summoned, through his computer, to meet the missing colleague of his reverie, Geneva Crenshaw, how he had traveled to her ancestral home, and how they had discussed the nine chronicles that constitute the discourses of his packet. The chronicles are accounts of Crenshaw's adventures in time and in parallel universes through the agency of a Celestial Curia that has deputized her to make sense of the history of racial justice in America. The title of the material in the packet is "The Civil Rights Chronicles as related by Geneva Crenshaw and reviewed with a friend." The tenth chronicle of Bell's book is presented to the bicentennial meeting by Crenshaw herself.

With this format, we are in the middle of a number of literary and discursive traditions, from the frame story as familiar to us as the "Arabian Nights" and the philosophical *consolatio* of the Middle Ages, through allegorical personification, to the found-manuscript devices so popular throughout the history of the novel. The effect is that of "jerry-rigging" a pseudogenre in the absence of a set of conventions within which the author can work. Tzvetan Todorov has suggested that new genres appear not as "normal" evolutions from the nearest forms but as grafts forming around new elements of an emerging discourse that were not obligatory to former texts. While some aspects of new generic forms appear similar to others, as some of Bell's discussion reads like a law text, the new genres arise to meet the necessity of encoding new discussions through textual practices removed from those ordinarily encountered by the author (Todorov 47–48 and passim). Such clearly is the case for Bell and his text here.

As the issue develops in the text, it becomes clear that Bell cannot carry on his discussion in the frame provided him by the case study, the brief, the decision, or the legal essay. In this instance, Bell draws on forms that have assumed for the quotidian what we could only describe as the fantastic: the dream tale, time travel, parallel universes, beings endowed with superhuman knowledge and compassion. And he uses these as they are often used, to frame discussions of contradictions in human experience. In Bell's case, the contradictions are those between the texts he has known as the law and the life of his race. His formal problem is that the law as positivistically written will allow no contradiction to go unacted upon, if not ultimately resolved. This formulation carries the intertextual critique of a legal epistemology a step beyond that which we found in Motley's novel. To pursue his inquiry, Bell must borrow or create a set of conventions that will allow him to present yet contain the legal arguments while providing a context for, if not privileging in the final instance, his extralegal experience. Thus Bell's choices, which are not only wonderfully appropriate for any discussion of textuality and intertextuality in the law, but also frame the same discussion we encountered as an effect of the experience of the text of Motley's novel. That is, throughout the frames and the discourses, the narrator and Geneva Crenshaw and the characters debate what kinds of information are acceptable as the bases for knowledge.

It is as if Bell/the narrator were the jury constrained by the epistemological requirements of institutional "legality" and Crenshaw were the lawyer in pursuit of justice for her client. Bell, however, by displacing his narrator from the necessity of finding for or against in a formal legal context, writes the contrapositioning of the legal and the just somewhat differently than does, let us say, Willard Motley in his defense of Nicky Romano. The displacement does not remove the constraints that Morton encountered in *Knock on Any Door*, but the narrator is somewhat more liberated from an ideational rigidity imposed by ideology than was the Romano jury. Similarly, Crenshaw is given a number of narratives through which to argue, not just the record of one young man's marginalized life. She is allowed to ring significant changes on a theme.

In these discussions, "the law," as represented by the narrator, will accept only case law and reasoning from that law based on traditional practice. He is opposed by another tradition, experiential and emotive, with which he is familiar but in which he does not easily participate. The text is more elusive in identifying this tradition, but there are early clues. Describing the facilities at the mysterious meeting center, the narrator ends with the Great Hall, site of the plenary sessions of their convocation. It was, he writes, "designed to reflect the architecture and atmosphere of both church and courtroom. It was both the focal point and an almost sacred nucleus of the conference complex" (Bell 16). Later, his reminiscence of Geneva Crenshaw contains a memory of her contemplation of pictures of Harriet Tubman and Sojourner Truth, to whose physical appearance the narrator had just compared hers:

> I've seen those pictures, . . . and were I give to vanity, I would hardly find the resemblance complimentary. But those women had an inner vision that enabled them to defy the limits on their lives imposed by the world around them. I try to be a good lawyer, but my devotion, too, is to an inner vision that makes me feel close to old Harriet and Sojurner—so your thinking that I resemble them is not only a compliment, it is an honor. (19)

Finally, when we meet the Celestial Curia in its Great Hall, we realize we are in the presence of powerful black women, robed as gospel singers, presiding over a mighty congregation. It is here that the issue of the book is joined, for the Curia presents two responses to racial injustice that the narrator as litigator must argue against in his encounters with Geneva Crenshaw: total emigration of black Americans to another, better land, or total revolution in this land. Throughout the book, through frames and chronicles, the "rational," precedental, litigative approach to achieving racial justice is represented by the male law professor and is opposed by female figures enshrouded in religious imagery, "testifying" to one or another totalizing vision of a reordered society in which white hegemony is decentered and black Americans become authors of their own destinies. The text seems always to cast these latter visions as a different order of experience, the products of a different way of knowing than that available to the law.

Early on, the narrator remembers that Crenshaw had once been an excellent lawyer, but as a consequence of a vicious physical attack in the Deep South had suffered a breakdown, and "for more than twenty years, her mind wandered in realms where medical science could not follow" (21). Needless to say, those twenty years produced the chronicles she asks him to consider. Her message to him, after those decades in the wilderness, appears without a prompt on his terminal:

> Dearest friend, I have folded my wings for a little while and returned to this world. I have learned all I can about our people's condition. . . . For the moment you must not share word of my return. I have no time for reunions, for I have come back with a purpose. My mind is filled with allegorical visions that, taking me out of our topsy-turvy world and into a strange and more rational existence, have revealed to me new truths about the dilemma of blacks in this country. To be made real, to be potent, these visions—or Chronicles, as I call them—must be interpreted. (22)

And it is the narrator who must help Crenshaw interpret the chronicles, although she has not counted on his practice of the law having been transformed into a profession of the law:

> "Of course, when I selected you, I did not know that you had left civil rights work and become a law teacher. Your interpretations are clearly different from mine, but discussing those differences helps me clarify my views. . . . The Curia was right [to warn] me that Western peoples simply reject anything not explicable in scientific terms. But, for me, friend"—Geneva spoke slowly, emphasizing every syllable—"it was neither vision nor dream, and no more fantasy than some of the beliefs that you have said you hold." (100–101)

It helps here to imagine the same argument posed by Crenshaw to the women on Nicky Romano's jury. Morton/Crenshaw could have claimed openly that which was implicit in the Romano defense from the start, namely that his/her version of the crime and antecedents and the relative importance of those antecedents to an understanding of the crime were "neither vision nor dream, and no more fantasy than some of the beliefs" about their own lives and the ideologized system of explanation that framed them, which would prevent them from admitting Nick's narrative to the realm of justified experience. Of course, the beliefs to which Crenshaw is referring are beliefs in the ultimate value of litigation and of Western jurisprudence. The purpose of Bell's book is to throw that tradition into relief against the imperatives of black American experience and to make it justify itself if possible. Near the end of the book, all the players come together in the Great Hall of the conference center, Geneva, the narrator, his fellow conferees, and the Curia Sisters, who make the following point:

> "Of course, some of you"—and the Curia Sisters nodded solemnly at the audience assembled—"will view [the chronicles] as merely metaphorical essays on the plight of blacks—and will leave here seeking theories of liberation from white legal philosophers, who are not oppressed, who do not perceive themselves as oppressors, and who must use their impressive intellectual talent to imagine what you experience daily. Black people, on the other hand, come to their task of liberation from the battleground of experience, not from the rarefied atmosphere of the imagination. Do you understand?" (253)

In the end, it seems that both Geneva and the narrator understand only in part, and the book closes with all assembled rededicated to "keep on keepin' on," apparently to continue to play the hand dealt them but informed by their unique experience as strangers in this land. The book that had begun with the solitary voice of the narrator, discussing the painfully alienating reality of a law school so dominated by the appetites and fears of patriarchal white males that he had contemplated leaving his faculty position, ends with a Great Hall full of black men, hands joined in brotherhood, singing:

> Done made my vow to the Lord,
> and I never will turn back.
> Oh, I will go. I shall go.
> To see what the end will be.
>
>   (258)

While a critique of the implications of the Critical Legal Studies movement is almost incidentally placed in Bell's book, it is at the center of Patricia J. Williams's article. Williams, too, chooses a literary frame for her discussion, but her reasons are not as readily accessible as Bell's seem to be. He has written a book that challenges the practice of the ordering of experience through a positivistic system of social description governed by rules of formal interpretation applied to texts, and the profession of the methods through which that ordering is accomplished. He does so with a diametrically opposing epistemological system and casts the written record of that conflict, his text, in literary forms historically used to encase and privilege the oppositional system. Williams attempts something similar when she adopts the frames of literary fictions for her argument.

Because Williams's essay is so rich in argumentation and detail, the small section of her discussion that I address here should not be taken to represent the complexity of her presentation. I want to focus on what seems to me to address the epistemological issue most directly. In this section, Williams compares her attempts to rent an apartment in New York with those of her white, male colleague Peter Gabel. When each had found a place, each went about securing the lease in very different ways. Gabel, she says, "handed over a $900 deposit, in cash, with no lease, no exchange of keys and no receipt, to strangers with whom he had no ties other than a few moments of pleasant conversation" ("Alchemical Notes" 406). He did so, she argues, because Gabel is extremely self-conscious of his power and authority as a white or male or lawyer and is willing to go to great lengths to remove these barriers of privilege from between himself and a world of trust, a trust, he would argue, built on the obvious willingness of the powerful to give up power. She, on the other hand, dealt with friends but demanded and got the right to draw the contract, set the terms, and specify responsibilities. For Williams, these relationships are part of a lifelong struggle for all blacks to establish patterns of transaction that portray each person as a "bargainer of separate worth, a distinct power, with sufficient *rights* to manipulate commerce, rather than to be manipulated as the object of commerce" (408).

At this point, we ought to consider the frame for this essay. To a certain extent it functions, as does Bell's, to privilege a kind of discourse for which the profession has no conventions. This is accomplished through the use of the "fabulous" tale and the discourse of the philosophical treatise as narrative. But one aspect of the frame is unlike any we see in Bell's book. Williams introduces sections of her discussion with versions of the chapter headings common to novels of the mid–eighteenth century: "In Which Peter Gabel and I Set Out to Teach Contracts in the Same Boat While Rowing in Phenomenological Opposition"; "In Which, by Virtue of My Own Mortality, I Am Dragged from a Great Height in Order to Examine the Roots of My Existence"; and so on. In each of these cases, the headings gloss the content of the ensuing section and provide a personalized flavor and distance from the realm of traditional legal essays. In fact, the sections they introduce have little of the personal flavor the headings promise; there are no continuing characters, no plot lines, no rising and falling action of the sort Bell attempted in his imitation of a fully realized framing fiction.

Williams's postmodern use of these headings functions to privilege the ensuing discourse not so much by evoking any specific eighteenth-century English novel, but by hauling up old discursive templates, patterns from storerooms of literary and cultural history that somehow speak to the imperatives of the problem at hand. For example, the concerns of the European novel during its development at the height of the era of mercantile capitalism were similar to those of Williams, the accurate representation of human relationships as aspects of commerce or commercial relationships. What was a cultural problematic for Fielding and Richardson in the eighteenth century, however, is a political necessity for Williams. For similar reasons, such formal devices as chapter headings privileged *Tom Jones* by allowing the text to aspire to kinship with history. Henry Fielding, arguing for acceptance of the prose novel, claimed that it was like history and even a little better because it showed you what happened in people's lives; novels were, in fact, personal histories. For that reason, the conventions of the early novel were those of verisimilitude: Fielding's chapter headings in which he claimed that these things really happened to the narrator, or Richardson's letters that seemed to be from real people telling real personal histories. These were, and for Williams's text are, epistemological devices, ways of knowing what is and what isn't true.

Williams is concerned with that problem because it is at the center of her quarrel with Critical Legal Studies; that is, the deconstruction of rights by CLS is accomplished from a privileged, experiential base that is not that of blacks and does not describe their relationship to civil rights. This way of knowing, from privilege, is not sufficient for her needs, and she cites Mary Ann Caws's gloss of Wittgenstein:

> Suppose someone were to say: "Imagine this butterfly exactly as it is, but ugly instead of beautiful"?! The transfer we are called on to make includes . . . stretching not just of the imagination, but of the transfer point: . . . It is as if I were told: "Here is a chair. Can you see it clearly?—Good—now translate it into French!" (411)

Suddenly, it is as if we are back in Bell's book, and the Curia Sisters are telling us that white male legal philosophers who try to imagine black life and its relation to justice will fail. Williams shows us why they will fail: because what is required is not just a stretch of the imagination, but of the transfer point as well; the experiential life of racial injustice is not just the philosophical exercise of rights defined, then written under erasure—it is the other language of pain, loss, and dispossession of identity that whites cannot speak or imagine. This, then, is the position Morrison defends in *Beloved*, that it is through the narrative of romance, not of law, that the race will be understood. Here, too, we can read Motley against the implications of Bell and now against Williams. If, as the Curia Sisters and Williams would argue, the substance of African American life lies, for whites, beyond a point of experiential and discursive transfer that has proved historically impossible to negotiate, what is the argument of Motley's text? It is, most clearly, that the class realities of Nick's life lie beyond the ideological mythology of daily life in mid-twentieth-century America. And the Romano jury may not be indictable for a failure of moral imagination if we are to take up Williams's argument. No lives as marginalized as those of Nick and the great majority of African Americans are accessible to ordinary white Americans, particularly when you circumscribe the exercise of any interpretative faculty by the epistemology of American law.

It is because of this isolation that Williams wants to insist on the right to rights. Where Gabel would forgo any formal structure rather than introduce distrust into his relationships, risking alienation and loss of self, Williams knows that the lack of formal relationship leaves her estranged from whites and without status, since she has no historical base of privilege from which to redefine relationships; she points out that whites, not black slaves, wrote the laws that defined the status of the dispossessed. Her only alternative in this society is to take part in "creative commerce," a part, but only one part, of the indices of privilege of whites. As Williams says, it is that relationship alone within "which I may be recognized as whole, with which I may feed and clothe and shelter myself, by which I may be seen as equal—even if I am stranger. For me, stranger-stranger relations are better than stranger-chattel" (408).

When I read these critiques by Patricia Williams, I always feel as though I were reading yet another palimpsest. But it is not Bell she is overwriting; it is Ellison. If there is a line from Ellison at the close of the classical period that is the beginning of modernist fiction in the black tradition, it extends to Williams as a postmodern writer. Like Ellison's protagonist, Williams's persona lives a private life that is, as she imagines it and formulates it for us, the life of the race, historically and of her moment. Between Ellison and Williams, as a writer who is more fully "modern" than Ellison and anticipatory of Williams's postmodern conflations of theory and narrative, is James Alan McPherson, lawyer and fiction writer. From his 1987 collection of stories, *Elbow Room*, two pieces will illustrate the position his fictions occupy in the evolution of the African American narrative critique of American law.

In "A Sense of Story" (193–214), a judge reviews the transcript of a murder case in which a black employee had shot his white boss. This story reaches back beyond Ellison, to echo the third section of *Native Son* in which Bigger rejects Boris Max's version of his crime and its motivation. Here McPherson has Charles blurt out a confession in court to counter the impression of him that was being woven by his white lawyer's defense. In so doing, McPherson places his protagonist in the line of black figures who will not testify against their true sense of self: Nat Turner, Towns in Du Bois's *Dark Princess*, Bigger, John Pearson in Zora Neale Hurston's *The Jonas Gourd Vine*, and Janie in Hurston's *Their Eyes Were Watching God*. In this case, the judge's review is McPherson's device to allow us access to the story through a controlled narrative, that is, the judge's selective reading of the transcript. That control is not unlike the control exercised over the text by Ellison's narrator. That is, between the "real world" writer and the narrative of record being presented to us is an intervening persona who has his own, if unstated, reasons for editing the text.

Even so, we see enough to understand the crime and Charles's motivations, for the killing and the confession. Whether the judge does or does not understand is ambiguous, since his "last words" on the case are "guilty as charged"—what that means in terms of the law being one thing, in terms of the narrative another, in terms of "real life" perhaps a third. McPherson makes clear to us what I posited in the introductory chapter as a consideration to be made about how law and fiction move to closure. "Guilty as charged" should be read as a sign of approval that the case closed appropriately in terms of what could be said in the law. The irony of the ending for us as readers of fiction is that the judge's conclusion is not epistemologically satisfactory, however ontologically satisfying it may be to the law. And here McPherson is steadfastly operating in the tradition of moralistic irony that characterized the Wright and Motley books discussed in the previous chapter: the novelist's reproduction of the law/lawyer's failure to convince authority of innocence not only succeeds in establishing that innocence in the eyes of the reader of the fiction but condemns the law's failure to read the text the same way.

What is particularly "modern" about the story, except for the use of the intervening consciousness of the judge to allow the story the kind of control that "back-paced" or flashback narratives provide, as in *Invisible Man*, is the implicit focus on the story qua story, on the textuality of the experience. McPherson's attention, and our own, is on the functioning of narrativity itself, as *meta*narrative. From the outset the presenting problem is one of what a text, in this case the transcript of Robert Charles's trial up to the moment of his unsolicited public confession, will reveal. The judge's task is to determine from the transcript whether the jury, as "readers" of the case to that point, would have found a preponderance of evidence against Charles prior to his outburst or whether that outburst would have contaminated the process such that it would unnecessarily tip the scales of justice against the defendant. The story that McPherson writes, then, is the story of a man reading a story with a directed purpose. It is also, as we see, the story of the creation of that story that is being read, as McPherson produces questioning, testimony, rulings, discussions at the bench from the transcript, such that the transcript is revealed as a record of its own composition.

At the same time, it does not appear as if we as readers experience everything the judge is experiencing as reader because someone, McPherson or the judge, "edits" the transcript. That is, not all of the transcript is available to us; many ellipses pepper the text we are reading. The sidebar is called for, for example, but not presented in McPherson's text of the transcript. Yet the judge knows that part of the story two ways: once through his participation in it and twice because he "reads" it, even if we don't. Later, we are allowed to read in the transcript an allusion to the judge's decision in that sidebar when he reminds the defense of some not fully explained point concerning race and standards of proof in the court. At one point the transcript reports something like the heart of the matter as far as the judge, and McPherson, are concerned, that there is here a "sense of a story" that needs attending to if that story is to emerge:

> Ladies and gentlemen, I feel I must apologize to you for these lengthy excursions. I have attempted to grant leeway to counsel for both sides, because it seemed to me that my own decisions, based

solely on the rules of evidence as I know them, would prevent you
from hearing the cross-light of competing views, which I consider
to be essential to the adversary process. But it seems to me that this
trial has lost its direction. Still, in my mind, law is an art, and my
function here should ideally be no different than that of a literary
critic. But as I have said, I have probably . . . (210)

The judge's reading of this part of the transcript is interrupted by a
call from his clerk, and we never return to the judge's admission that he
has lost control of the trial. But it is at this point that the story we are
reading takes on its final dimension. The transcript as we have seen it
has revealed to us the minimal validity of the state's case: Robert
Charles did shoot and kill the victim. It also reveals that the jury would
have found that to be so without the confession in court. But hanging
from this case is the possibility that Charles will be the first criminal
executed under the state's new capital-crimes law. His attorney was
hoping to show mitigation, and the judge did, indeed, give him a lot of
room to do so. But the essential revelation of the text is the deeply ironic
one that while the defense fails in its attempt to argue mitigation on the
grounds of Charles's illiteracy, his drinking, and the ingrained "customary violence" of the transplanted southern Negro, it succeeds in a
more authentic manner. That is, the transcript to which we have access
shows nobility of character, perfectionism, commitment to hard work,
genuine creative intelligence, and patience on the part of Charles and
blind racial insensitivity, class privilege, institutional racism, and personal betrayal in the larger world around him. We come away with
solid intimations of the etiology of the crime. But, of course, that is not
in any way admissible, nor was it even visible to Charles's own attorney. Nor did the judge admit it even on his review of the transcript.
What was allowed to be told was enough to convict, though not
enough to create an accessible and "true" story of a man's life. Charles
saw and understood that during the trial. Given the irrelevance of the
truth of his life to the case, he refused to allow the lie about him that
was being spun out in his lawyer's summation. It was then and there
that he stood and claimed the responsibility for the death of his
employer.
     On one level, the actual content of the case is irrelevant. Its details
of life on the color line are so familiar to us by this point that the story's
social argument could have been written by Charles W. Chesnutt. But
McPherson's story argues once again a larger point, one we saw in

Wright, Motley, Bell, and Williams: the law is no lens through which to view the lives of African Americans. In McPherson's text we see perhaps more clearly than in the others where the narrative shortcomings of the law may lie.

The title story of McPherson's collection, "Elbow Room," investigates the problem of narration again. If the implication of "A Sense of Story" (which immediately precedes "Elbow Room" in the collection) is that the formal constraints of the law fail to capture the reality of black life, this story goes a bit further. McPherson opens with this italicized paragraph:

> Narrator is unmanageable. Demonstrates a disregard for form bordering on the paranoid. Questioned closely, he declares himself the open enemy of conventional narrative categories. When pressed for reasons, narrator become shrill in insistence that "borders," "structures," "frames," "order," and even "form" itself are regarded by him with the highest suspicion. Insists on unevenness as a virtue. Flaunts an almost barbaric disregard for the moral mysteries, or integrities, of traditional narrative modes. This flaw in his discipline is well demonstrated here. In order to save this narration, editor felt compelled to clarify slightly, not to censor but to impose at least the illusion of order. This was an effort toward preserving a certain morality of technique. Editor speaks here of a morality of morality, of that necessary corroboration between unyielding material and the discerning eye of absolute importance in the making of a final draft. (215)

This story is not overtly concerned with points of law, yet McPherson's speculations throughout it on the nature of narration are shaped by his understanding of African American experience as a part of America's legal narrative. Issues that emerged in nineteenth-century discussions of black citizenship and identity reemerge in McPherson's story of an interracial marriage: romantic self-identification, authenticity, ironic self-perception, separation, segregation, freedom, and imaginative capacity. For McPherson, the primary ontological activity is narration, the crafting of a record for the future, the establishment of precedent, the making possible the act of stare decisis. That narrative act, however, is not just a naturalistic recording of what was but an imaginative figuration of as much of the complexity inherent in the moment as is possible for the narrator:

If I approached a stranger and said, "Friend, I need your part of the story in order to complete my sense of self," I would have caused him to shudder, tremble, perhaps denounce me as an assailant. Yet not to do this was to default on my responsibility to narrate fully. There are stories that *must* be told, if only to be around when fresh dimensions are needed. . . . A narrator cannot function without new angles of vision. I needed new eyes, regeneration, fresh forms, and went hunting for them out in the territory.

A point of information. What has form to do with caste restrictions?
 Everything.
You are saying you want to be white?
 A narrator needs as much access to the world as the advo-
 cates of that mythology.
You are ashamed then of being black?
 Only of not being nimble enough to dodge other people's
 straightjackets.
Are you not much obsessed here with integration?
 I was cursed with a healthy imagination.
What have caste restrictions to do with imagination?
 Everything.
A point of information. What is your idea of personal freedom?
 Unrestricted access to new stories forming. (220)

McPherson's narrator recapitulates for the artist/advocate the same imperative that underlay the restrictions on literacy for enslaved people: language-as-narrative enables the imaginative creation of identity and community. As McPherson's narrator attempts to understand and limn the new dimensions of black identity in the 1970s, he seeks access to as many lives as possible so he can imagine the new community of which they will be a part. His job is to set down as many of these "new stories forming" as he can find. Unlike the "whispered consolations" of which Mrs. Mossell wrote three-quarters of a century before, McPherson seeks to leave an inscribed, permanent record of how black people were in the world, as he imagined that being and that world. "A Sense of Story" then becomes clearer to us as one of these records, a record of a record of a life, imperfectly imagined by all of the principals except Robert Charles himself, and McPherson the narrator-artist-lawyer.

 As for the story "Elbow Room" itself, little is resolved, although much is imagined. Anticipating the arguments made by Patricia Williams and Derrick Bell, McPherson points out how difficult it is for a white man to successfully imagine black experience. His story of a young white Kansan married to a worldly black woman exemplifies Williams's point about the impossibility of the translation of perspective. Williams had cited Mary Ann Caws, and I repeat that brief passage from the discussion earlier in this chapter:

> Suppose someone were to say: "Imagine this butterfly exactly as it is, but ugly instead of beautiful"?! The transfer we are called on to make includes . . . stretching not just of the imagination, but of the transfer point: . . . It is as if I were told: "Here is a chair. Can you see it clearly?—Good—now translate it into French!" (411)

Whereas Williams and Bell are less than sanguine about the ability of whites to make that transfer successfully, McPherson imagines the possibility of a genuine effort on the part of his white protagonist to do so. At one point in the story, McPherson's narrator loses interest in the lives of the interracial couple because he thinks the man is failing to see the reality of his wife's life as a woman of color and the woman is failing to sustain the authenticity of that life; these are no longer "new" stories but old anecdotes. But he revisits them at the end of his ruminations on the dialects of narration and tells us that they are struggling in ways that less dramatic than he had imagined, but no less authentic, to shape new lives.

The end of the story, set in the rural Midwest and evocative of the romance of the local, reminds me, ironically, of the ending of W. E. B. Du Bois's *Dark Princess*. Du Bois's novel, if read through the lens of McPherson's speculations on narrative, is clearly his attempt to imagine new caste relations, new stories, new freedoms. As McPherson's story is set at a moment of transition in American culture, so was Du Bois, some fifty years earlier. Both take their characters into a wider, cosmopolitan world, and both end their narratives with the same scene: the nuclear couple, joined across racial barriers, transplanted from the urban world of affairs back to the ancestral "land" and the bosom of the "folk," with a new son whose presence represents the potentiality of a new order of experience for an undefined future people. This kind of community is, as Benedict Anderson has explained and we have explored in the opening chapters of this study, the product of imagination. Both McPherson's and Du Bois's notions of the imagined nation to which their protagonist's experiences point are radical, in the word's sense of "root." Both authors ultimately move their characters to a world as far removed from that of positivist constructions of reality, away from positivist law, to the closest thing to nature and natural law one can have and still maintain civility, the family group situated on the ancestral land, governed by narratives of the past and figuring forth some sort of equally "natural" future.

McPherson reiterates this vision in an essay called "Junior and John Doe," which he wrote for a collection of essays on the theme of Du Bois's 1903 *Souls of Black Folk* trope of "double consciousness." Reflecting on the potential loss of internal sources of integrity among black people as they lose their separateness and assimilate into everyday white American life, McPherson seems to echo the arguments of Frances Harper, Sutton Griggs, and Pauline Hopkins, as well as those of Du Bois, about the rectitude of black folks and their purer vision of the promises and implications of the Constitution and the laws that ought rightly to flow from it, visions purer than those of the whites who used the law to abuse them. McPherson writes:

> Our slave ancestors were familiar with this distinction. Their very lives depended on the ability to distinguish between moral fashions and meaningful actions. They survived by having sufficient vitality of imagination to pass over the present scene, if its currents were not moving in their direction, and identify their meaning with an age that was yet to come. In this way they kept alive the hope of eventually being able to continue moving toward their own goals. In this way a defeated people kept alive a sense of integrity, a sense of self, even if their bodies were bought and sold. During the worst of material times they provided a standard for the best of material times. (189–90)

Both McPherson and Gerald Early, whose introduction opens the volume for which McPherson wrote, conceive of their enslaved ancestors as those whose acts of self-definition were rooted in the future, in an age yet to come, a people they would be once history righted itself. Early reads Du Bois's trope as a depiction of blacks "as being caught, Hamlet-like, between the issue of a nationalistic and an assimilated collective identity," neither of them yet realized (*Lure* xx). To Du Bois, as Early understands him, this unrealized future holds the entire ironic condition of African American life, a life in which the Negro in America not only knows of the existence of each option, to be Negro or to be American, but *already* knows what it is to be each, (and I would add) without knowing what it is to be both.

At the close of the twentieth century, a rising black middle and professional class could argue that the legal war is over. The litigative and legislative struggles over affirmative action that dominated the 1990s are last skirmishes, perhaps. Many, maybe most, black conservatives would say that America can never go back to the racial uses of law that characterized slavery, the counter-Reconstruction, and Jim Crow. For the Shelby Steeles, the Clarence Thomases, the Stephen Carters, there is no ironic contradistinction in theory or practice between being Negro and being American; they know what it is to be both; they claim not to know what it is to be each.

Bebe Moore Campbell, on the other hand, a woman writing in the realist-naturalist tradition of the classic African American narrative, is not so sanguine. In 1992, Campbell wrote *Your Blues Ain't Like Mine,* a novel based loosely on the Emmett Till case. Young Till was killed by whites in Mississippi in 1955. He was beaten, one eye gouged out, shot in the head, and thrown into the Tallahatchie River with a seventy-five-pound cotton gin fan wired around his neck. He was fourteen years old and had spoken to, maybe whistled at, a white woman. The men who killed him were acquitted by an all-white jury after deliberating one hour. Campbell's novel explores the consequences of the murder in the lives of black and white Mississippians, and she brings the story line down to contemporary Mississippi, where black and white poor still struggle and compete for resources while trying to learn to live together as members of the same class. Writing in the persona of a woman worker of mixed racial background, years after the event, Campbell looks back:

> Ida thought about the irony of poor black people suing the town.
> Everyone else on the committee was exultant, as though they had
> already won the case, but the more Ida thought about the lawsuit,
> the more enraged she became. Suing the town should be just the
> beginning. She should file a lawsuit against Barnes for trying to
> rape her. The blacks ought to sue because the dilapidated schools
> hadn't taught them to read and write. Odessa and Delotha could

sue the Coxes for Killing Armstrong. There weren't enough
lawyers in Mississippi to give black folks the justice they deserved.
(391)

That is the epilogic conclusion to which I would like to come. In at
least some of the contemporary black narrative that carries on the critique of American law begun in the traditional African American narrative, the racialization of poverty and pathology continues in the public life of the nation. The black poor increase in number and in distance
from the white wealthy. And an activist Supreme Court, much like that
decried by the Brotherhood of Liberty in the 1880s, seems intent on
returning the legislative and police power of government back to the
states and the counties and the cities, to re-create the United States that
existed when the Court wrote its Edenic text of American life, *Plessy v.
Ferguson.*

Amid these depredations, in popular genres removed from law
schools and reviews, from best-seller lists and MLA conventions, popular African American narrative still engages the law, but not as
directly athwart these issues as earlier works had done. Gangsta rap
epitomizes the commercialization of alienation in the conflict between
social order and male desire as a reification of race. Black-oriented
comic books epitomize the other end of the fantasy of the breakdown of
social order by positing black superheroes who seek to enforce stability
through a kind of anxiety-ridden populist vigilantism. In both genres,
women's bodies objectify the desire for chaos and for order. As postmodern narratives, the word balloons in the comics and the meter of
rap break out of their frames in every track, on every page, carry with
them the randomized accumulation of historical and cultural references that are the semiologic frames of their stories.

On television, black situation comedies, as they have always done,
use vocabulary rather than invention to signify blackness, and the law
functions as it has always done in comedy, as the blocking humor, there
of necessity, to be overcome. In film, black experience with the law,
when it is not a fantasy of integrated police work or of the outlaw life,
is historical. In these ways film and television replicate and extend
some of the traditional narrative practices of the previous century of
African American prose fiction. In addition, narrative has made its way
into the academy, coincidental with the rise in the number of black aca-
demics, and law, history, political science, even economics boast con-

ventions and festschrifts dominated by tales that exemplify the contradictions of practice and theory.

These extensions of the great interrogative project of classical African American literature against American law notwithstanding, that critique has shifted in interesting ways. White (and black) conservatives have appropriated much of the vocabulary of traditional political critique, so that no real language to challenge the law's ability to write the lives of African Americans leaps to the pen or tongue. Fully possessed now of all the romantically authentic and ironic indices of selfhood, African America's literature has become both American and Negro. But as it has done so, it may have finally lost the ability to frame its challenges to the law and the law's narrative. Law no longer exists in the African American narrative as a metanarrative to be confronted or embraced or patched together, not when law can be seen in every possible demythologized form on television any night. In the last half of the last decade of the century, classical African American narratives are more likely to be found protecting the legal order than attacking it. Like the Brotherhood of Liberty over a century ago, black men and women concerned about the law are not interested in breaking it but in salvaging it, protecting it from dismemberment.

As the radical Right of America, in its secular and Christian personae, seeks to dismantle the remnants of the New Deal and the civil rights legislation of the Lyndon Johnson presidency, postproperty African American narrative turns from traditional fiction to other forms. As, for example, the memoir and the autobiography reach the novel's audience, literary narrative becomes a vehicle for the neoromantic politics of individual identity, a record of how the individual American, black or white, male or female, was formed.

Gangsta rap, comic books, and popular television and film share a common vocabulary, also romantic in its situating of the autonomous individual, and it is through these that a black narrative clearly interrogates American law. In each of these "radicals of presentation," black writers and artists produce postapocalyptic visions of a culture in which African Americans are only one fragment of a deconstructed society. As romantic as its heroes are, the tone of these representations is as deeply ironic. Gangsta rap in particular stakes out territory at the margins of the law, disdaining not only the structures of American law but the bourgeoisification of black American life that has brought much of it within those structures. Robin D. G. Kelley writes:

[L]iving in the lap of luxury is not what renders the black bourgeoisie bankrupt, but rather their inability to understand the world
of the ghetto, black youth culture and rap music. . . . And to be fair
. . . wealthy African Americans are often guilty of the kind of social
labeling associated with white suburbanites and police. (211)

Kelley's analysis, written in the early 1990s, sees the phenomenon
of gangsta as a mixture of previous black literary conventions, social
anomie, and hucksterism. The degree to which gangsta rap performers
emerge from authentic criminal environments or themselves actively
espouse criminal activity is imprecisely understood, according to Kelley. By 1993, he thought that g-rap was on its last legs (225) but the continued celebrity of Tupac Shakur until his death, the posthumous reputation of the Notorious B.I.G., the media blanketing of America by the
group Bone Thugz-N-Harmony, and the alleged aesthetic, economic,
and cultural rivalry between the schools of East and West Coast
gangsta rap have kept the genre fresh, if not vital.

Certainly some of the conventions of g-rap have, as Kelley suggests, origins in "bad-nigger" folklore and toasting, the extended oral
narration popular in urban communities since the turn of the century.[17]
The subject position of the narrator, however, is significantly different.
The rapper as first-person narrator takes on the law and challenges its
relevance to his life. The ironic vision of these narratives undercuts
their romanticism, but the outlines of the romantic hero are present: the
gangsta-artist whose sensibilities pinpoint the contradictions between
overwhelming forces of control and "natural" impulses to action,
appetite, and desire. The gangsta-artist operates on the basis of need,
not of rights, and his argument against the state is that it has no right to
deny him the pursuit of the satisfaction of his desires.[18] That those sat-
isfactions are often cruel, dangerous, and socially as well as self-
destructive is a fact explained by the class position of the gangsta-artist
and the people for whom he speaks.

Generalizations about the maleness of this genre are inevitable,
although I am aware there are some women who practice in it. The very
real misogyny of the genre is striking, and the objectification of women
as well as their victimization in it are signifiers, perhaps, of how far outside bourgeois values and the systems that support them gangsta rappers want to position themselves. In doing so in the arena of gender
relationships, rappers "have it" both ways. Because the biggest market
for gangsta rap is among white males in late adolescence and early

adulthood, the popularity of antisocial and specifically misogynistic material suggests that the position is not really outside the frame of bourgeois reference at all.

One of the problematics of gangsta rap as a form of cultural critique is that created by the financial positioning of g-rappers after they become popular. The money that flows into the rappers and to the companies that produce and distribute their records and videos has the tendency to isolate them from the street origins on which they built their first images. The promise of a share of that money also may attract rappers who are performers but not "authentic" gangstas, not real "niggaz" but "studio gangstas." This debate about who can speak to and for the putative audience, young, black, working-class males suffering from un- or underemployment, racial discrimination, and police repression, is a 1990s analogue to the prolit discussions of the early and mid-1930s and similar to that of the Black Arts movement of three decades past. In the 1930s, leftist political writers argued over the nature of proletarian fiction in terms of class-based authenticity, some believing that only workers could write about the working class and only politicized worker-writers could write politically about their class interests. Others took the position that middle-class writers who took the class position of the workers could create a viable literature of that class, particularly if that class position was informed by a Marxist analysis of the workers' role at that historical moment. G-rap debate has not become that arcane, but the issues are much the same, particularly when the lyrics of gangsta rap evoke class and race as positions from which to critique and resist the criminalization of black experience.

On another popular cultural front, comic books in the 1990s create narratives of black men (and some women) as superefficient guardians of order and justice, either as legal minions or as vigilantes. Written and drawn by black artists such as Dwayne McDuffie, Christopher Priest, Kyle Baker, Michael Paris, Mark Bright, Bob Washington, and Rob Simpson, these comics feature the technological age's version of the romance hero, the character for whom some natural laws are suspended so that he or she can pursue a personal or social quest.

"Steel," for example, whose adventures were written primarily by Christopher Priest and published by DC Comics, is in "real life" Dr. John Henry Irons (a name made up out of the iconography of black heroic legend), an engineer and medical researcher whose work has allowed him to construct a steel exoskeleton that gives him superhuman strength, mobility, and stamina. Donning his mechanical suit, Irons becomes Steel and fights the metaphysical forces of evil in the universe, especially as they manifest themselves in social chaos in the black community of Jersey City, New Jersey (*Steel,* January 1997). Among the DC stable are other black superheroes written or edited by black men. There do not seem to be any black women writing or editing comic books today, although some white women do, including Louise Simonson, who conceived the idea for *Steel.*[19]

"Deathlok" and "Xombi," each heroes of their own eponymous comics written and/or edited by Dwayne McDuffie, are Osiris figures, men who have died and come back to life whole or in parts to return value to the universe. Deathlok, for example, is a creature of destruction created by the military-industrial complex. However, the human brain that serves as its contextual center is that of Michael Collins, black pacifist, who struggles against the programming of destruction by the "lawful' authorities to impose his own will on the death machine he inhabits.

The most ironically imprisoned black male hero of them all is Christopher Priest's "Xero." In ordinary life, if the world of professional basketball superstardom can be called "ordinary," Xero is Trane Walker, power forward for the East St. Louis Vipers. When he is called on to act as a force for justice, the force that can close a case, permanently, he becomes a blonde-haired, blue-eyed "Closer." Priest says of the ironic dilemma his character faces, "As the lines separating Xero and basketball begin to blur, Trane Walker becomes lost in the collision of ethics and values and ends up paying a terrible price for his emerging moral conscience" ("Creating"). The superficial characteristics of the narratives, the technology, hardware, and cold-war espionage context of the plots are geared to the conventions of the genre, but the ironic struggle is less conventionally at the moral level, especially at the level of identity. The basic humanity of the black athlete Trane Walker is constantly being submerged beneath the amoral destructiveness of the white "Closer" Xero. Thus the real struggle in the series is that of Trane to retain his humanity and his racial identity.

While *Steel* and *Xero* are mainline publications of DC Comics, others such as *Hardware, Icon, Blood Syndicate, Static,* and *Wise Son* are products of its "multicultural" line, Milestone Books. The editor in chief and executive vice president of Milestone is Dwayne McDuffie. He oversees the ongoing storyline that carries the actions of the black, Asian, and Latino superheroes his writers and artists create. That storyline is set in the city of Dakota, primarily in its ghetto, Paris Island. Paris Island has been devastated by the Big Bang, a plan by the mayor to use a radio-active-laced tear gas on a street gang battle so her police could trace gang members easily after the fight. Something went wrong and 90 percent of the gang-bangers died. The survivors mutated into monsters or superheroes. The comic books in the Milestone series follows the lives of the survivors and the citizens of Paris Island, some of whom serve as the heroes of the series. "Static," for example, is Virgil Hawkins, a black teenager with electromagnetically enhanced abilities; "Wise Son" is Hannibal, leader of the Blood Syndicate and a troubled man of tragic stature; "Icon" is Augustus Freeman IV, a wealthy black lawyer who is in fact an extraterrestrial. Freeman came to Earth in the nineteenth century and took the identity of an African American male.

The Milestone series books are urban-oriented, contemporary narratives of the conflict between organized systems of social control and personal morality. All of the heroic characters are flawed and struggle with the implications not only of the inhumanity of the system under which they live but of the powers that separate them from the ordinary people of their community. In this they are similar to, but more reflective than, their nineteenth-century counterparts in African American romantic responses to American life, Madison Washington (Douglass's *The Heroic Slave*), Henry Blake (Delany's *Blake*), and Bernard Belgrave and Belton Piedmont (Griggs's *Imperio in Imperium*). The earlier romance heroes are less troubled by the distance between their endowments and those of the ordinary men and women they seek to serve. There is no anxiety over becoming "white" or less human as a consequence of their abilities to prevail in their environments. To them, their abilities to prevail are proofs of the humanity of their people; for the heroes of the Milestone series, the ability to prevail is a reason for anguish and concern at times, coming as it does from the outside, from some external accident of technology or nature. However, like the protagonists of every classical African American narrative we have discussed, the Milestone heroes are all trying desperately to remain both black and American, and neither seems a workable option much of the time.

Although the heroes and narratives of gangsta rap and black comics occupy different ends of the spectrum of critiques of the law in black popular narrative, the two genres share some common ground. Each is distinctly urban and sees the law not as an organic realization of the ethoi of the community but as a system of social control devised externally. They each privilege the romantic vision of the individual while attempting to maintain valued ties to "the community." Each focuses its attention on the intersection of law as an instrument of social order and the expression and realization of desire. Their differences are equally important. One, g-rap, is almost starkly naturalistic and cynically ironic. Another, the comics, are elaborate romances and are painfully ironic.

An example from the ironic romances of the Milestone series emphasizes this difference. In the series, the forces of oppression and bondage that mark the deepest ironic narrative are personified by characters; forces that can only be alluded to and named as abstractions in gangsta rap can be drawn and colored in comics, as are the members of the "Beli Mah," a cult, appearing in the *Xombi* comic, whose central belief is that the world can be made ideal by reducing everything to an abstraction of what it represents, a true form of itself, with no masks to be misinterpreted. They feel that the world is full of masks behind masks behind masks. Among the Beli Mah are the Painful Inscriptions, warrior figures who are physical embodiments of certain abstract concepts: Manuel Dexterity is a product of all the unfulfilled intense desires in the world, and he is accompanied by his twin sister Manuella, the embodiment of deep-rooted shame; Bludgeon is crafted from misdirected rage; Blister Ed is a creature constructed out of words spoken in anger, which cannot be unsaid ("Milestone").

This drift into allegory is an extreme response to the opportunities that comic narratives offer writers, but it exposes the romantic heart of these stories. The only black narrative writers who have attempted to create a critique in the same quasi-allegorical style have been Sutton Griggs and George Schuyler, Chester Himes in *Plan B,* a posthumously published novel, and Ishmael Reed throughout his career.

These parallels highlight the most contemporary characteristic of both black comics and gangsta rap, their extensive exploitation of the literary absurd. While Griggs is a forefather of black American apocalyptic fiction, it is Schuyler who truly appreciates the usefulness of absurdity as a tool for social criticism in extended narrative.[20] In his hands, however, the device remains playful; it is Chester Himes who uncovers the morbid power of the absurd and uses it unsparingly in his fiction. It remained only for Reed and then black comic books to combine Schuyler's comedic use of the hyperextension of absurdity with Himes's unflinching stare directly into the pain of the absurdity of urban black life. It is in this way that the critique of law in African

American life found in black comics is carried on in a more consciously "literary" manner than are the narrative critiques of the law found in gangsta rap. Nevertheless, both respond to traditions of representation particular to their genres and to the African American transformations of those traditions.

From the transcript of the trials of Phillis and Mark, who poison their master in 1755, to the postmodern comics tracking the despair of "Flashback" and "Wise Son," who are poisoned by drugs and toxic waste served up by a malevolent legal system sometime after the turn of the second millennium, narratives of law and African American life are inextricably bound up in one another. Is there a master narrative to be made of all of these intertextualities? In the 1950s, Norman Mailer thought that there was. He thought it was an existential tale of mindless energy and ahistorical sensation, and he said so in the complexly racist and misogynistic essay, "The White Negro." Mailer's world of nuclear anxiety and bourgeois complacency called out, or so he argued, for whites to abandon rationality and embrace the implications of black America's encounter with the law. Those implications required that whites become outlaws, hipsters, marginal beings, as he thought American blacks had become.

Certainly Mailer was right to suspect that the black encounter with the legal life of America was unlike anything whites could have experienced. But his assumptions about African American responses to that encounter were typically simplistic and predetermined by white assumptions about black people. Mailer's "appreciation" of the Negro as a psychopath, a child, and an intuitive idiot savant of the netherworld is only a mid-twentieth-century recasting of the romantic images of antebellum and post-Reconstruction racism. The record I have tried to reconstruct here, however, shows that black Americans wrote themselves into the life with authenticity, irony, imagination, and care, with a fine ear and eye for the absurdity of the law as an epistemological tool, and with a love of and devotion to the rule of law nevertheless unequaled by any of their fellow citizens. Time and again black Americans turned to the law for protection, for justification, for consolation, and for a weapon or two. Time and again they have inscribed their hopes for outcomes that would be just as well as legal.

As I write the end of this study, black Americans are watching as many whites abandon programs based in law that were intended to bring to realization the promises of Emancipation. Once again African

Americans are called on to argue the validity of their claim to an equal identity in this nation. Hundreds of thousands of black men languish in prisons or are wards of the parole system. The death penalty has returned to the criminal-justice system with an intensity of application not seen since the 1950s, despite fears that the distribution of that penalty is skewed by race throughout the population. Black communities seek segregated schools for their boys and girls, and something like a resigned separatism informs the workaday world of many African Americans.

The attempt to read the lives of black folks through the law is a sobering one. Even more sobering, yet provocative and exciting for its richness and its insight, is the critique of American law we discover in African American narrative. From the first appeal to the natural rights of man and the promises of the Declaration of Independence to the bleak absurdity of unnatural men of steel and static and urban decay in contemporary black comic books, that critique gives evidence of the dignity and forbearance of black people living under a system of laws not of their own making.

Because of the very existence of that critique and the testimony it gives to the steadfastness through which black Americans have focused on the reality of life under the law, it demands to be read. We are still two nations, black and white, and the law and literature of black experience emerge, as they are read, as our true national history.

Small consolation. Whispered consolation.

Notes

Introduction

1. Ellison uses his early years in Oklahoma as a jumping off point for his discussion of black inequality before the law. For a more detailed account of the law in Oklahoma at the same period, as seen through the eyes of an African American lawyer, see the autobiography of John Hope Franklin's father, B. C. Franklin.

2. Compare the often cited passage from Robert Cover's "Nomos and Narrative": "No set of legal institutions exists apart from the narratives that locate it and give it meaning. For every constitution there is an epic, for each decalogue a scripture. Once understood in the context of the narratives that give it meaning, law becomes not merely a system of rules to be observed, but a world in which we live" (95–96). Kleinhans's unpublished paper argues the necessity for a narratival analysis of the "self" in law.

3. See the Wittgensteinian explanation of grammar employed by Woolgast: "the grammar of a term includes a variety of practices connected with its use and the criteria and background conditions that govern its normal application. Thus it is part of the grammar of 'chair,' Wittgenstein says, that *this* is what it is to sit in one" (x).

4. But see Toni Morrison's discussion of black character on trial in the O. J. Simpson case in "The Official Story." See Alexander and Cornell for a more traditional explanation of the jury's verdict.

5. That some viewers found the character Flynt contemptible because of his representation of women, despite the extraordinary performance of the actor Woody Harrelson, exemplifies another aspect of narrative: its power. Complaints against the film took the line of argument that such a medium of representation should not be used to validate the career of a man whose actions endangered women exactly because of narrative's power to convince on the basis of character, not action.

6. Considering how influence happens in culture, Ann Douglas writes, "But I do believe, with Freud and Fitzgerald, that history works as much by something like telepathy as by cause and effect, as much by the apparent coincidences of what Hegel called the Zeitgeist as by calculable economic or cultural influences; in an important essay of 1893, Twain christened this view of history-as-mind-reading 'mental telegraphy'" (201). While I am less mystical than Douglas, I do assume that some paradigms through which cultures arrange experience become embedded in the design of everyday life, almost as matrices or templates through which the raw material of cultural production passes everywhere on its way to becoming law, novel, poem, advertisement, hymn,

video game. This is how romanticism continues to shape our representations and perceptions.

7. For a more traditional line of inquiry in a search of sources and influences from the literature of English romanticism on slaveholders and their legislative allies, see Osterweis. For a critique of, and corrective to, Osterweis, see O'Brien. His references constitute a comprehensive bibliographic record of the inquiry into romantic impulses in both the Old and New South.

My questions are more argumentative and suggestive than they are amenable to documentation, having to do with the presence within the general culture of discourse of attitudes and assumptions so sympathetic to the perceived realities of the historical moment that most of the participants in the life of that moment would not think to question or even remark on the centrality, even universality, of their content, whatever side any given participant might take on a specific issue. The presence of those assumptions must be teased out of the social texts of the period, if they are to be seen at all, by intertextual readings. Nevertheless, see Jehlen for her reading of the founding experience as an encounter with "entelechy," or endless possibility, making America the most romantic site in European experience.

8. I do not mean to suggest that there were no whites sympathetic to one degree or others with the conditions of people of African descent, free or enslaved, in the American nineteenth century. The abolition movement alone shows that not to be the case. See, for example, as one of the latest studies, Harrold. I do suggest, however, that the attitudes I address in this chapter were endemic and predominant.

9. For example, consider, which I do not in the body of this book, Abrams's study of literary romanticism, *The Mirror and the Lamp*. Abrams presents two metaphors for the perception of reality: art is either a mirror of reality (Enlightenment view) or it is a lamp illuminating and exposing reality (romantic view), even transforming it when the lamp is seen to be the interior light that shines through the creating intellect's faculties and produces art. I would argue that 'law' is like any other text of experience, real or potential, in that it is susceptible to the same influences as its sister arts. So, what would a romantic theory of law look like? That is, if paradigms for the organization of experience exist at a historical moment that carry the weight of authority, as say romanticism did in the first half of the English and American nineteenth centuries, and as it does now in many elided formulations, how might legislators and lawyers and judges and law professors (now, not then) understand law's capability to figure forth reality? Or are all lawyers always ironicists? It does not help to claim to be realists, perhaps, because in American literary history of the nineteenth century, realism is understood generally to emerge from romanticism (via regionalism) and passes on soon enough to naturalism. None of this is to say that the formulations of literary history are any more (or at all) useful to legal historians. But it is to suggest that to consider reality and its discovery in the context of the discussion of a textual system without considering paradigms that apply to other and similar textual systems may be to miss a bet here and there.

10. Similarly, Countryman makes the argument that "romantic American democracy" was contradictory from the beginning, depending as it did on the

denial of rights, property, and freedom to blacks, women, and Indians while extending unprecedented levels of personal and social liberty and equality to white males.

11. Wolgast opens her critique of the autonomous identity in American culture by noting the antiauthoritarian bases of its development:

[S]uch a point was located in the autonomous, unconnected, rational human individual. . . . Thus a new kind of moral, political, and epistemological justification came into being, one that was derived from the natural, free, rational, and morally autonomous individual" (2). How this putatively "Enlightenment"-driven justification can be better understood as a romantic paradigm is the story of this chapter.

12. Tomlins addresses in another context the action of law as constitutive of reality.

Chapter 1

1. Ironically, later slave law as developed in the South suggests that many if not all of Horsmanden's convictions would have been impossible. In an 1834 case, 7 La. 586 (O.S.) [336 vol. 4] (June 1834) *Hart & Co. v. St. Rames et al.,* the court noted that because slaves were not persons they were not liable for damage they might cause, but "[o]n the other hand, it is urged that if the slaves were persons, *sui juris,* they would be liable, *in solido,* for damages committed by them jointly" (588–89). As they are property, owners are only liable proportionally, as though three separately owned carts broke loose and caused damage; since property cannot collude or conspire, owners have no responsibility in solido, only for a proportional share of the damage done by their witless property. Similarly, property could not collude or conspire to commit an illegal act.

2. Goodell cites a letter from Revere to the corresponding secretary of the Massachusetts Historical Society of January 1, 1798, to this effect.

Goodell's recovery and recapitulation of the trial of Mark and Phillis is given as a pretext for his advocacy of a more enlightened penal code. Having discovered the cases of Phillis and Mark, he uses their outcomes to argue "that it is not necessary to multiply extreme penalties in order to prevent crime, but that we are to look for the amelioration of manners and the diminution of public and private wrongs to the mental and moral education of the people rather than to the terrors of the law" (37).

In an email message of October 20, 1995, Linda K. Kerber wrote:

[J]ust as regicide is worse than "normal" treason, so the murder of a master by a servant or of a husband by a wife was worse than "normal" murder, and the penalties were harsher. Under the old law of domestic relations [the law of baron and feme, parent and child, master and servant] at marriage the husband became, in effect, the wife's lord, and stood to her as king did to subject. The killing of a wife by her husband, however, remained murder. The concept was not much enforced in early America, but neither was it eliminated from the statutes until the Revolution. *Petit treason* involving the killing of a master by a servant endured in the slave South much longer than in the North.

Massachusetts abolished the distinction between murder and petit treason in 1785; only the punishment for murder would be imposed, in these cases, hanging. The irony of the silent corpse of Mark watching over the figure of Paul Revere in full gallop and voice cannot be avoided. Revere's warning, "The British are coming! The British are coming!" meant something other than danger to some American blacks, who allied themselves with the Crown or with Tory masters. After the Revolution, it was England that abolished slavery first.

3. Victoria Bynum points out that some slaves responded to the inherent violence of slavery by becoming more aggressive, even murdering masters. Often it was the slave women who were the principal aggressors. In the Norwood murder in 1857 in Granville County, North Carolina, slaves poured boiling water down Norwood's throat while holding a cloth over his mouth and nose, because he beat his slaves so and sold their families away (114).

4. An invaluable collection is Finkelman, *Free Blacks, Slaves, and Slaveowners.* Volume 1, for example, contains not only the transcript of "The Trial and Execution of Mark and Phillis," but reports of the trials, variously, of Abraham Johnstone (hanged in New Jersey), Cato (a slave executed in 1803), *Alms-House v. Alexander Whistelo* (a case of bastardy), and Susanna (for the murder of her infant child) among others.

5. Besides the narratives, autobiographies, and fictions discussed in this study, African Americans produced essays, articles, plays, and short fictions in numbers too great to survey here. In nineteenth-century African American newspapers alone, over one hundred short fictions were published between 1820 and the end of the Civil War. Hundreds more were published between 1865 and 1952, the terminal date for this study.

6. Grant reprints a number of these documents, including the April 20, 1773, petition for freedom signed by the Boston slaves Peter Betses, Sambo Freeman, Felix Holbrook, and Chester Joie (28–29) and the 1793–94 petition against the South Carolina poll tax made by "Free Negroes Mulattoes and Mustizoes" (31–32).

7. See Siler 94–168. As Siler notes in unpublished research on the legal implications of slavery, not even conversion to Christianity was sufficient to ensure one's liberation: "The legal process of depriving slaves of human rights began with the Virginia statute which declared that baptism was no grounds for a slave's claim to freedom, and continued—with law after law, in colony after colony—until the time of the Revolution" (99). The march of prohibitory acts seems inexorable in retrospect: owning guns was first prohibited in Virginia in 1680, Pennsylvania in 1706, and North Carolina in 1729; ownership of property first prohibited in Virginia in 1692 and in North Carolina in 1741; trading prohibited in New York in 1703 and again in 1712 and 1726; assembly in Virginia in 1680, New York in 1702, Pennsylvania in 1706, and North Carolina in 1729; "leaving their condition" (i.e., being anything but a slave) was prohibited in

Virginia in 1688. Schwarz, however, argues that Africans shaped the customary law, the informal code, through which whites governed in Virginia and that those practices in turn influenced statutory law.

8. See, for example, United States Circuit Court (2d Cir.), *The African Captives* (1839); Adams; for a fictional treatment of antebellum white lawyers representing black clients, including appellate representation, see Stowe.

9. The docket book of Benjamin Montgomery, justice of the peace at Davis Bend, Warren County, Mississippi, and first black man appointed to public office in that state, on September 10, 1867, provides another kind of record. In a typical case, "Robert Johnson made affidavit that Mary Hudson used vulgar language toward his wife. Arthur Glass complained that Isaiah Hunter had killed his dog. A woman charged that Harvey Green rode her horse without her permission." Violence was reported in more cases than any other violation, one-third alleging assault. A quarter of the cases alleged theft. All of the participants in these cases were black, and none owned taxable property. (From a manuscript in preparation, "Law and the Lash: Race and Criminal Justice in a Mississippi County, 1817–1880," Christopher Waldrep, H-Law, May 1, 1996, 07:39.)

10. The *Amistad* case of 1839–41 is one, and *Thomas Sim's Case*, 61 Mass. 285 (1851) is another. John Quincy Adams successfully argued for the return to their homeland of a community of enslaved Africans in the first of these, and in the second Lemuel Shaw, father-in-law of Herman Melville, returned Thomas Sims, an escaped slave, to his "owner" under the compulsion of law. The 1842 case involving the claim against George Latimer caused Massachusetts to pass a law forbidding state officials from participating in actions against fugitive slaves. In another area of litigation, Shaw had, in *Roberts v. City of Boston*, 5 Cush. 198 (1849), decided that school segregation by race was not illegal because it was not a matter of law. This finding was later cited as case law by Justice Fenner of the Louisiana Supreme Court in *Plessy*. In 1854 an angry crowd failed to rescue Anthony Burns from Sims's fate, but Burns was the last black man or woman to be returned to slavery from Massachusetts. *Scott v. Sandford* is the most remarked of these "national" cases and one of the very few to be brought outside of Massachusetts. See cases as well in Finkelman, *Slavery, Race*.

11. Bynum notes:

The slaveholding elite's notions about status and honor conformed to the traditional English model, which stressed family lineage, wealth, and, for men, physical prowess, sexual virility, and intellectual leadership. Power and honor went hand in hand; one could hardly achieve one without the other. The southern version of honor was also grounded, however, in the need to maintain racial distinctions within institutions of the family, law, politics, and the economy. . . . Slaveholders devised laws to limit interracial social contact, and the ideology of paternalism posited slavery as the stewardship of infantile, uncivilized blacks by noble, beneficent whites. Paternalist ideology effectively denied adult status to all blacks; it denied the rights of manhood to black men and the rights of womanhood to black women. (4)

12. Note also that between 1850 and 1860, the number of fugitive slaves reported declined by 20 percent. In 1850, one in every thirty-one hundred slaves was a fugitive, but by 1860, one in every five thousand was a fugitive (Census of 1860).

13. See previous remarks in this chapter, including Bynum, for this pattern of response in the actions of enslaved women.

14. When the mistress dies, her son refuses to pay the note, claiming the estate is insolvent and "the law prohibited payment. It did not, however, prohibit him from retaining the silver candelabra which had been purchased with that money" (Jacobs 9).

15. Flint, the master, is echoing the words of Chief Justice Thomas Ruffin's 1829 decision in North Carolina's infamous *State v. Mann*, 2 Dev. (N.C.) 263 (1829), which furnished this often quoted summary of the slave's condition vis-à-vis the master: "The power of the master must be absolute to render the submission of the slave perfect. . . . This discipline belongs to the state of slavery. They cannot be disunited, without abrogating at once the rights of the master and absolving the slave from his subjection."

16. The strength of expression of these opinions about one's status as property contradicts the humor of such anecdotes as the following, reported in the *New York Tribune* and reprinted in *Pine and Palm* for June 22, 1861:

> The decision of the Government, that the slaves of the enemy are to be treated as "contraband goods," is carefully suppressed by the newspapers; but the general feeling is that expressed by an old and trusted slave in Louisiana, since the war broke out: "Sam," said his master, "I must furnish some niggers to go down and work on the fortifications at the Baline. Which of the boys had I better send?" "Well, massa," replied the old servant, shaking his head oracularly, "I doesn't know about dat. War's coming on and dey might be killed. Ought to get Irishmen to do dat work, anyhow. I reckon you'd better not send any ob de boys; tell you what, massa, *nigger property's mighty onsartin dese times!*" ("Sage Conclusion")

The ironic humor of Sam's remark notwithstanding, the Union's policy of treating slaves held by them as a consequence of the war as property underlines how crucial the advent of Emancipation two years later was to black Americans. The use of the antebellum Negro commentator as an ironic observer of the regimen of slavery and the complexities of labor relations when some workers are free and others are not has not, to my knowledge, been commented on. The moral earnestness of the slave narrative and fugitive autobiography leaves little room for humor, it would seem.

17. For the history of the novel's revisions and published versions, see the introduction to Brown, *Clotel.*

18. See primarily J. C. Smith, "Justice and Jurisprudence." I have gone to Smith's sources and to records at the Enoch Pratt Free Library in Baltimore. The history of the Mutual United Brotherhood of Liberty of the United States begins essentially with the ministry in Baltimore of Reverend Harvey Johnson. His biographer, A. Briscoe Koger, claims that Johnson had read the basic documents of American law and had concluded that "within the already existing

law of the land, may be found for all citizens, ample protection and safety, if this law but be carried out, respected and obeyed by all the body politic" (9). The Brotherhood was founded in the summer and fall of 1885, and its first formal meeting was held over the three days of October 19–21, 1885, with Frederick Douglass as its first speaker and Henry Highland Garnett in attendance (12–13).

19. James G. Blaine, who lost the 1884 presidential election. Here is some of the passage to which the preface is referring:

> I must relate, before we separate, a curious incident, in connection with the foremost man in the republican class—to follow my figure of the school,—who was about to graduate with its highest honors. One day he went to New York; and while in the society of his friends there, he received from a zealous advocate and admirer, who familiarly styled his old classmate the "Plumed Knight," a decoction of his own invention which he thought would operate as a sort of [political] elixir. Mr. Blaine, without noticing the label, swallowed the contents of the bottle. The next day, upon examining it, he discovered it was labeled "Rum, Romanism, and Rebellion." He instantly feared that, in the condition of his own system and of the public atmosphere, this mixture would prove a deadly poison. It was such a whimsical compound, however, that we at first thought no harm would come of it. In a few days we saw our mistake. (120)

20. See Roediger for an extended analysis. Bernstein notes the public opposition to racist trade unions by black leaders at the end of the century, but cites Frederick Douglass as early as 1871 (91–96).

21. Whittier's "Howard at Atlanta" is collected among his "antislavery" poems, although it appeared in 1869. Sixty-six years later, in his June 25, 1935, address to the annual meeting of the NAACP, Joel Spingarn cited Whittier's poem and used its central metaphor to end his speech, reminding the conference in St. Louis that the association's hope and message was "that the colored race is rising, rising, rising, forever." See the Joel E. Spingarn Collection, box 9, folder 3, "NAACP 1915–29," New York Public Library.

22. Mrs. Mossell's poem replaces Whittier's own emendation, "General," with "Massa." The boy was Richard R. Wright, who went on to become a major in the U.S. Army, a minister, and president of the Georgia State Industrial College. Although she gets some of the facts of the event wrong, see the note to Mrs. Mossell's poem (64–65). In his autobiography, General Howard gives his recollection of the event. He suggests that Wright was disturbed that Whittier had him addressing Howard as "Massa." Later editions of Whittier's poem replace "Massa" with "General" (414).

23. Shain uses his observation to argue against the importance of "individualism" during the formative years of the republic, and I disagree with that line of thought. However, Shain's point that an "Enlightenment" individualism was not central is more to the issue, since I argue that the romantic psychology of the monadic, autonomous romantic and individualistic hero-as-self is at the base of republican, antebellum, and postbellum American identity.

24. Page numbers in the text refer to the 1988 paperback edition.

25. Harper was a temperance lecturer as well as a race woman; many ante-bellum black newspapers were financed by white temperance organizations battling liquor as a danger to reenslave the free Negro.

26. Some thirty years later Alain Locke, in his now famous 1926 essay, "The New Negro," revisits the idea that black Americans have a unique opportunity to address the promise of America when he calls for turning to race, not in separatism, but as a source of necessary energy arising from obstacles to human aspiration transformed into "an efficient dam of social energy and power" (967). Race as a form of value-generating experience is enhanced, he suggests, by a "warrantably comfortable feeling in being on the right side of the country's professed ideals" (967). This perspective was resurrected on October 16, 1995, at the Million-Man March in Washington, D.C. In his address to the crowd of black men on the Mall, Nation of Islam minister Louis Farrakhan argued that African Americans alone could make America truly American, could create the "more perfect Union" called for in the Preamble to the Constitution.

27. Dr. Harvey Johnson, one of the founders of the Brotherhood of Liberty, found himself of the same opinion at the close of the century:

> In order to further show the falsity and unconstitutionality of Judge Taney when he declared that the "negro had no rights that the white man was bound to respect," and also to further show that the colored men were already in full possession of all rights of American citizens for a year or more before the decision of the socalled learned Judge, I will here quote from "Justice and Jurisprudence," a very elaborate work issued by J. B. Lippincott Co. in 1889: see page 528. It reads as follows:
>
> > "In early times free colored persons exercised the right of suffrage in New Hampshire, Massachusetts, New York, New Jersey and North Carolina, and this was the case in New Hampshire and Massachusetts in 1856, and colored aliens could be naturalized. It is not true that the Constitution was made exclusively for and by the white race; it was established by the people of the United States for themselves and their posterity, and, as free colored people were then citizens of at least five States, and in every sense part of the people of the United States, they were among those for whom and for whose posterity the Constitution was established."
>
> What more do I need to say to prove that the white man is selfgoverning in theory only, and is for that reason, in every practical sense, unfitted to have in his keeping the rights of the people? (22–23)

28. The most famous exception to this observation is the career of Frederick Douglass, who, by the 1850s, had come to believe that the Constitution provided a ground for successful claims by blacks for equality, thus abandoning his earlier "Garrisonian" disdain for the document. See Rushdy for a recent account of a black writer's critique of the nineteenth-century constitutional argument.

29. See the Collections of the Massachusetts Historical Society, III, 5th series,

1877. From a white writer's perspective, the Declaration might undergird resistance rather than solicitation. Harriet Beecher Stowe's 1856 novel, *Dred: A Tale of the Great Dismal Swamp*, contains a speech by an educated mulatto to a group of rebellious slaves about the principles of the Declaration, particularly about the right and duty of revolution (2:225–56).

30. See Kaminski, *A Necessary Evil?* for a survey of the documents undergirding this argument.

31. Langston's position was similar to that of Frederick Douglass by the 1850s, in that Douglass had not only abandoned the anti-Constitution position of Garrison, but had also abandoned his passive evolutionism for a belief in armed action if necessary.

32. This excerpt from the prospectus of the *Pine and Palm*, a publication out of Boston and New York, provides an even more radical approach to "Constitutional" America than Garrison's in calling for

> I. The immediate eradication of Slavery from the soil of the United States by the Federal Government, and failing that, by John Brown expeditions, and simultaneous and extended Negro Insurrection.
>
> II. The calling of a National Convention for the revision of the Federal Constitution, to place it unmistakably and forever on the side of freedom: to erase from it its lingering remnants of royalist ideas; to enable the North to share the taxation and new duties (as they have shared the guilt and the folly of Slavery) which must necessarily result from a forced emancipation; and finally, believing that the people of the Cotton States, east of the Mississippi, are, in every essential respect, a different and hostile nation to us, to take measures for their temporary secession from the Union, *after* the abolition of Slavery in their territory; that is to say, if, by a fair vote, their inhabitants shall decide, as we believe they would decide, in favor of an independent government. ("Prospectus" n.p.)

The newspaper goes on to argue for a Negro emigration to Haiti and the creation of a confederation of Caribbean Negro states in alliance with the United States and with Canada, which would be asked to join the Union. The prospectus closes with a call for "THE COSMOPOLITAN GOVERNMENT OF THE FUTURE, which, superseding Nationalities and rendering war unnecessary, shall establish and secure forever the 'reign of peace on earth and good will to men'" (n.p.).

33. About the legal context emerging between 1820 and 1830 Ascher remarks,

> The new context of slavery as a legal condition was created by the transformation that had begun in property and contract law, rather than to [sic] the immediate economic needs or security of the South. And it was as much that institutionalized acceptance of slavery as an acceptable legal condition rather than a necessary and circumstantial "curse" that excited the passionate reaction of its opponents in the North. In the 1840s and 1850s slavery as a legal issue made it most clear that American law was no longer within the natural law tradition of the *Declaration of Independence*, that it was no longer an immutable rule of justice that transcended the peculiarities of local economic and political conditions. (161–62)

34. Some discussion questioning the importance of *Marbury* has developed over the past few years, but it still remains an iconographic reference for the first defining moment in the history of the Court.

35. But sympathy with the aims of the Constitution was such that an anonymous reviewer in 1887 could write on the publication of Reverend Charles W. Mossell's *The Supremacy of the Constitution, and the Sovereignty of the People,* delivered before a mass meeting of the citizens of Hagerstown, Maryland:

"It is by such papers as the above that the negro American is to win the respect of the white American. There is no begging or whining about it. Thoroughly manly, it is an appeal to law, natural and statutory" (Review 344).

36. Fortune, an African American newspaperman and entrepreneur, combined a youthful radicalism with a long-held admiration for Booker T. Washington. Johnson and his friends, while militant for the rights of their people, were not political radicals. Neither did they share Fortune's admiration for Washington's policies of racial appeasement.

37. The bibliography of black nationalist thought of the nineteenth and twentieth centuries is an extensive one. See these studies for a sense of the range of nationalist sentiment: J. S. Wright; Ullman; Moses, *Crummell;* Moses, *Wings;* Moses, *Black Messiahs;* McAdoo; Allen; Elder; Dubey; Stuckey; V. P. Franklin; Helmreich; Herod and Herod; Jenkins and Phillips.

Chapter 2

1. In 1888, thirty years after *Scott v. Sandford* and twenty years after the ratification of the postwar amendments, Aaron A. Mossell, lawyer and brother-in-law of Mrs. N. F. Mossell, found it necessary to refute Taney's assumption of Negro inferiority and lack of qualifications for citizenship with a statement of the effect of the amendments: "The Negro by the force of them became an adopted citizen, a member of that body politic termed the people of the United States, and as such is entitled to all the privileges and immunities that are other citizens[']" (73). Mossell's use of the word "adopted" suggests that the rhetoric of citizenship contained more than ample room for intimations of degrees of citizenship. That Mossell must argue *ab novo* the case for black citizenship even after the events of the previous three decades may also be taken as evidence of the difficulty African Americans had even then establishing as a *premise* their "American-ness."

2. For an argument on whiteness as property interest growing out of the Enlightenment, see Radin 957.

3. This observation about Emerson is Jeffrey A. Steele's, from an email posting on T-AMLIT of July 11, 1995.

4. See Morrison, *Playing* 34–37, as well.

5. I am grateful for John Nickel's unpublished paper, "Race, Class, Gender, and Eugenics in the Fiction of Pauline Hopkins" for introducing me to the term "Adamic multigeneity."

6. Michele Gates Moresi of George Washington University notes in an email

communication of April 9, 1996, that "the right to free one's slaves in Georgia was restricted and from the 1830's through 1850's, it became increasingly difficult. The free black population in Georgia was small due to laws restricting employment, residency and manumission." A Louisiana case (*Mary, F.W.C. v. Morris et al.*, vol. 7 O.S., 135) notes that Georgia's law against manumission was dated 1810 and was "enacted for the security of the public peace, and good order of the community" (135). Mary had filed for freedom on the grounds that her previous owner had freed her in his 1809 will. The will existed, but the proviso was void in Georgia because of the law, which did, however, allow an owner to petition the legislature for special permission. It appears that, having been brought to Louisiana, Mary argued that Louisiana law's permission for manumission altered the condition of the original will and that, in any case, it was only the failure of her owner's heirs to file the necessary request before the Georgia legislature that prevented her emancipation in 1814 under the terms of the will. She lost on appeal. See also Alexander.

7. Paul Finkelman, University of Florida, noted in email, April 8, 1996:

> From 1780 until 1847 Pennsylvania allowed visiting masters to keep slaves in the state for six months, after which they became free. . . . Until the 1830s most, but not all, southern states accepted the idea that slaves became free by being brought to free states. I do not recall the situation in Georgia, but I believe this was the case in the 1830s. . . . Thus, a slave taken to Pa. and kept there more than six months and returned to Ga. would be free under Pa. law and Ga. would probably have accepted that; I believe in the 1830s it was still possible to emancipate a slave in Ga., but by the 1850s it certainly was not; you had to remove the slave from the state.

And see Finkelman, *Imperfect.*

Two important North Carolina cases from the same era suggest that the law on these matters was a discretionary tool at best. In *Newlin v. Freeman* (1841), Newlin, a Quaker, sued for a slave owned by Sarah Freeman, deceased, who willed him to Newlin because, barred from emancipating the slave herself, she felt Newlin would treat him as though he were free. Sarah Freeman's widower had refused to hand over the slave. "[U]nder Chief Justice William Gaston, the state supreme court ruled that Freeman had a right to bequeath her slaves to whomever she chose because a deed of separate estate filed at the time of her first marriage gave her the right to acquire and dispose of personal property without the consent of her husband. Justice Gaston represented a dying generation of southern leaders who tolerated criticism of slavery" (Bynum 53 n. 55).

In 1844, in *Thompson v. Newlin*, Sarah's widower sued Newlin for repossession of the slave. This time the husband won, because Gaston had died and Chief Justice Thomas Ruffin presided. Ruffin defended the court's decision on grounds that it was the state's duty to protect its most fundamental institution. "Slaves can only be held as property," he wrote, "and deeds and wills having for their object their emancipation, or a qualified state of slavery, are against public policy, and a trust results to the next of kin" (Bynum 54 n. 56).

8. Wills were often contested by heirs. In Kentucky, for example, such appeals were heard in review by a circuit court that could review all manumis-

sion decrees. Sometimes slaves could petition a circuit court for freedom under an instrument or will. In *Hill v. Squire*, 12 B. Monroe 557 (1851), in Madison County, Kentucky, slaves successfully sued the executor of their master's will to free them under a provision of that will.

More to the point of Webb's novel, however, in Louisiana, in *Poulard, C. P. et al. v. Delamere et al.* (12 La. 267 [542 vol. 6] Feb. 1838), the former slaves of the deceased Julien Poydras lost their appeal to be emancipated by the terms of his will. Several Poydras cases reached the courts over the better part of a decade. Poydras had wanted his slaves maintained with his lands and not sold away; he wanted them emancipated at age sixty or after twenty-five years of service, and he wanted an annual stipend given each. The slaves lost the manumission and money issues and could be sent to work on another plantation, but in a partial but significant victory, could not be sold away from the plantation by either the heirs or by the first vendee of any property of the estate.

9. All data in this discussion of black Philadelphia between 1830 and 1860 is from Salvatore 15–25. See also his extensive notes 16–34, pp. 331–33. See also Du Bois, *Philadelphia* 25–45, which gives details of income and property holdings. His discussion also provides names of persons who may have contributed to the composite portrait of the black philanthropist Walton; foremost of these would be Stephen Smith, a lumber merchant who endowed a home for aged and infirm Negroes (35–36). Du Bois also notes that blacks were prohibited from riding the streetcars in Philadelphia until 1867 (38).

10. Or as Roediger phrases a similar observation, "Blackness . . . almost perfectly predicted lack of the attributes of a freeman. In 1820, 86.8 percent of African Americans were slaves—in 1860, 89 percent" (56).

11. The conceptual barriers created by these cultural ideograms of privacy, difference, and liberty have not only prevented African Americans from enjoying full citizenship, they have made it easy to overlook the constrictive power of the ideology they undergird. It is easy to misconstrue the implications of American legal and social history where these terms are employed. Cornel West observes the situation of black Americans defined as "other" and describes that condition as having been "somehow" left out of the weave of what he calls America's "one garment of destiny." But his "somehow" misjudges how deeply ingrained in American self-definition has been the historical rejection of blacks by Eurocentric romanticism's obsession with the "other" as an agent in the white male quest for self. This "Eu-romantic" privileging of self-creation in American cultural narratives deliberately places all African Americans at the margins of the imagined community, never at the center as subject-citizen. The "weave of the garment" that West believes need only be adjusted to create destiny's true pattern, was not, we should argue, designed to show any black thread.

12. It is commonly believed that the last six chapters of this work are missing. The impact of the Fugitive Slave Act can be noted in William Wells Brown's *Clotel,* as remarked earlier, and on the composition of Frederick Douglass's "The Heroic Slave" (1853). See Takaki; Andrews, "Novelization."

13. In Webb, discussed previously, the white lawyer-villain Stevens's son is

portrayed as a dull, loutish child who catches and tortures insects. He also reflects the attitude of whites toward blacks that Baker alludes to:

> "Ah!" said he, in a tone of exultation, "father took me with him to the jail to-day, and I saw all the people locked up. I mean to be a jailer some of these days. Wouldn't you like to keep a jail, Liz?" continued he, his leaden eyes receiving a slight accession of brightness at the idea. (127)

14. Arnold Rampersad ("W. H. Thomas") has suggested that literacy was not the single key to personal liberation; rather, he sees some Faustian desire for power in the narratives of black hero/intellectuals of the nineteenth and early twentieth centuries. Rampersad would then "rate" these figures on the success of their abilities to negotiate such deals without giving away too much in the bargain.

15. The case here is *County of Santa Clara v. Southern Pacific R.R.*, 118 U.S. 394 (1886). The matter of citizenship and corporations had been settled in *Paul v. Virginia*, 8 Wall. 168 (1869) in which it was held that a corporation is not a citizen within the meaning of the comity clause. Nevertheless, the issue of personhood contra citizenship was part of the subtext of the *Santa Clara* controversy. For a brief discussion of *Santa Clara* and related cases, see Fairman 726–29. The major studies of the origins and implications of *Santa Clara* et al. are Graham; Horwitz 65–107.

16. *Dartmouth College v. Woodward*, 17 U.S. 518 (1819).

17. *Dartmouth College v. Woodward* at 636, cited in Mark 1441.

18. *Girod v. Lewis*, 6 Mart. (O.S.) 559 [3 Mart. (N.S.) 291], Louisiana, May 1819.

19. Consider here the probability that impulses toward escape were as gendered as any other complex relationship, especially one involving the removal of oneself from the site of children and parents. What, for example, is a useful reading of the multiplicity of male voices that extol literacy as a part of the impulse to freedom and the absence of any similar number of women's voices expressing or even suggesting the same supposed relationship?

20. See Kaplan. A previous version of this article suggested to me Douglass's attitude toward the right to marriage.

Bynum discusses the ambivalence toward marriage of some free women of color in the South:

> [Black and white women] lived in a patriarchal society that merged the legal identities of wife and husband into one: the husband's. In North Carolina, as in virtually the entire United States in this period, English common law provided the basis for the system of law. Where women were concerned, common law provided a simple directive. In the words of Sir William Blackstone: "By marriage, the husband and wife are one person in law: that is, the very being or legal existence of the woman is suspended during the marriage, or at least is incorporated and consolidated into that of the husband; under whose wing, protection, and *cover,* she performs everything." (60n. 6)

Suzanne Lebsock's observation that some free black women were reluctant to marry because "women so recently emancipated . . . did not give up their legal autonomy lightly" (109) is probably true also of some married free black women. Although [Sally] Fane had chosen to marry, she was unwilling to trade the legal bondage of slavery for that of marriage (Bynum 62 n. 16)

21. For a brief discussion of this approach and a comparison of it to other historiographic approaches, see Schiller, particularly the opening section, "Historiography," 1209–16. Schiller also makes a useful comparison of the development of slave law in North Carolina and Georgia on the basis of the differences of local conditions of economy and demographics (1247). A full-length study of the conflict between intellectual and moral understanding of the law in the rulings of various nineteenth-century jurists is Karsten's *Heart versus Head*.

22. An ironic reading of these dynamics suggests that for enslaved people slavery was just as much a local, municipal experience. No slave residing on the site of his or her birth would have any more of an active universal paradigm of "slavery" than would his or her owner admit a larger, national design of slavery. Thus the fear of being sold might not be wholly driven by a fear of the known, as to a worse system, but of the unknown and the fear of how more heartless it might be.

23. Some of my thinking about romanticism most recently, specifically my discussion of belonging and individualism, was stimulated by two lectures by Charles E. Larmore given at Columbia University on October 17 and 24, 1994, and subsequently published. See also Karst, especially chapters 1–6.

24. For a discussion of Herder and American, particularly southern antebellum, romanticism, see O'Brien, "Lineaments." O'Brien's discussion of the implications of Euromanticism generally coincides with my own, but his discussion of the interweaving of themes from the Scottish Enlightenment is useful as well. His brief discussion of the "Romantic dialectic of passion and reason" and of "psychological individualism" and the desire for community (45) is sketchier but parallels my own discussion in subsequent pages of this chapter.

25. But it may be noted that a moral vision that is more universal in its genesis can contradict the local values a jurist might share with his colleagues. Schiller cites the "humanizing decision" in *State v. Caesar*, 31 N.C. (9 Ired.) 391 (1849) as an example in which the highest court allowed a slave the limited right to resist excessive authority from whites. Such decisions, he observes, "protect neither masters' property interests nor society's security," by "allowing a slave, who was not himself attacked, to kill a white and escape with a lesser penalty" (1227). He cites Justice Ruffin's dissent in the appeal:

> It seems to me to be dangerous to the last degree to hold the doctrine, that negro slaves may assume to themselves the judgment as to the right or propriety of resistance. . . . First denying their general subordination to the whites, it may be apprehended that they will end in denouncing the injustice of slavery itself, and, upon that pretext, band together to throw off their common bondage entirely. (427–28)

Justice Pearson, in finding that a slave could resist aggression from a man who was not his owner nor an official of the law, even if he killed the white man (Caesar had killed a man who was beating a fellow slave), portrayed the slaves involved as "friends quietly talking," "comrades," capable of "generous indignation" at the gratuitous violence. "[A]re we not forced, in spite of stern policy, to admire, even in a slave, the generosity, which incurs danger to save a friend?" (400, 404, 405).

26. The inability to make these connections stunts the lives of those so marginalized. As Tocqueville wrote in 1831:

> The emancipated negroes, and those born after the abolition of slavery [in the northern states] remain half-civilized, and deprived of their rights, in the midst of a population which is far superior to them in wealth and in knowledge; where they are exposed to the tyranny of the laws and the intolerance of the people. . . . [T]hey are haunted by the reminiscence of slavery, and they cannot claim possession of a single portion of the soil: many of them perish miserably, and the rest congregate in the great towns, where they perform the meanest offices and lead a wretched and precarious existence. (Cited in J. S. Wright 304 n. 113)

27. While I am writing generally here about whites north and south imagining their community, it is important to note that some white Americans, abolitionists, imagined themselves as part of a moral community that paralleled their national community. And in that community, romantic notions of identity formation allowed them to accept blacks as fellow beings, although not all abolitionists would offer American citizenship as well. Membership in the moral community was based at least in part on one's capacity for participating in "the Romantic agon, the life and death contest of the spirit of revision against all that represses it" (Andrews, "Representation" 64). Abolitionists' appetite for the slave narrative that exhibited evidence of the agon and revision suggests that they granted to the African in America capacities for self-realization that the majority of their fellow citizens would not. An interesting discussion of *intra-national* racial dynamics and romanticism goes on in Doyle (35–53).

28. This argument is not about the creative or imaginative capacities of African Americans as a race or as individuals; it is about how social and legal constraints can exclude a people from a specific exercise of those faculties within specified parameters.

29. The role of black reading societies in the North (and in the South prior to 1830 in some urban areas) in nurturing just such imaginative practices are being studied now by Elizabeth McHenry in a series of unpublished papers. McHenry's research suggests that previous definitions of literacy are inadequate and must include the practice of unlettered members of such societies as the listening audience for oral presentations of texts and active participants in subsequent discussion sessions. In this way, people who could not read or write could be a part of the "reading" community. She suggests that such participation explains the apparently contradictory facts that Anna Douglass was a member of a Baltimore reading society when Frederick Douglass met her, yet she never learned to read or write. Such societies, then, were sites of imaginative re-creation of the act of literacy through performance, reception, reenactment, and revision, through discussion, of the performed text.

30. This is true, for instance, in "slave correspondence," as collected by

Starobin. In his preface, Starobin notes that letters from enslaved people must be read carefully, since the relationships of the messages to the potential as well as the intended readers (whites who might intercept letters to black addressees, for example) were complex: "[T]hey are loaded with subtleties of meaning, irony, double entendres, and outright put-ons" (xx). Even the fact that some letters were transcribed by amanuenses affects our reading of the voice of the enslaved person.

31. Two twentieth-century novels, Sherley Anne Williams's *Dessa Rose* and Toni Morrison's *Beloved,* deal specifically with narrativity of the enslaved experience as property, specifically in each case as a woman's property, echoing perhaps issues raised by the Linda Brent narrative a century and a half earlier. See Salvino for the limitations of literacy in the escape from economic bondage.

32. A possible source for some of Delany's plot here might be found in the newly "rediscovered" German-American novel *The Mysteries of New Orleans* by Ludwig von Reizenstein, serialized first in the *Louisiana Staats-Zeitung* in 1854. I have not seen the novel, which is forthcoming from Johns Hopkins University Press but it is described as having as part of its plot a conspiracy to create a worldwide slave rebellion under the leadership of a mysterious figure named Hiram. Since Delany traveled as a free black in the South in the 1850s, he may have seen the story as he was collecting and shaping the material that was to become *Blake* (Zalewski).

33. By 1860, this meant 233,073 black people in the "free" states of the North, the federal territories and the District of Columbia; it meant 247,971 free people of color in the "slave" states of the South ("Census of Colored Americans" n.p.).

34. Delany's advice is somewhat different from his position two decades and more earlier. In an important passage in *Blake* (1859–61) in which religion stands synecdochically for all organized systems of oppression, Henry Blake explains to his Cuban cousin, Placido, that a revolutionary moment is approaching, a moment Henry can recognize because of his role as romantic hero, a self-created, ironic personality:

> "The difference will be just this, Placido—that we shall not be disciplined in our worship, obedience [sic] as slaves to our master, the slaveholders, by associating our mind with that religion, submission to the oppressor's will."
>
> "I see, Henry, it is plain; and every day convinces me that we have much yet to learn to fit us for freedom."
>
> "I differ with you, Placido; we know enough now, and all that remains to be done, is to make ourselves free, and then put what we know into practice. We know much more than we dare attempt to do. *We want space for action— elbow room; and in order to obtain it, we must shove our oppressors out of the way.*" (197; emphasis added)

35. The idea of the Supreme Court as the "grave of liberty" is echoed in a letter from Albion Tourgee to Louis Martinet on October 31, 1891, in which Tourgee notes that the Court had "always been the foe of liberty until forced to move on by public opinion" (Olsen, *Carpetbagger's* 326).

36. Freeman assumes that John Henry Keene, "one of Baltimore's leading white lawyers," (55) wrote the bulk (some 530 pages) of the book, citing only an unpublished manuscript, "The Brotherhood of Liberty" by Warner T. McGuinn, undated. J. Clay Smith argues for several black authors, most of whom were lawyers (1104 n. 41).

37. We know, however, that the book had no observable effect on its times. Published by Lippincott in Philadelphia, its sole major review was in the weekly *Science*, after which, despite reviewer T. B. Wakeman's positive response to its argument, it sank from sight in print.

38. See also Sanda (Walter H. Stowers and W[illiam] H. Anderson), *Appointed: An American Novel*. Stowers and Anderson were staunch supporters of Martinet, Tourgee, and the plan to test the Louisiana Jim Crow car law.

39. Here is the relevant passage from *Plessy:*

[P]etitioner was a citizen of the United States and a resident of the state of Louisiana of mixed descent, in the proportion of seven eighths Caucasian and one eighth African blood; that the mixture of colored blood was not discernible in him, and that he was entitled to every recognition, right, privilege and immunity secured to the citizens of the United States of the white race by its Constitution and its laws. (163 U.S. 537, 538 [1896])

Chapter 3

1. The racialization of puritanical intolerance of, and ire against, sexuality is a recurring aspect of black-white relationships in American society, although intolerance and ire are not always clearly racially embossed. American women's sexuality in general has been circumscribed by structures of social control putatively directed at the good of society. See, for example, Omolade; Jordan, "New Politics."

2. Somerville's larger argument, that *Contending Forces* encodes homosexual desire as well (141–43), is convincing, but that narrative line falls outside the scope of my study.

3. How ought this reading of the marriage practices of slaves to affect a historical analysis of "the black family" as a pathologically stricken unit? See R. T. Smith 274ff.; Hudson. For a fascinating African American text of antebellum white marriage, see Thomas Detter's *Nellie Brown or The Jealous Wife* (1871). Detter's discussions of law, lawyers, and divorce are unusual for their period.

4. In his original study of black family life and from the survey of scholarship which informed it, Herbert Gutman noted that there was a paucity of knowledge of eighteenth-century African marriage and family patterns to allow us to resolve the question of "borrowing" of white marriage practices by blacks. He does note that in the communities he studied, black exogamy contradicted white endogamy. However, his assertion that black families were not, in practice, "matriarchal," begs the question that should be addressed: whether

enslaved people from different sections of West Africa brought with them matrilineal or patrilineal descent systems in the eighteenth century. Patterns of descent as well as endo- and exogamous marriage rules and matri/patrilocal residence rules all influence marriage practices, even under duress. Whatever the specifics of the answers to such questions, it is clearly a mistake to assume that all narrative of black life represents wholesale adoption of white domestic patterns by enslaved people (45–143, 185–229).

5. Wilfred M. McClay notes the confluence of a sacral and secular identity in the American nation-self: "This amalgamation of holiness and freedom, . . . of the sacred order and the secular nation, suggests the distinctive contours of the American (or at any rate northern) political religion" (19). For McClay, this sacralization seems to begin with the victory of the Union over the Confederacy, but I believe the mimetic seed was sown in early American romantic thought.

6. For example, the *New York Age* for March 2, 1911, reported an ironic recapitulation of the problem of miscegenation under slavery. Many prominent Virginians were forbidding their children to attend history classes at Roanoke College, then one of the largest Lutheran colleges in the South, and the Confederate Veterans of America were "expressing the highest indignation" over the use of a text that stated,

> The most revolting feature of slavery in America, one that the historian blushes to record (but history must deal with facts), is that too often the attractive slave woman was a prostitute to her master, that their children bore the stamp of her countenance, and yet, according to the inflexible rule of the slave States they shared the condition of the mother and were sold by their own father; this evil was widespread at the South, as the mixed condition of the black race to-day will testify.

> A sister of President Madison declared that though the Southern ladies were complimented with the name of wife, they were only the mistresses of the seraglio. A leading Southern lady declared to Harriet Martineau that the wife of many a planter was but the chief slave of the harem.

Complaints were referred to the professor who had assigned the text.

7. But also see Aaron A. Mossell's argument that the law prohibiting mixed marriages is discriminatory. He does not argue the efficacy of miscegenation, only its permissibility under the Constitution because of the citizenship of Negroes. Mossell's description of the constitutional bases of black citizenship is among the more effective I have seen from the period.

8. The book to which Viola responded was John H. Van Evrie's polemic, published first in 1861 as *Negroes and Negro "Slavery": The First an Inferior Race: The Latter its Normal Condition.* The second edition, which Viola would have owned, was published in New York by Van Evrie, Horton and Company in 1868 with the title *White Supremacy and Negro Subordination; or, Negroes a Subordinate Race, and (So-called) Slavery its Normal Condition, with an Appendix, Showing the Past and Present Condition of the Countries South of Us.*

9. I would omit Delany's *Blake* from this discussion, as he creates from experiences of a personal trip through Louisiana in the late 1850s several mulatto characters whose status in white society has corrupted their sense of fellow-feeling for both free and enslaved blacks.

10. Forty-five years later, Chester Himes, a writer as unlike Ms. Hopkins as one can imagine, allowed the same sentiments to move his protagonist in the bitter, despairing novel *If He Hollers Let Him Go:*

> I'd learned the same jive that the white folks had learned. All that stuff about liberty and justice and equality. . . . All men are created equal. . . . Any person born in the United States is a citizen. . . . Learned it out of the same books, in the same schools. Learned the song too: ". . . o'er the land of the free and the home of the brave . . ." I thought Patrick Henry was a hero when he jumped up and said, 'Give me liberty or give me death,' just like the white kids who read about it. I was a Charles Lindbergh fan when I was a little boy, and thought George Washington was the father of my country—as long as I thought I had a country. (151)

11. For a sense of Hopkins's general appreciation of the fate of Negroes under white law, this passage from a 1901 short story, "Bro'r Abr'm Jimson's Wedding," might do: "A nigger can't holp himself. White folks can run agin the law all the time an' they never gits caught, but a nigger! Every time he opens his mouth he puts his foot in it" (142).

12. For example, Louisiana cases: *Adelle v. Beauregard* (1810), *Metoyer v. Metoyer* (1819), *Catin v. Orgenoy's Heirs* (1820), *Marie Louise, F.W.C. v. Marot et al.* (1835); Virginia cases: *Maria v. Surbaugh* (1824), *Crawford v. Moses* (1839), *Henry v. Bradford* (1842), *Ellis v. Jenny* (1844); Kentucky cases: *Esther v. Aikens' Heirs* (1842), *Johnson v. Johnson* and *Stewart v. Wyatt* (1848), *Spurrier v. Parker* (1855); U.S. cases: *Fanny v. Kell* (1823), *Samuel v. Childs* (1831), *Brooks v. Nutt* (1834). See also Spillers's discussion throughout her essay, "Mama's Baby, Papa's Maybe."

13. Maryland's 1661 anti-intermarriage law forbade marriage between white women and black men because the children of such a relationship would be free, the condition of the children following that of the mother.

14. An eyewitness account is Clawson. Clawson was city editor of the white newspaper, the *Wilmington Messenger,* at the time of the riot, and his account is clearly partisan, on the side of the Democratic Party plotters who had engineered the coup. Clawson writes:

> A defamatory and disgusting editorial in a newspaper published by negroes in Wilmington brought the situation to a climax. This editorial was properly construed as a base slander of the white womanhood of the South. Following it's [*sic*] publication, the white men of Wilmington considered that the time for action had arrived. And act, they did. (N.p.)

The "situation" that came to a climax was life for whites in a city run by an integrated fusion administration. Clawson writes: "The course determined upon was to take charge of the municipal government, and to make same an agency to be guided and conducted by the white race" (n.p.). A look at the contexts out of which these events grew can be found in Evans, a reprint of the 1965 edition resetting that study in the light of current historical emphases via a foreword by Charles Joyner.

15. No citation from Prather; this may be from Wilbur J. Cash, *The Mind of the South* (New York, 1941). See Clawson's account of the Alexander Manly editorial in the *Wilmington Record*, August 18, 1898. Manly's editorial was part of his ongoing defense of black men from defamation as part of a white propaganda campaign during the election year. In particular, whites (Democrats) raised the specter of black rapists violating white women.

16. County court dockets reveal that the mingling of poor whites, slaves, and free blacks included the trading of goods, liquor, and sexual favors. Blacks and whites fought and gambled together, and they sometimes cohabited. With varying degrees of success, county magistrates curbed the interracial exchange of goods and favors by indicting the most flagrant offenders of both races on charges of gambling, illicit trading, prostitution, and fornication (Bynum 47 n. 38).

17. Manly's response survives in Clawson as exhibit A. Clawson's exhibit is a notarized transcript of the editorial "defaming the white women of North Carolina and of the South." Whereas Prather reports the speaker as Mrs. Felton, Manly calls her Mrs. Fellows in his editorial.

18. Another contemporary fictional account by a black writer, a man from Wilmington who had moved to New York, is Thorne's (pseud. David Bryant Fulton) *Hanover*. Thorne's novel is less polished than Chesnutt's, but it is full of local lore and is closer to experimental reportage than to a traditional novel. A third fictional treatment is by a white writer, Gerard.

Chesnutt's three published novels written after the *Plessy* decision, *Marrow*, *The House Behind the Cedars*, and *The Colonel's Dream*, echo the Brotherhood's pre-*Plessy* fear of the abandonment of the protections of the Thirteenth, Fourteenth, and Fifteenth Amendments. In particular Chesnutt may be looking to the "badges and indices" clause of the Thirteenth Amendment; passages in *Marrow* and *House* replicate a white argument that slavery has been proof of the degraded nature of blacks. Thomas *(American)* probably puts more weight on these and similar passages than their presence in the texts will bear when he claims that Chesnutt is pressing for a specific Thirteenth Amendment response to *Plessy*, but locating Chesnutt in the stream of anxiety about the gutting of the postwar amendments is correct and important (156–90). Matthewson suggests that Chesnutt apparently seeks to give both sides of the *Plessy* argument in the "train trip" chapter of *Marrow*.

19. Dr. Miller's wife, Janet, is the issue of an act of miscegenation, and the emotional and property issues that undergird the Miller story arise in great part from the effect her presence in town has on her white half sister, Olivia. Consequently, reading the appeal to Dr. Miller through the text of his wife's story produces an equally normative text on the inherent moral superiority of black women. Janet Miller's ability to approach her husband with her half sister's request, after years of rejection by her sister, is a moral centerpiece of the episode.

20. In contrast, Thorne clearly and purposefully ties the event to race and class tensions heightened by white obsession with miscegenation.

21. Schiller notes, however, that in cases in which responsibility for injury to slaves was an issue, judges tended to admit that slaves had intelligence, reasonableness, capacity for observation, experience, knowledge, skill, and an instinct for self-preservation, and the presence of those capacities in slaves hired out to industry or commerce allowed judges to find in behalf of laissez-faire capitalism in the cases involving the fellow-servant rule and the concept of ordinary care (1239). In effect, he notes, the contractarian nature of court ideology threw responsibility back on the owner of the property (slave) that had a reasonable capacity to care for itself. The same qualities had no weight or even existence in a rights context.

22. Larmore suggests one look at Rousseau and Stendhal for the clearest expression of this. Another version of the implications of "authenticity" as applied to black experience can be found in hooks's "Postmodern Blackness" (11); she would posit romanticism as one of the "master narratives" that are the objects of postmodernism's interrogation (9ff.).

23. In her novel *Jazz*, Morrison writes of her antebellum mulatto character Golden Gray:

> How could I have imagined him so poorly? Not noticed the hurt that was not linked to the color of his skin, or the blood that beat beneath it. But to some other thing that longed for authenticity, for a right to be in this place, effortlessly without needing to acquire a false face, a laughless grin, a talking posture. (160)

Morrison is a consistent practitioner of the romance and of the romantic in her tales.

Patricia Williams observes that so-called universal truths are given voice in our culture by supposedly "unmediated" and objective voices and that such voices

> [are] also given power in romanticized notions of "real people" having "real" experiences—not because real people have experienced what they really experienced, but because their experiences are somehow *made* legitimate. . . . The Noble Savage as well as the Great White Father, the Good-Hearted Masses, the Real American, the Rational Consumer, and the Arm's-Length Transactor are all versions of this Idealized Other whose gaze provides us with either internalized censure or externalized approval; internalized paralysis or externalized legitimacy; internalized false consciousness or externalized claims of exaggerated authenticity. (*Alchemy* 9)

24. Gillman makes a somewhat different argument, focusing her attention on the conscious use by black women writers of the period to appropriate literary conventions and adapt them to a political argument. I would hold that, conscious or not, the use of the unadapted conventions of melodrama was enough to subvert the hypergentility of the novels.

25. Quoting Jameson 171. His chapters "Magical Narratives" and "Realism and Desire" are important to Gillman's reading of melodrama.

26. Missing from both antebellum and postwar fiction, narrative, and legal records are any extensive portrayals of domestic violence among free or enslaved black Americans. Rapport notes that the bureau did record some "cases stemming from gender conflict between black women and men" but that such cases appeared infrequently. She attributes this to either the likelihood that "freedpeople simply did not experience a great deal of sex antagonism" or that blacks saw no reason to parade their personal problems before whites (39).

27. Louisiana Civil Code ca. 1820: 40, art. 17—a slave can contract no engagement, cannot bind herself in any respect "because she [is] without will" (8 Mart. [O.S.] 161 [82 vol. 4], *Livandac's Heirs v. Fon & al.* [May 1820]: 83 in vol. 4).

28. *Poulard, C. P. et al. v. Delamere et al.,* 12 La. 267 at 270 (542 vol. 6) Feb. 1838; similarly *State v. Mann* (13 N.C. [2 Dev.] at 266) (1829), in which the court found that the slave does not labor for his own happiness.

29. *State v. Caesar,* 31 N.C. 391, 400, 402 (9 Ired.) 49, 50 (1849), cited in Fisher 1078.

30. Stephenson cites the case, as he found it reported in the *Boston Post,* May 22, 1909, as *Griffin v. Brady,* a 1909 New York case referred to in 117 N.Y. Supp., 116.

31. Darwin T. Turner notes in unpaginated comments at the front of the 1969 reprint: "All Dunbar's novels are marred by stereotypes, sentimentality, and melodrama. . . . In this work he was the first significant Negro novelist to attempt a realistic representation of the Negro in northern cities. . . . Dunbar viewed cities as traps for the souls of the innocent. . . . If this book had been published anonymously, it would have been considered a bitter protest and the author might be heralded as the first major Negro ironist."

32. In Webb's *The Garies and Their Friends* (1857), underground railroad operatives working as porters in a hotel con white southerners who are slavery sympathizers out of money to support the escape route by pretending to be freemen or escaped slaves who long to go back South and remand themselves into slavery because life in the heartless North is so terrible (41).

33. As, perhaps, in *State v. Gilbert* (2 La. Ann. 244) of March 1847, in which the Louisiana Supreme Court found that a slave acquitted of a capital crime may be punished by the same sitting court (by the act of 1846 a capital court consisted of two justices of the peace and ten slaveholders) for any lesser offense established by the evidence without being remanded to a lesser court. Since this seems not to require the second charge be part of the first indictment nor require a second indictment, and since it places the slave in the grip of the company of men who hold dominion over him daily, it is no real surprise that Gilbert, acquitted (because of lack of unanimity on the court) of attempted rape of a white woman, was sentenced by the same court to life in prison for assault.

Chapter 4

1. The romantic genesis of such a figure is suggested in lines from Byron's *Childe Harold's Pilgrimage,* canto 3, stanza 97 (1817), in which Byron, like Douglass, connects the moral and physical superiority of his hero with the forces of

nature. This stanza follows five that do for Byron's hero what the first paragraph quoted above does for Douglass's:

> Could I embody and unbosom now
> That which is most within me, could I wreak
> My thoughts upon expression, and thus throw
> Soul, heart, mind, passions, feelings, strong or weak,
> All that I would have sought, and all I seek,
> Bear, know, feel, and yet breathe—into *one* word,
> And that one word were Lightning, I would speak;
> But as it is I live and die unheard,
> With a most voiceless thought, sheathing it as a sword.

2. In a March 22, 1899, letter to Frederick Goff, Charles Chesnutt expresses similar views of the Supreme Court:

> "I will say . . . that the Supreme Court of the United States is in my opinion a dangerous place for a colored man to seek justice. He may go in with maimed rights; he is apt to come away with none at all" (Cited in Andrews *Literary* 214).

3. *Blake* must be read as though the missing six chapters do not exist. Delany's text ends on the eve of a slave and free-black revolt in Cuba and an anticipated exportation of the revolutionary moment to the slave states of the South.

4. Chief Justice Waite said, before oral argument, that he would accept a reading that extended Fourteenth Amendment protection to corporations, based on testimony from Congressman Roscoe Conkling that the Joint Congressional Committee, in drafting the amendment, used "persons" consciously to cover corporations. The manuscript journal of the committee's deliberations does not support Conkling's assertion, and his distortion of the point is well known to legal historians.

5. This latter condition, in which the apparently human is actually not so, became the premise of another great romantic monster's story, Bram Stoker's *Dracula*. See Alan Hyde's chapters "The Body as Property" and "The Racial Body."

6. *Adelle v. Beauregard*, 1 Mart. (O.S.) 183 (fall 1810). The irony of Adelle's suit was that she had been brought to New York from the Caribbean as a young girl and raised in a private school, paid for by Beauregard. When she reached adulthood, he brought her to New Orleans and placed her in his household as his mistress. Adelle sued for her freedom on the basis there was no proof she had ever been enslaved, and she asked not only for her freedom but back wages for services to Beauregard. She won her freedom when Beauregard could show no papers of sale for her, but she was denied wages in arrears because the court felt she should consider the cost of the education Beauregard had provided for her as compensation for the three months she had spent with him. See also Morris 22–29.

7. *Forsyth et al. v. Nash*, 4 Mart. (O.S.) 385 (180 vol. 2) (La., June 1816).

8. *State v. Treadaway, et al.*, 126 La. 300, 52 So. 500 (April 25, 1910).

9. See *Pierce v. School Trustees,* 46 N.J. Law, 79, for example, on forbidding the exclusion of a mulatto child from school, in which the court said, "Counsel further urges that since, under the rule of the trustees, an Italian (for example) as dark as the realtor's children would have been admitted, the exclusion was therefore owing, not to 'color,' but to race, which the statute does not prohibit. But I think the term 'color,' as applied to persons in this country, has had too distinct a history to leave possible such an interpretation of the law. Both in the statute and in the regulations of the respondents persons of color are persons of the negro race" (cited in *Treadaway* 507; see 500–507 for literally hundreds of definitions, statutes, and cases to this matter).

10. In February 1911, Luella Lettridge was returned to a "home for colored children" despite a petition by her sister to have her released on the grounds that she had white parents. A birth certificate was produced by the state of Maryland indicating that her father was a Negro. Included in the testimony for her "whiteness" had been that of a "prominent medical expert" who held that "with the exception of a bluish tint in the 'half moon' of one of her finger nails" there was no indication that "she was of negro parentage" (*Baltimore Independent,* March 2, 1911).

11. See Graham throughout. The case was *County of San Mateo v. Southern Pacific R.R.,* 116 U.S. 589 (1882). No decision was handed down, and in 1885 the case was dismissed and its issues folded into *Santa Clara.* Essentially, Conkling was guilty of some creative "back-formation" of the 1866 deliberations of the joint committee. The entire episode, as Graham reconstructs it, is more than a little evanescent, from Conkling's argument to Waite's notes to the recorder about how to report his comments prior to argument. See as well Thomas's argument to the contrary of my own (*Literary* 235, 339 n. 9).

12. But see *Paul v. Virginia,* 8 Wall. 168 (1869), which established that a corporation is not a citizen within meanings of the comity clause. Soifer's general argument—that the failure of Reconstruction to provide "progress" in Maine's use of the term, for African Americans from status (enslaved) to functional contract capacity under the law, threw blacks *back* into servitude, one perhaps more virulent than before—is relevant to the general discussion of this chapter.

13. See Ascher 146–47; no citation in Ascher for Powell.

14. Stephenson had written to over three hundred counties of the Old South in which blacks constituted more than 50 percent of the population in 1900. Of 106 responses, only 16 reported any African Americans in the jury pool in the memory or records of the county clerks.

A Virginia clerk reported: "Negroes under our Constitution are not debarred from serving as jurors in Virginia, but owing to the nature and disposition of the Negro to follow and not to lead, we seldom place them on trial juries. The number of colored jurors has decreased in the last ten years" (270).

North Carolina: "I will say that Negroes do not serve on the jury in this county and have not since we, the white people, got the government in our hands" (265).

South Carolina: "In my experience covering ten years or more, I find it difficult to get a large array of competent jurors. We are careful and painstaking in making our lists; therefore, we never allow a Negro to serve for the reason of the general moral unfitness, and general depravity" (268).

15. Waldrep notes a case in which an all-white jury deliberated thirteen minutes before convicting a black defendant of rape. They complained that they had been delayed by a lack of ink and light. Waldrep also notes a report by McMillan of a case in 1911 in which a court took seven minutes to impanel a white jury, present evidence, and impose a ninety-nine-year sentence on a black man charged with attempting to enter the bedroom of a white woman.

16. There was some question in Pugh's mind as to the jurisdiction of this court to hear the case. Nor was she satisfied that the remanding of the case there was properly documented. She claims in her pretrial motions to have had "this case removed to the Federal courts by virtue of a petition filed April 20th in the Clerk's office. This petition is based on the fact that there was an unjust discrimination against the colored people in the selection of the jury" (*State v. Baby Poindexter* 2). Later, "Your Honor, I challenge the panel of the jury, the array of the jury, pursuant to Section 363 of the Code" (3). The challenge was disallowed.

17. See Schafer. Schafer has made use of court records found in a repository at the University of New Orleans.

18. For a brief but interesting discussion of the intersection of religious and legal experience in the eighteenth and nineteenth centuries, see T. H. Smith 81–109.

19. In the same year, Grosset and Dunlap in New York published a potboiler of a love story, *The Northerner*, by Norah Davis, that had the same basic theme as did Chesnutt's novel. In *The Northerner*, a wealthy northern businessman comes to a small southern town to transform it by his enlightened industrial capitalism. He is defeated by the backwardness, prejudice, and provincialism of the South.

Chapter 5

1. Race was implicated in all property assumptions in the new worlds of European colonialism, both in North America and Australia, where land inhabited by racially "inferior" people was deemed to be vacant.

2. That migration was predominantly into larger cities. In antebellum America, black residential patterns in the North had been inscribed in quite dissimilar places. Philadelphia with a black population of over twenty thousand was the largest black urban center because of its proximity to the slaveholding states. But Chicago in 1860 had only 955 Negroes in its population, and Boston only 2,261. New Bedford, because of its port status, was home to 1,515, while Cleveland had only 800 Negroes among its citizens (Salvatore 100).

3. W. E. B. Du Bois *(Souls)* notes that at the turn of the century the black "peasantry" (landowners) of southern Georgia constituted only 6 percent of the black population, while fully half of the remaining 94 percent "sit in hopeless serfdom." The only escape they could find, Du Bois notes, was migration to

urban areas, usually towns (121). Watkin-Owens notes that this migration was marked by its internal demographics: the numbers of black women in urban areas exceeded those of black men in every city but one. Watkin-Owens also suggests there was a higher rate of literacy among black women in cities than among black men there. If we can assume that the audience for African American narrative in the 1890s was literate blacks in urban areas, then we might expect that the majority of those readers were women of color. The causal relationships between audience demographics and literary production are not clear, but some influence on subject matter, genre, and style could be expected.

4. It is also clearly the case that the weight of illiteracy and unceasing labor in the rural South prevented the development of a regional romantic literature by African Americans. As Du Bois has noted, there was no black leisure class in the post-Reconstruction South, where fully 96 percent of the black population toiled with no chance of school, contemplation, or even of childhood (*Souls* 110).

5. Logan covered the following newspapers: *Boston Evening Transcript; New Haven Evening Register; New York Times; Philadelphia North American; Washington Star; Cincinnati Inquirer; Pittsburgh Dispatch; Indianapolis Journal; Detroit Tribune* (the *Post-Tribune* from October 1877 to July 1884); *Chicago Tribune; St. Louis Globe Dispatch; San Francisco Examiner.*

6. Butterfield argues that one of the legacies of the Scotch-Irish settlement of the South was an exaggerated sense of honor that produced incredible civil violence among whites in the late nineteenth century and that that paradigm of reputation wronged leading to violent retribution was absorbed as a lesson for living by black citizens who were, by practice and design, outside the law in any case.

7. Du Bois *(Philadelphia)* noted that the proportional responsibility for crime in general in the city that could be attributed to blacks was *less* in 1896 (4 percent of population, 9 percent of crimes) than it had been in 1850 (5 percent of population, 32 percent of crimes) (238–39).

8. Riis notes, "The [color] line may not be wholly effaced while the name of the negro, alone among the world's races, is spelled with a small n" (148).

9. In a paper presented at the American Literature Association conference in Baltimore, MD, on May 25, 1997, Virginia Whatley Smith noted that Horace Cayton's unpublished biography of Richard Wright indicates that Wright read both *The Philadelphia Negro* and *The Souls of Black Folk* sometime after 1927. There is a common tenor to Du Bois's story and Wright's short fiction of southern life in *Lawd Today!*

10. That Bowers had a black lawyer was a stroke of luck; in 1900, when the black population of the United States was approximately 7 million, there were 728 black lawyers. By 1940 there were 1,052 black lawyers to serve 12,865,518 African American citizens, or 1 to every 12,230. The ratio of white lawyers to white citizens was 1 to 670. The increase in black lawyers had occurred primarily in northern states, since the number of black lawyers in southern states declined overall between 1900 and 1940 (J. C. Smith, *Emancipation* 322–23, 625–35).

11. These periodicals are found on microfilm at the Schomburg Center for Research in Black Culture. These files are informative of matters of interest to the African American reading public. Issues of the *Colored American Magazine* for May through October 1900, for example, carry several articles on the legal status of black Americans, among them "The Separate Car Law in Virginia," "Shall the 15th Amendment be Repealed?" several pieces on lynching and lynch law, the denial of suffrage, penology and rehabilitation, and life under "an imperfect system of civil law."

12. Olsen notes that while there was not as much public outcry at the decision as there had been over the 1883 decisions in the Civil Rights Cases,

> The Negro press was unanimous in its denunciation [of the decision], and a random survey of the northern white press reveals that [it] almost invariably attracted some attention, that it aroused significant opposition, and that it seldom won strong support. Only three out of forty-three newspapers surveyed ignored the decision altogether, while twelve displayed some hostility . . . and four, two of which were south of the Mason-Dixon line[,] approved it. (*Thin Disguise* 25)

Only one of nine New York City newspapers endorsed the majority opinion, while four favored Harlan's dissent (25). Olsen notes that periodicals and journals of opinion seemed to have paid little attention to the decision, except where their readership had an interest in the outcome. Thus the Negro press and periodicals were vehemently on record in opposition to the decision, as were some Roman Catholic magazines interested in immigration and civil rights issues for foreign communicants. Methodists, it seems, were particularly strong against the decision and against segregation. Some examples:

> Equality of rights does not mean community of rights . . . if all rights were common as well as equal, there would be practically no such thing as private property, private life, or social distinctions, but all would belong to everybody who might choose to use it.
> This would be absolute socialism, in which the individual would be extinguished in the vast mass of human beings, a condition repugnant to every principle of enlightened democracy. (*New Orleans Daily Picayune*, May 19, 1896; Olsen, *Thin* 123)

> The announcement of this decision will be received by thoughtful and fair-minded people with disapproval and regret. It is not in harmony with the principles of this republic or with the spirit of our time. (*Rochester (N.Y.) Democrat and Chronicle*, May 20, 1896; Olsen, *Thin* 124)

13. In 1892 alone, over 255 black men, women, and children were lynched (Giddings 26); between 1882–1925 more than 3,513 African Americans were lynched, of whom 76 were women (Griffin 202 n. 21; *Women Lynched*).

14. *Wolfe v. Ry. Co.*, 1907 58 S.E. 899.

15. In Chesnutt's *Marrow of Tradition* (easily understood by most commentators as a novel written at least in part in reaction to *Plessy*), the passage in which Dr. Miller, the mulatto protagonist, travels south by rail with a white colleague

articulates the basic arguments on both sides of the *Plessy* case. A similar passage occurs in Frank J. Webb's *The Garies and Their Friends,* and has been discussed in chapter 2. The argument made in the hotelier episode here is actually in ironic counterposition to the argument derivable from Chesnutt's railroad chapter, that is, that Dr. Miller's rights to business and professional association are harmed by the separate-car law. The black hotelier is less concerned about protecting his rights than about retaining his customers. If there are going to be racial distinctions and an economic system based on those distinctions, then it is imperative that the authorities "get it right." Real life under Jim Crow was less amenable to idealized notions of "rights," but in this case it is almost more interesting than the problem that the noble Dr. Miller exemplified. The black press actively covered stories about Jim Crow disputes, preferring those in which black litigants won cases to have local ordinances and practices set aside, as in Baltimore in August 1912 (*Atlanta Freeman,* August 9, 1912) and those in which whites were taken for blacks and denied access to white facilities, as in the case of Miss Bella Kitchel, "a Jewess . . . unable to make the members of the train crew believe she was entitled to ride with white persons" (*New York Age,* October 17, 1912).

16. In an earlier story, "An Old-Time Christmas," Dunbar had evoked memories of holidays down South and the cruelty of New York City in comparison. Little Jimmy, a newsboy, is arrested on Christmas Eve for shooting dice for a few pennies after selling all his papers. His mother, who has saved all year to make "an old-time Christmas" for her son, puts up every cent she has saved to pay Jimmy's fine so he can come home for Christmas, albeit Christmas in a walk-up flat with no heat, no tree, no food, no presents. Dunbar clearly paints Jimmy as innocent and the law as mindless.

17. The reality of black underworld life in Hell's Kitchen and San Juan Hill may have been as desperate as this scene, but black criminals were also able to attain some celebrity status, at least among detectives and newspapermen. Alfred Woods, for example, born on Tenth Avenue, became known as the "Black Prince," "the subject of gossip in police circles all over the world." A pickpocket and "gentleman thief," Woods traveled the country and abroad, including, if his own account is to be believed, Australia, conning and "gunning" his way into and out of fortunes (*New York Telegraph* and *Montgomery Advertiser,* September 24, 1911).

18. In an email message dated November 23, 1996, Aukram Burton of the International Black Cinema Network (<www.coe.uncc.edu/~ibcnhp>) noted:

> Micheaux's work spans the period between 1918 to 1949. . . . The handful of companies producing "race movies" during this period were owned by whites. These productions were exclusively made for an AfricanAmerican population who attended approximately 400 Black movie theaters located predominately in the South. . . . It was very difficult for the few AfricanAmerican filmmakers that did exist to secure consistent financing. . . .
>
> Micheaux wrote his own scripts, directed all of his films, set up the lighting, edited the final production and handled his own distribution.

19. There were, however, black private detectives operating in New York as early as 1911. Shepard N. Edmonds had offices as "Edmonds National Detective Bureau" at 65 West 132d Street. Edmonds was called "the cleverest colored detective in existence" (*New York Age*, July 13, 1911).

20. Originally serialized in the *Pittsburgh Courier* between November 21, 1936, and July 3, 1937 (Schuyler, *Black Empire*, "Internationale") and October 2, 1937, and April 16, 1938 (Schuyler, *Black Empire*, "Empire").

21. Stowers and Anderson controlled the *Detroit Plaindealer*; W. H. Anderson was secretary of T. Thomas Fortune's Afro-American League (Penn 158–64).

22. This novel points to a telling gap in the "canon" of African American fiction of the Nadir/Gilded Age: there are no "Ragged Dick," Horatio Alger stories by, for, or about black Americans. One reason is clearly that the material reality of black life made such formulations of the consequences of hard work, temperance, and intelligence irrelevant. But another reason, one more directly reflective of how law operates to influence both literature and life, is the centrality in the Alger convention of the possibility for young men of no background to marry "up" out of their station, that is, to marry the boss's daughter. Of course, no such path existed for the young black worker. Antimiscegenation laws precluded any black man from such alliances with the daughters of his white employer. As for "indigenous" stories, color and caste discrimination within the black community controlled social advancement through marriage quite rigidly. Even if one could move into the "blueblood" circle (see Charles Chesnutt's short story "The Wife of His Youth"), African American wealth was limited and precariously situated by law and custom in trade rather than capital property. These conditions made marriage as an economic enterprise more likely to function as alliances between equals in the black community rather than as exercises in class mobility.

23. The North-South "dichotomy" as expressed in fiction of this period is significant. While *Appointed* argues for the North as a "utopia of place," Dunbar's "One Man's Fortunes" (*Gideon* 131–61) tells the story of Bertram Halliday, a young law student in the Midwest forced to move south to a teaching job as door after door closes in his face in his own hometown:

> I am still studying law in a half-hearted way for I don't know what I am going to do with it when I have been admitted. Diplomas don't draw clients. We have been taught [in the North] that merit wins. But I have learned that the adages, as well as the books and the formulas, were made by and for others than us of the Black race. (160)

And in Otis M. Shackelford's *Lillian Simmons, or The Conflict of Sections*, the northern Negro is portrayed as jealous of his privileges and antagonistic toward the southern immigrant who is more suspicious of northern white attitudes toward issues of race.

24. This faith in the white man's political machine was not shared by Paul Laurence Dunbar. In his short story "A Council of State," black lawyer Joseph Aldrich is betrayed by his light-skinned fiancée into suborning the upcoming "Afro-American Convention" for her boss, the white political power-broker of

the city. As a result of his actions and speech at the convention, an important resolution fails, courageous black men lose their jobs, and the "movement" dies aborning (*Gideon* 317–38).

25. In a better-known story, however, Rudolph Fisher's "City of Refuge" (1925), the South is once again the place you leave:

> Dey killed five o' Mose Joplin's hawses 'fo' he lef'. Put groun' glass in de feed-trough. Sam Cheevers come up on three of 'em one night pizenin' his well. Bleeson beat Crinshaw out o' sixty acres o' lan' an' a year's crops. Dass jess how 't is. Soon's a nigger make a li'l sump'n he better git to leavin'. And 'fo' long ev'ybody's goin' be lef'. (7)

26. There is no full-length study of Thorne (Andrews, "Jack Thorne [David Bryant Fulton]").

27. It is not known how widely known or read the novel was, but in 1917 Thorne presented a copy to black bibliophile Arthur Schomburg through the agency of an advocate of the book, Dr. R. R. Wright Jr. Thorne's dedication to Schomburg reads,

> Mr. Arthur A. Schomburg: This little volume Hanover is the outpouring of a heart full of love for the people of my race. In it I have attempted to relate the injustice done them in the year '98 at Wil. N.C. This is the work of one who was reared in Wil. and therefore knows the worth of the victims of mobs fury Yours sincerely Jack Thorne D. B. Fulton.

This copy is at the Schomburg Center for Research in Black Culture.

28. This case also caught the attention of John Edward Bruce, prominent black publisher and a man of considerable influence in his day. Bruce's papers contain dated notes to himself about the case:

> There is a strange streak in the Anglo-Saxon race—so called—despite its alleged contempt for the Negro the white man will not let Negro women alone. The Platt-Elias case in New York is the latest development of masculine white depravity[.] This lecherous old villain John R. Platt in an open confession admits he ruined Hannah Elias an octaroon when she was sixteen years of age. (He is seventy). (John E. Bruce Papers, May 23, 1904)

In fact, as Bruce notes, on June 8, 1904, Platt had paid Elias the $685,000 over some twenty years and had, at seventy, gone broke, while at thirty-six Elias was living well off her investments and real estate.

29. I would be remiss at the moment of this writing not to call attention to a couple of ironic parallels between this case and that of O. J. Simpson. One is the common name for the houseboy, Kato. The other is the way the case seemed to split New York City into its black and white components on the acquittal of Mrs. Elias. Unlike Simpson, however, Elias won her civil case as well. The accounts of the Elias-Platt case are contained in issues of the *New York Times* for June 1, 2, 3, 6, 7, 8, 9, 11 (including the editorial), and 28, 1904; September 11, 25, 1904; January 18, 19, 1905; February 2, 22, 1905; March 11, 1905; and May 2, 1905.

30. Thorne sent the manuscript of the novel to Nancy Cunard, along with the manuscript of "Cumberland," a historical novel of North Carolina. Cunard said she lost both (Hunter).

31. Fisher returns to the theme of the black policeman in 1933 in a slight comedy, "Guardian of the Law," celebrating the coming of age of the Negro civil servant (R. Fisher, *City*).

32. Walker lists, in part, Sarah Lee Fleming, *Hope's Highway* (1918), late-nineteenth-century history and growth of Jim Crow; W. E. B. Du Bois, *Quest of the Silver Fleece* (1911), a school for Negroes in the South and how to keep it going; John E. Bruce, *The Awakening of Hezekiah Jones* (1916), Negro politician, set in 1896 presidential election; Oscar Micheaux, *The Forged Note* (1915), law and the courts; Joshua Henry Jones, *By Sanction of Law* (1924), law and the courts; Sutton Griggs, *Souls of the Infinite* (1911); William Ashby, *Redder Blood* (1915); Clayton Adams, *Ethiopia, the Land of Promise* (1917).

33. In 1925 Dr. Ossian Sweet bought a home for his family in a heretofore white neighborhood of Detroit. Whites surrounded his house, shots were fired, and Sweet and everyone in his house at the time were arrested. As he wrote to L. M. Hussey on September 14, 1925, Walter White found himself

> hustling off to take a train to Detroit where a group of some five thousand Nordic gentlemen have been demonstrating their biological and mental superiority by attacking [Sweet as] too prosperous "for a Negro." The police force kept their hand off and the mob got the surprise of its life when the colored doctor opened fire on the mob, killing one of the heroes and wounding another. Then the police got busy and slapped the doctor, his wife and children, and his friends in jail, refusing not only to permit them bail but even to let counsel see them. Thus is the Nordic glorified! (NAACP Papers, reel 9).

White finally convinced Clarence Darrow to defend Sweet, and all the defendants were ultimately acquitted.

34. See, for example, the NAACP pamphlet, *The First Line of Defense*, sent to all chapters, detailing the expenditures for, and outcomes of, NAACP lobbying and litigation since 1910. It also contained the following notice:

> [The Association] has maintained a publicity service reaching the principal magazines, leading news services including Associated Press, and leading daily newspapers of the U.S., as well as newspapers and magazines in Europe and Asia. A regular weekly press service goes to 250 colored editors acquainting them with developments important to colored people. (N.p.)

Defense also argues that the "legal work of the Association is directed to the affirmation of fundamental civil rights affecting not alone Negroes but every citizen of the country. The Negro represents the shock troops in this long struggle for democracy" (n.p.). Aside from the use of "shock troops," a trope popular at the time for designating the political avant-garde and borrowed from the cultural rhetoric of the Left, this passage is interesting because it carries forward the argument posited throughout the last quarter of the nineteenth century that African Americans occupied a special and privileged place in the political destiny of the country, a place closer to the heart of the promises implicit in the Declaration of Independence and the Constitution than could be occupied by whites.

Chapter 6

1. White later requested that "The" be dropped from the title in subsequent editions.

2. Ida B. Wells-Barnett's reports on lynching between 1892 and 1900 were already well known. Her analysis of lynching aimed at its practice as a form of political and economic oppression. See also Carby, "Threshold"; Brundage; Goings; Gunning; Hall; T. Harris; Zangrando.

3. The Dyer bill finally passed the House of Representatives in 1922 but died in the Senate without coming to a vote in the extraordinary fourth session that ran into 1923.

4. Even James Joyce found a use for a lynching episode in *Ulysses:*

Hanging over the bloody paper with Alf looking for spicy bits instead of attending to the general public. Picture of a butting match. . . . And another one: *Black Beast Burned in Omaha, Ga.* A lot of Deadwood Dicks in slouch hats and they firing at a sambo strung up on a tree with his tongue out and a bonfire under him. (328)

The joke on Joyce here is that his use of the term "Deadwood Dicks," while in keeping with the phallic imagery of the rest of the Cyclops episode (as this part of the book is called), is inauthentic not only because of regional differences, but because the historical "Deadwood Dick" was himself an African American whose real name was Nat Love (Suggs, "Deadwood").

5. See White's notes on lynching throughout his papers in the NAACP files. Note that White's version of his disagreements with the first publisher interested in the book, Doran, as related to McKay in the August 15, 1924, letter (NAACP Papers, reel 7) is not borne out by the correspondence record. Doran ultimately refused to publish the novel.

6. White supplements his own experience with previously published sources; in a letter to Louis R. Glavis of *Hearst's International* magazine, White asks for the specific oath of allegiance taken by initiates to the Klan; he wants to put it in his novel, apparently on 122 (April 9, 1924, NAACP Papers, reel 7).

7. But in an October 17, 1922, letter to the novelist Clement Wood (NAACP Papers, reel 7), White reports that he has just tried his hand at a story about blacks in the South: "It was my first attempt at creative writing in the field of imaginative literature. However, I shall rewrite and rewrite—if necessary twenty times—until I have, if possible, made something worth while."

8. Five months after writing Webster, on September 9, 1925, White writes to Joel Spingarn that his second novel is free of "propaganda" and that "[a]t only one point do white people enter the story at all and then only because certain experiences which this girl has in connection with white people profoundly

influence her life afterwards. I sought to give a dispassionate, objective picture" (NAACP Papers, reel 9).

9. The story of the dispute is a lengthy one, involving John Farrar, Mary Roberts Rinehart, Irwin Cobb, and the Spingarn Brothers. It is clear from the correspondence that Doran sought to tone down both White's condemnation of white southerners and his indictment of southern "law." In an August 21, 1923, letter to White, Saxton wrote: "I should be entirely willing to have ninety-five per cent of all you say remain in the book if there were some moderately fair presentation of the white man's case" (NAACP Papers, reel 7).

10. Whites were not the only readers likely to suffer from the arguments put forth in the novel. A request for *Flint* from the librarian at Hospital 91, the United States Veterans Bureau Hospital for black veterans at Tuskegee, was rejected by the bureau on the grounds that although

> "[i]t is a masterly stroke in the world of literature," and carries us to the heights of success and then places the bitter cup of race prejudice to our lips and commands us to drink—to drink deeply; and after having drunken, we wonder why it must be so—what is the use. . . . The men in this hospital are sick mentally as well as physically. The books given them to read must be such as to leave them in a pleasanter frame of mind than they were in when they started to read them. They must be books to make them feel that they have every thing for which to live, to make them know that right will prevail and not might. (S. M. Peterson, letter to Walter White, May 1, 1925, NAACP Papers, reel 8)

"Right" here means the law of the land, and while the sick must be kept from the truth, Miss Peterson notes that she circulated a personal copy among the staff and the doctors and nurses discussed the book at "Book Evening." Nevertheless, she fears for her job and asks White not to refer to her any further inquiries about the official fate of his book but to write to the bureau.

11. Lynching as a motif or as an episodic event in African American fiction did not begin with White, nor would it end with him, but his work for the NAACP investigating and compiling the record of white violence against black Americans was crucial to the NAACP's ongoing attempts to get a federal anti-lynching law passed. That they were never successful was a source of great pain to the black community and is a subtext to much of black fiction well into the 1980s.

12. White's treatment of commercial sex between the races resembles this passage from Du Bois's *Souls of Black Folks:* "[T]here on the edge of town are five houses of prostitutes,—two of blacks and three of whites; and in one of the houses of the whites a worthless black boy was harbored too openly two years ago; so he was hanged for rape" (98).

13. White's design for the sharecroppers' cooperative is taken from his experiences investigating the oppression of black farmers in Arkansas in 1919. There, the farmers set up the "Progressive Farmers and Household Union of America," one function of which would be to fund test cases to break the legal back of the shares system in Arkansas. The group did not prevail, but the

NAACP was able to save the lives of twelve men who had been sentenced to death in Arkansas as a result of a "riot" related to the challenges to the system (White, *A Man* 48–53).

14. White wrote to T. S. Stribling that he had composed two endings to the novel (September 6, 1924, NAACP Papers, reel 8), and in one Harper is rescued by the mother of the white child whom he had cured. Harper then leaves town and never returns. White submitted the escape ending to Spingarn and Mencken, and each, he claims, found it "false—everything in the book led to the tragic ending in the death of Kenneth."

15. White's full-length treatment of lynching is *Rope and Faggot: The Story of Judge Lynch.* White's book was not his only participation in the popular dissemination of information about lynching. In October 1928, he sent Clement Wood, a white southern writer with whom he was friendly, data and cases from NAACP files on lynching. Wood used that material as the core of his pamphlet "Sexual Relations in the Southern States" (White, letter to Clement Wood, October 24, 1928, NAACP Papers, reel 11).

16. The only known print of the film was found in Spain. The Spanish intertitles were translated and edited in accordance with English slang, diction, and syntax as found in Micheaux's three novels and his 1925 silent film, *Body and Soul.*

17. Chapter 8 of Du Bois's *Souls of Black Folks,* "The Quest of the Golden Fleece," gives as good an account as you are likely to find of how agricultural oppression to the point of serfdom was carried out in the South at that time.

18. W. E. B. Du Bois noted in an internal NAACP memorandum that the United States Census for 1920 listed twenty-eight states that forbade intermarriage of the white race with any other. In those states, Du Bois pointed out, lived some 1.4 million mulattoes (memorandum, 1926, NAACP Papers, reel 9).

19. I can only hazard a guess about this peculiar scene, but the legislation passed at the height of war fever allowed authorities to seize seditious materials, and as David Levering Lewis has pointed out in his biography of Du Bois, the black community was under special scrutiny by the intelligence branch of the War Department. *Crisis* was censored by Du Bois to prevent it from being shut down by the army. Micheaux may have feared that he would be unable to send his film through the mails if his criticism of racism and violence against black Americans was not alloyed with some old-fashioned flag-waving. My colleague Michelle Wallace has suggested to me that because Micheaux wanted the film to be a "response" to D. W. Griffith's *Birth of a Nation,* he presented the scene as an African American version of the patriotic couples with which Griffith closes his picture.

20. Contrast Micheaux's solution, and the fate of the "good" woman, to the darker view of American promise held by Vera Manning in Fauset's *There Is Confusion:*

> Oh, Janna [*sic*], this terrible country with its false ideals. So you see why I'm glad there's a South for me to go to—I've got to choose between life and death. Even if I should lose my life in Georgia or one of those other terrible places where they lynch women, too, I'll save it, won't I? (273)

Manning is passing for white to investigate lynchings in the South in Fauset's novel. Her view of America is not so different from that expressed by characters in Harper's *Iola Leroy* three decades earlier.

21. Ralph Ellison evokes the problematic of this term in a scene in which the young protagonist delivers a prizewinning speech to some white businessmen and accidentally uses the words "social equality" (*Invisible Man* 31). The menace in the response from the audience is frightening to the boy.

22. Johnson's *Autobiography of an Ex-Coloured Man* (rereleased 1928), Fauset's *Plum Bun* (1929), and Larsen's *Quicksand* (1928) and *Passing* (1929) were the most remarked of the period.

23. The obverse of this practice was the use by whites of blackface disguise for various reasons, from entertainment to crime. Chesnutt's novel, *The Marrow of Tradition*, contained a plot mechanism in which a young white ne'er-do-well impersonates a black servant to commit a robbery and a murder. A famous case at law of the early 1920s was that of Maurice F. Mays. Mays, a black man, was convicted of the murder of a white woman, Bertie Lindsey. Retried on appeal, he was convicted again. In 1927, almost six years after his execution, Sadie Mendil, a white woman, confessed that she had blackened her face and dressed like a man to break into Lindsey's home, where she killed her (*Crisis*, October 1927, 276). In 1912, the *New York Age* reported the case of assault on Mrs. Camilla Beach, in which her husband reported a Negro attacked her. Later, a warrant was issued in Aiken, South Carolina, for Mr. Beach for "assault and battery with intent to kill his wife." The Beaches, New York socialites, were by then in Europe, and the *Age* reported: "Meantime, many of the negroes of Aiken are locked up and held as witnesses" (April 14). Russell treats the phenomenon in late-twentieth-century America (the Charles Stewart and Susan Smith cases) in her examination of crime as a racial barometer.

24. In an aside, Cheryl Harris suggests that a black person entering the white world as white was "not merely passing, but trespassing" (1710). But legally that is not the case, there being no criminal or civil penalty for claiming to be white or, as "trespassing" actually connotes, for crossing onto property not your own. But in an informal sense, trespass does catch much of the sense of what passing actually involves as whites might perceive it.

25. *State v. Treadaway et al.*, no. 18, 149 (126 La. 300. 52 So. 500) (April 25, 1910).

26. *Hopkins v. Bowers*, 16 S.E. 1; III N.C. 175.

27. *Bell v. State*, 33 Tex. Cr. R. 163.

28. *State v. Chavers*, 50 N.C. 11.

29. *Hare v. Board of Education*, 113 N.C. 9. 18 S.E. 55, 56.

30. *State v. Miller et al.*, 224 N.C. 228, *229, 29 S.E.2D 751, **752. And in Georgia, in the late 1920s:

> I have just completed a week of jury duty in the Bibb County superior court. As is customary, the solicitor asks each juror whether he is related by blood or marriage to any of the parties in each case that is called. But in cases where only negroes are involved, the formula runs something like this: "As both of the parties in this case are of the African race, there can be no question of blood relationship." This is the stencil even where prosecutors or defendants

are obviously more white than black. (Aaron Bernd, in Oswald Garrison Villard, letter to Walter White, July 1, 1929, NAACP Papers, reel 12)

The point here is that all the jurors are always white and the assumption is that none of them could possibly be related to any "negro" defendant or plaintiff, no matter how light the contestants might be.

31. For a rich discussion of issues arising from cases like *Treadaway*, see Diamond and Cottrol.

32. Chesnutt returns to this topic in his last two novels, *Paul Marchand, F.M.C.* (published in 1998) and "The Quarry," both written in the late 1920s, late in his life and after he had struck up a corresponding friendship with Walter White.

33. Ironically, in 1910, the most popular novels at Booker T. Washington's Tuskegee Institute were Chesnutt's *House Behind the Cedars* and *The Marrow of Tradition.* Next, in position 3, was *Ivanhoe* (Farnsworth xvii).

34. After the 1873 legislation, the 1875 North Carolina constitutional convention criminalized miscegenation as it rewrote the major portion of the 1868 Reconstruction constitution. I thank here my colleagues at several institutions: Louis Anthes, Stephen Siegel, J. Douglas Deal, Paul Finkelman, Chris Waldrep, William A. Link, Peter Bardaglio, Michael McConnell, and Andy Grossman, all of whom, through H-NET, guided me to the citations given here: Clinton and Silber; Martyn; Cohen; F. Johnson; Wallenstein; Bardaglio; Alexander; Bank. I was also informed by Novkov's 1993 paper.

35. Such an attitude, we might add, is a direct contravention of the intent of the Thirteenth Amendment's "badges and indices" clause, which forbids legal discrimination against blacks particularly because of their former status or attitudes by the law derived from that status.

36. Nabokov's observation was first pointed out to me in an H-AMSTDY posting by Patricia Travis on November 25, 1996, to the thread "Black-White Interracial Romance." The other two plots are pedophilia and the long, happy, useful life of an atheist who dies in his sleep at the age of 106.

Nabokov's point is exemplified by the revision of *House* done by Oscar Micheaux in *The Masquerade* (1947). In 1921 Chesnutt had sold film rights to *House* to Micheaux, who claimed to have filmed it twice, once as a silent film and once with sound. In the mid-1940s, Micheaux turned Chesnutt's novel into his own novel, one in which Rena's and John's mother Molly is presented as the unwilling victim of a white master rather than mistress to a white lover. In Micheaux's version, Rena chooses Frank rather than Tryon.

Micheaux had definite ideas about the kind of films he wanted to make. In 1926 he wrote to Walter White about optioning his novel *Flight*. Micheaux's brother liked the novel, but the decision was Micheaux's alone to make. He wanted to make serious dramas about the real lives of black people, not just entertainments for white or black audiences. Race, however, was not enough. He hoped, he told White, that White had not written a novel "along the lines of the N. A. A. C. P., setting forth vigorously the white man's injustice to our group, a thing too well known to interest people anymore." Nor was he interested in tributes to the "progress and achievement" of the race. Finally, he refused to make the Negro comedies the distributors wanted (Micheaux to White, April 21, 1926, NAACP Papers, reel 9).

37. Larsen's other novel, *Quicksand,* while not a "passing" novel per se, is very much a study of the suppression of African American desire. See Monda.

38. Anderson's play was perhaps the first by a black playwright to be produced on Broadway. It ran twenty-three performances, toured, then returned to New York in 1929 for another month's run. *Appearances* was also the first play on Broadway to "cast colored"; black actors were cast for black roles that interacted with white roles (Hatch and Shine 100–134; Peterson 28–29).

39. Ironic complications abound when passing is the issue. Rudolph Fisher's 1925 short story "High Yaller" tells the story of Evelyn, who is so light that she is forced to pass for white in order to find someplace for herself in the world. In effect, it was easier for her to be white than not. To be accepted by Harlem, she would have to pass for *black,* an effort she could not pull off. In the final irony, her black boyfriend is taken in and beaten by white police because he is dating a "white" woman.

40. The 1889 article is referred to in a January 5, 1927, letter from Chesnutt to Walter White (NAACP Papers, reel 10). Chesnutt does not remember the name of the case in the letter, but believes it to be "the case of Polly Anderson against some school or county authority." Chesnutt does not identify the "later case." I have checked the article and find no citation of the case.

41. In 1886 the Brotherhood of Liberty had attacked Maryland's bastardy law. Black women had been covered by the law between 1785 and 1860 but were excluded after 1860. As a consequence no Negro woman could sue for child support or force marriage of her child's father through a paternity suit. The Baltimore black community felt that this left Negro women exposed to sexual exploitation by white men and broke down black family structure. (It also made it difficult if not impossible for illegitimate black children to inherit property from their white fathers.) The challenge worked indirectly. Black lawyer Everett Waring's arguments re the Civil Rights Acts of 1866 and the Fourteenth Amendment were rejected by the Baltimore County Supreme Bench, but later the Criminal Court declared the 1860 version of the law unconstitutional. That was reversed by the state's court of appeals. The Maryland legislature deadlocked on the matter, and finally in 1888, John Poe, in codifying (drawing together for official publication) the general laws of the state, simply omitted the word *white* from the provisions of the law, and the legislature left the change intact (Paul 209–10).

The 1875 North Carolina constitution was unusual in that its antimiscegenation statute explicitly prevented the father from legitimizing any children produced by a mixed marriage, thus denying the children a right to inherit. Other states allowed offspring of an interracial marriage to inherit, but this did not prevent legal challenges to such wills from taking place. The most interesting of these cases is *Smith v. DuBose,* 78 Ga. 413 (1887) (A. L. Alexander; email: Peter Bardaglio, H-LAW, "Re: Miscegenation," December 2, 1996).

42. See John McClusky Jr.'s introduction to Fisher, *City* xiv.

Chapter 7

1. It is interesting to note that while Du Bois is called the "most noted Negro man of letters in the United States" (6) in a course survey for public schools produced by the Service Bureau for Intercultural Affairs of New York City sometime between 1937 and the early 1940s, this novel is not listed among his works. The document, "The Negro in Literature," is a guide to classroom material for high schools to show "that Negroes have made contributions to American literature." The survey ranges from Jupiter Hammon to Zora Neale Hurston but not once mentions a political position other than abolitionism taken by any black writer, nor does it mention any work by a black writer in a political context. That the guide was "[p]repared with the assistance of the Works Progress Administration for New York City" may account for its politically denatured tone.

2. My favorite line from the book is exemplary of Du Bois's operating in this mode. He throws in this observation without developing it any further: "Baseball, movies, Spain, and Italy are ruled by Tyrants" (*Dark Princess* 283).

3. Du Bois puts the Republican Party at the center of black politics in Chicago, even at the local level. This contradicts the portrayal of local party politics in Corrothers's *Black Cat Club* of some twenty-five years previously. Corrothers had written that in national politics black Americans remained Republican but on the local level, particularly in Chicago, voted Democratic, for the graft. Du Bois specifically states in his novel that the Democratic Party is "anathema" in Negro Chicago: "It stood for slavery and disenfranchisement and Jim Crow cars" (179). Admittedly, Corrothers's piece was meant to be humorous, but it has the ring of truth.

4. In 1928, the year *Dark Princess* was published, Oscar Stanton DePriest, the first black congressman since Reconstruction, was elected from Chicago.

5. The overt internationalism of Du Bois's protagonists is unique among African American narratives of the first four decades of the century. Du Bois's own investment in pan-Africanism and later in Marxism explains this for the most part. Somewhat more obscure is the abortive attempt by Walter White, Alain Locke, and others (names proposed for trusteeship included, among others, James Weldon Johnson, Du Bois, Carter G. Woodson, and Roland Hayes) to create a foundation to support the exposure of "a few competent young colored men and women" to the "wider social vision and contact with progressive movements" available only in Europe. The goal was to create a young generation of "liberally trained leaders with world perspective, international outlook and contacts." The plan was submitted for funding to the American Fund for Public Service in May 1924; the fund declined the request. See Walter White's correspondence in the NAACP files for 1924.

Except for James Weldon Johnson's protagonist in *Autobiography of an Ex-Coloured Man,* no characters in black fiction to that date had traveled to Europe, much less come back imbued with progressive politics. Throughout the decade White, McKay, Fauset, and Hughes would create characters, veterans of the First World War for the most part, who had seen Europe, but their experience was broadly "cultural" rather than political. In his 1926 essay, "The New

Negro," Locke declares the problem of the color line a dead letter, made so by a new internationalism, a pan-Africanism that sweeps black Americans into the future, and by a new psychological consensus based on "an attempt to repair a damaged group psychology and reshape a warped social perspective" (966). Thus black Americans should recognize themselves as inheritors of the democratic ideals of the American past but should not dwell on the centuries of betrayal of those ideals through which they had suffered. Locke's position was antithetical to the political romanticism of Du Bois, and his art would be less directly engaged with the mechanisms of power than with the exaltation of race as the source of public identity and even citizenship.

6. See Bell's discussion of legal realism (*Faces* 99–105) and his notes to that discussion.

7. Nevertheless, Negroes did own property in every state in which they could be counted. In 1911, for example, Negroes in Pennsylvania had title to real estate valued at $20 million (*New York Age,* January 11, 1912). In Georgia that same year, blacks paid taxes on property worth $34,234,037 (*New York Age,* April 25, 1912). The fictional discussion of these "utopias of place" figures strongly in the literature of Toni Morrison at the end of this century, finding its most complex form in her 1998 novel, *Paradise,* set in an all-black town in Oklahoma.

8. When black Americans did encounter the law in Shreveport, real life was more painful. Sometime in 1910, John Hope Franklin's father, B. C. Franklin, went to Shreveport from Ardmore, Oklahoma (a real town where he practiced law) to represent a client in court. When Franklin stepped to the bar as his client's case was called, the judge asked why he was standing in his court. Franklin replied that he was the attorney in the case just called, "whereupon the judge shook his head and declared that no 'nigger' could represent anyone in his court. He then ordered [Franklin] to leave the courtroom" (B. C. Franklin xvii–xviii).

9. A rich line of inquiry to follow would be the physician as character in African American fiction. From the various doctors in *Iola Leroy* through *Fire in the Flint* and *Dark Princess* to *The Chinaberry Tree* and beyond, the physician challenges "social" law in the name of the laws of science.

10. See Scruggs for a masterful discussion of urban "alternative spaces"; Scruggs does not discuss the spaces created by Micheaux, White, or Fauset discussed here, as they are not urban spaces, but his treatment of the city is insightful.

11. Studies of Harlem abound, but for Harlem as a site rather than a movement, see J. Anderson; De Jongh; Douglas; J. W. Johnson, *Manhattan;* Kellner; Kisselhoff; Lewis, *Vogue;* McKay; Ottley; Schoener; Allen; Thurman, *Life;* Watkin-Owens.

12. The line between the criminal world and the literary was not always clearly visible. For instance, the May 1925, awards banquet for prizes in literature sponsored by *Opportunity* was underwritten by Caspar Holstein, the "numbers king" of Harlem (De Jongh 13–14). Holstein may also have underwritten some of the costs of Arthur Schomburg's book and artifact collections.

13. John McCluskey, in his introduction to *The City of Refuge: The Collected Stories of Rudolph Fisher,* suggests that John Edward Bruce's "Black Sleuth," an adventure series serialized in 1907–8 in *McGirt's Reader,* was the first detective story published by a black writer.

14. The Archer-Dart symbiosis is clever, as Archer the intellect propels Dart the instrument into action. The relationship is similar to, or perhaps a foreshadowing of, the one Mickey Spillane creates for his equally cathected characters, Mike Hammer and Pat Chambers. Hammer's impact on Chambers has the same effect as in the workings of a pistol, setting the law into action with explosive, reactive force.

15. Archer appears again in Fisher's fiction in a 1935 short story, "John Archer's Nose," in which science defeats superstition in a Harlem setting, primarily through Archer's efforts, with the help of Detective Sergeant Dart.

16. Hurston is subtle in her depiction of the impact of white law on black life. For example, one proof of a man's interest in a woman is spelled out in terms of old contract labor sentences. Under the South's legalized form of economic slavery, a black man arrested for vagrancy was auctioned off to the highest bidder according to a formula of court costs in relation to the amount of time the "employer" wanted him for. The transaction was called by the black victims of the system "makin' time," and it meant, in practice, the amount of time you were contracted to the boss-man by the state or county to pay out your fine and court costs. So:

> DAVE: "Well all right, less prove dis thing right now. We'll prove right now who love dis gal de best. How much time is you willin' tuh make fuh Daisy?"
> JIM: "Twenty yeahs!"
> DAVE: "See? Ah told yuh dat nigger didn't love yuh. Me, Ah'll beg de Judge tuh hang me, and wouldn't take nothin' less than life."
>
> *(Eyes, 60)*

Later, when Tea Cake is helping bury hurricane victims, the whites get coffins, but black folks get a mass grave, and he is warned not to misidentify the race of any corpse: "They's mighty particular how dese dead folks goes tuh Judgment," Tea Cake observed to the man working next to him. "Look lak dey think God don't know nuthin' 'bout de Jim Crow law" (140–41).

17. See M. H. Washington 237–54 and 290–93 for an account of this problem and a bibliographic guide to it.

18. Almost as a postscript, Hurston has the male members of the black community speculate on all the possible reasons for the acquittal. These boil down to the observation that there is some natural (unmediated) affinity between white men and black women, the two freest things on earth.

19. I am indebted to Professor Judi Newman of the University of Newcastle on Tyne for her discussion with me of the Boas-Hurston relationship. An informative reading of another anthropological aspect of this novel is in Professor Newman's unpublished paper.

Chapter 8

1. African American modernism, it could be said,

was concerned preeminently with removing the majority of the black population from the poverty, illiteracy, and degradation that marked southern, black, agrarian existence in the United States at the turn of the nineteenth century. AfroAmerican scholars, intellectuals, and activists of the late nineteenth and early twentieth centuries were faced with a task substantially different from that of their AngloAmerican, British, and Irish counterparts. Rather than bashing the bourgeoisie, such spokespersons were attempting to create one. Far from being rebellious dissenters against existent AfroAmerican expressive forms, they sought to enhance these forms and bring them before a sophisticated public. And far from repudiating the emergent age as "an old bitch gone in the teeth," AfroAmerican spokespersons welcomed a new century as a time when shackles of slavery and impoverishment would fall decisively away. (Baker, *Poetics* 4)

2. Wright's novel has been reissued with corrections from his original manuscripts and proofs (*Early Works* 443–850). This edition restores sections cut at the request of the original publisher. The 1966 edition used for this chapter has been checked against the 1991 restorations.

3. I want to point out that it is the argument of marginalization that overcomes an obvious problem, the fact that Nicky Romano is Italian-American, not African American, in describing the novel as "African American" for first-time readers of *Knock on Any Door*. Wright explored the problem of race narratively in the first two sections of *Native Son* and the question of class argumentatively in the last third of the novel. Motley's novel, however, seems to ignore race and devotes its considerable length to the effects of socioeconomic conditions on the development of personality among children of the working poor. Is his, then, an "African American" fiction? For the purposes of this study, insofar as we can say that an African American writer, working within identifiable conventions of the classical African American novel and in the context of recent practice in his genre by other African American writers, produces a text, suffused with law, that explores the effects of social marginalization, we ought not to bother that the protagonist is a white boy. By deliberately, and/or necessarily to his purpose, avoiding race as an issue in the specific and generic telling of his tale, Motley causes us to consider class among the primary causes of the marginalization he recognized as the condition of black Americans and that eventually drove him to self-imposed exile. Motley's choice is not unusual; the three strongest marginalizing forces in American society, class, race, and sex/gender rarely appear fully articulated in the same fiction.

4. In his novel *Iron City*, Lloyd L. Brown, a black Marxist, parodies white social scientists with the news account of an address by a sociologist to a women's civic club. Having stated, "We are confronted by fourteen million Bigger Thomases," Dr. Canfield, the sociologist, reports to the ladies that when rats and sheep are trained by rewards of food to follow a specific path, they react visibly when that path is blocked:

"The rats," said Dr. Canfield, "were observed to become maddened by the imposed frustration. Frantic, confused, desperate, they battered themselves to death against the barrier. Sheep, who normally are docile and gregarious, became sullen, morose, and solitary, pathologically warped by the continuous cycle of hunger-hope-frustration.

"This explains," the lecturer pointed out, "why we have among the Negro race both the destructive Bigger Thomas type and the helpless, hymn-singing passive type familiar to us all." (208)

5. Alan France's idea that part of the conflict in the novel is that which is fought out by men over the bodies of women depends on the positioning of women as male property. An example is Mary's position as Jan's "girl" and then Bigger's victim (414; Blake 198 n. 24).

6. Like Ellison after him, however, Wright seemed to need to believe that he was the first black writer to attempt to deal seriously with African American life. He wrote, for instance, "[M]y race possessed no fictional works dealing with such problems, had no background in such sharp and critical testing of experience, no novels that went with a deep and fearless will down to the dark roots of life" ("Bigger" 862–63). Even the turn to documentation began in the nineteenth century with the "appropriation of the fact" by African American novelists. Beyond the practice of the authenticating preface established in antebellum slave narratives and revived by Wright here. Webb, Jacobs, Delany, "Sanda," Thorne, Griggs, and Chesnutt all used such documentary devices as footnotes, trial transcripts, "found" manuscripts, correspondence, newspaper accounts, and census data to establish the authenticity of their texts.

7. Material on the Double V campaign comes from research done by William F. Yurasko, who was a student in Ford Risley's COMM 401 Mass Media in History course. He is a student of Media Studies, with a focus on journalism and political science at Penn State University in the College of Communications.

8. It is in this early novel, for example, that Himes anticipates the racial-economic centerpiece of Lyndon Johnson's Great Society some twenty years down the road: affirmative action. Because of their historic deprivation in the face of democratic and laissez-faire rhetoric, the blacks Himes's protagonist Lee Gordon is trying to coerce into the union want not only equal treatment under the rules (law) but special status:

For while their cold racial logic told them that the union also was another racial barrier, their deep yearning for democracy caused them to expect from it not only the opportunity for full-fledged participation but in addition special consideration and privileges. They did not want to be just members; they wanted to be special members with rights and privileges above all other members. (138)

Of course, Gordon/Himes can and does anticipate the tensions this status would create, but in his mind the demands of democracy are simple, reparations under law on the work floor (139–40).

9. Yet Alain Locke, as we have seen, announced the agenda of the New Negro as early as 1926 to be "an attempt to repair a damaged group psychology . . . a warped social perspective" (966). Ironically, Locke's method, turning to

race as a center of value-generating experience, is not available to Himes's protagonists, since it is race that is driving them mad.

10. It requires no real leap of reasoning to follow Himes's argument to that of Grier and Cobbs and the periodic attempts to raise the question of that rage as a defense in the courtroom (P. Harris).

11. Just to show how Ellison did use his own experience, compare the first paragraph of the novel's treatment of the 1943 riot with his own *New York Post* lead paragraph from August 2, 1943:

> When I reached Morningside the shooting sounded like a distant celebration of the Fourth of July, and I hurried forward. At St. Nicholas the street lights were out. *(Invisible Man)*

> At 3 a.m. this morning I left the Eighth Av. subway at 127th and St. Nicholas Av. When I came out, there was the sound of gunfire and the shouting as of a great celebration. ("Eyewitness Story of Riot: False Rumors Spurred Mob," 2)

12. Compare this episode (231–50) with George Schuyler's *Black No More.* Both procedures at the heart of their respective stories change the social identity of the patient. That the electronic lobotomy of *Invisible Man* is supposed to make you "black no more" can be seen in this exchange:

> "[T]he result is a complete change of personality as you'll find in your famous fairy-tale cases of criminals transformed into amiable fellows after all that bloody business of a brain operation. . . ."
>
> "But what of his psychology?"
>
> "Absolutely of no importance!" the voice said. "The patient will live as he has to live, and with absolute integrity. Who could ask for more? He'll experience no major conflict of motives, and what is even better, society will suffer no traumata on his account."
>
> There was a pause. A pen scratched on paper. Then, "Why not castration, doctor?" a voice asked waggishly, causing me to start, a pain tearing through me. (236)

13. The 1995 Vintage edition here omits a line of text from the original, which I have replaced.

14. Ellison returns to this depiction of men with guns standing for law in "Perspective of Literature." Writing of his childhood in Oklahoma, he recalled: "In our common usage, law was associated more with men than with statutes. Law-enforcement officers in our usage were 'Laws,' and many were men with reputations for being especially brutal toward Negroes" (323).

15. Ellison reflects in "Perspective of Literature" that during his boyhood there was great respect for the law, despite the "persons and forces that imposed the law undemocratically" (323). His people then, as represented in editorials by a local black newspaperman, believed that

> the real clue, the real ground for solving the racial predicament, rested in the Constitution. I read his editorials, but I must confess that with my youthful cynicism, I didn't quite believe them. But anyway, the men in the barbershop believed in the spirit of the law, if not in its application. (323)

The other "texts" alluded to here are, I believe, the Masonic movement, black nationalism/separatism, and the back-to-Africa movement.

16. Walter White began work on a boxing novel, the only such novel attempted by an African American writer, in the late 1920s but abandoned it when he became the permanent executive secretary of the NAACP in 1930. I am currently editing the manuscript of that novel for publication.

17. Ellison had asked the same question much more prosaically nine years earlier: "Much in Negro life remains a mystery; perhaps the zoot suit conceals profound political meaning; perhaps the symmetrical frenzy of the Lindy Hop conceals clues to great potential power—if only Negro leaders would solve this riddle" ("Editorial").

18. These connections are ironic in themselves. The folklore of black music has it that Razaf wrote the song in an hour after the white mob boss that controlled the Cotton Club told him he wanted a "coon" song for the evening's performance there. And it seems pretty well established that one way Louis Armstrong adapted to the pressures of his life as a black man lionized by whites was to smoke marijuana every day. See the marijuana-induced reflections on the history of slavery (Ellison, *Invisible Man* 9–12).

19. But his grandfather had once recited the entire United States Constitution as a text "of his fitness to vote" (*Invisible Man* 315). Still, they denied him a ballot.

Epilogue

1. Two essays suggest how, in fact, the two threads of development are the same skein: Peller; Calmore.

2. The term *Black Arts movement* is not meant to subsume all writers or movements in the black community in the two decades after Ellison. The novelists Rosa Guy, John O. Killens, Sarah E. Wright, and Paule Marshall, for example, were members of the Harlem Writers' Guild in the late 1950s and throughout the 1960s (J. Campbell).

3. See the entries and bibliographies in Decker. Important figures of the movement were Larry Neal, Hoyt Fuller, Clarence Major, Joe Goncalves, Marvin Jackman, LeRoi Jones (Amiri Baraka), Askia Muhammad Toure (Roland Snellings), Tom Dent, Calvin Hernton, Addison Gayle Jr., Don L. Lee, Ishmael Reed, Sonia Sanchez, Mari Evans, Carolyn M. Rogers, Nikki Giovanni, Mae Jackson, Jayne Cortez, Jackie Earley, Toni Cade (Bambara), Audre Lorde, June Jordan, Ellease Southerland, and Alice Walker. The summer 1968, issue of the *Drama Review* carried significant examples of Black Revolutionary Theatre and of the Theatre of Black Experience as well as Larry Neal's essay "The Black Arts Movement," in which he states:

> The Black Arts Movement is radically opposed to any concept of the artist that alienates him from his community. Black Art is the aesthetic and spiritual sister of the Black Power concept. . . . The Black Arts and the Black Power concept both relate broadly to the Afro-American's desire for self-determina-

tion and nationhood. Both concepts are nationalistic. One is concerned with the relationship between art and politics, the other with the art of politics. (29)

4. Henry Louis Gates Jr., has argued, however, that "the dirty little secret of the Black Arts movement was that it was a project promoted and sustained largely by the Ford Foundation." Gates's position is that there was no authentic "populist modernism" in the movement; rather it was a showcase for the intellectual elite (Gates, "Chitlin'").

5. However, poetry and drama actually "outranked" prose fiction in the movement, at least in part because they were more communal forms, and more participatory. Even in theater, though, traditional expository techniques generally prevailed, the notable exception being the plays of LeRoi Jones.

6. In a subplot, Jim Minsk, a Jewish director, gets killed by a cabal of white Protestant fundamentalists seeking revenge on Jews for the death of Mary Phagan in the Leo Frank case.

7. A. Leon Higginbotham Jr. discusses the general impact of these acts on black life in general and on blacks in the legal profession in his essay "Opening Argument" (7–19).

8. Morrison, Reed, Baker, Johnson, and others are engaged in a complex reappropriation of the African American origins, as they see them, of nineteenth-century American romanticism, especially that of the Transcendentalists. See Hardack.

9. Morrison's use of detail is effective and, apparently, rooted in history. In an important thematic scene, one in which the slave-training "schoolteacher" teaches the slave Sixo with a beating that "definitions belonged to the definers—not the defined," Sixo had claimed that he had not stolen a shoat from his master, although he had eaten it, because he was actually improving the master's property by making himself more fit, and so more productive: "Sixo plant rye to give the high piece a better chance. Sixo take and feed the soil, give you more crop. Sixo take and feed Sixo give you more work" (*Beloved* 190). This passage is a direct parallel to the following in which a slave claims he is only recycling the master's wealth: "If chicken eat corn, only turn massa corn into massa chicken; he no tief. If hog root through potato row, he no tief; only turn massa potato into massa hog. If nigger eat corn, chicken, and hog, he no tief; all massa's yet." David Oshinsky cites this speech as exemplary of slave attitudes toward their masters' property (33). His sources, one of which may have been Morrison's, are Eugene Genovese's *Roll, Jordan Roll* (1972) and Claude Nolan's *The Negro's Image in the South* (1967). Note, however, that Morrison changes the character of the act itself by having Sixo claim what historical slaves seem not to have claimed, that he was *improving* the master's property, not simply recycling it. The lesson Sixo learns from the schoolteacher proceeds from that overreaching, then. Ownership permits definition; to presume to define presumes ownership, a status in no way "grammatically constructable" in the schoolteacher's universe of masters and slaves.

10. Compare, for instance, another infanticide, that related in Art Spiegelman's *Maus*. There, as the Jewish community in Zawiercie is being transported,

Tosha kills not only herself but the three children with poison: "I won't go to their gas chambers! . . . And my *children* won't go to their gas chambers" (109).

11. Morrison also makes use of the Isis-Osiris myth when Paul D remembers Sixo saying of the Thirty-Mile Woman, "'She was a friend of my mind. She gather me, man. The pieces I am, she gather them and give them back to me in all the right order'" (*Beloved* 272–73). See Lock for a discussion of the Isis-Osiris myth and the Afrocentric detective novel.

12. Morrison revisits this theme in *Jazz:* "Get a hold of yourself. A son ain't what a woman say. A son is what a man do" (172).

13. One story circulating in the community was that the baby ghost "came back evil and sent Sethe out to get the man who kept her from hanging" (*Beloved* 267).

14. Sabrina Lecky, a student in my course on African-American Literature and American Law, observes that Beloved stands for the entire legal world of slavery—the Fugitive Slave Law, the local ordinances, the overarching institution of it, the consequences of its institutionalized existence.

15. Williams's article was included, in reworked form, as part of chapter 8 of *Alchemy*. See also the formative articles from the late 1980s and early 1990s in which gender and race positions within Critical Race Theory were contested, among them Barnes; P. C. Davis; Kennedy; and Scales-Trent.

16. Bell's stormy relationship with Harvard, which resulted in the revocation of his tenure there in 1993, gives some weight to his argument.

17. See, for example, the poetry sampled from James Corrothers's *The Black Cat Club* in an earlier chapter of this study.

18. See Marshall Berman's chapter, "Justice/Just Us: Rap and Social Justice in America," for a discussion of how self-experienced group oppression translates to identification with a larger justice community.

19. Other black writers and artists working in the comic book industry are Kyle Baker, whose graphic novels *Why I Hate Saturn* and *The Cowboy Wally Show* are cult classics, Bob Washington, and Rob Simpson. Black comics go back at least as far as the 1940s; the 1960s and 1970s saw mainstream publishers such as Marvel *(Black Panther)* and DC Comics *(Black Lightning)* approach the black reading market. In an email message of June 5, 1998, Catherine Yronwode brought to my attention the career of Don McGregor, a scriptwriter for *Black Panther* in the mid-1970s who broke with Marvel over editorial policy and founded Eclipse Publishers to bring out his own comic, *Sabre. Sabre* featured an interracial couple as heroic protagonists and was the first comic to depict child-birth "on-panel."

20. Some strains of African American humor have always relied on the ironic recognition by blacks of the absurdity of white claims to superiority and to the implicit absurdity of the system of regulation whites invent to support those claims (Levine 310ff).

References

Abrams, M. H. *The Mirror and the Lamp.* New York: Oxford University Press, 1953.

Adams, John Quincy. *Argument of John Quincy Adams before the Supreme Court of the United States, Appellants, vs. Cinque, and Others, Africans, Captured in the Schooner "Amistad," by Lieut. Gedney, Delivered on the 24th of February and 1st of March, 1841. With a Review of the Case of the "Antelope," Reported in the 10th, 11th, and 12th Volumes of Wheaton's Reports.* New York: Negro Universities Press, 1969.

Alexander, Adele Logan. *Ambiguous Lives: Free Women of Color in Rural Georgia, 1789–1879.* Athens: University of Georgia Press, 1991.

Alexander, Nikol G., and Drucilla Cornell. "Dismissed or Banished? A Testament to the Reasonableness of the Simpson Jury." In *Birth of a Nation'hood: Gaze, Script, and Spectacle in the O. J. Simpson Case,* ed. Toni Morrison and Claudia Brodsky Lacour, 57–96. New York: Pantheon, 1997.

Allen, Robert L. *Black Awakening in Capitalist America: An Analytic History.* Garden City, N.Y.: Doubleday, 1969.

Anderson, Benedict. *Imagined Communities: Reflections on the Origin and Spread of Nationalism.* Rev. ed. London: Verso, 1991.

Anderson, Jervis. *This Was Harlem: A Cultural Portrait, 1900–1950.* New York: Farrar, Straus and Giroux, 1982.

Andrews, William L., ed. *Collected Stories of Charles W. Chesnutt.* New York: Mentor/Penguin, 1992.

———. "Jack Thorne [David Bryant Fulton]." In *Dictionary of American Negro Biography,* ed. Rayford W. Logan and Michael R. Winston 589–90. New York: Norton, 1982.

———. *The Literary Career of Charles W. Chesnutt.* Baton Rouge: Louisiana State University Press, 1980.

———. "The Novelization of Voice in Early African American Narrative." *PMLA* 105.1 (1990): 23–34.

———. "The Representation of Slavery and the Rise of Afro-American Literary Realism, 1865–1920." In *Slavery and the Literary Imagination,* ed. Deborah E. McDowell and Arnold Rampersad, 62–80. Baltimore: Johns Hopkins University Press, 1989.

Armstrong, Nancy, and Leonard Tennenhouse. *The Imaginary Puritan: Literature, Intellectual Labor, and the Origins of Personal Life.* Berkeley and Los Angeles: University of California Press, 1992.

———. "The Literature of Conduct, the Conduct of Literature, and the Politics of Desire: An Introduction." In *The Ideology of Conduct: Essays on Literature and the History of Sexuality,* ed. Armstrong and Tennenhouse, 1–24. New York: Methuen, 1987.

Ascher, Allen. "'No Respecter of Persons': Law and the American Renaissance." Ph.D. diss., City University of New York, 1993. Ann Arbor: UMI, 1993.

Attaway, William. *Blood on the Forge.* 1941; New York: Macmillan, 1970.

Bailyn, Barnard. *The Peopling of British North America: An Introduction.* New York: Knopf, 1986.

Baker, Houston A., Jr. *AfroAmerican Poetics: Revisions of Harlem and the Black Aesthetic.* Madison: University of Wisconsin Press, 1988.

———. *Modernism and the Harlem Renaissance.* Chicago: University of Chicago Press, 1987.

———. *Singers of Daybreak.* Cambridge: Harvard University Press, 1974.

Bank, Steven. "Anti Miscegenation Laws and the Dilemma of Symmetry: The Understanding of Equality in the Civil Rights Act of 1875." *University of Chicago Law School Roundtable* 2 (1995): 303–21.

Bardaglio, Peter. *Reconstructing the Household: Families, Sex, and the Law in the Nineteenth-Century South.* Chapel Hill: University of North Carolina Press, 1995.

Barnes, Robin D. "Race Consciousness: The Thematic Content of Racial Distinctiveness in Critical Race Scholarship." *Harvard Law Review* 103 (1990): 1864–71.

Barrett, Lindon. "Hand-Writing: Legibility and the White Body in *Running a Thousand Miles for Freedom.*" *American Literature* 69 (1997): 315–36.

Bell, Derrick. *And We Are Not Saved: The Elusive Quest for Racial Justice.* New York: Basic, 1987.

———. *Faces at the Bottom of the Well: The Permanence of Racism.* New York: Basic, 1992.

———. "Xerxes and the Affirmative Action Myth." *George Washington Law Review* 57 (1989): 1595–1613.

Berlant, Lauren. *The Anatomy of National Fantasy: Hawthorne, Utopia, and Everyday Life.* Chicago: University of Chicago Press, 1991.

Berman, Marshall. "Justice/Just Us: Rap and Social Justice in America" In *The Urbanization of Injustice,* ed. Andy Merrifield and Erik Swyngedouw, 161–79. New York: Washington Square and New York University Press, 1997.

Bernstein, David E. "Roots of the 'Underclass': The Decline of Laissez-Faire Jurisprudence and the Rise of Racist Labor Legislation." *American University Law Review* 43.1 (1993): 85–138.

Blake, Caesar R. "On Richard Wright's *Native Son.*" In *Rough Justice: Essays on Crime in Literature,* ed. M. L. Friedland, 187–99. Toronto: University of Toronto Press, 1991.

Brooks, Peter. *The Melodramatic Imagination: Balzac, Henry James, Melodrama, and the Mode of Excess.* New York: Columbia University Press, 1985.

———. *Reading for the Plot: Design and Intention in Narrative.* New York: Vintage, 1984.

Brotherhood of Liberty. *Justice and Jurisprudence: an Inquiry concerning the Constitutional Limitations of the Thirteenth, Fourteenth, and Fifteenth Amendments.* Philadelphia: Lippincott, 1889.

Brown, Jeffrey A. "Comic Book Masculinity and the New Black Superhero." *African American Review* 33.1 (spring 1999): 25–42.

Brown, Lloyd L. *Iron City*. New York: Masses and Mainstream, 1951.

Brown, William Wells. *Clotel, or The President's Daughter*. 1853; New York: Arno Press and the New York Times, 1969.

Bruce, Dickson D., Jr. *Black American Writing from the Nadir: The Evolution of a Literary Tradition, 1877–1915*. Baton Rouge: Louisiana State University Press, 1989.

Brundage, W. Fitzhugh. *Lynching in the New South: Georgia and Virginia, 1880–1930*. Urbana: University of Illinois Press, 1993.

Bryant, Edward. "Our Duties, Responsibilities;—Negro Literature." *A.M.E. Church Review* 1.3 (1885): 257–67.

Burke, Kenneth. *A Grammar of Motives*. Berkeley and Los Angeles: University of California Press, 1969.

Butterfield, Fox. *All God's Children: The Bosket Family and the American Tradition of Violence*. New York: Knopf, 1995.

Bynum, Victoria E. *Unruly Women: The Politics of Social and Sexual Control in the Old South*. Chapel Hill: University of North Carolina Press, 1992.

Byron, George Gordon, Lord. *The Works of Lord Byron*. Poetry. 7 vols. Vol II. Ed. Ernest Hartley Coleridge. 1898–1904; New York: Octagon Press, 1966.

Cade, Toni. "On the Issue of Roles." In *The Black Woman: An Anthology*, ed. Cade, 101–10. New York: Mentor, 1970.

Callcott, Margaret Law. *The Negro in Maryland Politics, 1870–1912*. Baltimore: Johns Hopkins University Press, 1969.

Calmore, John O. "Critical Race Theory, Archie Shepp, and Fire Music." In *Critical Race Theory: The Key Writings That Formed the Movement*, ed. Kimberle Crenshaw et al., 315–29. New York: New Press, 1995.

Campbell, Bebe Moore. *Your Blues Ain't Like Mine*. New York: Ballantine, 1992.

Campbell, Jennifer. "'It's a Time in the Land': Gendering Black Power and Sarah E. Wright's Place in the Tradition of Black Women's Writing." *African American Review* 31 (1997): 211–22.

Carby, Hazel V. "'On the Threshold of Women's Era': Lynching, Empire, and Sexuality in Black Feminist Theory." In *Race, Writing, and Difference*, ed. Henry Louis Gates Jr., 301–16. Chicago: University of Chicago Press, 1986.

———. *Reconstructing Womanhood: The Emergence of the Black Woman Novelist*. New York: Oxford University Press, 1987.

Castronovo, Russ. *Fathering the Nation: American Genealogies of Slavery and Freedom*. Berkeley and Los Angeles: University of California Press, 1995.

Catterall, Helen Tunnicliff, ed. *Judicial Cases Concerning American Slavery and the Negro*. 5 vols. Washington, D.C.: Carnegie Institution of Washington, 1926–37.

"Census of 1860." *Pine and Palm*, June 8, 1861, n.p.

"Census of Colored Americans." *Pine and Palm*, September 7, 1861, n.p.

Chesnutt, Charles W. *The Colonel's Dream*. 1905; Boston: Gregg, 1968.

———. *The House Behind the Cedars*. 1900; New York: Collier-Macmillan, 1969.

———. *The Marrow of Tradition*. 1901. Ann Arbor: University of Michigan Press, 1969.

————. *Paul Marehand, F.M.C.* Jackson: University Press of Mississippi, 1998.

————. "The Web of Circumstance." In *Collected Stories of Charles W. Chesnutt,* ed. William L. Andrews, 249–65. New York: Mentor, 1992.

————. "What is a White Man?" *New York Independent,* May 30, 1889, 5–6.

————. *The Wife of His Youth and Other Stories of the Color Line.* New York: Houghton Mifflin, 1899.

Clark, Alexander. "Socialism." *A.M.E. Church Review* 3.1 (1886): 49–54.

Clark, Edgar Rogie. "Psalmnettes for the Dark Seraph." *Masses and Mainstream,* ca. March 1951. Undated photocopy from the Schomburg Center for Research in Black Studies.

Clawson, Thomas. "The Wilmington Race Riot in 1898. Recollections and Memories." PC.777.1. Louis T. Moore Collection, Department of Archives and History, State of North Carolina Department of Cultural Resources, Raleigh.

Clinton, Catherine, and Nina Silber, eds. *Divided Houses: Gender and the Civil War.* New York: Oxford University Press, 1992.

Cohen, William. *At Freedom's Edge: Black Mobility and the Southern White Quest for Racial Control.* Baton Rouge: Louisiana State University Press, 1991.

Corrothers, James David. *The Black Cat Club: Negro Humor and Folk Lore.* New York: Funk and Wagnalls, 1902.

Countryman, Edward. *Americans: A Collision of Histories.* New York: Hill and Wang, 1996.

Cover, Robert. *Narrative, Violence, and the Law: The Essays of Robert Cover.* Ed. Martha Minow, Michael Ryan, and Austin Sarat. Ann Arbor: University of Michigan Press, 1993.

Crane, Gregg D. "The Lexicon of Rights, Power, and Community in *Blake:* Martin R. Delany's Dissent from Dred Scott." *American Literature* 68 (1996): 527–53.

Crenshaw, Kimberle, et al., eds. *Critical Race Theory: The Key Writings That Formed the Movement.* New York: New Press, 1995.

Davis, Norah. *The Northerner.* New York: Grossett and Dunlap, 1905.

Davis, Peggy C. "Law as Microaggression." *Yale Law Journal* 98.8 (1989): 1559–77.

De Jongh, James, *Vicious Modernism: Black Harlem and the Literary Imagination.* New York: Cambridge University Press, 1990.

Decker, Jeffrey Louis, ed. *The Black Aesthetic Movement.* Vol. 8 of *Dictionary of Literary Biography Documentary Series.* Detroit: Gale, 1991.

Delany, Martin J. *Blake, or The Huts of America.* 1859–61. Ed. Floyd J. Miller. Boston: Beacon, 1970.

Detter, Thomas. *Nellie Brown or The Jealous Wife, with Other Sketches.* 1871; Lincoln: University of Nebraska Press, 1996.

Diamond, Raymond T., and Robert J. Cottrol. "Codifying Caste: Louisiana's Racial Classification Scheme and the Fourteenth Amendment." *Loyola Law Review* 29.2 (1983): 255–85.

Douglas, Ann. *Terrible Honesty: Mongrel Manhattan in the 1920s.* New York: Farrar, Straus and Giroux, 1995.

Douglass, Frederick. "The Heroic Slave." In *Violence in the Black Imagination:*

Essays and Documents, ed. Ronald Takaki, 37–77. Expanded edition. New York: Oxford University Press, 1993.

———. *Narrative of the Life of Frederick Douglass, an American Slave, Written by Himself.* 1845; New York: Signet, 1968.

Doyle, Laura. *Bordering on the Body: The Racial Matrix of Modern Fiction and Culture.* New York: Oxford University Press, 1994.

Du Bois, W. E. B. "Criteria of Negro Art." In *The Norton Anthology of African American Literature,* ed. Henry Louis Gates Jr. and Nellie Y. McKay, 752–59. New York: Norton, 1997.

———. *Dark Princess, a Romance.* 1928; Millwood, N.Y.: Kraus-Thomson, 1974.

———. *The Philadelphia Negro: A Social Study.* 1899; Philadelphia: University of Pennsylvania Press, 1996.

———. *The Souls of Black Folk.* 1903; Greenwich, Conn.: Fawcett, 1961.

Dubey, Madhu. *Black Women Novelists and the Nationalist Aesthetic.* Bloomington: Indiana University Press, 1994.

duCille, Ann. *The Coupling Convention: Sex, Text, and Tradition in Black Women's Fiction.* New York: Oxford University Press, 1993.

Dunbar, Paul Laurence. "An Old-Time Christmas." In *The Strength of Gideon and other Stories.* 1899; New York: Arno Press and the New York Times, 1969. 229–38.

———. *The Sport of the Gods.* 1902; New York: Arno Press and the New York Times, 1969.

———. *The Strength of Gideon and other Stories.* 1899; New York: Arno Press and the New York Times, 1969.

Early, Gerald. *The Culture of Bruising: Essays on Prizefighting, Literature, and Modern American Culture.* Hopewell, Va.: Ecco, 1994.

———. *Lure and Loathing: Essays on Race, Identity, and the Ambivalence of Assimilation.* New York: Penguin, 1993.

———. *Tuxedo Junction: Essays on American Culture.* Hopewell, Va.: Ecco, 1989.

Edwards, Laura F. "'The Marriage Covenant Is at the Foundation of All Our Rights': The Politics of Slave Marriages in North Carolina after Emancipation." *Law and History Review* 14.1 (1996): 81–124.

Elder, Carol E. "'The Discovery of America': Literary Nationalism in the Criticism of Black American Literature." Ph.D. diss., University of Pittsburgh, 1972. Ann Arbor: UMI, 1973.

Ellison, Ralph. "Editorial." *Negro Quarterly* 1.4 (1943): 301.

———. *Invisible Man.* 1952; New York: Random/Vintage, 1995.

———. "Perspective of Literature." In *Going to the Territory.* New York: Random House, 1986. 321–38.

Ernest, John. *Resistance and Reformation in Nineteenth-Century African-American Literature: Brown, Wilson, Jacobs, Delany, Douglass, and Harper.* Jackson: University Press of Mississippi, 1995.

Evans, William McKee. *Ballots and Fence Rails: Reconstruction on the Lower Cape Fear.* 1965; reprint with a foreword by Charles Joyner, Athens: University of Georgia Press, 1995.

Fairman, Charles. *Reconstruction and Reunion, 1864–88.* Vol. 2, pt. 2 of *The Oliver*

Wendell Holmes Devise History of the Supreme Court of the United States. New York: Macmillan, 1987.

Farnsworth, Robert M. Introduction to *The Marrow of Tradition,* by Charles W. Chesnutt. Ann Arbor: University of Michigan Press, 1969.

Fauset, Jessie Redmon. *The Chinaberry Tree: A Novel of American Life.* New York: Stokes, 1931.

———. *Plum Bun: A Novel without a Moral.* 1928; Boston: Beacon, 1990.

———. *There Is Confusion.* 1924; Boston: Northeastern University Press, 1989.

Fede, Andrew. *People without Rights: An Interpretation of the Fundamentals of the Law of Slavery in the U.S. South.* New York: Garland, 1992.

Ferguson, Alfred R. "The Abolition of Blacks in Abolitionist Fiction, 1830–1860." *Journal of Black Studies* 5.2 (1974): 134–56.

Ferguson, Robert. *Law and Letters in American Culture.* Cambridge: Harvard University Press, 1984.

Finkelman, Paul, ed. *The Age of Jim Crow: Segregation from the End of Reconstruction to the Great Depression.* Vol. 4 of *Race, Law, and American History, 1700–1990.* New York: Garland, 1992.

———. "Exploring Southern Legal History." *North Carolina Law Review* 64.1 (1985): 77–116.

———, ed. *Free Blacks, Slaves, and Slaveowners in Civil and Criminal Courts: The Pamphlet Literature,* Vols. 1 and 2, series 6, of *Slavery, Race, and the American Legal System, 1700–1872,* ed. Finkelman. New York: Garland, 1988.

———. *An Imperfect Union: Slavery, Federalism, and Comity.* Chapel Hill: University of North Carolina Press, 1981.

———, ed. *Slavery and the Law.* Madison, Wis.: Madison House, 1994.

———. *Slavery in the Courtroom: An Annotated Bibliography of American Cases.* Washington, D.C.: Library of Congress, 1985.

———, ed. *Statutes on Slavery: The Pamphlet Literature* Vols. 1 and 2, series 7, of *Slavery, Race and the American Legal System, 1700–1872,* ed. Finkelman. New York: Garland, 1988.

The First Line of Defense. New York: National Association for the Advancement of Colored People, 1929.

Fisher, Rudolph. "City of Refuge." In *The City of Refuge: The Collected Stories of Rudolph Fisher,* ed. John McClusky Jr., 3–16. Columbia: University of Missouri Press, 1987.

———. *The Conjure-Man Dies: A Mystery Tale of Dark Harlem.* 1932; New York: Arno Press and the New York Times, 1971.

———. "High Yaller." In *The City of Refuge: The Collected Stories of Rudolph Fisher,* ed. John McClusky Jr., 81–97. Columbia: University of Missouri Press, 1987.

———. "The South Lingers On." In *The City of Refuge: The Collected Stories of Rudolph Fisher,* ed. and introduction by John McClusky Jr., 30–39. Columbia: University of Missouri Press, 1987.

———. *The Walls of Jericho.* New York: Knopf, 1928.

Fisher, William W., III. "Ideology and Imagery in the Law of Slavery." *Chicago-Kent Law Review* 68 (1993): 1051–83.

France, Alan W. "Misogyny and Appropriation in Wright's *Native Son*." *Modern Fiction Studies* 34 (autumn 1988): 413–23.

Franklin, Buck Colbert. *My Life and an Era: the Autobiography of Buck Colbert Franklin*. Ed. John Hope Franklin and John Whittington Franklin. Baton Rouge: Louisiana State University Press, 1997.

Franklin, H. Bruce. *Prison Literature in America: The Victim as Criminal and Artist*. Rev. ed. Westport, Conn.: Lawrence Hill, 1982.

Franklin, Vincent P. *Black Self-Determination: A Cultural History of the Faith of the Fathers*. Westport, Conn.: Lawrence Hill, 1984.

Freeman, Elaine Kaplan. "Harvey Johnson and Everett Waring: A Study of Leadership in the Baltimore Community, 1880–1900." M.A. thesis, George Washington University, 1986.

Freund, Paul. *On Law and Justice*. Cambridge: Belknap Press of Harvard University Press, 1968.

Frye, Northrop. *Anatomy of Criticism*. Princeton: Princeton University Press, 1971.

Garvey, John, and Noel Ignatiev, eds. *Race Traitor: Treason to Whiteness Is Loyalty to Humanity*. Nos. 1–5. 1995–96.

Gates, Henry Louis, Jr. "Dept. of Disputation: The Chitlin' Circuit." *New Yorker*, February 3, 1997, 44–55.

———. *The Signifying Monkey: A Theory of Afro-American Literary Criticism*. New York: Oxford University Press, 1988.

"General Orders, No. 8} Marriage Rules." Headquarters, Assistant Commissioner, Bureau of Refugees, Freedmen, and Abandoned Lands. South Carolina, Georgia, and Florida. Beaufort, South Carolina, August 11, 1865.

Gerard, Philip. *Cape Fear Rising*. Winston-Salem, N.C.: John F. Blair, 1994.

Giddings, Paula. *When and Where I Enter: The Impact of Black Women on Race and Sex in America*. New York: Morrow, 1984.

Gillman, Susan. "The Mulatto, Tragic or Triumphant? The Nineteenth-Century American Race Melodrama." In *The Culture of Sentiment: Race, Gender, and Sentimentality in Nineteenth-Century America*, ed. Shirley Samuels, 221–43. New York: Oxford University Press, 1992.

Gleason, Philip. "American Identity and Americanization." In *The Harvard Encyclopedia of American Ethnic Groups*, ed. Stephan Thernstrom, 31–58. Cambridge: Belknap Press of Harvard University Press, 1980.

Goings, Kenneth W. *"The NAACP Comes of Age": The Defeat of Judge John J. Parker*. Bloomington: Indiana University Press, 1990.

Goodell, Abner Cheney, Jr. *The Trial and Execution, for Petit Treason, of Mark and Phillis, Slaves of Capt. John Codman*. Cambridge, Mass.: John Wilson and Son, 1883.

Goodrich, Peter. "*Antirrhesis:* Polemical Structures of Common Law Thought." Unpublished paper.

Graham, Howard Jay. *Everyman's Constitution: Historical Essays on the Fourteenth Amendment, the "Conspiracy Theory," and American Constitutionalism*. Madison: State Historical Society of Wisconsin, 1968.

Grant, Joanne, ed. *Black Protest: History, Documents, and Analyses, 1619 to the Present*. Greenwich, Conn.: Fawcett, 1969.

Greenfield, Nathan Monte. "'Their Position (S) Must Be Mined': Charles W. Chesnutt's Assault on Racial Thinking." Ph.D. diss., McGill University, 1994.

Grier, William H., and Price M. Cobbs. *Black Rage*. New York: Basic, 1968.

Griffin, Farah Jasmine. *"Who Set You Flowin'?": The African-American Migration Narrative*. New York: Oxford University Press, 1995.

Griggs, Sutton Elbert. *Imperium in Imperio: A Study of the Negro Race Problem, A Novel*. 1899; Salem, N.H.: Ayer, 1992.

Grimes, William. *Life of William Grimes, The Runaway Slave, Brought Down to the Present Time. Written By Himself*. 1855. In *Five Black Lives: The Autobiographies of Venture Smith, James Mars, William Grimes, the Rev. G. W. Offley, James L. Smith*. Middletown, Conn.: Wesleyan University Press, 1987. 61–128.

Grossberg, Michael. *Governing the Hearth: Law and the Family in Nineteenth-Century America*. Chapel Hill: University of North Carolina Press, 1985.

Guild, June Purcell. *Black Laws of Virginia: A Summary of the Legislative Acts of Virginia from Earliest Times to the Present*. Richmond: Whiltet and Shepperson, 1936.

Gunning, Sandra. *Race, Rape, and Lynching: The Red Record of American Literature, 1890–1912*. New York: Oxford University Press, 1996.

Gutman, Herbert G. *The Black Family in Slavery and Freedom, 1750–1925*. New York: Vintage, 1977.

Hall, Jacquelyn Dowd. *Revolt against Chivalry: Jessie Daniel Ames and the Women's Campaign against Lynching*. New York: Columbia University Press, 1974.

Haney, Craig. "Criminal Justice and the Nineteenth Century Paradigm: The Triumph of Psychological Individualism in the 'Formative Era.'" In *Law and Jurisprudence in American History: Cases and Materials*, ed. Stephen B. Presser and Jamil S. Zainaldin, 479–91. 3d ed. American Casebook Series. St. Paul: West, 1995.

Hardack, Richard Bryan. "'The Seductive God': Pan and Transcendental Individualism in American Literature." Ph.D. diss., University of California, Berkeley, 1994.

Harper, Frances E. W. *Iola Leroy, or Shadows Uplifted*. 1892; New York: Oxford University Press, 1988.

Harris, Cheryl I. "Whiteness as Property." *Harvard Law Review* 106 (June 1993): 1707–91.

Harris, Paul. *Black Rage Confronts the Law*. New York: New York University Press, 1997.

Harris, Trudier. *Exorcising Blackness: Historical and Literary Lynching and Burning Rituals*. Bloomington: Indiana University Press, 1984.

Harrison, Alferdteen, ed. *Black Exodus: The Great Migration from the American South*. Jackson: University Press of Mississippi, 1991.

Harrold, Stanley. *The Abolitionists and the South, 1831–1861*. Lexington: University of Kentucky Press, 1995.

Hatch, James V., ed., and Ted Shine, consultant. *Black Theatre, U.S.A. Forty-five Plays by Black Americans, 1847–1974*. New York: Free Press, 1974.

Heinzleman, Susan Sage. "Riding the Black Ram: Custom and Law." Paper presented to the conference "Law, Literature and Culture: The Letter of the Law," University of Southern California, Los Angeles, February 28–March 1, 1997.

Helmreich, William B. *Afro-Americans and Africa: Black Nationalism at the Crossroads.* Westport, Conn.: Greenwood, 1977.

Herder, Johann Gottfried von. *Outlines of a Philosophy of the History of Man.* Trans. T. O. Churchill. 2d ed. 2 vols. London, 1803.

———. *Reflections on the Philosophy of the History of Mankind.* Trans. Frank E. Manuel. Abridged ed. Chicago: University of Chicago Press, 1968.

Herod, Augustina, and Charles C. Herod. *Afro-American Nationalism: An Annotated Bibliography of Militant Separatist and Nationalist Literature.* New York: Garland, 1986.

Higginbotham, A. Leon, Jr. "Opening Argument." In *Black Judges on Justice: Perspectives from the Bench,* ed. Linn Washington, 3–23. New York: New Press, 1994.

Himes, Chester. *If He Hollers Let Him Go.* 1947; New York: Thunder's Mouth Press, 1993.

———. *Lonely Crusade.* 1947; New York: Thunder's Mouth Press, 1986.

———. "Negro Martyrs Are Needed." In *Black on Black: Baby Sister and Selected Writings.* New York: Doubleday, 1963. 230–35.

———. *Plan B.* Ed. Michel Fabre and Robert E. Skinner. Jackson: University Press of Mississippi, 1993.

Hine, Darlene Clark. "Rape and the Inner Lives of Black Women in the Middle West: Preliminary Thoughts on the Culture of Dissemblance." In *Words of Fire: An Anthology of African-American Feminist Thought,* ed. Beverly Guy-Sheftall, 380–87. New York: New Press, 1995.

Hodes, Martha. "Sex across the Color Line: White Women and Black Men in the Nineteenth Century American South." Ph.D. diss., Princeton University, 1991.

Hoffman, David. *A Course of Legal Study; Respectfully Addressed to the Students of Law in the United States.* 1817; New York: Arno Press, 1972.

hooks, bell. "Postmodern Blackness." *Postmodern Culture* 1.1 (1990): 1–15.

Hopkins, Pauline E. "Bro'r Abr'm Jimson's Wedding, A Christmas Story." 1901. In *Invented Lives: Narratives of Black Women, 1860–1950,* ed. Mary Helen Washington, 130–46. Garden City, N.Y.: Anchor, 1987.

———. *Contending Forces: A Romance Illustrative of Negro Life North and South.* 1900; New York: Oxford University Press, 1988.

Horsmanden, Daniel. *The New-York Conspiracy, or a History of the Negro Plot with the Journal of the Proceedings against the Conspirators at New-York in the Years 1741–2.* Ed. Thomas J. Davis. 1810; Boston: Beacon, 1971.

Horwitz, Martin. *The Transformation of American Law, 1780–1860.* Cambridge: Harvard University Press, 1977.

Howard, Oliver Otis. *Autobiography of Oliver Otis Howard, Major General, United States Army.* 1907; Freeport, N.Y.: Books for Libraries Press, 1971.

Hudson, Larry E., Jr. *To Have and to Hold: Slave Work and Family Life in Antebellum South Carolina.* Athens: University of Georgia Press, 1997.

Hughes, Langston. *The Ways of White Folks.* 1933; New York: Random, 1990.

Hunter, Eures. "David B. Fulton—Jack Thorne—His Interesting Career as a Writer." *Cape Fear Journal,* February 10, 1930. Typescript. David Bryant Fulton Papers, Schomburg Center for Research in Black Culture.

Hurston, Zora Neale. *Jonah's Gourd Vine.* 1934; Philadelphia: Lippincott, 1971.

——. *Their Eyes Were Watching God.* 1937; Greenwich, Conn.: Fawcett, 1969.

Hutchinson, George. *The Harlem Renaissance in Black and White.* Cambridge: Harvard University Press, 1995.

Hyde, Alan. *Bodies of Law.* Princeton: Princeton University Press, 1997.

Ignatiev, Noel. *How the Irish Became White.* New York: Routledge, 1995.

Jacobs, Harriet Brent (Linda Brent). *Incidents in the Life of a Slave Girl.* Ed. L. Maria Child. 1861; New York: Harcourt Brace Jovanovich, 1973.

James, Henry. *The American.* New York: Scribners, 1907.

Jameson, Fredric. *The Political Unconscious: Narrative as a Socially Symbolic Act.* Ithaca: Cornell University Press, 1981.

Jehlen, Myra. *American Incarnation: The Individual, the Nation, and the Continent.* Cambridge: Harvard University Press, 1986.

Jenkins, Betty, and Susan Phillips. *Black Separatism: A Bibliography.* Westport, Conn.: Greenwood, 1976.

Johnson, Franklin. *The Development of State Legislation Concerning the Free Negro.* N.p.: n.p., 1918.

Johnson, Harvey. *White Man's Failure In Government.* "This pamphlet is a Chapter from a book to be published in the near future, entitled: 'The Nation From a New Point of View.' Press Of AfroAmerican Co., 307 St. Paul St., Baltimore, 1900." Schomburg Center for Research in Black Culture.

Johnson, James Weldon. *The Autobiography of an Ex-Coloured Man.* In *Three Negro Classics.* New York: Avon, 1965.

——. *Black Manhattan.* 1930; New York: Atheneum, 1972.

Jordan, June. "A New Politics of Sexuality." In *Words of Fire: An Anthology of African-American Feminist Thought,* ed. Beverly Guy-Sheftall, 407–11. New York: New Press, 1995.

——. "On Richard Wright and Zora Neale Hurston: Notes toward a Balancing of Love and Hatred." *Black World* 23 (August 1974): 4–8.

Joyce, James. *Ulysses.* New York: Modern Library, 1946.

Kahn, Robert M. "The Political Ideology of Martin Delany." *Journal of Black Studies* 14.4 (1984): 415–40.

Kaminski, John P., ed. *A Necessary Evil? Slavery and the Debate over the Constitution.* Madison: University of Wisconsin Press, 1995.

Kaplan, Carla. "Narrative Contracts and Emancipatory Readers: *Incidents in the Life of a Slave Girl.*" *Yale Journal of Criticism* 6 (1993): 93–119.

Karst, Kenneth L. *Belonging to America: Equal Citizenship and the Constitution.* New Haven: Yale University Press, 1989.

Karsten, Peter. *Heart versus Head: Judge-Made Law in Nineteenth-Century America.* Studies in Legal History. Chapel Hill: University of North Carolina Press, 1997.

Kelley, Robin D. G. *Race Rebels: Culture, Politics, and the Black Working Class.* New York: Free Press, 1994.

Kellner, Bruce. *The Harlem Renaissance: A Historical Dictionary of the Era.* New York: Methuen, 1987.

Kennedy, Randall L. "Racial Critiques of Legal Academia." *Harvard Law Review* 102 (1989): 1745–1819.

Kilson, Martin. "Dynamics of Nationalism and Political Militancy among Negro Americans." In *Racial Tensions and National Identity,* ed. Ernest Q. Campbell, 97–114. Nashville: Vanderbilt University Press, 1972.

Kisselhoff, Jeff. *You Must Remember This: An Oral History of Manhattan from the 1890s to World War II.* New York: Harcourt, 1989.

Kleinhans, MarthaMarie. "The Creative Self as a Site of Internormativity: A Nonessentialist Aesthetic Approach to Legal Pluralism." McGill Faculty of Law, 1996. Typescript.

Koger, A. Briscoe. *Harvey Johnson—Pioneer Civic Leader.* Baltimore: A. Briscoe Koger, 1957.

Larmore, Charles E. *The Romantic Legacy.* New York: Columbia University Press, 1996.

Larsen, Nella. *Passing.* 1929; New York: Collier, 1971.

Lauter, Paul. "Little White Sheep, or How I Learned to Dress Blue." *Yale Journal of Criticism* 8 (1995): 103–29.

Lears, T. J. Jackson. *No Place of Grace: Antimodernism and the Transformation of American Culture, 1880–1920.* 1983; Chicago: University of Chicago Press, 1994.

Lebsock, Suzanne. *The Free Women of St. Petersburg: Status and Culture in a Southern Town, 1784–1860.* New York: W. W. Norton, 1985.

Leonard, Walter J. "The Development of the Black Bar." *Annals of the American Academy of Political and Social Science* 407 (May 1973): 134–43.

Levine, Lawrence W. *Black Culture and Black Consciousness: Afro-American Folk Thought from Slavery to Freedom.* New York: Oxford University Press, 1977.

Lewis, David Levering. *W. E. B. Du Bois: Biography of a Race, 1868–1919.* New York: Henry Holt, 1993.

———. *When Harlem Was in Vogue.* New York: Knopf, 1981.

Lock, Helen. *A Case of Mis-Taken Identity: Detective Undercurrents in Recent African American Fiction.* New York: Peter Lang, 1994.

Locke, Alain. "The New Negro." 1926. In *The Norton Anthology of African American Literature,* ed. Henry Louis Gates, Jr. and Nellie Y. McKay, 961–70. New York: Norton, 1997.

Logan, Rayford W. *The Negro in American Life and Thought: The Nadir, 1877–1910.* New York: Dial, 1954.

Lynch, John. *The Spanish-American Revolutions, 1808–1826.* New York: Dutton, 1973.

Mailer, Norman. *The White Negro.* San Francisco: City Lights, [1957].

Marcus, Lisa. " 'The Pull of Race and Blood and Kindred': American Narrative, 1850–1940." Ph.D. diss., Rutgers University, 1995.

Mark, Gregory A. "The Personification of the Business Corporation in American Law." *University of Chicago Law Review* 54.4 (1987): 1441–83.

Marren, Susan Marie. "Passing for American: Establishing American Identity in the Work of James Weldon Johnson, F. Scott Fitzgerald, Nella Larsen, and Gertrude Stein." Ph.D. diss., University of Michigan, 1995.

Martyn, Byron. "Racism in the United States: A History of Anti-Miscegenation Legislation and Litigation." Ph.D. diss., University of South Carolina, 1979.

Matthewson, Gwen C. "In Dialogue with the Law: *The Marrow of Tradition.*" Paper presented to the conference "Law, Literature and Culture: The Letter of the Law," University of Southern California, Los Angeles, February 28–March 1, 1997.

McAdoo, Bill. *Pre–Civil War Black Nationalism.* New York: D. Walker Press, 1983.

McClay, Wilfred M. *The Masterless: Self and Society in Modern America.* Chapel Hill: University of North Carolina Press, 1994.

McClusky, John, Jr. Introduction. *The City of Refuge: The Collected Stories of Rudolph Fisher.* Columbia: University of Missouri Press, 1987. xi–xxxix.

McDonald, Forrest. *Alexander Hamilton: A Biography.* New York: Norton, 1979.

McHenry, Elizabeth. "Re-reading Literary Legacy: New Considerations of the Nineteenth-Century African American Reader and Writer." Paper presented to the Annual Meeting of the Modern Language Association, Washington, D.C., December 29, 1996.

McKay, Claude, *Harlem: Negro Metropolis.* New York: Dutton, 1948.

McLaurin, Melton A. *Celia, a Slave.* Athens: University of Georgia Press, 1991.

McMillan, Neil R. *Dark Journey: Black Mississippians in the Age of Jim Crow.* Urbana: University of Illinois Press, 1989.

McPherson, James Alan. "Elbow Room." In *Elbow Room.* New York: Scribner's, 1987. 215–41.

———. "Junior and John Doe." In *Lure and Loathing: Essays on Race, Identity, and the Ambivalence of Assimilation,* ed. Gerald Early, 175–93. New York: Penguin, 1993.

———. "A Sense of Story." In *Elbow Room.* New York: Scribner's, 1987. 193–214.

Meier, August. *Negro Thought in America, 1880–1915: Racial Ideologies in the Age of Booker T. Washington.* 1963; Ann Arbor: University of Michigan Press, 1988.

Merrifield, Andy, and Erik Swyngedouw, eds. *The Urbanization of Injustice.* New York: Washington Square and New York University Press, 1997.

Michaels, Walter Benn. *Our America: Nativism, Modernism, and Pluralism.* Durham: Duke University Press, 1995.

Micheaux, Oscar. *The Masquerade.* New York: Book Supply Co., 1947.

———. *Within Our Gates.* 1919. Preserved and edited 1993. United States Library of Congress.

Middleton, Stephen. "The Fugitive Slave Crisis in Cincinnati, 1850–1860: Resistance, Enforcement, and Black Refugees." *Journal of Negro History* 72 (winter–spring 1987): 20–32.

Midnight Shadow. Dir. and prod. George Randol. Distributed by Sack Amusement Enterprises, 1939.

"Milestone." <www.cs.sfu.ca/ ~npd/ personal/ comics/ milestone/ htm1>. April 20, 1999.

Minutes of the State Convention, of the Colored Citizens of Ohio, Convened at Columbus, January 15–18, 1851. In *A Documentary History of the Negro People in the*

United States: From Colonial Times through the Civil War, ed. Herbert Aptheker, 316–17. New York: Citadel, 1962.

Monda, Kimberly. "Self-Delusion and Self-Sacrifice in Nella Larsen's *Quicksand.*" *African American Review* 31 (1997): 23–39.

Montgomery, Maxine Lavon. *The Apocalypse in African-American Fiction.* Gainesville: University Press of Florida, 1996.

Morris, Thomas D. *Southern Slavery and the Law, 1619–1860.* Chapel Hill: University of North Carolina Press, 1996.

Morrison, Toni. *Beloved.* New York: Knopf, 1987.

———. *Jazz.* New York: Plume/Penguin, 1993.

———. "The Official Story: Dead Man Golfing." In *Birth of a Nation'hood: Gaze, Script, and Spectacle in the O. J. Simpson Case,* ed. Toni Morrison and Claudia Brodsky Lacour, vii–xxviii. New York: Pantheon, 1997.

———. *Paradise.* New York: Knopf, 1998.

———. *Playing in the Dark: Whiteness in the Literary Imagination.* Cambridge: Harvard University Press, 1992.

Moses, Wilson Jeremiah. *Alexander Crummell: A Study of Civilization and Discontent.* New York: Oxford University Press, 1989.

———. *Black Messiahs and Uncle Toms: Social and Literary Manipulations of a Religious Myth.* University Park: Pennsylvania State University Press, 1982.

———. *The Wings of Ethiopia: Studies in African-American Life and Letters.* Ames: Iowa State University Press, 1990.

Mossell, Aaron A. "The Unconstitutionality of the Law against Miscegenation." *A.M.E. Church Review* 5.2 (1888): 72–79.

Mossell, Mrs. N. F. "Tell the North that We are Rising." *A.M.E. Church Review* 6.1 (1889): 64–65.

———. *The Work of the Afro-American Woman.* 1894; Philadelphia: Geo. S. Ferguson, 1908.

Motley, Willard. *Knock on Any Door.* 1947; New York: Signet, 1950.

NAACP Papers. Microfilm. Schomburg Center for Research in Black Studies.

Nabokov, Vladimir. *Lolita.* 1955; New York: Vintage, 1989.

Neal, Larry. "The Black Arts Movement." *Drama Review* 12.4 (1968): 29–39.

The Negro in Literature. Service Bureau for Intercultural Education. New York City. WPA for NYC Project 65–97–295. Sub-project 15. (Ca. 1937). Schomburg Center for Research in Black Studies.

Newman, Judi. "'Dis ain't Gimmee, Florida': Zora Neale Hurston's Indian Givers." Paper presented to the Annual Meeting of the American Literature Association, San Diego, May 28, 1998.

Nickel, John. "Race, Class, Gender, and Eugenics in the Fiction of Pauline Hopkins." Paper presented to the Annual Meeting of the American Literature Association, Baltimore, May 23, 1997.

North, Michael. *The Dialect of Modernism: Race, Language, and Twentieth-Century Literature.* New York: Oxford University Press, 1994.

Novkov, Julie. "Toward a Racist Theory of the State: Post–Civil War Anti-Miscegenation Prosecutions." Paper presented to the Annual Meeting of the Law and Society Association, Chicago, May 27, 1993.

Nunn, Kenneth B. "The Trial as Text: Allegory, Myth, and Symbol in the

Adversarial Criminal Process—a Critique of the Role of the Public Defender and a Proposal for Reform." *American Criminal Law Review* 32.3 (1995): 743–822.

O'Brien, Michael. "The Lineaments of Southern Antebellum Romanticism." In *Rethinking the South: Essays in Intellectual History*. Baltimore: Johns Hopkins University Press, 1988. 38–56.

Offley, G. W. *A Narrative of the Life and Labors of The Rev. G. W. Offley, A Colored Man and Local Preacher.* 1860. In *Five Black Lives: The Autobiographies of Venture Smith, James Mars, William Grimes, the Rev. G. W. Offley, James L. Smith.* Middletown, Conn.: Wesleyan University Press, 1987. 131–37.

Olsen, Otto H. *Carpetbagger's Crusade: The Life of Albion Winegar Tourgee.* Baltimore: Johns Hopkins University Press, 1965.

———, ed. *The Thin Disguise: Turning Point in Negro History—Plessy vs. Ferguson—a Documentary Presentation, 1864–1896.* New York: Humanities Press, 1967.

Omolade, Barbara. "Hearts of Darkness." In *Words of Fire: An Anthology of African-American Feminist Thought,* ed. Beverly Guy-Sheftall, 362–78. New York: New Press, 1995.

O'Neill, William. *Divorce in the Progressive Era.* New Haven: Yale University Press, 1967.

Oshinsky, David. *"Worse Than Slavery": Parchman Farm and the Ordeal of Jim Crow Justice.* New York: Free Press, 1996.

Osterweis, Rollin. *Romanticism and Nationalism in the Old South.* New Haven: Yale University Press, 1949.

Ottley, Roi. *The Negro in New York: An Informal Social History, 1625–1940.* New York: Praeger, 1969.

Owens, Leslie Howard. *This Species of Property: Slave Life and Culture in the Old South.* New York: Oxford University Press, 1976.

Parker, Kellis E., and Betty J. Stebman. "Legal Education for Blacks." *Annals of the American Academy of Political and Social Science* 407 (May 1973): 142–52.

Parnham, Geo. D. Letter, July 25, 1837. Slavery Collection. Schomburg Center for Research in Black Culture.

Paul, William George. "The Shadow of Equality: The Negro in Baltimore, 1864–1911." Ph.D. diss., University of Wisconsin, 1972. Ann Arbor: UMI, 1977.

Peller, Gary. "Race Consciousness." In *Critical Race Theory: The Key Writings That Formed the Movement,* ed. Kimberle Crenshaw et al., 127–58. New York: New Press, 1995.

Penn, I. Garland. *The Afro-American Press, and its Editors.* Springfield, Mass.: Willey and Co., 1891.

People vs. Larry Flynt. Dir. Milos Forman. Columbia/Phoenix, 1996.

Peterson, Bernard L., Jr. *Early Black Playwrights and Dramatic Writers: A Biographical Directory and Catalog of Plays, Films, and Broadcasting Scripts.* New York: Greenwood, 1990.

Porter, Horace A. *Stealing the Fire: The Art and Protest of James Baldwin.* Middletown, Conn.: Wesleyan University Press, 1989.

Powell, Adam Clayton, Jr. *Marching Blacks: An Interpretive History of the Rise of the Common Man.* New York: Dial, 1945.

Prather, H. Leon. *We Have Taken a City: The Wilmington Racial Massacre and Coup of 1898.* Rutherford, N.J.: Fairleigh Dickenson University Press, 1984.

Priest, Christopher. "Creating a Super Hero: Interview with Christopher Priest." *Mediadome.* CNET. <www.cnet.com>. March 26, 1997.

"Prospectus." *Pine and Palm,* June 29, 1861, n.p.

Radin, Margaret J. "Property and Personhood." *Stanford Law Review* 34 (1982): 957–1015.

Rampersad, Arnold. "Langston Hughes and Approaches to Modernism in the Harlem Renaissance." In *The Harlem Renaissance: Revaluations,* ed. Amritjit Singh et al., 49–71. New York: Greenwood, 1989.

———. "W. H. Thomas, W. E. B. Du Bois, and the Struggle for the Black Soul." Paper presented to the Annual Meeting of the Modern Language Association, Washington, D.C., December 30, 1996.

Rapport, Sara. "The Freedmen's Bureau as a Legal Agent for Black Men and Women in Georgia: 1865–1868." *Georgia Historical Quarterly* 73.1 (1989): 26–53.

Reddick, Lawrence Dunbar. "The Negro in the New Orleans Press, 1850–1860; a Study in Attitudes and Propaganda." Ph.D. diss., University of Chicago, 1939.

Reed, Ishmael. *Reckless Eyeballing.* New York: St. Martin's, 1986.

Review of *The Supremacy of the Constitution, and the Sovereignty of the People,* by Charles W. Mossell. *A.M.E. Church Review* 4.3 (1887): 344.

Riis, Jacob. *How the Other Half Lives.* New York: Scribner's, 1902.

Rodgers, Lawrence R. *Canaan Bound: The African-American Great Migration Novel.* Urbana: University of Illinois Press, 1997.

———. "Dorothy West's *The Living Is Easy* and the Ideal of Southern Folk Community." *African American Review* 26 (1992): 161–72.

———. "Paul Laurence Dunbar's *The Sport of the Gods:* The Doubly Conscious Worlds of Plantation Fiction, Migration, and Ascent." *American Literary Realism* 24 (spring 1992): 42–57.

Roediger, David R. *The Wages of Whiteness: Race and the Making of the American Working Class.* New York: Verso, 1991.

Rushdy, Ashraf H. A. "Representing the Constitution: Embodiments of America in Barbara Chase Riboud's 'Echo of Lions.'" *Critique: Studies in Contemporary Fiction* 36.4 (1995): 258–81.

Russell, Katheryn K. *The Color of Crime: Racial Hoaxes, White Fear, Black Protectionism, Police Harassment, and Other Macroaggressions.* New York: New York University Press, 1997.

"A Sage Conclusion." *Pine and Palm,* June 22, 1861, n.p.

Saks, Eva. "Representing Miscegenation Law." *Raritan* 8.2 (1988): 39–69.

Salvatore, Nick. *We All Got History: The Memory Books of Amos Webber.* New York: Random House/Times Books, 1996.

Salvino, Dana Nelson. "The Word in Black and White: Ideologies of Race and Literacy in Antebellum America." in *Reading in America: Literature and Social*

History, ed. Cathy N. Davidson, 140–56. Baltimore: Johns Hopkins University Press, 1989.

Sammons, Jeffrey. *Beyond the Ring: The Role of Boxing in American Society*. Urbana: University of Illinois Press, 1988.

Samuels, Shirley. "The Identity of Slavery." In *The Culture of Sentiment: Race, Gender, and Sentimentality in Nineteenth-Century America*, ed. Samuels, 157–71. New York: Oxford University Press, 1992.

Sanda [Walter H. Stowers and W. H. Anderson]. *Appointed: An American Novel*. 1894; New York: AMS, 1977.

Sarat, Austin, ed. *Race, Law, and Culture: Reflections on Brown v. Board of Education*. New York: Oxford University Press, 1997.

Scales-Trent, Judy. "Black Women and the Constitution: Finding Our Place, Asserting Our Rights." *Harvard Civil Rights-Civil Liberties Law Review* 24 (winter 1989): 9–44.

Schafer, Judith Kelleher. *Slavery, the Civil Law, and the Supreme Court of Louisiana*. Baton Rouge: Louisiana State University Press, 1994.

Schiller, Reuel E. "Conflicting Obligations: Slave Law and the Late Antebellum North Carolina Supreme Court." *Virginia Law Review* 78.5 (1992): 1207–51.

Schoener, Allen, ed. *Harlem on My Mind: 1900–1968*. New York: Random House, 1969.

Schuyler, George. *Black No More: Being an Account of the Strange and Wonderful Workings of Science in the Land of the Free, A.D. 1933–1940*. 1931; Boston: Northeastern University Press, 1989.

———— [Samuel Brooks]. *Black Empire: Comprising "The Black Internationale, Story of Black Genius against the World" and "Black Empire, An Imaginative Story of a Great New Story in Modern Africa."* Ed. Robert A. Hill and R. Kent Rasmussen. Boston: Northeastern University Press, 1991.

Schwartz, Bernard, ed. *American Law: The Third Century: The Law Bicentennial Volume*. South Hackensack, N.J.: Published for the New York University School of Law by F. B. Rothman, 1976.

Schwarz, Philip J. *Slave Laws in Virginia*. Studies in the Legal History of the South. Athens: University of Georgia Press, 1996.

Scruggs, Charles. *Sweet Home: Invisible Cities in the Afro-American Novel*. Baltimore: Johns Hopkins University Press, 1993.

Seipp, David J. "The Concept of Property in the Early Common Law." *Law and History Review* 12.1 (1994): 31–34.

Shackelford, Otis M. *Lillian Simmons, or The Conflict of Sections*. Kansas City, Mo.: R. M. Rigby, 1915.

Shain, Barry Alan. *The Myth of American Individualism: The Protestant Origins of American Political Thought*. Princeton: Princeton University Press, 1994.

Shelley, Mary. *Frankenstein, or The Modern Prometheus*. 1818.

Siler, Ann. "Research Notes on a Book on Slavery." Chapters 9–12. Schomburg Center for Research in Black Culture. Typescript.

"Slave Contracts in Court. Charge of His Honor Judge T. J. Mackey, Sixth Circuit South Carolina, to the Jury in Case of W. M. McCollum, Administrator, vs. J. G. Robinson and Avery Jaggers. Money Demand." In *Free Blacks, Slaves, and Slaveowners in Civil and Criminal Courts: The Pamphlet Literature*. vols. 1

and 2, series 6, of *Slavery, Race, and the American Legal System, 1700–1872,* ed. Paul Finkelman, 307–12. New York: Garland, 1988.

"Slaves Petition for Freedom during Revolutionary War." In *Black Protest: History, Documents, and Analyses, 1619 to the Present,* ed. Joanne Grant, 28–30. New York: Fawcett, 1968.

Smith, Barbara Herrnstein. *On the Margins of Discourse.* Chicago: University of Chicago Press, 1978.

Smith, Gail K. "Reading with the Other: Hermeneutics and the Politics of Difference in Stowe's *Dred.*" *American Literature* 69 (1997): 289–313.

Smith, J. Clay, Jr. *Emancipation: The Making of the Black Lawyer, 1844–1944.* Philadelphia: University of Pennsylvania Press, 1993.

——. "Justice and Jurisprudence and the Black Lawyer." *Notre Dame Law Review* 69 (1994): 1077–113.

Smith, James L. *Autobiography of James L. Smith, Including, Also, Reminiscences of Slave Life, Recollections of the War, Education of Freedmen, Causes of the Exodus, Etc.* 1881. In *Five Black Lives: The Autobiographies of Venture Smith, James Mars, William Grimes, the Rev. G. W. Offley, James L. Smith.* Middletown, Conn.: Wesleyan University Press, 1987. 141–240.

Smith, Raymond T. "Race, Class, and Gender in the Transition to Freedom." In *The Meaning of Freedom: Economics, Politics, and Culture after Slavery,* ed. Frank McGlynn and Seymour Drescher, 257–90. Pittsburgh: University of Pittsburgh Press, 1992.

Smith, Theophus H. *Conjuring Culture: Biblical Formations of Black America.* New York: Oxford University Press, 1994.

Smith, Valerie. *Self-Discovery and Authority in Afro-American Narrative.* Cambridge: Harvard University Press, 1987.

Soifer, Aviam. "Status, Contract, and Promises Unkept." *Yale Law Journal* 96.8 (1987): 1916–59.

Somerville, Siobhan. "Passing through the Closet in Pauline E. Hopkins's *Contending Forces.*" *American Literature* 69 (1997): 139–66.

Southerland, Ellease. "Zora Neale Hurston: The Novelist-Anthropologist's Life/Works." *Black World* 23 (August 1974): 20–30.

Spiegelman, Art. *Maus: A Survivor's Tale.* Vol. 1, *My Father Bleeds History.* New York: Pantheon, 1986.

Spillers, Hortense J. "Mama's Baby, Papa's Maybe: An American Grammar Book." *Diacritics* 17.2 (1987): 65–81.

Starobin, Robert S. *Blacks in Bondage: Letters of American Slaves.* 1974; New York: Markus Wiener, 1988.

State v. Baby Poindexter. Transcript. Court of General Sessions of the Peace, 1551 (old number 1848), May 15, 1912.

State v. Leroy Poindexter. Transcript. New York Supreme Court, 3196 (old number 1847), April 22, 1912.

Staves, Susan. "Chattel Property Rules and the Construction of Englishness, 1660–1800." *Law and History Review* 12.1 (1994): 123–53.

Stephenson, Gilbert T. *Race Distinctions in American Law.* New York: Appleton, 1910.

Stepto, Robert. *From behind the Veil: A Study of Afro-American Narrative.* Urbana: University of Illinois Press, 1988.

Stewart, T. McCants. "The Afro-American as a Factor in the Labor Problem." *A.M.E. Church Review,* July 1889, 30–38.

Stowe, Harriet Beecher. *Dred: A Tale of the Great Dismal Swamp.* Boston: Phillips, Sampson, and Co., 1856.

Stroud, George M. *Slave Laws; extracted chiefly from Stroud's "Sketch of the laws relating to slavery in the United States of America."* New York: American Anti-Slavery Society, 1837.

Stuckey, Sterling, comp. *The Ideological Origins of Black Nationalism.* Boston: Beacon, 1972.

Suggs, Jon-Christian, ed. *American Proletarian Culture: The Twenties and the Thirties.* Vol. 11 of *Dictionary of Literary Biography Documentary Series.* Detroit: Gale, 1993.

———. "Epistemology and the Law in Four African American Fictions." *Legal Studies Forum* 14.2 (1990): 141–62.

———. "Joyce's Deadwood Dick." *James Joyce Quarterly* 10.3 (1973): 344–46.

Takaki, Ronald, ed. *Violence in the Black Imagination: Essays and Documents.* Expanded ed. New York: Oxford University Press, 1993.

Thomas, Brook. *American Literary Realism and the Failed Promise of Contract.* Berkeley and Los Angeles: University of California Press, 1997.

———. *Cross Examinations of Law and Literature: Cooper, Hawthorne, Stowe, and Melville.* New York: Cambridge University Press, 1987.

Thorne, Jack [pseud. David Bryant Fulton]. "Hannah Elias." In *"Eagle Clippings."* Brooklyn: David B. Fulton, 1907. 25–26.

———. *Hanover; or The Persecution of the Lowly, A Story of the Wilmington Massacre.* [Brooklyn]: M. C. L. Hill, 1900.

———. "Mr. Thomas Dixon, Jr., The Alienist." In *"Eagle Clippings."* Brooklyn: David B. Fulton, 1907. 33–34.

Thurman, Wallace. *Infants of the Spring.* 1932; Boston: Northeastern University Press, 1992.

———. *Negro Life in New York's Harlem.* Girard, Kansas: Haldeman-Julius, 1928.

Todorov, Tzvetan. *The Poetics of Prose.* Trans. Richard Howard. Ithaca: Cornell University Press, 1977.

Tomlins, Christopher L. *Law, Labor, and Ideology in the Early American Republic.* New York: Cambridge University Press, 1993.

Trachtenberg, Alan. *The Incorporation of America: Culture and Society in the Gilded Age.* New York: Hill and Wang, 1982.

Trotter, Joe William, ed. *The Great Migration in Historical Perspective: New Dimensions of Race, Class, and Gender.* Bloomington: Indiana University Press, 1991.

Tushnet, Mark. *The American Law of Slavery, 1810–1860: Considerations of Humanity and Interest.* Princeton: Princeton University Press, 1981.

———. *The NAACP's Legal Strategy against Segregated Education, 1925–1950.* Chapel Hill: University of North Carolina Press, 1987.

Ullman, Victor. *Martin R. Delany: The Beginnings of Black Nationalism.* Boston: Beacon, 1971.

United States Circuit Court, 2d Circuit. *The African Captives. Trial of the Prisoners of the Amistad on the Writ of Habeas Corpus, before the Circuit Court of the United States, for the District of Connecticut, at Hartford; Judges Thompson and Judson. September Term, 1839.* New York: N.p, 1839.

Van Evrie, John H. *Negroes and Negro "Slavery": The First an Inferior Race: The Latter its Normal Condition.* 1861.

———. *White Supremacy and Negro Subordination; or, Negroes a Subordinate Race, and (So-called) Slavery its Normal Condition, with an Appendix, Showing the Past and Present Condition of the Countries South of Us.* 2d ed. New York: Van Evrie, Horton and Company, 1868.

Wakeman, T[haddeus] B[urr]. "Justice and Jurisprudence: an Inquiry concerning the Constitutional Limitations of the Thirteenth, Fourteenth, and Fifteenth Amendments. Philadelphia, Lippincott." *Science: A Weekly Newspaper of All the Arts and Sciences,* January 10, 1890, 26.

Wald, Priscilla. *Constituting Americans: Cultural Anxiety and Narrative Form.* Durham: Duke University Press, 1995.

Waldrep, Christopher. "The Impact of Race on Law in Kentucky: A Research Note." *Register of the Kentucky Historical Society* 90 (spring 1992): 165–82.

Walker, Alice. "In Search of Our Mothers' Gardens." *Ms.,* May 1974, 64, 67–68, 70.

Walker, Grace Elena. "Novels by Negro Authors: A Study of Subject Matter." M.A. thesis, Fisk University, 1933. Schomburg Center for Research in Black Culture.

Wallenstein, Peter. "Race Marriage and the Law of Freedom: Alabama and Virginia, 1860s–1960s." *Chicago-Kent Law Review* 70 (1994): 371–437.

Waring, E. J. "The Judicial Function in Government," *A.M.E. Church Review* 2.4 (1886): 437–40.

Washington, Mary Helen. *Invented Lives: Narratives of Black Women, 1860–1950.* Garden City, N.Y.: Anchor, 1987.

Watkin-Owens, Irma. *Blood Relations: Caribbean Immigrants and the Harlem Community, 1900–1930.* Bloomington: Indiana University Press, 1996.

Webb, Frank J. *The Garies and Their Friends.* 1857; New York: Arno Press and the New York Times, 1969.

Wells-Barnett, Ida B. *"Southern Horrors" and other Writings: The Anti-Lynching Campaign of Ida B. Wells, 1892–1900.* Ed. Jacqueline Jones Royster. Boston: Bedford, 1997.

West, Cornel. "Learning to Talk of Race." *New York Times Magazine,* August 2, 1992.

White, Walter. *The Fire in the Flint.* New York: Knopf, 1924.

———. *A Man Called White: The Autobiography of Walter White.* 1948; Athens: University of Georgia Press, 1995.

———. *Rope and Faggot: The Story of Judge Lynch.* New York: Knopf, 1928.

Williams, Patricia J. "Alchemical Notes: Reconstructing Ideals from Deconstructed Rights." *Harvard Civil Rights, Civil Liberties Law Review* 22.2 (1987): 401–33.

———. *The Alchemy of Race and Rights.* Cambridge: Harvard University Press, 1991.

———. "Spirit-Murdering the Messenger: The Discourse of Fingerpointing as the Law's Response to Racism." *University of Miami Law Review* 42.1 (1987): 127–57.

Williams, Sherley Anne. *Dessa Rose*. New York: William Morrow, 1986.

Willis, Susan. *Specifying: Black Women Writing the American Experience*. Madison: University of Wisconsin Press, 1987.

Wilson, Theodore Brantner. *The Black Codes of the South*. Tuscaloosa: University of Alabama Press, 1965.

Wolgast, Elizabeth H. *The Grammar of Justice*. Ithaca: Cornell University Press, 1987.

Women Lynched in the United States since 1889. New York: National Association for the Advancement of Colored People, 1925.

Wood, Clement. *Sexual Relations in the Southern States*. Little Blue Book Series 1343. Girard: Haldeman-Julius, 1929.

Wright, John Samuel. "Ethiopia in Babylon: Antebellum American Romance and the Emergence of Black Literary Nationalism." Ph.D. diss., University of Minnesota, 1971. Ann Arbor: UMI, 1977.

Wright, Richard. "Blueprint for Negro Writing." *New Challenge* 1 (1937): 53–65.

———. *Early Works*. New York: Library of America, 1991.

———. "How Bigger Was Born." In *Early Works*. New York: Library of America, 1991.

———. "Lawd Today!" In *Early Works*. New York: Library of America, 1991.

———. *Native Son*. 1940; New York: Harper and Row, 1966.

Zalewski, Daniel. "Tongues Untied Translating American Literature into English." *Lingua Franca* 7.1 (1997): 63–64.

Zangrando, Robert L. *The NAACP's Crusade against Lynching, 1909–1950*. Philadelphia: Temple University Press, 1980.

Index